THE TRUTH ABOUT TRUMP

THE TRUTH
ABOUT TRUMP

Michael D'Antonio

St. Martin's Paperbacks

The Truth About Trump was formerly published in hardcover with the title *Never Enough.*

THE TRUTH ABOUT TRUMP

Copyright © 2015, 2016 by Michael D'Antonio.

For information address St. Martin's Press, 175 Fifth Avenue, New York, NY 10010.

ISBN: 978-1-250-11695-6

Our books may be purchased in bulk for promotional, educational, or business use. Please contact your local bookseller or the Macmillan Corporate and Premium Sales Department at 1-800-221-7945, ext. 5442, or by e-mail at MacmillanSpecialMarkets@macmillan.com.

Printed in the United States of America

St. Martin's Press hardcover edition / September 2015
St. Martin's Griffin trade paperback edition / May 2016
St. Martin's Paperbacks edition / July 2016

St. Martin's Paperbacks are published by St. Martin's Press, 175 Fifth Avenue, New York, NY 10010.

10   9   8   7   6   5   4   3   2   1

For Toni

CONTENTS

Preface to the 2016 Edition   ix

Introduction   1

1. The Trumps of Brooklyn, Queens, and the Klondike   19

2. The Boy King   46

3. Apprentice   73

4. Fear City   95

5. Donald Saves Midtown   127

6. Towering Trump   156

7. Celebrity Donald   187

8. Donald in Suckerland   204

9. Luck Runs Out   228

10. Trump the Spectacle   276

11. New Trump   298

12. Candidate Trump   312

13. Trump the TV Show   333

14. "The Beauty of Me"   363

15. A Not-So-Innocent Abroad   387

Postscript: Understanding Donald   418

Acknowledgments   453

Notes   455

Bibliography   481

Index   485

In mean-girl fashion, Donald Trump had decided we would never talk again. Five sessions into a scheduled seven interviews, the great dealmaker had an assistant break our deal. We would never speak again. The reason? I had spoken to someone he hated. Given his temperament, I wasn't surprised. Don, as he insisted I call him, feels offended when people don't serve him. And when he feels offended, he considers you dead. As he told me, "When somebody does something to me, they died. It's over. There's no coming back. That's okay. There are billions of people in the world. You don't need them."

Months passed and then the caller ID screen on my ringing phone flashed "Trump Tower." The call came from one of Trump's lawyers—he employs many of them—named Michael Cohen. He wanted the manuscript for this book because he was certain it was filled with errors. He wanted to "help" me avoid publishing inaccuracies. We talked about how books are fact-checked and about the reader's reliance on a writer's independence. A subject who gets final review of a manuscript may as well be coauthor of the work, imposing his self-serving perspective and bias. In the case of Trump, who uses lawsuits like weapons, there was also the strong possibility of a courtroom battle over my words.

When Cohen realized he wasn't going to get the text,

he started asking questions. Does the book mention certain famous women? Does it say that he is a racist? As I refused to answer, Cohen's voice grew huskier and more menacing until he sounded like the fictional mobster Tony Soprano, albeit with a law degree. Finally, Cohen seemed to recognize he was stymied and broke character.

"You're not really giving me anything," he said with an exasperated tone.

"Michael, I'm not supposed to," I answered.

I think he chuckled.

After our jousting conversation, Cohen followed up with calls to the legal department at my publisher's offices and at least one letter. Somewhere along the line, he announced, "You just bought yourself a fucking lawsuit." This was a classic Trump move. Throughout his career, he had made so many threats to sue journalists that reporters felt neglected if they were left out. In our very first meeting, amid the small talk and banter, Trump had mused about the prospect of suing me.

No lawsuit came, which also was not a surprise. A few weeks later, on a sunny day in June 2015, Cohen's boss called the press to the lobby of Trump Tower. At the appointed hour, he rode down an escalator, many steps behind his wife, Melania, to announce that he was running for president. This was why Cohen had called, I suspected. He was worried about how Trump would be portrayed and thought he would employ a little defensive menace.

Menace has long been a defining characteristic of the Trump modus operandi. This includes employing very large armed men who pose conspicuously—they all but flex their muscles and flash their weapons—in the waiting room of his office and accompany him when he leaves. This practice, which Trump has used for decades, may be unique to him. It is certainly not common among powerful executives. However, Trump often points out the members of his security squad and brags about their training as former police officers and detectives. The effect, of course, is to make others feel physically vulnerable, if not threatened.

Threat was often in the air as Trump conducted perhaps the most bizarre presidential campaign that America has ever seen. He fulminated against undocumented immigrants, whom he threatened to deport by the millions, and growled about Muslims, whom he would bar from entering the country. Little was out of bounds for candidate Trump, who retweeted a racist canard about murder in America. According to the faked "data" credited to a nonexistent "Crime Statistic Bureau," black assailants were responsible for 81 percent of murders of white Americans. (In fact, FBI statistics for 2014 show 82 percent of whites were killed by whites.) Trump's transmission of the race-baiting lie came days after his supporters kicked and punched a black protester who interrupted his stump speech in Birmingham, Alabama. Trump shouted (apparently to anyone and everyone), "Get him the hell out of here, will you, please? Get him out of here. Throw him out!" A Trump campaign spokesperson told CNN that the Trump campaign "does not condone his behavior," but Trump himself put it differently: "Maybe he should have been roughed up, because it was absolutely disgusting what he was doing." At another rally, he used his microphone to narrate the removal of a lone dissenter. "The guards are being very gentle with him," he said. "I'd like to punch him in the face, I'll tell you that."[1]

Delivered without notes, or any apparent preparation, Trump's campaign speeches were devoid of policy details and resembled comedy shows offered to eager fans who weren't asked to pay for tickets. He lacerated other politicians, demonized journalists, and crowed about polls that showed him outpacing his rivals. All of this was done in the staccato style of an insult comic. Consider his performance before a crowd gathered on January 20, 2016, in South Carolina, as reported by *The Kansas City Star:*

> I look at this guy Jeb Bush. He spent $59 million on his campaign and he is down in the grave. He is nowhere. No, no. Think of it. It's got to be much more than that. It was actually $59 million a while ago.
>
> Every time I turn on an ad, I see an ad about Trump. I mean, it's not that bad an ad either. It's like—you know.
>
> (Laughter)
>
> If you're going to do an ad, do an ad. But he's a low-energy person. Let's face it. We don't need low-energy. We need lots of energy.
>
> (Applause)
>
> But he spent—think of it. Think of it. He spent $59 million. I spent nothing, right? Nothing.
>
> (Applause)
>
> Now, I'm going to be spending. You probably saw I'm going to spend—now, we're going to start spending a lot of money because I don't want to take any chances. You know, it's—I love getting up—and for the last couple of months, I have been leading from practically the time I announced, right? And for the last—and leading a lot. I'm going to go over that because I go over polls. I love polls. I love polls.[2]

A spectacle of distortion, disjointed speech, and hyperemotional style, Trump's campaign defied the usual kinds of political analysis. As he talked about his great wealth, his superior intelligence, and his innate ability to "win" at everything, he seemed more like a character in a Hollywood farce than a legitimate candidate. He used his rubbery face to communicate disgust, anger, rage, and self-satisfaction. And he used his body to illustrate points he wanted to emphasize. When discussing a reporter who happened to be disabled, he mocked him by imitating the man's movements. To punctuate his charge that another candidate, Marco Rubio, sweated during a debate, he splashed water around and then pretended to gulp from a plastic bottle.

The approving laughter and cheers that greeted Trump's water bottle performance was informed by the fact that Rubio, an actual United States senator, had started all the talk about bodily fluids. Overwhelmed in the campaign by Trump, who had already won three state primaries, Rubio co-opted his techniques in February 2016. He told an audience that during a break in a televised debate Trump had "asked for a full-length mirror . . . maybe to make sure his pants weren't wet." This is what the presidential campaign had come to: two grown men talking about who may have sweated profusely or who might have become incontinent. And then it got worse.

As Trump and his rivals courted voters in the Deep South, the most famous racist in U.S. politics said that for white Americans to oppose Trump was "treason to your heritage." David Duke is a former national leader of the Ku Klux Klan, a white supremacist group, which in various incarnations has terrified and terrorized blacks, Jews, Catholics, and others. In 2000, Duke's name was mentioned by Trump himself as he ticked-off his reasons for leaving the Reform Party. (He called him "a bigot, a racist, a problem.") However, in 2016, as primaries in the Deep South approached, Trump could not seem to recall who Duke was. He also said he didn't understand the nature of the white supremacy movement. In a live interview with Jake Tapper of the CNN television network, he said, "I don't know anything about what you're even talking about with white supremacy or white supremacists . . . so I don't know. I don't know—did he endorse me, or what's going on? Because I know nothing about David Duke; I know nothing about white supremacists."[3]

When Trump failed to simply reject the support of racist organizations, and insisted he didn't know anything about a man he had once condemned as a bigot, many of his fellow Republicans recoiled. Speaker of the House of Representatives Paul Ryan of Wisconsin said, "If a person wants to be the nominee of the Republican Party, there can be no evasion and no games. They must reject any group or cause that is built on bigotry. This party does not prey on people's prejudices." In the heated controversy around the issue, Trump pointed to other instances where he had disavowed Duke.[4]

The controversy prompted a frenzy of press reports, which did not cast Trump in a favorable light. Nevertheless, he continued to speak to big crowds, and on so-called Super Tuesday, when ballots were cast in eleven states, Trump won seven. Mainstream leaders of the Republican Party faced the prospect of following the most divisive candidate in decades into the November election, where they feared they would lose not just the race for the White House but also cede control of the United States Senate. In this nightmare vision of the future, the party itself could break apart and sink like a ship overwhelmed by a hurricane sea.

◆

Trump's campaign was a carefully plotted and successful effort to exploit the grievances and ire of frightened people who harbored deep suspicions about a political system that was dominated by those who donated huge sums to election campaigns.

The fears that Trump exploited included, among others:

- Fear of Islamist terrorists—Trump would temporarily bar Muslims from entering the United States and begin massive military actions in the Middle East.
- Fear of unemployment—He would deport 11 million undocumented Mexican immigrants, build a huge border wall, and force Mexico to pay for it.
- Fear of crime—Trump would seek to impose the death penalty more widely, which is not something a president can order.
- Fear of globalization—He would start trade wars with China and Mexico.

Trump exploited the anger and suspicions people felt by:

- Mocking former prisoner of war and Senator John McCain's military service.
- Declaring climate change a hoax.
- Spreading the lie that "thousands and thousands of people" in New Jersey cheered the collapse of the World Trade Center towers in the terror attacks of 9/11.
- Demonizing reporters as "absolute scum. They're totally dishonest."

The sum of Trump's appeal could be found in the title of his swiftly assembled campaign manifesto, a book called *Crippled America,* and his slogan "Make America Great Again." At his rallies, people waved placards that referenced the Nixon-era "Silent Majority" and the phrase "take our country back" was a common refrain.

The inference was that millions of Americans had felt powerless and even silenced by some foreign force that had taken over the country. However, with Trump they had found a voice. As Trump voter Patricia Aguilar of Everett, Massachusetts, told *The New York Times,* Trump was expressing what "people really feel" but "we're all afraid to say it."[5]

Inspired by Trump's rhetoric and flamboyant style, which distinguished him in a crowded field, people flocked to his speeches and rallies. Television producers gave him far more time on their broadcasts than other candidates. Whenever he appeared, ratings for programs soared so much that Trump began to complain about the revenue bonanza enjoyed by the networks. In the online world, groups of Trump supporters clustered by the thousands and passed around faked news items and endorsements. Posters used photo-editing software to fake pictures of Trump supporters. (One manufactured image showed a black man in a T-shirt decorated with a pro-Trump slogan.) Bloggers faked articles under the bylines of established writers at *The Wall Street Journal* and *The New Yorker.* This lying was considered by many to be acceptable in the lawless space of the Internet. It was also consistent with Trump's own social media posts, which often featured mockery, anger, and distortions. As one follower wrote on Reddit, with apparent admiration, "He's shitposting, just like he does all day every day."[6]

What conventional politicians didn't understand was that "shitposting" can bind believers together and inoculate them against the influence of facts supplied by outsiders. In these groups of Trump fans, no outside critic was granted a hearing, and internal dissent was punished with a torrent of abusive comments. Unaware of the power residing in this alternative universe, pollsters and power brokers underestimated Trump for many months. In June 2015, Mara Liasson of National Public Radio said, "I think this is Donald Trump's biggest day. And he will be ignored from henceforth." In November, the chief political writer for *U.S. News & World Report* predicted "Trump's lead will fade," and number-cruncher Nate Silver advised the press to stop "freaking out" because Trump's base of support was less than 8 percent of the voters. As late as January 2016, the odds makers who bet on the presidential nominating process favored Marco Rubio.[7,8]

The truth about Trump's appeal began to dawn on the experts when he won the New Hampshire primary by almost twenty points. Next came victories in South Carolina and Nevada. On the first Tuesday in March, he won in seven out of eleven contests and Trump seemed on his way to the nomination. This reality, unthinkable to them months earlier, was so alarming to the party establishment that they began a mad scramble to find ways to avert a Trump nomination. Their concern was that despite the intensity of Trump's core supporters, he would not be able to attract enough independents and Democrats to win against the likely nominee from the other party, Hillary Clinton.

GOP leaders were concerned because after the 2012 election, a formal "postmortem" study had determined that the party had alienated certain large groups—Latinos, blacks, women, Asians, and others—that held the key to a national candidate's chances. As Trump pushed these voters further from the GOP, longtime leaders of the party, especially those who had been involved in nominee Mitt Romney's 2012 campaign for president, became alarmed. One, Kevin Madden, said that Trump should be considered "a litmus test for character" and that supporting him meant failing the test. Another, Stuart Stevens, urged people to vote for the Democrat Hillary Clinton because she would make a better president. One-time U.S. Senate candidate Meg Whitman called Trump "a dishonest demagogue."[9]

When Trump continued to win, the sober-minded members of the GOP establishment came together to try to stop him from becoming their party's leader. An anyone-but-Trump coalition, led by Romney and others, formed to stop him either during the primary elections or, failing that, at the party convention where the rules governing the proceedings could be used to thwart him. "Dishonesty is Trump's hallmark," said Romney. (Trump responded with a joke remark about how when they met in 2012, Romney would have performed oral sex on him to get his endorsement.) William Kristol, editor of the conservative *Weekly Standard,* said he would work to help an alternative independent or third-party candidate seek the White House, and GOP Congressman Scott Rigell of Virginia declared, "Not only could I not vote for him, but I couldn't sit and be silent as I watched him advance." A similar sentiment came from sixty Republican foreign policy experts, many of them former diplomats and presidential advisors who denounced him as a threat to America's standing in the world.[10,11]

The foreign affairs experts who finally recognized the problem Trump posed to America's global interests would have been informed by the TV news crews and correspondents who had, since the start of 2016, brought their worry about Trump to my home in suburban New York. Many, like Suh Yong Ha from the Korean Broadcasting System, had attended Trump rallies where he had pointed to reporters, called them "scum," and his supporters responded with boos and catcalls. Others had witnessed Trump's fans seizing protesters and forcefully ejecting them from events. In their conversations with me, three different reporters from Germany used the word "Nazi" as they described what they saw in Trump.

Every single interviewer pressed me to explain what was going on and offer some insight into the man.

Is he a racist?

Is he mentally ill?

Is he evil?

Unlike Trump, I wouldn't answer with simple declarations. That is *his* method. However, it is possible to study Trump and develop reasonable insights. I had put three years into the task of investigating his personal life, businesses, politics, and more. I had identified the influences and experiences that seem to explain his penchant for bullying, manipulation, deception, and megalomania.

Trump believes that much of what we are can be found in our genes and early childhood. He was born to a mother who was attention-seeking, obsessed with social status, and so money-conscious that she personally visited the basement laundries of Trump buildings to collect coins from the washers and driers. She was also sick during much of young Donald's early life. His father was, by many accounts, extremely strict and demanding but also preening, manipulative, and deceptive. Two government investigations revealed that he consistently bent the rules to wring excess profits out of programs designed to house war veterans and middle-class Americans.

Fred Trump's most creative business activity involved not the construction of his cookie-cutter housing but the development of a web of corporations to obscure what he was doing with his government-subsidized financing. When called to account, he owned up to his greedy and unseemly behavior and offered the immoral explanation that the system let him do it. There was nothing wrong with violating the spirit of taxpayer-supported housing programs so long as it was legal.

At home, Trump the elder demonstrated his methods

and priorities as he conducted business late into the night. One of his telephone tricks involved lying about his identity—he called himself "Mr. Green"—in order to gain some advantage over the people he called. When he did interact with his offspring, he taught them to be ruthlessly competitive and aggressive. Donald was to be both a "killer" and a "king." As befit his status, he was driven along his paper route in a big limousine. Not surprisingly, he became an argumentative, bullying, and physically aggressive little boy.

Donald attended a genteel private school where he was required to wear a little coat and tie every day. He was disruptive and unruly, and the school, called Kew-Forest, did not break him of these tendencies. Trump would not be moderated, either, by the spiritual lessons preached at the Marble Collegiate Church, which he sometimes attended with his family. Marble Collegiate was home to the famous Reverend Norman Vincent Peale, who taught that salesmanship was next to godliness and ambition was practically a form of worship. Peale almost never spoke of sin or moral obligations and offered anti-Catholicism in opposition to John F. Kennedy's bid for the White House. His followers constituted what could be regarded as a cult devoted to the messages in his book, which was called *The Power of Positive Thinking*.

Encouraged to feel superior by so much of what he experienced outside of school, Donald Trump bullied his schoolmates and teachers. For eighth grade, he was packed off to distant New York Military Academy, where he was put in uniform and deposited in a spare little room. Gone were family and friends and the opulence of the Trump mansion. In its place was a system of hierarchy and authoritarian discipline. The adults and NYMA, many veterans of World War II, governed with physical and psychological brutality. As Donald told me, "They'd smack the hell out of you."

In addition to confirming that bullying was the way of the world, NYMA reinforced for Trump the idea that competition and winning was everything. His old mentor at the school, "Maje" Theodore Dobias, would tell me that Trump had to be first at everything, including first in line at the chow hall. He also recalled that his father "was really tough on the kid. He was very German."

At NYMA, the corps of cadets included sons of mafia figures and boys whose fathers served Latin American dictators, but not one black or Asian student. In Donald's senior year, the ritual hazing at the school got so bad that a junior-level student was hospitalized after an upperclassman whipped him with a heavy chain. With the brutal culture of academy exposed to the outside world, three top officers at the school resigned.[12]

Having thrived at NYMA, Donald Trump treated college as if were a trade school, heading home every weekend to apprentice in the family business. There he saw how his father manipulated politicians with donations and worked his connections to get ever-richer. While young men from poor and minority communities fought and died in Vietnam, he was able to avoid service because of a minor medical problem. (His heel spurs didn't prevent him from playing sports, but somehow meant he couldn't fight.)

In his life after college, Donald settled in Manhattan, where he prowled the precincts of greed, deception, and depravity. In his own telling, he watched orgies in the celebrity quarters at Studio 54 and witnessed, firsthand, the corruption of New York politics. (He would later note how Governor Hugh Carey would do "anything" for a campaign donation.) One of Trump's earliest close associates was the mob lawyer and political hatchet man Roy Cohn, who was notorious for his racist and anti-Semitic (despite being Jewish himself) statements. Operating under Cohn's tutelage, Trump soon demonstrated an ability for using the press to build a false image of success. With a little manipulation, he got the blessing of *The New York Times,* which presented him as handsome and brilliant, and he got attention from the city's most important TV talk show. The press needed good stories, whether they were entirely accurate or not, and it didn't hurt that Donald photographed well.

At every turn, whether he was looking for it or not, young Trump saw how those who were willing to violate old-fashioned notions of decency benefited. In his 1970s New York, newspaper columnists traded attention for certain favors, mobsters enjoyed a celebrity comparable to star athletes, and values like fidelity and sincerity were relics of the past. His world was a gilded gutter where he became convinced that human beings are essentially venal creatures. The more he expressed greed and self-regard, the more people seemed to like it. He had hired someone to write a book and then paraded himself as an author and it became a bestseller. He publicly betrayed his first wife and the resulting scandal subjected his children to ridicule and scorn. His companies went through four massive bankruptcies and he failed at any number of businesses. And, according to countless lawsuits, reports, and individual accounts, he and his organization have victimized thousands of investors, consumers, and bystanders.

And now, in 2016, Trump is a candidate for president who is devoid of ideals and committed to little beyond his will to power. Without a strong foundation of empathy and ethics, he exploits racial hatred, dabbles in misogyny, and tacitly encourages violence. As the election approaches, his view of humanity is being affirmed again and again. And the important questions that must be answered are not about Trump. What lurks in him is apparent. Less certain is what resides in us.

◆

INTRODUCTION

*For the most part, you can't respect people because
most people aren't worthy of respect.*
—DONALD TRUMP

In profile, which was how TV viewers saw him that
night, Donald Trump resembled nothing as much as a
rooster in a tuxedo. His posture, developed in military
school, was firmly erect. His eyes were focused, with
narrowed intensity, on a distant challenger. And arcing
from his forehead back to his neck, his famous helmet of
golden hair evoked the cockscomb of a Rhode Island
Red. For the rooster, this beacon is meant to attract female attention and warn off enemies. For Trump, who sat
among admirers and detractors at the 2011 White House
Correspondents' Dinner, it drew the television camera
that caught his reaction to the public ridicule heaped on
him in the name of entertainment, by both comedian
Seth Meyers and the president of the United States.

The only hint that Trump was suffering came as
Meyers mocked him for a full two and a half minutes.
As the people laughed and strained to catch a glimpse
of Trump, he leveled a look that could kill at the comedian. His face remained unmoving, and glowering, as
even the diners at his own table found themselves unable to resist the tide of laughter. Meyers revealed the
reason for all the derision when he spoke of a poll that
found that only 38 percent of Americans were certain
the president had been born in the United States. Since

the Constitution requires that presidents be native born, the issue, which had been manufactured by conspiracy theorists, was a blatant attempt to paint Obama as an "other" whose claim to office was illegitimate.

Through his long, strenuous effort to promote this "birtherism," Trump had made himself a target of those who believed this talk was divisive, destructive, and perhaps a veiled form of racism. He objected to this criticism, insisting that he was not prejudiced and that he was posing important questions. "When it comes to racism and racists," Trump said, "I am the least racist person there is."

When it was his turn to address the White House correspondents and their guests, the president confronted the birthers head-on, but with remarkable humor, even presenting a video clip borrowed from the animated movie *The Lion King* as "my official birth video." Obama then mentioned Trump by name, praising the leadership he had demonstrated while performing as host of a reality TV show and making the "kinds of decisions that would keep me up at night." Obama added that with the birther issue resolved, Trump could "get back to focusing on the issues that matter—like, did we fake the moon landing?"

Confronted by a critic who stood rungs above him in the status hierarchy, Trump did not offer the killer stare. Instead he allowed the corners of his mouth to turn up, ever so slightly, which deepened the crow's-feet that framed his eyes. He then offered a wave to the president. Trump could take a joke. Afterward he took pains to seem unperturbed and spoke as if he had achieved something by gaining the president's notice. "I was actually very honored by the way I was treated," said Trump. "They treated me with great respect. They joked and they clowned, but I was the topic of conversation and that's perhaps not so bad."[1]

In one way or another, Donald Trump has been a topic of conversation in America for almost forty years. No one in the world of business—not Bill Gates, Steve Jobs, or Warren Buffett—has been as famous as Trump for as long. First associated with high-profile real estate development in 1970s Manhattan, his name soon became synonymous with success defined by wealth and luxury. Placed on skyscrapers, casinos, and commercial airliners, the name TRUMP (usually spelled in gold-colored, capital letters) became a true personal brand that connected one man to a seemingly endless number of offerings. In time it would be stamped on hotel rooms, furniture, neckties, meat; almost anything that might be sold as high quality, high cost, and high-class.

The kind of class Trump sought to deliver was defined not by social standing but by cash. Eagerly catering to the nouveau riches and the aspiring, he dismissed those who belonged to what he called "the lucky sperm club" while glossing over that he had been born into one of the wealthiest families in the country. Trump cast himself as the everyman's rich friend, who shunned high society, except when it was helpful to sell expensive apartments. In such cases he dropped the role of the anti-snob and readily referenced the Astors, Whitneys, Vanderbilts, and other blue bloods of a bygone age. It was understood, however, that he brandished these names out of commercial interest and that his heart was really aligned with Middle America. These were the people who followed him on TV, bought his products, and might even give him their votes should he ever get off the fence and actually run for office.

Today, according to the best available data, 96 percent of Americans recognize the name Donald Trump, but most don't like him. Henry Schafer of the firm that defines celebrities with its Q Score ratings called Trump the "quasi-celebrity people love to hate." In 2014,

61 percent of those polled in Trump's hometown of New York City viewed him unfavorably. Comedians find him an irresistible target. Jon Stewart, the former host of the long-running satirical news program *The Daily Show,* routinely jabbed Trump, calling him, among other things, Fuckface von Clownstick. The television host and comedian Bill Maher famously offered Trump $5 million if he could prove he wasn't "the spawn of his mother having sex with an orangutan."[2]

The level of commentary offered by Stewart and Maher says much about the rancor of our age. It's hard to imagine Mark Twain requiring the censor's bleeps that accompanied Stewart's rants. Of course Twain may never have met anyone quite like Trump. Gleefully aggressive, Trump looks for opportunities to take offense and then wrestle a supposed enemy into the gutter. When Stewart offered a generic juvenile taunt, Trump replied in a deeply personal way, asking, "If he is so above it all & legit, why did he change his name from Jonathan Liebowitz? He should be proud of his heritage! Jon Stewart @TheDailyShow is a total phony. He should cherish his past, not run from it." After Maher's comment, Trump filed a $5 million lawsuit. Although he eventually dropped it, the filing required a court's attention, at taxpayer expense, and a defense by Maher.[3]

But even as he appeared to appease his critics, Trump's views and bully persona made him exceedingly popular with people who believed he represented important ideals, especially the American promise of success represented by great wealth. His image was amplified as he hosted a TV game show—*The Apprentice*—and maintained a constant presence on the social media site Twitter, where millions followed his commentary and many implored him to seek the presidency.[4]

Ever provocative, Trump gained attention by expressing raw and unrefined thoughts rather than nuanced reflections. In his calculation, honesty comes from the corner of his heart that is willing to fling insults and divide the world into enemies and friends. As veteran gossip columnist Liz Smith sees it, Trump is often ruled by the needy child who resides in his psyche and would rather get negative attention than be ignored. Of course Trump does profit financially as he gives this part of himself free rein, and he has little patience for reflection or analysis. He just presses on, defying science with his criticism of immunizations for children and battling against the facts on climate change.

Trump has denied facts others accept and pushed the limits of propriety throughout his long and hyperactive life. In his parents' home, at school, and in the worlds of business and politics, he has continually asserted his superiority with only the barest hint of doubt. Perhaps nothing in nature is more voracious than this man's hunger for wealth, fame, and power. And it is this force that has allowed him to endure considerable mockery and substantial setbacks in business and still come back for more. Indeed, in the time after his humiliation at the correspondent's dinner, Trump nurtured an ambition to mount his own campaign for the American presidency—a real campaign and not another of his flirtations—and thereby claim the greatest accomplishment available to a mere mortal in the twenty-first century.

The Trump candidacy would be planned and plotted for 2016 when he would make it official in an address to well-wishers and journalists gathered in the lobby of his Trump Tower skyscraper in Manhattan. The most unconventional kick-off speech in many election cycles, the announcement—particularly his claim that Mexico is "sending" criminals across the U.S. border—would launch Trump on a rapid ascent to the top of the Republican field. For many weeks to come, Trump would outrage his critics and baffle his opponents as he held the nation's attention with one outrageous statement after another. As some Republicans speculated that he was a Democratic Party plant, many liberals said Trump's popularity reflected the irrational fears of the GOP base. All could agree that his ability to disrupt the status quo was breathtaking in its power and efficiency. Trump was unrivaled, it seemed, in his ability to capture and hold the attention of the American public.

◆

Although he seems like a unique and completely modern figure, Donald Trump actually emerges from this country's long tradition of rich-but-rough high-achievers, which Alexis de Tocqueville recognized in 1831, writing, "Love of money is either the chief or a secondary motive at the bottom of everything Americans do." By the end of the nineteenth century, the rich in America had become so wealthy that their power and influence equaled that of the aristocracy in Europe. Thanks to the rise of mass-circulation newspapers, the very rich became a source of widespread fascination as the press was filled with the comings and goings of Carnegies, Rockefellers, Goulds, and others whose fortunes permitted great displays of luxury. (Hence Mark Twain's term for the era, the Gilded Age.) J. P. Morgan favored ever-bigger yachts, each of which was named *Corsair* and painted a menacing black, as a means of showing off his ever-increasing wealth. The Vanderbilts also owned yachts, but they were better known for their houses. In 1883 they astonished the country with the largest house ever built in New York City. The family also owned a seventy-room "cottage" in Newport called The Breakers, and the Biltmore Estate in North Carolina, which has more than two hundred and twenty rooms.

The wealthy men of the Gilded Age knew that while their countrymen loved money, they regarded the excesses of high society as both foreign and suspect. Wilbur Fisk Crafts, a popular writer of the time, expressed it this way: "Is there anything more un-American than what we call 'society,' whose aristocratic code was imported from Paris and London into New York and thence spread to other large cities of our land?" To distance themselves from this vision, great men made certain that the public saw that the balls and galas were feminine affairs, in which they participated only to please their wives and daughters. In their biographies and public remarks they associated themselves with virtues such as hard work and determination. Andrew Carnegie counseled that success depended more on motivation than talent. John D. Rockefeller, founder of Standard Oil, advised "singleness of purpose."

Similarly, captains of industry and finance downplayed their intellectual pursuits and education. It was enough for a man to have attended college, if he had, but it was not necessary. After he finished school, it was best to talk about practical things and leave the world of art and books to those who couldn't handle the hurlyburly of business. By the start of the twentieth century, when Elbert Hubbard coined the term "school of hard knocks," everyday experience and common sense were widely accepted as equal if not superior to book learning. This belief affirmed both an American sense of equality and the increasingly popular idea that the accumulation of wealth made one a success in life.[5]

Eventually America's first great era of wealth led to countless books on the ways of making money. In 1914 preacher/author William Woodbridge posed the question of the day: "What is it that the upper ten possesses that the under ten thousand does not possess?" His book, *That Something,* revolved around an encounter between a fictional beggar and a financier who gives the beggar his business card and says the beggar doesn't need food but rather "that something" that all successful men have. Inspired, the young beggar discovers the value of "Faith, Confidence, Power, Ambition . . . " and, finally, the power of his own will, which is "the talisman of success." It is the will of the soul, writes Woodbridge, that explains why a few men are destined to be carried "on our muscle" like men upon horses. Another book of this sort, *Letters from a Self-Made Merchant to His Son* by Chicago pork-packer John Graham, stressed personality and appearance, explaining, "Two thirds of success is making people think you are all right."

While the masses sought to divine the secrets of success—willpower? personality? faith? confidence?— some at the top came to believe their success was either divinely distributed or a matter of superior morals. John D. Rockefeller claimed, "God gave me my money." When J. P. Morgan was questioned about his empire, which was built in large measure through stock manipulation, he said its source was "character."

◆

The first Gilded Age faltered with various recessions and panics and finally died, at about age sixty-five, after the stock market crash of 1929. Out of the ruins of the subsequent Great Depression emerged a safer financial system, more progressive taxes, and Social Security. In the decades that followed, the middle class expanded at an unprecedented rate. A new era of prosperity dawned in 1946, the year Donald Trump was born. (This makes him a founding member of the baby boom generation.) With World War II ended, America's industrial competitors lay in ruins and more than 10 million servicemen came home to resume civilian life. As export markets clamored for goods and domestic demand for consumer comforts exploded, a golden age began. Housing was required for the millions of new families begun as fighting men returned, and developers such as Trump's father, Fred, grew rich providing it. Through shrewd business practices and sheer determination, Fred came to be worth an estimated $100 million by 1975, when he turned seventy.[6]

The postwar golden years, which allowed men such as Fred Trump to live out a financial miracle, were marked by an unprecedented level of equality as the various income groups—upper, middle, and lower—each claimed a proportionate share of the expanding economy and the gaps separating them remained essentially constant. This happy state of affairs continued until the recession of 1973–75. Years of economic stagnation and crisis then fed a conservative political movement that was determined to use tax cuts and deregulation to promote the development of new great fortunes. Theoretically a flood tide of wealth flowing to the few would "lift all boats" and thereby save the middle class.

With the election of Ronald Reagan in 1980, firebrand conservatives got what they wanted. Washington began slashing the tax rates imposed on the rich and easing the regulations on industries and financial institutions. All this was done in the name of growth and fairness for the rich. To emphasize this latter point, President Reagan's budget director David Stockman gave cabinet members copies of his new favorite book, *Wealth and Poverty* by George Gilder, which proclaimed the moral basis for the accumulation of great wealth. Gilder lionized entrepreneurs and excoriated the poor, declaring that "the current poor, white even more than black, are refusing to work hard." As they turned Gilder's passion into policies, the Reagan administration targeted social programs for cuts, reduced taxes, and sought to unleash businesses from regulations. Thus began America's Second Gilded Age.[7]

◆

At first hardly anyone noticed that something significant was happening. In the early 1980s everyday Americans were primarily concerned with double-digit inflation and unemployment rates that flirted with 10 percent. As these menaces receded, many credited pro-wealth policies, and despite various financial crises, most of which were linked to speculation and lax regulation, the "second Gilded Age" wasn't described as such until 1990, when Kevin Phillips published *The Politics of Rich and Poor.* Phillips declared that America had been swept by "a plutographic revolution comparable to that of the late 19th century," and though he predicted an eventual end to the trend, he could not say when it might occur. As of 2015 it hadn't happened. In the first decade of this century those in the middle actually lost income and the top 1 percent came to control more wealth than the bottom 90 percent. In 2014 the five hundred richest people in the world controlled $4.4 trillion in assets. The sum exceeded the annual economic activity of India (population 1.2 billion) and Brazil (population 200 million) combined.

As in the past, fortunes were expressed in mansions—actually "mega" or "monster" mansions—and opulent parties, including the $3 million birthday celebration that investor Stephen Schwarzman threw for himself in 2007. Once again, giant yachts signified success. A prime example was the steel-hulled *Rising Sun,* launched in 2004. Owned by Larry Ellison and David Geffen, it was built with eighty-three rooms, an indoor pool, and a slip space for a private submarine. In comparison, Donald Trump's yacht was a modest, three-hundred-foot-long, traditional steamer. Preferring luxury travel by private jet, Trump spent little time aboard the *Trump Princess.* In modern times, private aircraft, which wealthy Americans buy with generous tax incentives, grab more public attention. Private-jet traffic jams became common at airports near resort towns such as East Hampton, New York, and Aspen, Colorado, and billionaires sought to one-up each other by purchasing ever-faster and ever-more-luxurious planes. Donald Trump made his statement with a $100 million Boeing 757. Built to carry two hundred or more passengers when configured for airline service, Trump's plane was fitted out for just forty-three people, whose seat belts clicked together with gold-plated buckles.

Often parked at LaGuardia Airport in a spot that made it as visible as a billboard, Trump's 757 announced his status as a rich and successful man. Hardly anyone argued with the proposition that wealth equaled success. In the new Gilded Age, 81 percent of college freshmen surveyed by the Pew organization in 2006 said their primary goal in life was to become rich. This was roughly double the number who expressed this notion in the 1960s. In the same survey more than half said that one of their main goals was to become famous. Fewer than one-third indicated that they wanted to "help others who needed help."[8]

Talent and intelligence were recognized as essential in the quest for success, but as in the past, higher education and intellectualism were deemed to be of limited value. Much was made of the entrepreneurs and inventors who dropped out of college and became wildly successful. (Microsoft founder Bill Gates was one.) Even more attention was lavished upon those who gained great fame as well as riches. No one achieved these two goals quite like Donald Trump, who became, quite literally, the face of modern success.

Dozens of men and women with several times Trump's holdings are unknown to those outside the world's billionaires. Donald Bren, Dan Duncan, and Leonard Blavatnik each ranked more than fifty spots higher on the 2014 *Forbes* list of the world's wealthiest, but they can walk the streets of any American city unnoticed and unmolested. Trump cannot go anywhere without attracting attention. More remarkable is that his fame has persisted for more than four decades, through success, failure, shame, and glory. By thrusting himself into one issue after another, and speaking with unequaled audacity, he has made himself one of the most quoted men of his time. Early in his fame, Trump enjoyed such broad public approval that the US Gallup Poll determined that he was the seventh most admired man of the 1980s, outranked only by the pope, the Polish nationalist Lech Walesa, and the four living presidents.

Although he often sought to use his fame to influence public affairs, Trump has always claimed that notoriety has real monetary value. According to him, the name Trump, just like that of Disney or Ford, added value to products, services, and assets he offered in the marketplace. Brand names are worth money. Apple is the most valuable brand name in the world, estimated in 2013 by the ranking service Interbrand to be worth $28 billion. Interbrand pegged the value of the Gap clothing brand at $3.9 billion. Trump didn't show up in the firm's public rankings of valuable names, but in a 2010 deposition he testified that an independent evaluation set it at $3 billion. This figure would have made his name the single most valuable item in his portfolio.[9]

Trump stressed that if the brand stood for any one thing, it was "luxury." However, he took pains to avoid being perceived as too elitist to appeal to the masses. This sensitivity, which served him well when he catered to slot-machine addicts in Atlantic City, could be traced to Trump's father, Frederick—he always went by "Fred"—a hard-knocks alumnus who built a personal fortune in excess of $100 million by selling and renting homes to working-class New Yorkers. Trump Sr. wanted his children to earn college diplomas. However, he was generally suspicious of intellectuals and valued hard work above all else. Ever his father's son, Donald Trump acquired an exquisite blend of attitudes that allowed him to flaunt his Ivy League diploma but also use his father's sharp-elbow tactics to prevail against competitors and opponents.

Seemingly committed to the notion that all publicity was good publicity, Donald Trump came to display a personality that was practically all id, all the time, and truly an expression of the American urge to forge empire from ambition. Flying from place to place in his TRUMP helicopter and TRUMP jet, he offered opinions on everything from politics to sex, and continually declared himself to be superior in every way. He frequently referred to the many people who thought he should run for president and sometimes acted as if he were a real candidate. During one especially tense Cold War moment, he even offered himself to the world as a nuclear-arms-treaty negotiator. His reasoning? A man who can make high-end real estate deals should be able to bring the United States and the Soviet Union into agreement.

If he had acted with a bit more humor, Donald Trump could have been a P. T. Barnum for his time, universally beloved despite his bombast because everyone would be in on the joke. But those who compared him to the nineteenth-century showman, who was more famous than any president of his era, missed the mark by a few degrees. Trump occasionally smiled in a way that made you think he understood he was being preposterous, but he lacked Barnum's sunny playfulness. Instead he was often combative and sometimes mean. He sued or threatened to sue those who offended him, and he declared certain female critics unworthy because they were "grotesque" or "fat" or "ugly." He once sent writer Gail Collins of *The New York Times* a copy of her column with her photo circled and the message "The Face of a Dog!" scrawled beside it.[10]

When questioned about this kind of behavior, Trump justifies it like a boy in a fight, complaining that the other guy struck first. He is often right about this. Comedians, politicians, and others *have* picked on him for everything from his ego to his extravagant swoosh of bright blond hair. But his policy of always answering a pesky jab with a roundhouse punch reveals remarkable sensitivity for someone so accustomed to verbal brawls. As a man who says he considers money to be a way to "keep score" in life, he has been especially bothered by those who suggested he wasn't all that rich. Gail Collins received the dog-face clipping after she called him a "financially embattled thousandaire." When the writer Timothy L. O'Brien published a book that quoted unnamed sources who estimated Trump's net worth at under $250 million, Trump sued the author and publisher seeking $5 billion in damages. Trump's level of fame made it difficult for him to win his case because, as a "public figure," the law treats him as fair game for any writer. The court dismissed Trump's lawsuit after it concluded that Trump had failed to come forward with sufficient evidence showing that O'Brien knew that his sources' information was false or that O'Brien had serious doubts about its accuracy. However, the mere filing of a legal complaint does inflict financial and, perhaps, emotional pain on the opposition, and these outcomes probably please Trump. He prefers to win, but victory isn't necessary. "I always loved to fight," he told me during a discussion about his youth, "all types of fights, including physical."

◆

What does one make of a grown man who, when he argues with women, stoops to insulting their appearance and speaks so proudly of his pugnacious past?

What if the same man is one of the most prominent people in the world, and a privately generous person who once handed a dying child a $50,000 check so that he could enjoy the last months of his life? Add to the picture a resilience that has allowed him to stage countless comebacks from defeat and a boundless optimism, and you get a figure so compelling that he cannot be dismissed simply because of his braggadocio's personality.

Indeed, for all of his excesses Donald Trump is a man perfectly adapted to his time.

Coming of age in New York City in Tom Wolfe's "Me Decade" of the 1970s, he fashioned himself into one of the most effective self-promoters in a city that was filled with them. In the 1980s, as the fictional Gordon Gekko announced that "greed is good," Trump invited the press, and therefore the public, to view and envy the lavish lifestyle he enjoyed thanks to his own relentless pursuit of profit. Then, after some scandal and very public troubles in business, he spent the 1990s engineering that most American of accomplishments, a comeback. In this he had much in common with other noteworthy men, including disgraced evangelists, the convicted bond trader Michael Milken, and the impeached president Bill Clinton. In the 1990s these men proved that fame can help a man overcome almost any disgrace.

In every period of his adult life, Trump maintained his real estate business, but he also dabbled in everything from sports to beauty pageants. The one consistent element in all of these interests was the value he placed on publicity, which he sought with the skill of someone who understood that celebrity is power, reporters are often lazy about facts, and image can trump reality. He moved from supplying the press with quotes and interviews to telling his own story in a 1987 book, *Trump: The Art of the Deal,* which he coauthored with a professional writer.

More than a dozen Trump-authored books followed the first. Each one advanced the notion that he was brilliant and successful. His face appeared on every cover, which meant that he beamed out from shelves in thousands of stores and airport newsstands across America. But the recognition they generated paled in comparison with the attention he received for his off-stated political ambitions. Although many political observers dismissed Trump's aspirations, his flirtations generated valuable publicity. Politics also prepared Trump for the greatest role of his life—playing himself on a TV show called *The Apprentice*.

Premiering in 2004, the series arrived as a genre called reality TV was drawing huge numbers of viewers. The show was conceived as a contest between two teams, which would ultimately produce a single winner who would get a job with Trump. The focal point of each episode was the moment when Trump announced, "You're fired," and one or more players departed the game. A genuine hit, *The Apprentice* was a top-ten program in its first season, attracting almost 30 million viewers on the final night of its run. Trump's "You're fired" catchphrase became such a sensation that a toy company developed and sold a doll in a blue suit and red tie that uttered it at the push of a button.

The Apprentice added "television star" to Trump's long résumé and confirmed, at last, that he was as much entertainer as businessman. The program showed his remarkable grasp of popular culture and the value of celebrity. It also made him known to a new generation of Americans. Trump came to represent wealth mixed with vulgarity and a hedonism that was refreshingly honest. Like the top-hatted Uncle Pennybags figure in the board game Monopoly, Trump's image was often used in the news media to signal that a report was about money, wealth, or luxury. The word Trump became synonymous with both unabashed success and unseemly self-promotion. To say that someone was "the Donald Trump" of this or that, which happened often, was either a high compliment or a put-down. By 2014, Trump was a walking inkblot test. In him one could see extreme examples of ambition, obsession, aggression, and insecurity. He also exhibited creativity, strength, and candor. Trump's peers in business reported that he was honorable and consistent, although he has sometimes been criticized for being slow to pay his bills (who hasn't?). With a few exceptions, employees described him as demanding but generous with pay and benefits. In our time together I found him to be quick-witted, funny, and charming. Words flowed from him like water from a spigot, even if some of the anecdotes he told have been repeated for decades.

Trump also gave the lie to the notion that he doesn't care what people think of him. His many feuds and conflicts suggest he worries a great deal about how he is perceived and whether he is judged to be a winner or a loser, handsome or hideous, strong or weak. While he says that he is driven by the thrill of competition, his bully-boy quality is a sign that something else has pushed him to overwhelm his opponents, run up the score, and dismiss those who speak against him.

In his office aerie on the twenty-sixth floor, Trump grumbled a bit about how this would undoubtedly be a "bad book," which meant that it would fail to promote his story as an example of entrepreneurial genius. "People want inspirational," he said, "they want uplifting. If you give them that, you'll have a bestseller." But a "good book" resides in the eye of the reader, and Donald Trump may be the least qualified to judge one about him. Yet his sense of what the public wants may be unrivaled in our time. For decades, no one has made a more insistent claim on the nation's attention than this man. Trump begins each day with a sheaf of papers detailing where and how often his name has been mentioned in the global press. The reports are typically too numerous for him to actually read, but the weight of the pages gives his sensitive ego a measure of his importance on any given day. This need to be noticed, and his drive to satisfy it, has made him a singular figure worthy of close inspection.

Who were the people who shaped him in his early years and aided him in his adult life? What values guided him through his professional and personal development? Is Donald Trump a product of his time, abetted by currents in our culture and our economy? And how much has he, through the force of his various identities—businessman, political gadfly, entertainer—influenced our society? Because he has become a stand-in for a set of ideals and attitudes, in examining Trump's life I am attempting to understand him as an idea. What does it mean that this remarkable man, who is at once so admired and reviled, is the most recognized businessperson of our time? How has he been able to offend so many and continue to garner so much attention? And why do his enemies find it so hard to ignore him?

◆

I
THE TRUMPS OF BROOKLYN, QUEENS, AND THE KLONDIKE

*He was a very difficult guy, but he was
a great teacher for me.*
—DONALD TRUMP ON HIS FATHER

Although he had been summoned by a US Senate committee to answer for $4 million in windfall profits he took from a government housing program for war veterans, things could have been worse for Frederick Trump. He could have been Roy Cohn.

For much of the previous month, Capitol Hill and the nation had been transfixed by the Army-McCarthy hearings, where military men battled with Joseph McCarthy, the notorious Red-baiting senator from Wisconsin, over the conduct of his belligerent chief aide, Cohn. (Things had gone so badly for Roy Cohn that his political career would be ruined. The hearings were just as bad for the senator. One witness became a sensation as he famously asked of the senator, "Have you no decency, sir?" Young Cohn would leave Washington in disgrace. Shunned by colleagues, McCarthy would soon die, at age forty-eight, of alcohol-related liver disease.)

The drama of the McCarthy hearings was still fresh on July 12, 1954, when Fred Trump sat at a witness table to answer questions about graft and profiteering in a Federal Housing Administration building program. In another time, corruption in an agency that subsidized builders who constructed apartments for World War II veterans might have riveted the nation's attention. But in McCarthy's wake, the American people could be forgiven if they took their eyes off the Capitol for a moment.

Trump had been called to answer questions raised by the first witness to testify before the committee. In his testimony, federal investigator William McKenna said Trump ranked near the top among builders who shared in excessively high payments approved by the FHA officials who were almost certainly on the take. Many of these bureaucrats had accepted expensive gifts—TVs, watches, appliances—from developers. Others lived so far above their means that it seemed obvious they had been bribed with substantial sums. The builders, in turn, got favors worth millions of dollars. According to McKenna, Trump had benefited, in particular, from the rule-bending practiced by a powerful Washington figure named Clyde L. Powell. Powell had allowed Trump to finish construction at Beach Haven six months before he had to start repaying his federally subsidized loan. In that time Trump pocketed $1.7 million in rent payments.

McKenna's testimony about Trump and others had appalled committee chairman Homer Capehart—the senator from Indiana used the word "nauseous"—who said that builders had taken advantage of both the federal government and countless vets. Capehart was taking cues from President Dwight Eisenhower, who had flushed red with anger when McKenna told him about the FHA troubles. The first nonpolitician to be elected president since U. S. Grant, Eisenhower had campaigned on a promise to root out corruption. The president had nothing against developers in particular. He had recently met with another big New York builder, William Zeckendorf, to urge him to take on the project that would become L'Enfant Plaza in southeast Washington. But Ike truly loved the fighting men he'd led to victory in World War II. When he had unleashed federal investigators with an executive order—calling the FHA developers "sons of bitches"—Senator Capehart, a more ordinary politician, had spied an opportunity.

Like Eisenhower, Capehart was a Republican. The FHA had been created by the Democrat Franklin Delano Roosevelt, and the events under investigation had all occurred while another Democratic president, Harry S. Truman, was in charge. If Capehart could make enough noise about the FHA, he might hurt the Democrats in the coming congressional election. So he said that the builders and the FHA were mired in "a grand scandal" far worse than the infamous Teapot Dome corruption case of the twenties, in which bribes were accepted by officials to grant rich oil leases on federal land. Teapot Dome, which involved oil reserves worth hundreds of millions—if not billions—of dollars, happened under a Republican, Warren G. Harding.

Capehart, who came to the Senate after a career selling jukeboxes and popcorn machines, was renowned as a self-promoter. He decided that the hearings would become a traveling show that would open in Washington and then cross the country so that more Americans could watch him grill colluding bureaucrats and builders. With a little luck, TV cameras might appear to broadcast the show live. As any astute politician understood, television would make the investigation and the scandal far more important to the general public. Committee lawyers, senators, and witnesses would be seen as dramatic characters, and the scandal would be understood as a narrative of good and evil. In the end, the acronym FHA might even enter the political lexicon and become as powerful as the words Teapot Dome, which everyone knew represented corruption.

In the days of testimony that preceded Fred Trump's

appearance, most of the witnesses had played their expected roles. After first explaining that he would not answer any questions because he refused to incriminate himself, Clyde L. Powell deflected his interrogators by repeating, "My answer is the same, sir" or "My answer is heretofore as given." Others tried, but failed, to explain the shocking returns made by the builders. In one case, every $5 put up by a developer quickly became $1,737. In another instance, $10,000 grew to $3.1 million. One builder pounded the witness table as he insisted upon his innocence. Another suffered a heart attack in the hours after his testimony.

No one performed more brilliantly than the witness who consumed most of the afternoon hearing on July 12. Dapper in a fine suit and carefully trimmed mustache, Fred Trump sat at the witness table flanked by attorneys. Like every other witness, Trump was seated at floor level and was thus required to look up to the dais where the chairman sat, like a judge in a courtroom or a king on his throne. But Trump didn't behave like a supplicant or an accused man. Instead, he spoke confidently of the convoluted, but legal, means he used to get the most for himself out of a program that seemed almost designed to benefit a builder who could read regulations as well as he could read a blueprint.

At times Trump's testimony proceeded with a "Who's on first?" quality worthy of Abbott and Costello. Asked when he had purchased some land, Trump answered, "Five or eight or ten years" prior. Questioned about a project estimate that included an extra 5 percent "architect's fee," which mostly went into his own pocket, Trump insisted it was included to satisfy the FHA. When a skeptical Senator Capehart pressed him, Trump added, "And it is provided by the regulation."

"What is provided by the regulation?" said Capehart.

"The five percent architect's fee."

"Have you ever seen a regulation that says that?"

"No, I'm a builder."

"Then how do you know these regulations provide for a five percent architect's fee?"

"They wouldn't have allowed it if they didn't."

So it went for much of the afternoon with Trump warning at times, "That is a very iffy question," and then launching into descriptions of the complex methods he used to squeeze maximum profit out of the taxpayers. He explained, for example, that the land under his Beach Haven development was held by a trust devoted to his children. The buildings, however, were owned by half a dozen corporations. Every year these six entities paid rent to the trust—really his children—for the use of the land. Under the terms of the lease the Trump kids might receive $60,000 or more in pure profits every year for ninety-eight more years. Then the lease could be renewed for another ninety-nine years.

With similar candor Trump explained how he had paid himself the general contractor's fee that had been included in the estimate he submitted to the FHA, and how he fattened his own wallet by having one of his corporations do business with another of his. To the senators this was the equivalent of a man mowing his own lawn and then insisting he should be paid for the chore. Trump insisted that he was more like the tailor who pays a low-wage assistant to sew a custom suit, then charges his customer full price. If the quality is the same, thanks to the tailor's supervision, why shouldn't he get the money?

In Trump's tailoring at Beach Haven he submitted a plan to the government that called for extra high construction costs, which allowed him to borrow more money and get the government's approval to charge higher rents. The final tally on the project showed that Beach Haven had been built for $4 million less than the estimate. (Worth $35 million in 2015.) The extra high rents set when the project was approved remained in place, even after the excess profits were revealed, because the FHA permitted it. Similarly, the cash left over from the FHA building loan stayed in a Trump bank account. As far as he was concerned, this money was fairly earned and, technically speaking, not personal income. As he explained, as long as he didn't put the cash in his pocket, the $4 million could be regarded as a rainy-day fund for Beach Haven.

With the occasional aid of his lawyers, Trump testified for more than two hours straight. Much of what he said would disturb anyone who believed that the taxpayer dollars invested through the FHA program were supposed to serve the noble public purpose of aiding veterans as much as possible. But Trump and other builders would say that their windfall profits compensated them for the excellent work they did creating tens of thousands of homes at a breakneck pace. Any suggestion that he had violated any regulations or laws was "very wrong, and it hurts me," said an indignant Trump. He was the one who ought to be vexed, not the senators, because of the "untold damage to my standing and reputation."[1]

◆

Although Fred Trump had clearly violated the spirit of the FHA program he had not been caught in any criminal act. Plenty of Americans might admire and even root for an ambitious and clever fellow who understood the ways of the world and exploited them for his own gain. Trump was just such a fellow; a classic New York character who could have been drawn from a Gilded Age memoir of political corruption called *Plunkitt of Tammany Hall*. The Plunkitt in question was George Washington Plunkitt, a nineteenth-century New

York State legislator who had famously declared, "I saw my opportunities and I took 'em." One of Plunkitt's most famous essays focused on what he called the "honest graft" practiced by politicians who made sure their friends received special favors, including help with real estate deals.

The rascal's humor in *Plunkitt* stood in sharp contrast to the acid observations of Thorstein Veblen, who also wrote a Gilded Age classic. In *The Theory of the Leisure Class,* Veblen showed that the American elite lived according to an ethic of utter greed and immorality covered by a veneer of proper education and manners. Far more powerful and thus more dangerous than Plunkitt's hacks and hangers-on, the members of Veblen's leisure class were enabled by great fortunes amassed by brutal men who enjoyed "freedom from scruple, from sympathy, from honesty and regard for life."

Known popularly as "robber barons," Veblen's subjects bore names such as Rockefeller, Morgan, Carnegie, and Vanderbilt. He saw in their conspicuous good works, lavish spending, and time-consuming leisure pursuits such as yachting and golf a concerted effort to distract others from their predations and inspire both admiration and imitation. Great fortunes also bought dependents and descendants access to the highest realms of business—finance, industrial monopolies, oil and minerals—where their status would be preserved with the aid of advisers, lawyers, and others who hoped to join the leisure class themselves.

◆

In the 1890s, as Plunkitt wrote his essays and Veblen lectured at Cornell University, Fred Trump's father could access neither Tammany Hall nor the leisure class. Born and raised in Germany, he had emigrated from Bremen via Southampton in October 1885 traveling in steerage aboard the new, Glasgow-built SS *Eider*. Just sixteen years old, Friedrich had been trained to work as a barber in a country already oversupplied with young men who knew how to use scissors and razors.

Donald Trump's grandfather first stepped on American soil at Castle Garden, where an immigration center occupied a former fort built on an island constructed of landfill off the southern tip of Manhattan. Arriving immigrants were put through a gauntlet of inspections before being permitted to walk across a bridge to the borough. Once safely in New York City they were free to travel anywhere in the United States and its territories. Like many other new arrivals, Friedrich Drumpf had his name summarily changed by immigration officers. According to government papers, he departed Castle Garden as Friedrich Trumpf, and he would carry this name for years to come.

After six years in New York, Friedrich followed news of a mining boom to the West, where new cities and towns were rapidly developing. In Seattle's red-light district he thrived as the owner of a restaurant that offered warm meals and prostitutes in private rooms. It wasn't quite the Horatio Alger myth come to life, but in a country that equated wealth with virtue, Friedrich was becoming a true and virtuous American. Seven years after his arrival in New York, he went to the US District Court for the Washington State and, after renouncing his "allegiance and fidelity" to "William II Emperor of Germany," signed the declaration that made him a US citizen. In this document the *f* in *Trumpf* disappeared.

Having become a citizen and a businessman named Trump, Friedrich looked for opportunities to become rich. He spied one in a Cascade Mountains mining camp called Monte Cristo, which was overrun by prospectors looking for silver and gold. Seeing a more reliable source of cash in the prospectors than in the dirt, Trump falsely claimed to have found gold on a plot of land, which allowed him to seize control of some prime real estate without actually paying for it. (A "strike" gave a prospector exclusive access to a parcel.) Trump never worked his claim but instead built a boardinghouse. The boardinghouse was a big success. Friedrich's profit was all that much greater because he had paid nothing for his location.

As he turned his nerve and hard work into wealth, Trump showed himself to be a genuine American. In the 1890s, much of the Pacific Northwest was practically lawless, and the landscape teemed with men and women who happily exploited civilization's not having quite taken hold. Formalities meant little in the isolation of the forests and mountains, so grit and audacity might be enough to bring success. The entrepreneurial outlaw was now gradually replacing the Indian fighter as the archetypal frontiersman, and no one in a place such as Monte Cristo would be shocked to learn that one man had simply occupied another's property. Trump may have been bolder than most as he accepted a shipment of lumber and built his business on another's land, but lots of men were living and mining on land they didn't own.

No one would have been surprised, either, that Monte Cristo turned out to be a false promise kept alive so that John D. Rockefeller, whose speculation had touched off the gold and silver rush, could escape with a big profit. In 1891 America's wealthiest man had invested in the mining region on the basis of a geologist's highly optimistic reports. Rockefeller built a large processing facility to prepare ore for shipment along a new railroad line. However, production was meager, and eventually Rockefeller and his syndicate partners learned that the geologist had been wrong. They quietly sold, at a profit, and took their money back East.

When Rockefeller's secret—there was no ore—got out and Monte Cristo was abandoned, few complaints were raised about the geologist's mistake and the New Yorker's stealthy retreat. What good would it do? Besides, a new gold rush had begun in the Klondike region of northwest Canada. Roughly one hundred thousand men stampeded north after two ships arrived in Seattle with prospectors bearing the equivalent of $1 billion in 2015 in gold. Friedrich Trump departed for the Yukon, intending to repeat his success at Monte Cristo. After landing in Alaska he endured one of the most demanding and deadly wilderness treks imaginable. Trump began by operating one of the tent restaurants that specialized in meals made of horses that had expired on the trail. Soon came a real establishment built out of shingles and planks—the New Arctic Restaurant and Hotel—where once again he made prostitutes available. The New Arctic was located first in a town called Bennett and then floated on lakes and streams to the larger settlement of White Horse. Again occupying land he didn't actually own, Trump kept his place open day and night and made far more money than all but the most successful prospectors. As the boom ended, he departed White Horse, leaving the New Arctic to a partner, who would soon lose the business.

Wealthy and twice the age he had been when he came to America, thirty-two-year-old Friedrich Trump traveled to New York, where he caught a steamer for Germany, intending to find a wife there. By one account he brought with him a fortune that would be worth more than $8 million in 2015. He returned to New York City in 1905 with his wife, Elizabeth Christ Trump. She was pregnant with the son who would be born in America and named Frederick (not Friedrich) Christ Trump.

Young Frederick's father used his Yukon riches to invest in real estate. He wisely focused on the sleepy borough of Queens, which was then home to fewer than two hundred thousand scattered souls. A new bridge to Manhattan was under construction along with a railroad tunnel. The bridge opened in 1909. By 1910, when the Long Island Rail Road began running trains from Queens to the glorious new Pennsylvania Station, 284,000 people lived in the borough. Developers put up apartments and homes as fast they could. Commercial blocks emerged along Hillside, Jamaica, and Atlantic Avenues. By 1920, Queens would be home to nearly half a million people.[2]

Friedrich Trump knew a gold rush when he saw it. Planning to get rich by investing in properties, he made regular visits to real estate agents, often walking to these appointments hand in hand with his son. On one of those walks, in March 1918, he began to feel sick. Within hours he developed the first symptoms of the flu. In some accounts, his death was attributed entirely to the "Spanish flu," which killed about 775,000 Americans between 1918 and 1919. But inside the family, alcohol would take a share of the blame.[3]

Suddenly the man of the family, young Frederick began working and contributing to the household as a national economic crisis—the depression of 1920–21—swept away much of the family's wealth. He attended night school, which he supplemented with correspondence courses, to learn various construction trades and went to work for a builder as soon as he finished high school. He began as an unskilled helper, hauling heavy loads of supplies. On good days he worked with a horse. On bad days, he replaced the horse. Conscientious and strong, he was soon promoted to carpenter and began learning both the tricks and the trade of construction and real estate.

Furiously ambitious, at age twenty-one Fred Trump went into business with his mother, whose maturity reassured those who would do business with E. Trump and Son. They couldn't have chosen a better moment. New York City had entered a period of exploding growth that would see its population increase by 20 percent in a decade. As it became the world's largest city, New York's economic and cultural influence rippled across America and around the globe. Thanks to newsreels and print photographs, the skyscrapers, theaters, and streets of Manhattan dominated the world's idea of New York City, and with the help of a rascal mayor named Jimmy Walker, the borough came to represent wealth, glamour, and corruption to an extent that was both breathtaking and intimidating. Although huge rewards awaited those who made it in Manhattan, the competition was fierce. The Trumps chose to play it safe, sticking to the outer boroughs of Brooklyn and Queens. From one-house-at-a-time projects they graduated to the development of small groups of houses on subdivided properties. Within two years they had finished and sold dozens of homes and were acquiring bigger properties near the border of suburban Nassau County.[4]

The fictional West Egg of F. Scott Fitzgerald's *Great Gatsby* was on Nassau County's North Shore, and new homes built anywhere near this tony district carried cachet. Growing even faster than it did in the previous decade, Queen's population pushed real estate prices to record levels. As the Roaring Twenties produced a bubble of wealth, the Trumps built bigger houses, on bigger lots, and embellished them with architectural details that appealed to those who wanted the look of success. At a time when the typical American home cost $8,500 the Trumps were building some valued at $30,000.

The stock market crash of 1929 changed what many readers saw in Fitzgerald's novel—it became a cautionary tale—and ended the real estate boom in Queens. Rippling out in every direction, Wall Street's woes became the Great Depression of the 1930s. So many workers were laid off that the unemployment rate, which had hovered around 5 percent, soared into double digits. As breadlines formed, almost everyone, including those with money, stopped spending. Stuck with properties that no one could or would buy, E. Trump and Son went out of business. Fred opened a grocery store, which he operated with the barest interest, and waited for a chance to get back into real estate.

◆

The American economy hit bottom in 1933, as the Great Depression pushed the official jobless rate to 25 percent and the drop in home values reached 20 percent. In many places conditions were far worse, and for the millions who'd lost their jobs and struggled to pay for food, clothing, and shelter, the data said nothing about their fears, anxieties, and desperation. Foreclosures forced record numbers of families out of their homes. On a single January day, fifteen properties, seized for nonpayment of mortgages, were sold at auction in New York City.

Remarkably, amid all the gloom, one of the most popular books of the time was the celebratory history called *The Epic of America,* which introduced the world to the concept of "the American dream." Author James Truslow Adams defined the dream as a shared belief that every citizen should have a chance to live "the fullest possible life of which they were capable." This concept wasn't merely economic. Adams stressed the dignity and respect sought by every human being—these were key elements of the dream—and rued "the struggle of each against all," which he blamed for the speculative excesses of the twenties and the Crash.[5] After his book was published in late 1931, Adams spent more than a year traveling and writing about his hope that the crisis would prompt a return to less materialistic values. By 1934, as the worst of the crisis seemed over, he noted that too many of his countrymen had resumed their obsession with "getting and spending" and warned of "another orgy" of speculation.

Adams wasn't alone in his fear. In March 1934, hundreds of residents of Brooklyn and Queens—fourteen busloads—would descend upon state lawmakers in Albany to demand they do something to help them keep their homes and to thwart real estate speculators. So many homeowners in the two boroughs had sought aid under an existing program that this agency was a year behind in processing the applications. "When the real estate market picks up, the loan shark and the speculator will reap," said Matthew Nappear, a spokesman for the petitioning homeowners. "Many of our great financial fortunes were built up that way. It should not happen again."[6]

Nappear was right about one thing. One man's real estate crisis is another's opportunity. All markets work in this way, providing investors with cash the chance to buy—stocks, bonds, real estate, and commodities—when prices are depressed. This reality is devoid of emotional weight and is the basic truth that keeps capitalist economies working. The difference, when it comes to real estate, is that the investment "instrument" might be someone's home. A home, unlike, say, a stock certificate, comes freighted with extra meaning. A source of safety, comfort, and even identity, home is not just a place but the heart's location. We do not dream of portfolios and mutual funds. We do dream of the houses and apartments we knew as children.

Additional factors distinguished real estate from other investments. For one thing, most property was bought with the help of a mortgage, which meant that a relatively small amount of ready cash could leverage a much larger purchase. Also, property, more specifically land, is permanent and fixed. Stocks and bonds and the entities they represent can and often do disappear without a trace. Except in the case of government accession, for which owners must be compensated, privately held land will always retain some value. "They ain't makin' any more of it," people say to communicate real estate's special appeal. The words convey something so primal that it is known, or rather felt, by any creature that ever defended a certain territory against a rival. Whether it is a house lot or a forest, no place is the same as *this* place.

Real estate's magic is no secret. In growing cities and towns, property owners understand that strong demand pushes values up, and many will sell to turn paper profits into cash. But as demand and prices continue to climb, and more owners seek to capitalize on the opportunity, markets enter a bubble phase. Supply then outstrips demand and the bubble bursts, sending prices down. Smart money gets into the game when prices are at rock bottom and exits before the pop.

In 1930s New York the smart money swirled around the courthouses, where judges resolved bankruptcies and foreclosures and disposed of real estate at extremely low prices. As political creatures themselves, judges understood that while rules governed their actions, well-connected players could be favored whenever possible. Friends and allies would be named as trustees when prime properties were forfeited in bankruptcies and get the first shot at them. With the right information, well connected investors might even approach a homeowner who was behind on payments and make an offer to buy a building or some land before a lender foreclosed or the city issued a tax lien. The seller would be spared the stress and embarrassment of an eviction, while the buyer acquired real estate without the hassle of working through the courts or competing with other investors.

Lacking the connections to seize the easy opportunities, Fred Trump watched the bankruptcy/foreclosure action hoping to see an opening he might exploit. He learned the names and habits of the powerful men who ran the city's Democratic Party clubs and checked courthouse dockets. At the end of 1933, Trump's eye was drawn to claims made against one of the biggest mortgage companies in Brooklyn, Lehrenkrauss & Co. Licensed as an investment bank by the state, the company was family owned and had operated for more than fifty years. In the 1920s, as Americans of every rank and class raced into the money boom, Lehrenkrauss sold everything from foreign currency to gold. However, the firm's main business was the sale of bonds backed by big bundles of mortgages. Many of the bondholders were recent German immigrants who were reassured, as they invested their savings, by the bank's good name.

The Lehrenkrausses were so prominent that their comings and goings were recorded on the society pages—Charles F. Lehrenkrauss entertained aboard his yacht in Manhasset Bay—and their divorces appeared in the news columns. (J. Lester Lehrenkrauss's wife, Beatrice, secured a divorce from him thanks to a court in Reno, Nevada.) A Lehrenkrauss Cup was awarded each year to the top student at a local school, and members of the family were sought to sit on various boards and committees. In April 1929 the most senior Lehrenkrauss, Julius, was named to the board of a new finance company called Brooklyn Capital. The very next month he joined the advisory board of the Hamilton Trust division of the Chase National Bank.

All three Lehrenkrauss men—Julius, Charles, and Lester—were named personally when investors filed their complaint against the firm in Brooklyn's federal court. According to the papers, investors suspected that the company was insolvent and that the notes the firm had sold were essentially worthless. Thousands of bond-holders were outraged by the tale of deception that emerged in the court hearings. As Julius explained, he had sold bonds worth many times the value of the mortgages that backed them. Dividends were paid with new revenues, Ponzi-style, and cash was shifted from account to account to give auditors the false impression that the firm's various operations were solvent. As the company was nearing collapse, Julius had withdrawn $1,900 in cash, all $20 bills, because, he said, he was "looking for the future."

Before the ordeal was over, investigators would discover that dozens of deeds were missing from company files, and unbeknownst to others in the firm, Julius had lost more than $450,000—worth roughly $8.1 million in 2015—in the stock market. (One of his investments had been in a copper company that had produced just $52.26 worth of ore.) A nephew said Julius had recently told him, "Stocks are bound to rise." Unable to pay for a vigorous defense and cornered by the evidence, Julius donned a formal wing-collar shirt, striped pants, and black jacket to attend the court session where he would plead guilty to grand larceny. His lawyer said that Lehrenkrauss would accept his punishment "like a man." The judge, a longtime friend of the accused's, sentenced him to a term of five to ten in the state prison known as Sing Sing.

Although Lehrenkrauss bonds were worthless, one small part of the business, which collected mortgage payments from debtors, retained some value. The court-appointed trustees invited bids for this business. One major mortgage-servicing company, Home Title Guarantee, entered the competition. Other bidders were less well-known but better connected to the Brooklyn political machine. Fred Trump, who had managed mortgages on many of the homes he sold, embellished his qualifications

by informing the court that he had been in the real estate and mortgage business for ten years. (This claim
would have had him selling houses as a high schooler.)
But even with this exaggeration, he could lose without a
special advantage.

Trump courted Brooklyn's political power brokers
and joined forces with another Queens-based bidder
named William Demm. Concerned that a large group
of Lehrenkrauss investors might hold up the sale, the
two men attended one of the investors' meetings at
Bushwick High School. The victims feared that the old
firm might one day be resurrected and they would be
deprived of any value left in the mortgage-servicing
business. Only a miracle would revive Lehrenkrauss,
but Trump understood the feelings of the creditors. He
and Demm promised that if Lehrenkrauss ever rose
from the dead, they would sell the mortgage-servicing
business to the creditors for a net profit of just $1,000.
All they asked in return was that the group endorse their
bid to the trustees. A deal was struck, and the court,
eager to avoid conflict with the victims of the Lehrenkrauss clan, accepted the Trump/Demm bid.[7]

Although they would make some money processing
mortgage payments, the real value in the business won
by Trump and Demm was in the information they
gleaned from the Lehrenkrauss operations. In the company's recent records they discovered which homeowners were behind in their payments and when foreclosures
were imminent. With this knowledge, they could offer
to buy distressed properties before they ever went on
the market.

As Fred Trump bought properties, he zeroed in on the
Brooklyn neighborhood of East Flatbush, where, just
thirty years before, farmers had grown produce to supply markets in Manhattan. The neighborhood's transformation from rural to urban began when a real estate

firm called Wood, Harmon and Company persuaded the Brooklyn Rapid Transit Company to extend trolley service that previously stopped at nearby Prospect Park. Wood, Harmon built fifty homes within a year. The neighborhood grew even more quickly when August Belmont's Interborough Rapid Transit Company brought its subway down Nostrand Avenue. Suddenly convenient to commuters who worked almost anywhere in Manhattan, East Flatbush bloomed with new single-family homes, duplexes, and apartment buildings.

By the late 1930s, Fred Trump was piecing together lots to create large tracts where he built developments ranging from a few dozen homes to hundreds. His largest project was built on a long-vacant lot where the Barnum & Bailey Circus had performed under a big top. When the circus last visited East Flatbush in 1938, the star of the show was a gorilla with the stage name Gargantua. Buddy, as he was known to his friends, had been raised by an eccentric Brooklyn woman, who used to dress him in a shirt and pants and drive around the borough with him in her car's passenger seat.

Close to two different subway stops, Trump's circus-lot development was subsidized by the very same Federal Housing Administration that would come under Senator Capehart's scrutiny in 1954. Created by Franklin Delano Roosevelt to help would-be home buyers, developers, builders, and construction workers, the FHA was a part of FDR's larger New Deal effort to stimulate the Depression-era economy with the kind of government spending that economist John Maynard Keynes called pump priming.

Prior to the 1930s and the creation of the FHA, the federal government had no real housing policy, and homeownership was not the bulwark of middle-class status that it eventually became. Mortgage lenders required down payments of 50 percent or more, and loans typically became payable in full—this was called a bullet payment—in five or ten years. (Most homeowners refinanced before the due date.) In 1940, just 43 percent of Americans owned their homes. In more urbanized states, even fewer people did. For New York the figure was just 30 percent. In addition to FHA support for new housing, New Deal programs sparked a steady increase in ownership by aiding the creation of twenty-year mortgages for up to 80 percent of a home's value and by insuring lenders against loss should a borrower default.

Although most Americans would struggle if asked to explain the difference between the FHA and Fannie Mae (the Federal National Mortgage Association), businessmen and politicians who followed the development of these programs recognized an opportunity. Real estate people saw a chance to do business on a much grander scale, with many more potential customers and greatly reduced risk. The pols saw big new bureaucracies that would be filled with Democratic appointees who would control millions and eventually billions of dollars' worth of financing that could be given to favored applicants, if one was so inclined. In New York, the top FHA job went to a high school football coach turned lawyer named Thomas "Tommy" G. Grace. A World War I army veteran and a gregarious mainstay of the party clubhouse in the Brooklyn neighborhood of Bay Ridge, Grace was just thirty-nine when he was appointed in 1935. His brother was Fred Trump's lawyer, and in August 1936 Tommy presented Trump with a plaque commemorating the federal government's commitment to back the financing for a four-hundred-home development.

The little ceremony, which was noted in *The New York Times,*[8] was a nonevent of the sort that businesspeople and politicians conceived and staged for the sole purpose of attracting publicity. Unlike real news events, which occurred spontaneously, these nonevents were preceded by "news" releases sent to editors and reporters, and they occurred at a certain hour with the participants following a preordained script. New York, where the first big public relations companies flourished in the 1920s, was the capital of this new business. The term *public relations* was coined by a New Yorker, Edward Bernays—a nephew of Sigmund Freud's—who taught the first course in this trade at New York University in 1923.

Bernays believed that with the right combination of manufactured events, celebrity endorsements, and allies in high places, he could not only stimulate sales for a client but actually create trends, change fashions, or alter public policy. When short flapper styles destroyed demand for a client's hairnets, Bernays got prominent women to declare they favored long hair, and he convinced regulators that hairnets should be required wherever women handled food or worked around machinery. Scant evidence existed that these new regulations were needed but Bernays was so persuasive that policies and attitudes changed and hairnet sales soared. He performed similar magic for luggage manufacturers who suffered because new styles allowed men and women to travel light. By the time Bernays was done, public health officials were telling people it was unsanitary to share a suitcase and luggage sales ticked upward.

Bernays was aided by what the critic Neal Gabler would call "the two-dimensional society," which came with the spread of photo-rich tabloid newspapers and movie-theater newsreels that made people and events memorable to millions of people who could never access them in real life. The PR pioneer's methods were so successful that in 1927 *The Nation* said he was ushering in "the Kingdom of heaven of the salesman." He soon had legions of imitators, including run-of-the-mill bureaucrats and businessmen who discovered they could do it themselves. By feeding reporters a steady diet of announcements and events, they gained access to the news columns of the local papers. The free ink they received was more valuable than paid advertising because it was delivered to the public as legitimate news, recognized as such by professional journalists. Much of this manipulation was harmless, but in some cases PR practitioners—particularly those in politics—created scapegoats and public enemies through negative stereotypes.[9]

Deploying news releases at a steady rate, Fred Trump sought free publicity for everything he did, including serving as host for a company picnic. He got a couple of free column inches by simply announcing that one development in Brooklyn was one year old—"Flatbush Builder Celebrates"—and more inches just twelve days later—"Selling Homes in Flatbush"—by announcing he had completed forty sales in three weeks. That a development was a year old, or that a real estate man was selling homes, was "news" of the dog-bites-man variety. But somehow Trump got these items published, and the cumulative effect was good for business. By 1940 he was hailed as one of Brooklyn's biggest builders in a report noting that his crews were bulldozing the last patch of forest in the borough. Paerdegat Woods, where Canarsie Indians once hunted, had been the site of a Revolutionary War skirmish between colonists and Hessian mercenaries during the larger Battle of Long Island.

Many of Trump's developments were built on properties that he purchased from public or publicly regulated sellers including the City of New York and, in the case of Paerdegat Woods, the Brooklyn Water Company. Trump was not hurt in these deals by being extremely well-known to the city's Democratic Party leaders. In any place or time, a real estate developer would be well advised to stay on good terms with local politicians. In 1940s New York it was also a good idea to stay on the right side of the mob.

As the end of Prohibition took away their liquor business, Italian American gangsters increased their presence in the construction industry and trade unions. These men used violence and the threat of violence to control the supply of materials and labor and determined which of the companies in their syndicate or "club" received contracts for major developments. The danger posed by these men was quite real. A double murder carried out by one group of Brooklyn mobsters against another brought unions representing painters and plumber's helpers under the control of Louis Capone and his associates. The executions also signaled the seriousness of organized crime's involvement in the trades. The mob bosses were so feared that with a word they could shut down a project and burden a developer with extra costs, or they could send cheap, nonunion workers to a site and thereby slash the price of labor. Sometimes the mob men required cash to keep the peace, or they forced a developer to pay for workers who never showed up. In other cases the cost was simply added to contracts. No matter the method, the Mafia's involvement made construction in New York City more expensive, and more dangerous, than anywhere else in America.

After World War II, when the FHA turned to funding homes for veterans, Trump teamed with a mob-connected masonry contractor to develop his big Beach Haven project. Prior to joining Trump, William "Willie" Tomasello had partnered with figures in the Genovese and Gambino crime families in a number of real estate developments in New York and Florida. Tomasello's presence at Beach Haven meant that Trump wouldn't have to worry about disruptions in the supply of bricks, cement, lumber, or hardware. It also assured him access to reliable labor, including men who were not union members and could be paid at lower rates. Trump never again partnered with Tomasello. In 1990 Tomasello's associate Louis DiBono, who worked with him on four subsequent projects, was found dead in a Cadillac parked in an underground garage at the World Trade Center in Lower Manhattan.[10]

More prosperous with every passing year, Fred Trump advertised his properties with billboards and air-dropped coupons promising discounts on his apartments. He began offering the press his opinions on issues of the day—including President Truman's policies—and talked about running for borough president of Queens. Practically unique to New York City, the office of borough president had been created at the end of the nineteenth century, when the city was consolidated. The presidents sat on a council called the Board of Estimate and controlled local land use, development, franchises, and other city business. By custom they exercised veto power over certain mayoral appointments and decisions. The office was tailor-made for an inside operator such as Fred Trump. But his desire would be thwarted as he ran up against a power that wasn't susceptible to the influences of the Brooklyn Democratic clubs or his friends at the courthouse.

◆

By 1954, various investigators had begun to reveal the widespread corruption of government and certain industries—construction, trucking, dock services—in many of America's big cities. Senator Estes Kefauver's Special Committee to Investigate Crime in Interstate Commerce had revealed the links between the Mafia and Tammany Hall and sketched the outlines of corruption in the construction business. A special New York State crime commission documented bribes to public officials, and a state senator from Manhattan called for a permanent grand jury to conduct a continual review of city business.

The reality revealed by Kefauver made Plunkitt's graft seem quaint. As the committee showed, gangsters were using extortion, violence, bribes, and payoffs to control both public officials and private businesses. The details outraged Dwight D. Eisenhower and a handful of clergy in New York, who denounced the greed and self-dealing. "We have become a city that is a civic sewer," said Rabbi William Rosenbaum of Temple Israel in Manhattan. However, the web of relationships that governed this shadowy world was so large and complex that only a true expert, and few existed, would know all the names of those involved. When Fred Trump appeared before the Senate banking committee, no one mentioned that his associate Willie Tomasello was also in business with organized crime figures. As the members of the banking committee and their aides amassed more than three thousand pages of testimony, they expressed no interest in the mobsters who hovered around the construction industry. They were concerned only with the windfall profits of developers and the bureaucrats who helped them.

Two of the committee's main targets, FHA officials Tommy Grace and Clyde L. Powell, had acted as the chief enablers for developers in New York, and Trump was involved with both of them. A Democratic clubhouse regular and political man about Brooklyn, Grace had bestowed upon Trump his very first FHA contract and the commemorative plaque noted in *The Times*. According to committee investigators, Grace had received $48,000 from the law firm where his brother George represented many FHA applicants, including Fred Trump. George would eventually admit that some "green" had been passed to "get something done," but in his official response to the government's inquiry he said that no one should believe the brothers Grace had done anything illegal.

Fred Trump's connection with Clyde L. Powell was documented by committee staffers, who found that Powell had acted on Trump's behalf. For example, when the agency's comptroller discovered problems in some of Trump's paperwork, Powell simply excused him from complying with the rules. Powell did the same for other developers and somehow, while his official government salary never exceeded $10,000 a year, managed to amass $100,000 in a bank account. The investigators suggested that the money had been accumulated as payoffs from those who wanted the FHA loans Powell controlled. Before he got his government job, Powell had been arrested several times on charges of embezzlement and check fraud. He also had a gambling problem so severe that he once lost $5,000—half his annual salary—in a single night.

Remarkably, neither Powell nor Grace were actually discussed when Trump appeared before the Senate committee, and he was never asked, directly, whether he had given them any money or gifts. However, Fred Trump would pay a price, for his involvement in the scandal, as he lost access to the FHA program. But in his spirited self-defense he made a much better impression than his fellow developers who, as the saying goes, "took the Fifth." Despite his convoluted answers, Fred Trump came across as cooperative. By the end of the afternoon Chairman Capehart had so thoroughly warmed up to Trump that he thanked him for appearing and assured him that the committee had been "glad" to listen to him.

Finished with his testimony before sundown, Fred Trump caught a flight to New York so he could end the day at his home with his family in the tony Jamaica Estates neighborhood of Queens. In one of those small-world moments that was more likely when only about three hundred flights were departing daily from National Airport, he ran into the senator, who was also headed for New York City. Capehart told him, chirpily, that America needed more housing so Trump should "keep up the good work."[11]

2
THE BOY KING

*When I look at myself in the first grade and I look
at myself now, I'm basically the same.
The temperament is not that different.*
—DONALD TRUMP

Perched above a sloping lawn and set beneath towering oaks, the home that welcomed Fred Trump
after his grilling in Washington was the one house in
Jamaica Estates, Queens, that could rightly be called a
mansion. It occupied two full lots on a graceful parkway
with a wide median for trees, shrubs, and flowers. An
American conception of a nineteenth-century British
garden suburb, Jamaica Estates was crisscrossed by
streets with properly English names. The parkway where
the Trumps lived was called Midland. The nearest cross
street was Henley Road.

Built by Trump himself, the Colonial Revival house
overwhelmed the land it occupied and stood out in a
neighborhood of more modest Tudor-style homes. Its red
brick exterior walls were topped by wide fascia boards
decorated with dentils and a steep slate roof. The door
was guarded by four massive columns, which supported
a pediment that bore a plaque painted with an ersatz
crest. Altogether, the design recalled a junior high in
some new suburb where the school board wanted something that looked stolidly institutional. But instead of yellow buses, the driveway sheltered fancy cars. A Cadillac
for him. A Rolls-Royce for her.

Visitors to the Trump home approached along a walkway flanked by two jockeys made of painted cast iron. Inside they found a foyer with a curved staircase leading to the second-floor family quarters. The stairway was impressive and formal looking, but none of the twenty-three rooms in the house were especially grand. Despite the decorations on the outside, this was a practical space, made to serve the needs of seven Trumps and their live-in housekeeper and chauffeur. Hence the nine bathrooms.

By the summer of 1954 the Trump family included five children—two girls and three boys—ages six to seventeen, who were shepherded by their mother, Mary Anne MacLeod Trump. Forty-two years old, Mrs. Trump was fair, tall, and slender with blue eyes and blond hair, and she spoke with a hint of a Scottish brogue. She was, in her quieter way, as tough, stubborn, and ambitious as her husband. "My mother was silently competitive," recalled Donald Trump, long after his mother had died. "She was a very competitive person but you wouldn't know that. She had a great fighting spirit, like Braveheart." She also loved the kind of excess represented by the British monarchy. Donald would recall that his mother had been fascinated by the coronation of Queen Elizabeth II, in 1953. As a boy he had been impressed by his mother's interest as she eagerly watched every minute of the live TV broadcast of the event. It was the first time that cameras had been permitted in Westminster Abbey.

The youngest of ten children, Mary Anne MacLeod was born in 1912 in her parents' home in the village of Tong on the rugged Scottish Isle of Lewis, which is closer to Iceland than London. She was descended from two clans, the Smiths and MacLeods, with deep roots in the Hebrides. On the Smith side, Mary Anne's forebears had been crofters who were forced off their tenant farms during the "clearances" of the nineteenth century. These mass evictions carried out by absentee landlords drove many rural families into poverty. One account from this time describes the landless people of Tong living in "human wretchedness" alongside arable land that was set aside for game preserves. The Isle of Lewis became poorer by the year, losing jobs, business activity, and population.

In 1917, virtually all of Lewis—683 square miles— was purchased by the soap magnate William Lever, who announced he would invest the equivalent of $500 million in 2015 dollars to turn the island into a paradise of industry, agriculture, and fisheries. A world-famous eccentric, Lever was a fresh-air fiend whose bedroom was open to the elements year-round. He was also a self-proclaimed social engineer, certain he could create the perfect way of life for great numbers of people, who would live as if they were his subjects, dependent on him for their employment, their homes, and their community life. Lever had made his vision real at Port Sunlight, in northwest England, where thirty-five hundred Leverites dwelled in his garden village and worked in his factories.

In Lewis, William Lever imagined another Port Sunlight, only bigger. In this Land of Lever, trained observers would circle the island in war-surplus planes, scanning the sea for shoals of herring. Boats sent to seize the catch would return to supply a giant cannery powered by a new electric plant, which would also energize spinners and looms in new textile mills. In the evenings all the spotters and fishers and spinners would go home to Lever-built homes where they would sup on foods produced by the lord's farmers. On weekends everyone would enjoy recreation or entertainments sponsored by their employer and benefactor.

Local burghers were excited by Lever's plan, which

they hoped would end the privation that began with the clearances. However, two years after his arrival, Lever had made almost no progress. No factories. No jobs. No fish-spotting planes. Many islanders, most especially those descended from crofters, grew both restless and suspicious. On March 10, 1919, landless men occupied Lever properties in several villages, including Tong. The occupiers staked out plots and scraped at the land to prepare it for planting. Made a peer by George V two years prior, Lord Leverhulme called on powerful friends in government. A government man sent to mediate the conflict would say of Lever, "I never met a man who was so obviously a megalomaniac and accustomed to having his own way." Nevertheless, the law was on Lever's side and the squatters were persuaded to retreat and wait for the great man to fulfill his promise. He would die in 1925 before developing even one of his promised projects.[1]

With all of its conflict and poverty, Lewis would seem to have endured more than its share of suffering, but the worst involved not an act of man, but one of nature. Having sent more than six thousand men to fight in World War I and losing nearly a thousand, Lewis awaited the return of their surviving soldiers. On New Year's Eve of 1918 a small ship called the *Iolaire* (Scots Gaelic for "eagle") joined the regular ferry that served the port of Stornoway to bring men home from the mainland train terminus at Kyle. Approaching Stornoway at night and in a storm, *Iolaire* struck an outcropping of rocks called the Beasts of Holme and slowly broke apart. On a night when many said they saw wild deer near their homes— local lore held that such sightings were ominous—205 men died within sight of the shore. The grief that swept across the island lasted for many years.[2]

Against the backdrop of such hard times, Mary Anne MacLeod's decision to leave Tong for America was as realistic as it was brave. Little work was available and marriageable men were in short supply on the isle. In 1930, at age eighteen, she boarded the three-funneled steamship *Transylvania* in Glasgow, bound for New York. A married sister already living in Astoria, Queens, welcomed her. The same sister would bring Mary Anne to the party where she met Fred Trump. The two married in January 1936 and honeymooned for a night in Atlantic City before returning to New York.

Fred and Mary Anne Trump's first child, Maryanne, arrived in 1937. She was followed by Fred Jr. (1938), Elizabeth (1942), Donald (1946), and Robert (1948). Hemorrhaging after the last birth led to a hysterectomy, followed by life-threatening peritonitis and several more surgeries. After Mary Anne recovered, she resumed command of the household and plunged into charity work. Strong-willed and energetic, she was charming and unafraid to be the center of attention at a party—a bit of a performer. In this she was very different from her husband. Fred Trump never developed the ease and grace necessary to win friends and influence people in social situations, though he worked hard at it and even attended a Dale Carnegie course, "Effective Speaking and Human Relations." Born Dale Carnagey in 1888, Carnagey changed his name to capitalize on the fame of the great tycoon and quit work as a salesman for Armour meat to pursue his dream of becoming a renowned writer and public speaker. Having studied the subject so intently, he made the art of public speaking the subject of his first book. In subsequent works he offered wide-ranging advice on everything from "how to make our listeners like us" to "the kind of smile that will bring a good price in the market place."

In his eight-page dissertation on smiling, Carnegie urged those who would succeed to offer others "a real smile that says, 'I like you. You make me happy. I'm glad to see you.' . . . An insincere smile? No. That doesn't fool anybody." As he implored followers to use artificial means—study, practice, repetition—to cultivate a sincere smile, Carnegie affirmed the triumph of personality, even one that is manufactured, over character, hard work, and quality. This was the tragic fact of life in twentieth-century America that was communicated in Arthur Miller's 1949 play, *Death of a Salesman*, in which Willy Loman declares, "Personality always wins the day." It may have been to Fred Trump's credit that he never mastered the Carnegie method.

Fred Trump made up for his social shortcomings by working exceedingly hard. He rarely went a day without conducting some sort of business, and he worked at home, by telephone, almost every night. A son or daughter who wanted his time would accompany him on a weekend trip to the office, or a tour of construction sites. He called it "making the rounds." Along the way they would hear about the importance of ambition, discipline, and hard work. Trump wanted his children to believe that they could, and should, accomplish a great deal in life. The family code barred coarse language and between-meal snacks and required obedience and loyalty. Infractions would be reported upon Fred's arrival home each evening, and he meted out the punishments.[3]

A gruff and demanding patriarch, Fred Trump required both his daughters and sons to work to earn their own money, but he was more keenly committed to training his sons for a life of fierce competition. "Be a killer," he told them over and over. But he also indulged them in the way that a man with hard-won riches might. They attended private schools and vacationed in Florida in the winter and in the Catskills in the summer. When it rained or snowed, he let the boys deliver their newspapers via chauffeured limousine. "You are a king," said Fred to Donald.[4]

Subject to this unusual combination of stern discipline, indulgence, and superiority, the five Trump children each reacted quite differently. The eldest, Maryanne, would develop into a studious young woman and realize an extremely successful career in law. Younger daughter Elizabeth would attend a small college, work in a bank, and eventually marry. Never suited to his father's template, Fred Trump Jr. would fail as his father's assistant and eventually have a career as an airline pilot. The youngest, Robert, would take a middle road through life, succeeding in business but without his father's drive and his need to dominate. This left Fred Trump's mantle available to his middle son Donald, who from an early age showed every sign that he was every bit the old man's boy, and then some.

◆

Erasers hurled at teachers and cake flung at birthday parties were notable examples of the problem-child behavior that separated Donald Trump from the other kids at the private Kew-Forest School, which he attended in the elementary grades. Kew-Forest had opened in 1918, as American educators shifted away from scholastic rigor and toward the child-centered approach advocated by psychologists John Dewey and G. Stanley Hall. Dewey and Hall believed that teachers should adjust the pace and content of their lessons to the students rather than simply demanding that they keep up. Kew-Forest became a training center for the children of the elite on the North Shore of Queens County, where wedding announcements often noted which brides and grooms had been educated there. A member of the board, Fred Trump had donated materials to construct a new wing for the school, which all of his children would attend.

At Kew-Forest, Donald Trump was a bit of a terror. He once said that he gave a teacher a black eye "because

I didn't think he knew anything about music." According to Trump, he was then already the person he would always be. "I don't think people change very much," Trump would tell me. "When I look at myself in the first grade and I look at myself now, I'm basically the same. The temperament is not that different."

Donald's sister Maryanne Trump Barry would describe her brother as "extremely rebellious" in his youth. A classmate recalled Donald as a boy who tested the rules, and the teachers, to their limits. A camp counselor was impressed by young Donald's "ornery" disposition, which compelled him to figure out "all the angles" so he could get his own way. His behavior wasn't any better at Sunday school, or at home, where he stood up to his father at moments when his older brother, Fred, would have retreated. In time Donald would credit the respect he won from the old man to the fact that "I used to fight back all the time."[5]

Father Trump liked that Donald was interested in the world of real estate development and construction. Every time Fred's middle son got the chance, he tagged along as Fred toured his many properties and building sites to make sure things were running smoothly. Having done most of the jobs himself at one time or another, Fred Trump was adept at negotiating with plumbers and masons, electricians, and maintenance workers. As he pressed for the best work at the best price on the best schedule, Donald absorbed his father's way of doing business. "He wouldn't say, 'Now listen to every word,' but I'd hear him talking . . . and I picked it up very naturally," Donald recalled. Much of what he "picked up" was the idea that a life of ambition and hard work was pleasurable. "He really liked his life, and yet he worked all the time."

The Trump work ethic was part of what both men would come to regard as a genetically transmitted talent for success. According to this view, some people are born to win. Seeing this trait in Donald, Fred Trump let the boy know that he was destined for greatness. "My father expected tremendous success out of me," Donald would put it later. But if Fred admired the child who was most like himself, it didn't win Donald any reprieve from his father's code of discipline. Fred Trump was especially bothered by the reports of bad behavior from Donald's teachers. As complaints about his son accumulated, he learned that Donald had been sneaking into Manhattan on the subway and acquiring a small collection of switchblades. (He and a friend had been inspired by the Sharks and the Jets of *West Side Story.*) Concluding that he could no longer manage the boy's behavior, Fred Trump decided that even though he was a trustee at Kew-Forest, seventh grade would be his boy's last at the school. In the fall of 1959 Donald was delivered to New York Military Academy (NYMA), a school for boys on the Hudson River just eight miles from West Point.

Private boarding schools had long supported the nation's elite. Located mainly in the Northeast, they provided places where the children of the rich and powerful could be trained, together, for their places in the world. Although they too served children from many of the same elite families, all-male *military* academies were more likely to receive boys who needed something sterner than Exeter or Andover. At these schools, cadets as young as six were required to don uniforms, obey orders, and submit to an intensely regimented way of life. Conservative in nature, military academies offered even more isolation from the outside world than ordinary boarding schools. The men who ruled these places believed in corporal punishment and discouraged individuality. They also required at least a display of respect, even from students who refused to grant them the real thing.[6]

At their best, old-fashioned military academies saved students from delinquency. At their worst, they drove boys to it by subjecting them to a culture that valued dominance, violence, and subversion of authorities. The experience is brilliantly told in Pat Conroy's novel *The Lords of Discipline,* which depicts life at a military college similar to The Citadel in South Carolina. Although Conroy writes with both dismay and affection, others have offered a more scathing evaluation of these places. In his memoir, *Breakshot,* former mobster Kenny Gallo noted that his military boarding-school experience transformed him from "a disorderly brat into an orderly outlaw." Recalling his career at Army and Navy Academy in California, Gallo writes, "I guess you could say my 'normal' social development stopped at military school when I was thirteen; I stopped developing as a healthy adult citizen and, first out of self defense and then out of pleasure, began honing my skills as a predator."[7]

As a thirteen-year-old newcomer at NYMA, fair-haired, baby-faced Donald Trump soon found himself confronted by a screaming US Army war veteran named Theodore Dobias. A former NYMA cadet, Dobias had enlisted in the US Army when he was seventeen to fight in World War II. Assigned to the Tenth Mountain Division, he had marched up much of the Italian Peninsula in a campaign that saw nearly one thousand of his fellow soldiers killed. After the war, Dobias returned to the New York Military Academy with stark memories of "the foxholes, the blood, the screaming," of combat. In Italy he had seen Benito Mussolini's mutilated body, and six others, hanging from the metal frame of a gas-station awning in Milan. Below them were piled almost a dozen additional bodies. Almost seventy years later, this grotesque scene would remain vivid in Dobias's mind when we met for an interview.

Dobias finished his education at NYMA then began

a lifelong career at the school. From the start he was an active disciplinarian. For new arrivals, Dobias's bark marked the moment when they realized the seriousness of their situation. "In those days they'd smack the hell out of you. It was not like today where you smack somebody and you go to jail," said Trump decades later. "He could be a fucking prick. He absolutely would rough you up. You had to learn to survive." Trump recalled that when he responded to an order from Dobias with a look that said, "'Give me a fucking break,' he came after me like you wouldn't believe."

At age eighty-nine Dobias was a bit stooped, but still sturdy, like a stout whiskey barrel on legs. In the spring of 2014 he scuttled around a house where a woodstove battled with the last chill of winter and a clock announced the hour with "Hey Jude" sounded by electronic chimes.

"The father was really tough on the kid," recalled Dobias when I asked about the Trumps. "He was very German. He came up on a lot of Sundays and would take the boy out to dinner. Not many did that. But he was very tough."

NYMA was in its heyday when Trump attended, and his fellow cadets included the sons of Wall Street bankers, Midwest industrialists, and South American oligarchs. The most homesick boy Dobias supervised in this time was the son of a Mafia boss. The grateful father sent boxes of cookies to the school at Christmas. Another dad sent cases of meat.

"I coached baseball and football, and I taught them that winning wasn't everything, it was the only thing," added Dobias, borrowing a cliché coined by Vince Lombardi, the pro football coach who became a paragon of mid-century manliness. "Donald picked right up on this. He would tell his teammates, 'We're out here for a purpose. To win.' He always had to be number one, in everything. He was a conniver even then. A real pain in the ass. He would do anything to win."

Describing a boy full of desire and drive, Dobias said Trump "just wanted to be first, in everything, and he wanted people to know he was first." Dobias would never forget the Columbus Day parade in New York City where NYMA was supposed to be first in the order of march, with Donald Trump leading the corps. "We got there and there were all these Catholic schoolgirls lined up ahead of us. He said, 'Maje, leave this to me.' He went off and talked to somebody, and when he came back, they put us first. That was the way he was."

A photographer sent by the school would snap a photo of Trump, smartly uniformed, down to his bright white gloves, right in front of Tiffany's iconic store on Fifth Avenue. A few blocks farther south, the NYMA cadets were greeted heartily by Cardinal Joseph Spellman, who stood on the steps of St. Patrick's Cathedral.

The assertiveness Trump showed as he cleared away the Catholic schoolgirls pleased Dobias, who said he tried to instill in his boys certain tenets of manhood. Included were:

> Respect for authority.
> Set a good example in your appearance, your
>   manners, and how you speak.
> Be proud of your family.
> Be proud of yourself.

"Trump was always proud of himself," said Dobias. "He believed he was the best." (When he reflected on this period, Trump would tell me, "I was an elite person. When I graduated, I was a very elite person.")

Theodore Dobias didn't tell the boys that they needed to accomplish anything significant in order to feel proud. It was enough to get in line with the program at the academy, present oneself well, and to appreciate one's status as a member of the NYMA community. This status was, in part, compensation for the strict discipline imposed there. Though an adult, Dobias was himself constrained by the rules. As a young man he could not leave the campus without permission, which made courting his wife-to-be a difficult and drawn out campaign. In midlife, Dobias was offered a free trip to Slovakia to visit the grandparents who had raised him up to age thirteen. He had last seen them through tears, from the deck of the ship that had brought him to America in 1939. His commander refused him permission to go. Dobias obeyed without complaint.

Eventually promoted to a rank just below superintendent, Dobias spent his entire adult life on the campus at Cornwall, where he even occupied an academy house with his wife and children. (His one son was a cadet.) Students called him "the Maje"—which was short for "major." Although, as he said, "sometimes I forgot there was an outside world," on occasion it came to him. When the first black cadet enrolled at NYMA in the 1970s, it fell to Dobias to ease his adjustment to the school, which required almost nightly discussions about the culture of the academy, racism, and the young man's struggles. "We had some really great talks."

Years later a lawyer in Pennsylvania called Dobias to discuss this same man. She said he was on death row, after being convicted of multiple murders, and he wanted Dobias to come visit. By this time, the Maje had become so rooted, in every sense, that he couldn't imagine traveling to Pennsylvania to see the former cadet. "It was far away," he explained, "and I didn't think I should get involved."

Despite the rough beginning of their relationship, Donald Trump came to regard Ted Dobias as his first real role model, aside from his father. Dobias helped him to adapt and thrive in an environment where macho concepts of strength and masculinity prevailed. One of Trump's fellow cadets, Harry Falber, would recall that the systematic bullying among the students was far more troubling than the discipline meted out by the staff. Though not quite *Lord of the Flies,* the culture at the school was "full of aggression," said Falber, and a mob mentality sometimes prevailed. He once saw a large group of cadets, who were being overseen by school staff, attack a car that had arrived on campus. "It was full of girls and these guys just pelted it with rocks," recalled Falber. "They took out at least one of the windows. Nobody stopped them. Discipline was very important there, but not always."

The rules the cadets were supposed to follow were set out in a booklet called "General Order No. 6," with the ominous subtitle "Scale of Punishment," which every boy received on his first day at the academy. This code of conduct noted that a boy could be charged with demerits for anything from lint on his uniform to a phone call longer than five minutes to holding hands "with a young lady." One major infraction, or an accumulation of small ones, would lead to an hour of military marching. Many offenses, including insubordination and "immorality" (assumed by cadets to mean homosexual acts) were so serious they could lead to a boy's dismissal.

Donald Trump apparently thrived at NYMA. He felt comfortable in uniform—spit-shined shoes and belt buckles polished with Brasso—and adjusted to mess-hall meals. Isolated in an all-male military environment, far from his mother and father and siblings, the boy quickly learned that "life is about survival. It's always about survival." A good but not stellar student, he became one of Dobias's favorites and absorbed the sense of superiority that was preached at NYMA with the consistency of a drumbeat. (Even the school catalog bragged that the academy was "superior" and "a school of distinction" where "each boy becomes familiar, through personal experience, with the problems of those who are led, and those who lead.")

Rigidly hierarchical and hypermasculine, the academy required physical sacrifice, and the cadets were denied a world of experiences and relationships enjoyed by friends back home. No moms and dads. No brothers and sisters. In school plays, female roles were played by boys in drag. All this was part of a plan of education devised to instill a sense of self-discipline and the ability to perform under duress. Athletes were revered, which was true at many, if not most, high schools in postwar America. As underpaid teachers struggled in overcrowded classrooms, football and basketball came to dominate the culture of secondary education, with marching bands and cheerleading squads adopting important supporting roles. All this and more was noted by Richard Hofstadter in a landmark book, *Anti-Intellectualism in American Life,* which was published in 1963, as Donald Trump hit his stride during his junior year at NYMA.

Hofstadter devoted much of his book to the modern American mode of child rearing and education, and he offered much to worry a reader who hoped for a humane and just society. He observed that in the name of child development, greater emphasis was placed on personality and social adjustment while character and scholarship were neglected. Influenced by the "prophets of practicality in business," wrote Hofstadter, teachers taught "not Shakespeare or Dickens, but how to write a business letter." One district in New York State was so committed to preparing socially successful young people that every student was required to attend a kind of self-improvement course where they would learn about "clicking with the crowd" and "how to be liked."[8]

At NYMA, educators strove to give cadets a feeling of confidence to match the military bearing— straight back, eyes forward, chin out—that would propel them through life with a sense that they deserved great success because the academy had made them better than everyone else. Donald Trump absorbed this lesson, rising to what he called "the top of the military heap" and excelling at baseball. ("Always the best player," Trump would say of himself. "Not only baseball, but every sport.") In his third year at the academy he earned a headline in the local paper—"Trump Wins Game for NYMA"—and the experience was almost electrifying. "It felt good seeing my name in print," he said fifty years later. "How many people are in print? Nobody's in print. It was the first time I was ever in the newspaper. I thought it was amazing."

This first brush with fame could be seen as the spark of a fire that would eventually light all of Trump's life. The notice in the paper made him real, and heroic to people who weren't even at the game. Fame also established that Donald Trump was a special boy. His deep appreciation for the experience shows that he understood that a great many people wanted fame but almost all of them fail to achieve it. Trump succeeded because of his athletic skill and because he was coming of age in a time when fame had been democratized by the mass media. For centuries only true leaders such as kings and queens and people with significant accomplishments could hope to be noticed by the public. The modern press changed all of this, making fame, however fleeting, possible for whole new categories of people—athletes, performers, criminals, beauty-pageant winners—and even animals such as Mrs. O'Leary's cow.

Trump would cling to his memories of athletic achievement and mention them in press interviews throughout his life. He believed that his ball-field experiences were formative because they made him locally famous and because they instilled in him the habit of winning. By his own estimate he was definitely "the best baseball player in New York," and he would have turned pro except that "there was no real money in it." In 1964 the median salary for a big leaguer was $16,000, which was the equivalent of $120,000 in 2015. It would double by 1970.[9] This was more than enough to allow a young man who loved the game to test himself against the best players and, when the adventure was over, chase wealth to his heart's content.

Was Trump in fact an elite player? Yes and no. In New York State, his high school contemporaries included Dave Cash, a future three-time National League All-Star from Utica and big leaguers Terry Crowley and Frank Tepedino. Crowley and Tepedino played high school ball in New York City, where the competition was fierce. NYMA, in contrast, battled against small private schools such as Our Lady of Lourdes in Poughkeepsie, which defeated the cadets 9–3 in Trump's senior year, when the team finished with a losing record.

Sports memories grow more gilded with time. Little League home runs fly farther and high school strikeouts are forgotten. What matters more is how large the ball-player identity looms in a man's imagination. In Trump's case, ball-field days are never far from his mind, and he's keen to make sure others understand that he was a great first baseman and that as a golfer he has won eighteen club championships, which are "really like majors for amateurs." This focus on athletic achievement is as much about establishing the man's interest in competition as it is about a desire to communicate some verifiable record. Trump wants people to know that he always had the heart and the ability of a winner, and these claims come with certain proof. Trump can prove too that he has always been especially interested in attractive women. At the academy, where hand-holding was forbidden, the cadets nevertheless identified him as the official "ladies' man" of his class in the academy yearbook, appropriately titled *Shrapnel*.

After NYMA came Fordham University in the Bronx, where Donald Trump distinguished himself by his military bearing and by his refusal to drink or smoke cigarettes, let alone experiment with the drugs that were increasingly evident on American campuses. (Like the teetotaler moguls of the Gilded Age, Trump would proudly claim abstinence his whole life.) The full extent of Donald Trump's college-years rebellion involved fantasizing about a career in the theater or film. Hollywood and Broadway were caught between the feel-good fifties and the angst of the sixties. *Mary Poppins* and *Dr. Strangelove* played on the same screens. *Hair* took over the stage at the Biltmore Theater on Broadway when *Barefoot in the Park* ended its run. For a military-school grad whose creative passion was far exceeded by his drive for wealth and conventional success, film and theater were in such flux that a career in business made much more sense.

Certain that his future would at least begin in his father's footsteps, Donald devoted much of his free time to working in the family business. He commuted to school from his parents' home in Queens and spent weekends either in the office or visiting Trump properties. While he learned the basics of managing buildings from his father, he looked to another real estate man for lessons in style. William Zeckendorf was the first New York builder who could also be considered a showman. A garrulous character who cruised Manhattan in a shiny Cadillac— license tag WZ—Zeckendorf often announced plans that were just shy of fantasy. One proposal included an airport atop new commercial buildings on Manhattan's West Side. Another was for a 102-story tower to be built over Grand Central Terminal.

Although his weight hovered around three hundred pounds, Zeckendorf was hyperactive and often in motion, both physically and mentally. His projects were daringly big, as in the case of the gigantic shopping development called Place Ville Marie in Montreal, which was built on an abandoned railroad yard and, with its sheer mass, shifted the center of the city in its direction. Zeckendorf's creative energy also led him to find novel ways to wring profit out of properties. For example, he realized he could buy a building and then sell the land beneath it, the future rent payments from tenants, and even the tax-depreciation benefits of the structure, all to separate parties.

Zeckendorf was also known for his eccentricities. He worked in a perfectly round, windowless office, which was paneled in teak and illuminated by skylights. A system of plastic filters, controlled remotely, allowed him to change the color of the light to suit his mood. He kept several telephones on his desk, and at his busiest he took dozens of calls per hour, scratching notes and making doodles on notebooks that were collected and filed by his assistants. He often purchased properties he had never seen and dove into new businesses with great enthusiasm. After he got interested in Broadway, he produced thirty shows.

Always courting publicity, Zeckendorf hired the famous press agent John "Tex" McCrary to keep his name in the newspapers and made a point of showing reporters that he was furiously active and successful and lived quite lavishly. He invited them to lunch in a private dining room where his personal chef, Eugene, prepared a daily menu set by Zeckendorf's wife that was served at a table set with the finest china and silver. Married four times, Zeckendorf's fondness for women was about equal to his appreciation for food.

At the height of his success Zeckendorf employed an all-star lineup of architects including Le Corbusier, William Lescaze, and I. M. Pei to complete major projects across North America. In the early 1960s he likely controlled more real estate than anyone else in the United States, including New York's Astor and Drake Hotels. However, he was often plagued by financial problems that required creative solutions. When he fell behind in his development of Century City for the Fox movie company in Los Angeles, he hired the movie star Mary Pickford to break a bottle of champagne over a shack that was to be demolished and thereby announced the start of construction. After the shack was bulldozed, nothing much happened at the site. However the publicity was so persuasive that Fox stopped pressuring Zeckendorf long enough for him to find a rich partner to help him move forward.

Zeckendorf's resilience and flamboyance showed Donald Trump the glories that might come with a showy approach to business. Other men offered what he came to see as cautionary examples of the fate that awaits the shy and the humble. In November of Donald's freshman year at Fordham, Trump *père et fils* attended the official opening of the grand Verrazano-Narrows Bridge. This outing, on a cloudless Tuesday before Thanksgiving, would offer a lesson young Trump would never forget.

For decades New Yorkers had flocked to ceremonies marking the completion of various public works projects—tunnels, highways, bridges—completed under the steely hand of construction czar Robert Moses. One of Moses's last significant projects, the great bridge was seventy stories tall and more than a mile in length, which made it the largest suspension bridge in the world.

Crossing the narrow point that marks the Hudson River's outlet to the sea, the bridge connected Staten Island to Brooklyn. When it was proposed, Brooklynites who lived where the bridge would be anchored protested that it would ruin their neighborhood. By the time it opened this conflict had dissipated, and no one appeared to protest and spoil the municipal pageantry. Flags and patriotic bunting flapped in the wind. The Sanitation Department band played. The ocean liner *United States* passed beneath the roadway.

The general public was welcomed to stand and gape at the bridge-opening festivities, and one carload of young men earned some recognition by dressing up in tuxedos and parking at the tollbooth for a week, so they might be the first to cross. However, the honored attendees were invited to stand close to the speakers and to the ribbon cutters, who included the governor, the mayor, Italy's ambassador to the United States, and the same Cardinal Spellman who had greeted the NYMA cadets from the steps of St. Patrick's Cathedral on Columbus Day.

From a spot that was close enough to give him a good view of the platform, Donald Trump noted that the elderly designer of the bridge, Othmar Ammann, was overlooked as Moses invited the assorted dignitaries to receive some applause. (*New York Times* reporter Gay Talese, who would one day be an acclaimed author, noted the oversight too.) The lesson Trump took away was that somehow Ammann was to blame for being overlooked. Trump decided he would remember the incident because "I don't want to be made anybody's sucker."

In the world of deals and schemes that Donald planned to inhabit, suckers were the ones who watched others get rich in a game that they didn't understand. His father was nobody's sucker. Denied access to federal programs because of the problems aired during the Senate hearings on the FHA, Fred had found another game called the Mitchell-Lama program, which had been created under the Limited-Profit Housing Companies act of 1955. Named for the New York State lawmakers who authored it, Mitchell-Lama allowed developers to build on land acquired by the government, supplied them with low-interest loans, and exempted them from certain taxes. Mitchell-Lama even guaranteed developers a 7.5 percent builder's fee and a 6 percent annual profit.

In the months before the Verrazano-Narrows Bridge was opened, Fred Trump had finished a Mitchell-Lama project called Trump Village, where he had maneuvered to take most of the land previously reserved for a nonprofit developer so Fred could put up thirty-seven hundred apartments. (The sprawling site was assembled through the government's condemnation of smaller properties. Those overseeing these condemnations, and setting the price paid for each parcel, were Brooklyn judges friendly to Trump.) Trump Village had served as a kind of operating-room theater for young Donald, providing him with an up close view of something few people ever saw. In countless conversations and many visits to the building site, he learned how government officials, politicians, contractors, and tradesmen could be managed and massaged. (Fred kept cigars in his pocket to offer at key moments.) Donald also saw how his father responded to an unexpected crisis.

Having never built anything taller than six stories, Fred Trump found himself operating beyond his area of expertise at Trump Village, where each building would rise twenty-three stories. His financial limitations and lack of experience with high-rise projects made it impossible for him to obtain a construction bond, which the state required as a guarantee for mortgage funding. Unable to proceed on his own, he turned to his advisers at a construction company called HRH. They obtained the bond and took over as general contractors. Under

HRH, Trump Village was completed ahead of schedule and at a cost below original estimates. Though still technically the boss, Fred was only an observer at his biggest-ever project.

Though designed by the renowned architect Morris Lapidus, the completed Trump Village showed none of the style of his famous Fontainebleau and the Eden Roc hotels in Miami. Instead Lapidus, working under constant pressure to reduce costs, produced spare, modernist structures with big windows and slots where residents could install their own air conditioners. The few design flourishes could be seen in the building interiors, where splashes of colored tile and bright paint relieved the monotony of brick and glass. Some of the furniture Lapidus designed for the lobbies at Trump Village was so artful it wound up in a museum.

The only project Fred ever put his name on, Trump Village became both his crowning achievement and a long-term headache. As his son Donald left Fordham in 1966 to finish his undergraduate degree (he majored in real estate) at the University of Pennsylvania, state officials began looking into the string-pulling Trump Sr. had practiced as he acquired both the land for his project and the government's help, which included $50 million in low-cost financing and valuable tax breaks.

As a scandal brewed, Donald worked at Trump Village on weekends and during school breaks, making apartments ready for occupants and responding to tenant complaints. Slender, with blue eyes and longish, blond hair, the fashionably dressed Donald stood several inches taller than his father, who still wore a fedora and a mustache that was clipped with razor precision. Fred had become so self-conscious about his German heritage that he had begun to tell people he was Swedish. Donald approached everyone he met with an easy confidence. But as different as father and son were in style, they were the same when it came to their ambitions and desires. Neither man seemed much interested in human pleasures such as fine food or art. And if they harbored any burning political or moral ideals, they were not in evidence, although privately they identified with the Republican Party and they both very much admired the Reverend Norman Vincent Peale.

Born and raised in the Midwest, Peale became pastor of the Marble Collegiate Church in Manhattan in 1932. In New York he worked with the aptly named psychoanalyst Smiley Blanton to develop a philosophy Peale called "the power of positive thinking." After soliciting financial support from luminaries such as Thomas Watson of IBM and Branch Rickey of the Brooklyn Dodgers, he built a one-man industry of exhortation to spread his ideas via books, magazines, and broadcasts. He reached 30 million Americans via his radio programs, and his 1952 book, *The Power of Positive Thinking,* sold 2 million copies in twenty-four months. It would remain in print for more than fifty years and became the foundational document in Peale's cult of success.

Peale's message could be boiled down to the proposition that self-confidence and visualization would overcome almost any obstacle life might place in your way. For a Christian minister, he devoted precious little attention to the Bible or to God, preferring instead to tell stories about individuals who followed his techniques to overcome everything from alcoholism to poverty. When God did appear in Peale's writings and sermons, He was often portrayed as a sort of life coach or an object of meditation. "I know that with God's help," wrote Peale, "I can sell vacuum cleaners."

Much of what Peale preached echoed the teachings of Napoleon Hill, whose *Think and Grow Rich* appeared in 1937 and counseled, "You can never have riches in great quantities unless you can work yourself into a white heat of desire for money." Peale was gentler in his prescriptions, urging meditative techniques borrowed from the theories of a famous French hypnotist named Émile Coué, who instructed his subjects to practice "autosuggestion" by repeating the phrase "Every day, in every way, I'm getting better and better." Coué's book *Self-Mastery Through Conscious Autosuggestion* was published in America in the year Peale was ordained as a Methodist minister. The author supported it with a much-publicized speaking tour that raised $16,000 (equivalent to $220,000 in 2015) for the founding of a Coué institute in New York. Its board would include a Vanderbilt, a Methodist bishop, a California socialite married to an Italian count, and a former city police commissioner.

Like Coué, Peale told believers to imagine themselves as they wanted to be and to overcome doubt by repeating such phrases as "God gives me the power to attain what I really want." These phrases and others should be repeated at least half a dozen times per day, wrote Peale, to "crowd your mind." His religion was, above all else, practical and useful in the pursuit of "power and efficiency." Peale rarely touched on Christian concepts of sin, suffering, or redemption. He preferred instead to preach that followers "be free of a sense of guilt" about their misdeeds. Speaking to the insecurities and anxieties of the people in his vast congregation, Peale noted, "Every normal person wants power over circumstances, power over fear, power over weakness, power over themselves." He said they would achieve this power through prayer, visualization, and action that would "actualize" their dreams of "prosperity, achievement, success." He wrote, "Learn to pray big prayers. God will rate you according to the size of your prayers."

Peale was as controversial as he was popular. Theologian Reinhold Niebuhr regarded Peale's various organizations as a cult. When leading psychologists criticized Peale—some warned that his methods could promote mental disorders—Smiley Blanton refused to defend him and barred Peale from using Blanton's name. Peale also ran into trouble when he opposed John F. Kennedy's presidential bid, saying, "Faced with the election of a Catholic, our culture is at stake." Amid the furor over this statement, Peale's congregation offered him almost unanimous support, but he quickly expressed regret and withdrew from a group of anti-Kennedy ministers. After Kennedy won, Peale's sin was quickly forgotten. By the following spring he was being celebrated for his forty years of service in the pulpit, and the elite of New York's business community were crowding the Easter service at Marble Collegiate Church.

Peale would remain a prominent figure and corporate America's favorite preacher as he offered both a moral argument for capitalism and inspiration for vacuum salesmen. In 1961, managers at more than 750 firms purchased subscriptions to his *Guideposts* for their employees. (In one year U.S. Steel alone spent $150,000 on the magazine.) In New York, Peale's Fifth Avenue congregation grew from six hundred to five thousand, and his services attracted bankers, political figures, executives, and business operators such as Fred and Donald Trump.

As nearly perfect practitioners of the power of positive thinking, they both wanted to achieve the kind of wealth and status that would elevate them above other men. In Peale they found a pastor who taught them that God wanted the same thing for them and that the "infinite forces of the universe" were available to them if only they used positive thinking and trained their minds "to think victory." Donald would demonstrate positive thinking throughout his life, as it became a true habit of his heart. His projects and creations would always be, in his words, "the best" and "the greatest," and when reminded of failures or inconsistencies in his claims, he would respond with phrases like "Yeah, whatever" and race on to describe another of his achievements. Positive thinking all the way.[10]

3
APPRENTICE

The business is, yes, about putting up buildings, but it's also about dealing with these people. It's about being friendly with politicians. It's about having them respect you. It's about having them like you.
—DONALD TRUMP

As a place of dreams, Fred Trump's office left much to be desired. Formerly occupied by a dentist, it was decorated with kitschy cigar-store Indians and furnished with battered desks, filing cabinets, and chairs. The cramped space felt even more claustrophobic from the addition of a cheap dropped ceiling and fluorescent lights that cast a bluish tinge on everything. The walls were filled with the businessman's version of a hunter's trophies—framed plaques and certificates—but otherwise the place was devoid of any human touches, except for the small collection of patriotic bric-a-brac, which included a statue of an eagle, wings spread, grasping a stars-and-stripes shield in its talons.

Coldly functional as it may have been, the Trump office was a haven from the surrounding neighborhood. Two blocks to the west, a sprawling subway yard complete with a twenty-four-hour repair shop occupied seventy-five acres crisscrossed by tracks. Immediately to the east, Coney Island Hospital welcomed a steady stream of ambulances, sirens blaring, day and night. To the south the elevated Belt Parkway, humming with traffic, cast a shadow and a cloud of exhaust fumes on the streets below. Known as Gravesend, the neighborhood was rarely in the news, except for the occasional murder or when, in 1970, the mayor announced a massive sewage-treatment plant would be built on the eastern end of Avenue Z.

Given the setting, young Donald Trump could be forgiven for letting his mind wander to Manhattan. Keenly aware of the value locked up in his father's eighty-or-so buildings, which were worth well over $100 million, Donald urged him to refinance and create a pool of cash for new endeavors. Fred believed in Donald's ability, considered him a natural successor, and was willing to use his equity to back his son's ideas. However, Fred was extremely wary of doing business in Manhattan, which was one of the most expensive places in the world for developers, and a locale where his friends from the Brooklyn Democratic clubhouses might run up against the limits of their powers.

Never truly comfortable as a public man, Fred had stopped pressing for media attention after his run-in with the US Senate banking committee. His instinct was confirmed on the rare occasions when he had contact with the men who operated at City Hall in Manhattan. When Fred attended a fund-raising luncheon for the reelection campaign of Mayor Robert F. Wagner, a Democrat, Fred's pledge of $2,500 wound up in the newspapers as Republicans assailed Wagner for taking money from people doing business with the city. (Wagner gave the donation back.) The fund-raiser had been organized by a politically powerful lawyer named Abraham Lindenbaum, who sat on the city's Planning Commission. Many New York real estate men, including William Zeckendorf, used Lindenbaum's firm. Fred Trump had engaged him for Trump Village, which was built under the Mitchell-Lama law. Lindenbaum and his partner Matthew Tosti submitted a ninety-nine-page bill for forty-five hundred hours in court appearances, to be paid out of public funds, even though the job they claimed to have done was actually handled by a city agency and another contractor. The invoice found its way into the local papers, where it became a scandal.[1]

Although Fred Trump was not accused of breaking the law in the Lindenbaum affair, he was required to testify before the New York State Commission of Investigation, which had been established in the 1950s to curb political corruption. In a setting less congenial than when he was questioned by the Senate banking committee, Fred had to contend with hours of questions about his state-subsidized Trump Village development. Much of what he said revealed an almost dazzling level of manipulation. For example, after first claiming ignorance, Trump consulted his lawyer and changed his testimony to explain how he had created an independent company to buy used equipment—backhoes, trucks, etc.—which was then leased to the Trump Village project at rates as much as twenty times their actual cost. (A truck valued at $2,600 rented for $21,000. Two tile-scraping machines valued at $500 apiece netted Trump $8,200.) Since Trump's fee as the builder was based on the ultimate final cost of construction, like a commission, he earned money once by renting the equipment at exorbitant rates and again when he got his final fee for developing the apartment complex.

Clever in the extreme, Trump's equipment scheme was technically legal under the rules of Mitchell Lama, and he was plainly irritated by the probing questions of the commission's lawyers. "I've got forty-three corporations I'm sole stockholder in," he explained. "These things escape my mind sometimes."

Trump was advised, as he testified, by the same Matthew Tosti whose name appeared on the contested ninety-nine-page bill. At some points Tosti sought to answer questions for his client and was admonished to let the witness speak for himself. The commission established that Trump had deliberately inflated estimates for the cost of construction and used excess subsidized funds to build a shopping center near the apartments. Other witnesses explained how he had received $500,000 in extra profits by exploiting certain provisions in the law. Finally, the director of a large, well-established nonprofit housing group testified that his organization had been authorized to build on the Trump Village site in 1957, but had run into a political trouble.

"We were told by members of the Board of Estimate that we couldn't get approval until we compromised with Mr. Trump," said Abraham Kazan of the United Housing Federation. "So we gave up more than half . . . and the Board of Estimate finally approved the amended plan in May 1960."[2]

Like the Eisenhower-administration investigators who probed the Federal Housing Administration, New York State's investigating commission revealed a program that seemed to be purposely designed to benefit builders guided by skillful lawyers. During the state hearings, the very same Senator MacNeil Mitchell who helped create Mitchell-Lama was required to answer for more than $400,000 in fees his law firm received from builders—including Fred Trump—who participated in the program. Once again a witness noted that his unseemly gain was perfectly legal and expressed a bit of outrage over the suggestion that anything improper occurred. Mitchell even described the work he had performed for builders as "a public service" and gave himself credit for not being one of many public officials who actually took cash from builders in exchange for their influence. He had actually worked for the money.[3]

No one was prosecuted as a result of the commission hearings, but the editorial page of *The New York Times* mentioned Fred Trump by name as it lambasted those it termed "profiteers" who had taken advantage of the taxpayers. The head of the commission criticized Trump and others as "grasping and greedy individuals" whose manipulations exploited the citizens of New York, drove up rents, and violated the spirit of Mitchell-Lama, which was supposed to create affordable housing with a combination of tax breaks and subsidized financing.[4]

Although he got to keep his profits and would reap the rents from both Trump Village and the shopping center for years to come, Fred Trump was bruised by his experience before the commission. Nothing in state or federal law would prohibit him from filing new applications to receive the tax breaks and subsidies that government programs offered. But the scent of scandal that had attached to him during the commission hearings would make it much harder for him to win approval. Competitors and enemies—every businessman has them—would surely use his record to oppose any new Trump applications in hopes of thwarting a rival or of boosting their own prospects for handouts.

Then there was the whole matter of politics. Though a Republican, the practical Trump had aligned himself with machine Democrats, who were subject to increasing scrutiny by good-government types. Weeks before Trump testified, Tammany's Mayor Wagner had been defeated at the polls by reform-minded Republican John V. Lindsay, whose campaign motto, borrowed from writer Murray Kempton, had been "He is fresh and everyone else is tired." During Lindsay's eight-year reign, the Lindenbaums, Mitchells, and others who had long wielded so much influence on behalf of builders would be sidelined. Any Trump plan that would require city approvals, and every big housing project required city approvals, would have to win the Lindsay administration's favor on its merits. Having never done business under such circumstances, Trump began to focus more on the task of training a successor.

In a family that honored male privilege, Fred Trump Jr. was first in line to take control of the business. Eight years older than Donald, Freddy had tried to become the killer king of his father's imagination but was too soft-hearted to succeed. He spent his high school years at a genteel Episcopal day school on Long Island instead of at a military academy. At Lehigh University he joined the Air Force Reserve Officers Training School and thought about becoming a pilot, but when he completed his studies, he dutifully began work as his father's assistant.

In the offices on Avenue Z and during their time in the field, Freddy Trump had trouble taking in the lessons his father tried to teach him. An enormously wealthy man who nevertheless picked up nails at his building sites, Fred Trump couldn't stand even a penny of waste. Somehow his eldest son missed the emphasis his father placed on thrift. Given the chance to renovate an old building, Freddy installed brand-new windows. His father berated him when he found out because he thought the old ones would have served well enough for a few more years.

As Donald watched his elder brother try to please their father, he felt sympathy for him. Freddy had been a kind and concerned sibling who lectured Donald on the dangers of smoking and drinking, two habits Freddy couldn't break. But as much as he loved his brother, Donald couldn't help but feel a bit exasperated by Freddy's problems. Their father and mother never drank to excess and probably considered such behavior a sign of bad character. (Fred Sr.'s own father may have been an alcoholic.) Donald wished Freddy would have tried harder to show them he could control himself. Also, Trump men were supposed to be tough, even when dealing with each other, but when his father lashed out at Freddy, he was so hurt he seemed to physically shrink. It was hard to watch.

Learning from what he saw, Donald resolved to stand up to anyone who challenged him, including his father. Years later he would say, "I used to fight back all the time. My father was one tough son of a gun." However, he added, "My father respects me because I stood up to him."

As Donald began working full-time in the family business, Freddy was assigned the daunting task of shepherding a proposed development on the site of the last big amusement park in Coney Island. Steeplechase Park had opened in 1897 on fifteen acres of seaside real estate. Founder George Tilyou had gone into the amusement business after getting bored with real estate. He developed a midway of games and concessions and decorated the place with the image of a demonically grinning character called either Tillie or Steeplechase Jack whose hair formed devil's horns and whose face surely hovered in many a child's nightmares. The park's main attraction was a mechanical "horse race" that allowed a dozen riders—mounted two per steed—to ride along tracks that encircled the entire lot. Attendants wore silks and a bugler announced the start of each race with the famous "Call to Post" tune. Racers cleared several hurdles and crossed a stream, getting sprayed with water. When they finished the ride, they were subject to a gauntlet of harassing clowns and "blowholes" that lifted women's skirts and prompted cheers from a crowd of people who were seated on a small set of risers.

Over the years millions of people had been entertained at Steeplechase Park, where Tilyou's parachute-jump attraction, and its 250-foot-high tower, became a landmark. Steeplechase thrived despite the rise of the bigger Luna Park, which was anchored by a ride in which thirty occupants of a winged "ornithopter" traveled to a papier-mâché moonscape where they were greeted by moon maidens. Together these amusement centers created a Coney Island mystique that made the gritty stretch of seaside an object of nostalgia even for people who had never been there. (Part of this phenomenon was due to Coney Island's many appearances in books, movies, and songs.) By the time Fred Trump bought the Steeplechase property, Coney Island's peak as a day trippers' resort had passed. Many of the middle-class Brooklynites who once flocked to the sands had left for suburbia. With business dropping off, honky-tonk joints closed. Properties were sold and apartment buildings began to sprout just off the boardwalk. George Tilyou's heirs sold the 12.5-acre Steeplechase Park to Fred for $2.5 million. Trump envisioned high-rise apartment buildings of the sort he had seen during vacations in Miami Beach.

Although apartments were being built in Coney Island, none were located in the blocks south of Surf Avenue where the amusement parks had operated and which city officials had reserved for recreational facilities. In this area, almost all the properties offered direct and unrestricted access to the beach, which poor and middle-class New Yorkers had come to view as their own. Over the generations the freely accessible Coney Island beach had become a symbol of egalitarian New York, one of its few amenities that didn't require one to purchase an admission ticket. As one local business advocate said, the city desperately required a "place where the low man on the totem pole can come and blow his top." For his part, Freddy Trump argued that Coney Island's days as a resort for even the low man had long since passed. "You and I wouldn't take our kids there," he argued. "People are afraid to walk on Surf Avenue at night."

Unfortunately for Freddy, the Steeplechase project became ever more difficult as time passed. The dashing Mayor Lindsay's Election Day defeat of an old-fashioned, cigar-chomping challenger named Abe Beame greatly diminished the power of the machine politicians who had made things easier for Fred Sr. Then there was Freddy's father's troublesome appearance before the investigations commission. No matter the outcome, the Trumps' prospects for overcoming the city's restrictions on the Coney Island property had dimmed as the grilling made Fred Sr. seem part of the corrupt Tammany past. He tried to induce Walt Disney and others to operate Steeplechase Park as an amusement center, but no one took him up on the offer. In the summer of 1966 he proposed dropping his plan in favor of a bigger development that would include housing and a year-round amusement and convention center enclosed by a glass or plastic dome. These facilities would be built on property that would have to be acquired by the city and cleared of businesses that were open and operating.

Sketched by Morris Lapidus, the "pleasure dome," as *The New York Times* called it, would be tall enough to house a Ferris wheel. In the drawings its swooping lines echoed Eero Saarinen's iconic new terminal at Dulles International Airport in Washington, D.C., which had opened in 1962. Of course an architectural drawing can be had quite cheaply, and the plan, which was presented at the Lapidus-designed Americana Hotel in Manhattan, wasn't much more than a vague vision of something that might occur under ideal circumstances. Lapidus even suggested that the recreation area be funded and operated by some new government agency, created for this sole purpose, which would also compensate the business owners displaced by the new development.

One voice raised in favor of Trump's grand vision for Coney Island belonged to Brooklyn borough president

Abe Stark, whose local claim to fame began with a bill-board for his tailoring business that made the promise HIT SIGN, WIN SUIT, posted beneath the scoreboard at Ebbets Field, which had recently been demolished. Seen by fans at the ballpark, in news photos, and in newsreels, the sign had made Stark so well-known that the voters promoted him from tailor, to city councilman, to bor-ough president. However, Stark was not a natural poli-tician and never gained the type of political power enjoyed by his predecessor (and Trump supporter) John "Cashbox" Cashmore. Stark was unable to rally even his fellow businessmen to support the Trump/Lapidus plan. The Coney Island Chamber of Commerce actively op-posed the idea and issued a scathing statement, which said in part, "Mr. Trump is stuck with the present Stee-plechase property on which he cannot build housing be-cause of the zoning. Under the plan he would exchange it for the city land. He's getting rid of a lemon. . . . The beach would become a personal haven for people who lease apartments from Mr. Trump."

Organized by Fred Jr., the Americana Hotel press conference yielded nothing more than a bit of publicity that promoted Fred Trump Sr. as a visionary. Weeks later Freddy invited his father's friends and associates to a wrecking party inside the huge glass-and-steel Pavilion of Fun, which once housed rides and attractions, which had since been sold to amusement operators across the country. (The park's towering parachute jump remained because the estimated cost of dismantling it and shipping it to a new locale discouraged would-be buyers.)

Although he was still stymied by city zoning regula-tions, Fred Trump Sr. acted as if he had already over-come his problems with the city. As guests sipped on champagne, six young women in bikinis and hard hats appeared to pull on ropes that toppled small pieces of a brick wall. The "girls," as the papers described them, then stood in the bucket of a giant earthmover and posed for photos. Fred took a turn in the operator's seat of a bulldozer. Onlookers then got the chance to hurl bricks at a section of pavilion glass where a huge painting of Steeplechase Jack had decorated the panes and welcomed visitors for more than fifty years.

The last publicity stunt of Fred Trump's career, the bikini/payloader/champagne extravaganza was a good example of a phenomenon that historian Daniel J. Boorstin had recently described in a landmark book called *The Image: A Guide to Pseudo-Events in America*. Boorstin was deeply concerned about how moral ideals, genuine relationships, and human experience were being replaced by images and "pseudo-events" that were manufactured by public relations experts, corporations, politicians, and governments. Americans, who were awash in these images and events, often accepted them as real and meaningful. One sign of this acceptance was the way people began creating more and more of their own posed photographs and staged home movies. These could then be compared with the images of famous people who were valued as "celebrities" and the concepts of the good life presented by advertisements for whatever was "new" and "modern." Of course advertising only succeeded when people bought a product, and this way the novelty was destroyed. Status seekers were thus frustrated until they acquired the next new thing to be advertised and sold.

The problems Boorstin described would occupy generations of future writers. Many sought to address the anxiety and ennui that were symptoms of what he called a "disease of extravagant expectations" caused by imagery and pseudo-events. Susan Sontag would observe in *On Photography* that inexpensive photos, produced by the hundreds, created a record that allowed an unprecedented level of self-examination—she called it "self surveillance"—that discouraged spontaneous human expression and encouraged posing and playacting. People were generally too busy to devote much time to considering how they were affected by the media bombardment and simply absorbed it or reacted as best they could.

Aside from their occasional complaints about the pressure to "keep up with the Joneses," most people were actually quite occupied with keeping up. Every day brought more images and pseudo-events that insisted that striving for the right possessions—a new suit, car, house—would bring fulfillment and even happiness. That few people ever reached this state, as defined by the manufacturers of this reality and illustrated on TV, was hardly ever mentioned, even in private, because to do so would cast doubt on the whole basis of commercial life.

In the accelerated marketplace that Boorstin and others described, a small number of energetic, talented, and resourceful men could achieve the high-status life depicted in the imagery that surrounded them. This was most true for those who, like Donald Trump, might enjoy the advantages of talent, family wealth, and useful connections inherited from a successful father. When still a student at the University of Pennsylvania, Donald was so confident in his future that he couldn't wait to begin life as his father's partner and fulfill the older man's dream for him. "My father was a businessperson that expected tremendous success out of me," he would eventually recall.

A month after the demolition celebration on Coney Island, Fred Trump appeared before the city's Planning Commission, which was leaning against the development scheme and toward the public purchase of the Steeplechase land for use as a park. Trump told the panel they were wasting "a valuable piece of property" because people would visit only in the summer. However, he didn't fight hard to save his project, and any pain he may have felt over the loss of the land was surely eased by the $1.2 million profit he made when the city paid him for the site.[5]

Although his gain of roughly 25 percent per year was more than triple the rate of growth in the Dow Jones Industrial Average for the same period, Fred Trump's profit on the Steeplechase property was much less than what he would have reaped from his original plan. He had envisioned a river of rent payments from apartments and businesses that would eventually pay off his financiers and yield millions of dollars in net revenues even as inflation drove up the value of the property. This formula—investment + time = revenue *and* higher value—was the magic of real estate. By following it, Fred Trump had amassed assets that allowed him to develop ever bigger projects while simultaneously reducing the risk to his personal fortune. Eventually these methods allow developers to use the equity in one project as a down payment on another and escape using any of their own cash. They could even avoid paying taxes on their profits by investing them in a new property. This provision of the tax code, originally written to aid farmers, made real estate an even better business.

The Trump variation on the basic real estate recipe often included a dollop of political grease and a little show-business spice, for the sake of publicity. The precise mixture depended on the location, the competition, and the level of public interest. A celebrated architect, for example, could win invaluable publicity for a planned development and encourage city officials to regard it as beneficial, and even prestigious. Good press could influence those who might buy or rent at a certain location. The Steeplechase project all but required Morris

Lapidus and bathing beauties in the bucket of a pay-loader. But as Fred Trump offered flutes of champagne and invited his guests to smash Jack's face, he showed that his feel for New York in general, and Coney Island in particular, was just a little bit off.

A proper pseudo-event to bid farewell to the old amusement park would have been a glass-of-beer occasion. Instead of being invited to hurl bricks at an emblem of the good ol' days, the invitees could have been offered a chance to flutter to the ground from the top of the parachute jump. What was being lost deserved to be recognized with a bit of respect. Instead, the event conflated Trump's desire for profit and the city's own needs. This approach ignored the value of an ocean beach that could be accessed by millions of people for the price of a subway token. And Trump's complaint about how the beachfront property would be wasted on a recreation area that received just two months of use ignored the many locals and tourists who walked the beach, gazed at sunsets, and cast for striped bass in the cooler months. This was the Coney Island they would lose to development, and it was the one they gained as the city denied Trump the zoning changes he needed to proceed.

Fred Trump Jr., who was supposed to help see the project through to completion, fled the family business after the Steeplechase proposal was killed. When TWA accepted his application, he began training for a career as a pilot, which he would pursue for many years. At the time TWA had retired the last of its prop planes in favor of an all-jet fleet. First-year pilots were paid the 2015 equivalent of $110,000 per year, and the most senior ones earned more than three times as much.

Glamorized in the media and respected by the public, pilots enjoyed high social status. Donald Trump would remember that his brother's work, and family life in Florida, made him happier than Donald had ever seen him. However, a happy life was not enough for a Trump man. The model of masculinity established by Fred Sr., which he surely inherited from his German immigrant father, called for extreme competitiveness and victories that yielded great wealth. Pilots were well compensated, but they were not rich by Trump standards. And given that the job mainly required the safe transit of an airplane and its passengers, how could one pilot prevail over another? He could not, which was why Fred Sr. and Donald couldn't help but torment Freddy when they were together. "What's the difference," asked Donald, "between what you do and driving a bus?"[6]

◆

With his eldest son striking out on his own and his dream project defeated, Fred Trump Sr. reached a turning point. At sixty-one he had lived twelve years longer than his own father, and he had, in less than three decades, built one of the largest real estate portfolios in New York City. But the game that he knew was changing. Old friends in politics and government were being squeezed out or leaving of their own accord. The city government was facing serious problems as budget deficits begun under Wagner continued with Mayor Lindsay. The middle-class workers and families who had once eagerly filled Trump's buildings in Brooklyn were joining the "white flight" to the suburbs. The neighborhoods they left were tumbling into poverty.

New York was hardly alone in this crisis. Much of urban America had begun a slow but steady decline in the 1950s. This accelerated in the 1960s and was accented by race riots that saw mostly white police forces battling black citizens. In 1964, thousands of black residents took to the streets in Harlem and other New York neighborhoods after a white off-duty officer shot a black teenager. In 1965, long-simmering racial animosity led to widespread rioting in the Watts neighborhood of Los Angeles, and in the following two summers riots occurred in Cleveland, Omaha, Newark, and Detroit. Bad as things were by '67, they got worse in 1968 after Martin Luther King Jr. was killed at the Lorraine Motel in Memphis, Tennessee. Fifty cities erupted in violence that summer. Police in Baltimore and Chicago were so overwhelmed that National Guard troops were called to patrol the streets.

The effects of the racial unrest of the 1960s were long lasting as urban centers lost businesses, jobs, and people. In the 1970s New York would suffer a 10 percent decline in population, the first time in its history that the city had endured a double-digit drop. Many businesses closed, and major employers, including manufacturing companies, moved to the suburbs and the Sunbelt, taking jobs with them. Other cities suffered similarly. In 1971 more than two hundred people were killed in race-related riots from Boston to Los Angeles. Cities suffered billions of dollars' worth of damage, and property values declined as arsonists burned individual buildings and entire blocks.

Although race was the most evident factor in both white flight and the civil unrest, poverty also loomed large. Discrimination in jobs, housing, and education hobbled minority Americans who sought any level of wealth and security. In the outer boroughs of New York City poor black and Hispanic newcomers moved into neighborhoods that were vacated by whites and their employers. Many of these communities became official "poverty zones" where 30 percent or more of the residents depended on government welfare payments. This problem was especially acute in the Flatbush, Greenpoint, and Coney Island areas of Brooklyn, where incomes fell and crime rates rose.[7]

Confronted with downward pressure on rents and

declining property values, homeowners, real estate investors, and landlords in certain New York neighborhoods faced the worst market conditions since the Great Depression. More than one hundred buildings per month were being abandoned, and in most cases tenants who found themselves without utilities and maintenance quickly departed. Squatters and scavengers would eventually be followed by city demolition crews. In this way, crime was followed by blight and entire blocks were devastated.

Some owners resisted selling their buildings to blacks or Hispanics who made inquiries, and some landlords refused to rent to them. Although a number of the landlords were genuinely racist, most would say they were motivated by financial concerns. They equated black and brown with poor and feared unpaid rents and the expense of eviction battles. Developers in New York's outer boroughs cut back their activities, especially in middle-class and poorer neighborhoods, and hoped that with time they might once again make real profits building homes and commercial space. By 1969 private developers had stopped building market-rate residences for all but the wealthiest New Yorkers (*The Times* described them as the top "7 percent"), and the only apartments being developed for the rest of the population were those subsidized by the government. These were going up at such a minimal rate that waiting lists were decades long.[8]

On Avenue Z, Fred Trump hunkered down, contenting himself with collecting rents and controlling costs on the thousands of apartments in buildings he owned and operated. With Freddy's departure from the business, Fred also focused on training his son Donald, who was spending his weekdays at the University of Pennsylvania and his weekends in New York in the family business. At Penn, where he enrolled after two years at Fordham, Donald studied real estate at the Wharton

School of Finance and Commerce. A decade earlier, editors at Penn's student newspaper had decried the Wharton School's influence on campus, describing it as "the first and most important destructive influence" on the study of science and liberal arts. In his time on the campus Donald Trump absorbed all he could from his professors, devoting special attention to the intricacies of high finance. At home in New York he studied his father's holdings to see where he might find opportunities for growth.[9]

Visiting various buildings with his father, Donald learned the mundane art of rent collecting, which, when done in person, required a step to the side whenever a door was opened just in case someone was armed with, say, a bucket of hot water. Such things did occur. Donald was also educated in the various ways that proper maintenance would extend the life of certain equipment and fixtures while preventing costly emergency repairs. Following his father's example, Donald never went to work without a jacket and tie, and he made certain that he understood enough about every aspect of the business to instruct employees and follow up on the tasks he assigned to them.

Given his choice, Donald would have preferred to forgo his formal education. He was not a natural student and wasn't much interested in the social opportunities available to him on or off the campus in Philadelphia. However his father insisted that Donald earn a degree. (It was a point of honor for him that his son was an Ivy League man.) If Donald had dropped out, he would have lost his student deferment and been subject to the military draft and, perhaps, combat duty in Vietnam.

As the war had dragged on, Trump's generation of young men had joined the armed services at a rate of more than 1 million per year. More than one-third would serve in Southeast Asia. With the American military death toll climbing toward its eventual total of nearly sixty thousand, opposition to the war also increased, and public rallies were organized at campuses from coast to coast. In some places colleges and universities were shut down by protesters. Students blocked streets with barricades and set fire to draft cards and, in a few cases, campus buildings. The worst would come in 1970 when four students were killed and nine were wounded as National Guard troops fired on demonstrators at Kent State in Ohio. Followed by hundreds of protests across the country, the Kent State killings galvanized opposition to the war among the young.

Although Ivy League schools such as Columbia and Harvard were hotbeds of activism, students at the University of Pennsylvania were not so restive. However, in 1965 more than a thousand students attended an antiwar "teach-in," and in 1967 about fifty students added black bands to their straw hats and covered their faces with gas masks during the traditional, springtime Hey Day festivities, which included parading, drinking, and picnicking. In 1968, Donald Trump's last year at Penn, a small group occupied a building and drove away recruiters for the Central Intelligence Agency and Dow Chemical, a manufacturer of napalm, which was being used to set vast swaths of the Vietnamese countryside ablaze.

Donald Trump did not join in the protests, sign petitions, or otherwise agitate against the power of the "establishment." Although he personally opposed the war, Trump would later say he was so intently focused on his future in business that he was not even aware of the campus protests. In light of Trump's political disengagement, you might conclude that he was more like a college man of the fifties than the sixties. But he showed no more enthusiasm for the old-fashioned version of college life than he did for the psychedelic style of his own generation. Assiduously sober, he didn't care for beer bashes at fraternities or druggy house parties. He generally stayed in after classes, watched the talk-show host Johnny Carson, whom he greatly admired, and went to sleep. This was his routine until he received his diploma and went home to New York. He would often say he graduated at the top of his class, but as the school does not issue official rankings, this claim cannot be confirmed or contested.

After Donald returned to New York for good, protests roiled the Democratic Party's National Convention in Chicago, and the number of American troops in Vietnam peaked at 541,000. Thousands of young men who were no longer excused from service as students fled to Canada to escape the draft. Like others who received their diplomas and left school in the spring of 1968, Trump's 2-S student deferment expired as of July 1968. For two months he was classified 1-A and ready for conscription, but when he reported for a military physical in September 1968, he was found medically unfit. His new classification, 1-Y, permitted him to be called only in case of national emergency.

Considering that roughly 60 percent of his peers also avoided wartime service, Trump's record was not especially remarkable. Roughly 10 million men in his age group were not drafted due to deferments and special status. However, as time passed, Vietnam-era service would become an issue for a generation of political figures including Bill Clinton, Dick Cheney, and Mitt Romney, who all had to explain the deferments that permitted them to escape the draft. When asked about his war years experience, Trump would often point to a lottery system begun in December 1969, which assigned men draft priority based on a random drawing of birth dates and gave him number 356. No one with a number higher than 195 was ever called to serve.

"I actually got lucky because I had a very high draft number," he would tell a TV interviewer in 2011. "I'll never forget, that was an amazing period of time in my life." In fact the lottery was not a factor in his experience. It didn't occur until fourteen months after he received his medical exemption, and eighteen months after he'd left Penn. Nevertheless he would recall, "I was going to the Wharton School of Finance, and I was watching as they did the draft numbers."

When the subject came up in conversation in 2014, he repeated the draft number story. But when offered the chance to work through the details, he seized it. Yes, he agreed, if the first lottery took place in 1969, he must have been mistaken about living in Philadelphia. And the gap between his graduation from Penn and the lottery could be explained by a medical deferment. As he talked, Trump slipped off his black loafer and pointed to his heel, where a little bulge pushed against his sock. "Heel spurs," he explained. "On both feet." The deformities qualified a would-be draftee for a medical deferment. Unlike others who dealt with the same question as public figures, Trump wasn't defensive about never having served. The war "was a mistake" he said, and he was grateful to have remained a civilian.[10]

But Trump also insisted that he had actually known military life. In a separate conversation he said, "I always thought I was in the military." He said that in prep school he received more military training than most actual soldiers did, and he had been required to live under the command of men such as Ted Dobias who had been real officers and soldiers. "I felt like I was in the military in a true sense," added Trump, "because I dealt with the people."

Probably not many other NYMA alumni would compare military school with actual military service. But the assertion was consistent with the self-image Trump often expressed. With ambition beyond measure, he would make the most of every experience and accomplishment and lay claim to excellence in almost everything he attempted. He wasn't just a baseball player, he was one of the best in New York State. He wasn't just a student at Penn, he was at the top of his class. That these claims can't be confirmed doesn't mean he is lying. He seems to genuinely believe them, and when he says something like "I always thought I was in the military," he is sharing the truth as he feels it.

No one would contest what Trump had to say about his state of mind when he took up adult life in New York City in 1968. Time and again he has said that he had gazed at Manhattan and thought about how he would change the most famous skyline in the world. Confident in his abilities and wholeheartedly optimistic, he wasn't hoping or dreaming. He believed—no, he knew—it was going to happen. It was just a matter of time.

4
FEAR CITY

I used to come over that bridge and I used to say,
"I want to be in Manhattan someday."
—DONALD TRUMP

Donald Trump's first Manhattan apartment gave him
a raptor's view of the city from seventeen stories
above the sidewalk. Completed in 1959, the building at
196 East Seventy-fifth Street was faced in the glazed
white brick that came into wide use in the mid-twentieth
century as developers imitated architect Gordon Bunshaft's stylish Manhattan House at Sixty-sixth Street
and Third Avenue. (Manhattan House was eventually
designated an official landmark.) Young Trump wasn't
much concerned with the aesthetics of postwar architecture on the East Side. He was mainly interested in
gaining a toehold in the place that had dominated his
imagination ever since he knew what waited on the western end of the Queensboro Bridge. To his delight, he
had landed in one of the borough's tonier precincts,
and thanks to rent-control laws it was a bargain.[1]

Reverse commuting in a Cadillac convertible, Donald spent his days in Brooklyn with his father where
anyone could see that blight was spreading out from the
poverty zones and threatening previously stable communities. Were the downturn a typical part of the real
estate cycle, the depressed prices would have been attractive to a developer with cash on hand. However, the
trouble in Brooklyn was more fundamental. Most of

New York City's decline in population was occurring there. When newcomers did fill the homes and apartments vacated by would-be suburbanites, they were less affluent and less educated.[2]

A similar process was occurring across the country as cities emptied and real estate development in the suburbs boomed. The contrast between the urban and suburban experience was especially pronounced for the middle class. In the cities, midrange home values stagnated and even fell because demand declined. In the suburbs, new-home buyers who made low-down-payment purchases often saw the value of their home rise quickly and then traded it in for a bigger and fancier residence. As people caught on to the seeming magic of "trading up" with the help of rising values, houses became not just homes, but assets that could be leveraged to produce wealth. In California, a real estate speculator named Albert J. Lowry began renting hotel ballrooms where people paid to attend his seminar called "How to Be Successful in America."

Lowry taught that with a little cash and a lot of nerve, anyone could achieve success by locating undervalued or foreclosed properties, improving them with low-cost renovations and repairs, and selling them at a profit. Naturally, if everyone who attended a local Lowry seminar immediately put his lessons to work, they would compete for the same number of bargain houses. Demand would outstrip supply and bargains would disappear. But only a small percentage of his students would actually follow through. Some became so successful that they became the subjects of stories Lowry told in his classes, although none could match his own orphanage-to-mansion biography. A few became his partners in the seminar business. This enterprise was so successful that Lowry, decked out in a three-piece suit and toupee, taped a thirty-minute TV commercial that he paid stations to air in the middle of the night.

When he appeared in New York City, Lowry offered his seminars on weeknights, which made it easier for suburban commuters to attend. As they went home by train, they passed through parts of the Bronx, Brooklyn, and Queens where almost no one was investing in real estate. Although few knew it at the time, New York City had entered a period of profound economic change. Private-sector employment, which peaked in 1969, had begun to slide and wouldn't fully recover for more than forty years. For most of the same period, rising top-tier salaries received extravagant attention in the press, but median incomes for city residents remained below the national average. In time, Manhattan's rich would push out from their bastions in Midtown and on the East Side to claim, block by block, new territories for luxury apartments and high-end shops. The displacement of the poor and the middle class would be recognized as a threat to the rich culture of the borough. However, in the late sixties and early seventies, the threat of blight was a far more urgent concern.

Keen to protect the center of the city's economy, officials of the Lindsay administration pushed a host of ideas to aid development in Manhattan. New expressways were proposed to replace the crumbling West Side elevated highway and to link the Holland Tunnel and the bridges to Brooklyn. According to proponents, these highway projects would create jobs and, supposedly, aid business. However, they would also displace tens of thousands of people, which is why they met fierce resistance among local citizens. Opponents were joined by preservationists, who agreed with Ada Louise Huxtable, the architecture critic. She noted that the highway route through lower Manhattan seemed designed to create

"the most possible historical and architectural damage."
When the highway plans were presented at neighborhood meetings, angry residents often shouted down
city officials as they tried to speak.

In the end, despite great sums invested in planning
and studies, neither of the Manhattan freeways would
be built. The construction industry would survive, instead, on the development of offices and residential
buildings. The Twin Towers of the original World Trade
Center, which became the tallest buildings in the world
when they were completed in 1973, led this activity. For
a moment this prompted envy among the real estate
elite. The owners of the Empire State Building, which
saw its forty-year reign as "world's tallest" end when the
Twin Towers were completed, even announced a plan
to add eleven stories and recapture the title. But the idea
never progressed beyond talk. In the meantime the Port
Authority of New York and New Jersey, which owned
the Trade Center, struggled to fill them with tenants.
The two towers wound up contributing to a glut in office
space, which suppressed rents.

Housing construction spent the early 1970s in the dol-
drums as well. Only two significant projects were completed in this period, including a complex of 1,470
apartments called Waterside Plaza and a development
to house twenty thousand on Roosevelt Island in the
East River. Both were overseen by Richard Ravitch,
whose firm, HRH Construction, had completed the development of Trump Village. Both were also financed
by low-cost state bonds.

Despite the glimmers of hope represented by the
HRH projects on the East Side, a fortress-Manhattan
mentality prevailed in many discussions about the future of the city as frightening reports of crime and de-
spair arrived from the outer boroughs. In the South
Bronx, where 40 percent of the population depended on

welfare, law-abiding people feared
ments even during the day. In build
abandoned by their landlords, tenants
the winters without heat. Eventually
people found themselves without relia
were, at times, forced to haul buckets to from fire
hydrants. Packs of dogs roamed the streets. Trash accumulated in vacant lots. A local physician declared the
Bronx "a necropolis." Manhattanites saw shades of the
necropolis in parts of Harlem and in the Lower East
Side slums and in the peep-show-and-crime district
around Times Square. By 1975, real estate executives
would have to fight a sense of panic as prices for some
residential buildings dropped as much as 50 percent and
demand all but disappeared.[3]

While others watched fear and anxiety wash over the
real estate business, Donald Trump saw opportunities.
In his block-by-block exploration of Manhattan he had
noted several sites where he could imagine a better use
for the available space. This exercise required a creative
mind that could recognize that a neighborhood needed
more high-end housing or a low-rise block was ready for
a big, mixed-use development. Traffic flow, access to
mass transit, and the value of nearby parcels all played
into the calculations. These imaginings were just the
start. Once he identified a spot, Trump would have to
acquire it, and that could mean negotiating with a number of owners who might raise their prices as soon as
they figured out what game was afoot.

Given the extreme difficulties posed by sites with
multiple owners, developers in Manhattan were most interested in those rare big parcels controlled by single
entities. In many cases these owners were government
agencies and large corporations, which rarely parted
with property. In Manhattan, in the early 1970s, one exception was the remnants of the Penn Central railroad.

rising several formerly great lines, Penn Central as careening toward bankruptcy. But the railroad still controlled hundreds of pieces of real estate that could be sold to raise cash. Trump, like others in New York real estate, was especially interested in the railroad's little-used train yards on the West Side of Manhattan. One was in Midtown. The other was on the Upper West Side. They were the last large undeveloped tracts in the borough. A bankrupt railroad might make the yards available at an extremely attractive price for the buyer with foresight.

Years would pass while the Penn Central shed assets and died a slow death. Trump would bide his time, enjoying what New York could offer a young man with a good income, a rich father, and no real responsibilities. In the winter of 1969–70, he dabbled in the entertainment business as the coproducer of a Broadway play. The critics did not find much to like in *Paris Is Out!,* which told the story of a squabbling, middle-aged suburban couple. "I neither hated it nor liked it," wrote Walter Kerr. "I simply sat there and looked at it."[4] Closed soon after it opened, the play did succeed in giving Donald Trump the title of "Broadway producer" to carry with him as he traveled a circuit of nightspots that included 21, the Four Seasons, and a members-only restaurant-bar-discothèque called Le Club.

Le Club was renowned for attracting beautiful women, who commanded Trump's attention in ways that drink and drugs could not. (He would eventually confess that sex was his one real indulgence.) As he would write, "Some were vain, some were crazy, some were wild, and many of them were phonies." Trump would live up to his NYMA "ladies' man" designation, expending much time and energy in the pursuit of models, flight attendants, and others he found attractive. He also made fast friends with older, powerful men who might help him advance. First among them was the owner of the New York Yankees, George Steinbrenner. A bombastic bully who was a perfect subject for the tabloid press, Steinbrenner had used outbursts and tantrums to make himself into a national household name, which was a rarity for baseball owners of the day. He doubtless considered his personal fame to be good for business, and the recognition suited his ego.[5]

The whole point of Le Club was to be noticed as powerful or beautiful and to be photographed alongside a celebrity and thereby become one yourself. The place was founded and operated by the fashion designer Oleg Cassini and his brother, Igor, who had previously written a celebrity-gossip column under the name Cholly Knickerbocker. Igor claimed to have coined the term *jet set* and for a brief time published a magazine called, simply, *Status*. Le Club was all about status. It claimed the names of thirteen princes and four barons on its rolls, and its board of directors included the Maharaja of Jaipur and the Duke of Bedford. Although twelve hundred people belonged to Le Club, half were out of towners, and the place was so small that it couldn't accommodate more than two hundred in a night. The exclusivity meant that once you got inside, you stood a good chance of meeting certain first-tier celebrities— Diana Ross, Al Pacino, various Kennedys—or one of the real regulars. This latter group included Trump, Steinbrenner, and the most famous/infamous lawyer in New York City, Roy Cohn.[6]

With his McCarthy hearings well in the past, Roy Cohn of the 1970s was the ultimate wheeler-dealer attorney. Raised, quite literally, in the political clubhouses where his father traded in favors and influence, Cohn was fixing speeding tickets while still in high school. As a grown-up lawyer he devoted much of his time and energy to proving that he was extremely well connected to powerful people who could get things done. Forever gathering and disseminating gossip as well as meaningful information, Cohn spent his days on the phone with local judges, city officials, New York's Catholic cardinal, and politicians around the country. He tape-recorded many of these conversations and would later use the contents of calls to pressure people. When he couldn't fix a problem through his connections, or his clients' money, he went to court, where, in most cases, he performed quite brilliantly, whether he was defending organized-crime figures or defending himself against charges of unproffessional conduct. "A total genius" was how Donald Trump would describe him, adding, "But he would kill for somebody that he liked."[7]

For much of his life Cohn faced an almost constant threat of prosecution on charges related to his tax returns—IRS officials ultimately pegged his debt at $7 million—and his professional conduct. (He once put a pen in a comatose man's hand in an attempt to get a signature on an amendment to his will.) Although repeated efforts were made to prosecute or discipline him through the bar association, all but one failed. The last, which ended with the revocation of his law license, occurred just prior to Cohn's death in 1986 at age fifty-nine.

More than most, Cohn was a man of seemingly irreconcilable contradictions. Although he was gay, he befriended homophobes, opposed gay rights efforts, and helped persecute other gay men. Though Jewish, he often spewed anti-Semitic remarks. His bulging eyes were ringed with dark circles, and his face, made leathery by too much sun, was scarred by plastic surgery. But he dressed impeccably—fine suits, silk ties, matching handkerchiefs—and was so vain that he never appeared in public with a hair out of place. He looked like a gangster who had worked his way up through the ranks the hard way. He spoke in a soft, conspiratorial voice, and his accent, though mild—"open da door," go out "fuh lunch"—betrayed a bit of the New York streets. Some of his favorite phrases, including "along those lines" and "at a given time," made him sound like someone trying hard to sound like a fancy lawyer. Although obviously brilliant, he sometimes stumbled on common terms. In a radio interview he granted to promote a book he wrote, Cohn said that Joseph McCarthy's main problem was that he "would not observe the social amenities."

Cohn's style appealed to those who thought they needed a tough guy on their side, and it helped him to fit in with a clientele that included plenty of genuine mobsters. Among others, he represented reputed crime bosses and shady characters he helped to skim free cash out of X-rated-movie houses. Because authorities were never permitted to bug an attorney's office, his were sometimes used by suspected criminals seeking to avoid surveillance. Cohn's own businesses included a scam that cheated the City of New York out of the part of the rent due on parking-lot leases. A parking lot employee manager eventually confessed that Cohn was the ultimate beneficiary of the scheme and that he had pocketed thousands of dollars every week.[8]

Like many of the gangsters he represented, Cohn possessed a kind of charm that many who would have preferred to hate him found compelling. Loyal and generous, the gossip he shared over drinks or in the backseat of his rattletrap Rolls-Royce—his initials RMC were on the vanity license plates—made anyone who listened feel privileged and a little bit powerful. At Le Club, Cohn and Trump could have traded stories about mutual friends and acquaintances, including a host of political bosses such as Fred Trump's old friend Abe Beame, whom Cohn had known for many years. Cohn and Trump were also connected by a mutual interest in the outcome of a housing-discrimination case brought against the Trump Organization in the fall of 1973 by the federal government.

Based on complaints from officials of the Urban League's Open Housing Center, who sent black and white applicants to test landlord practices, the Justice Department had asked agents of the Federal Bureau of Investigation to probe the Trumps' operation. This work led the Department of Justice to sue the family's real estate company, Trump Management Corporation, alleging that the company had refused to rent to prospective tenants "because of race and color." The Trumps weren't singled out for this attention. In 1971 the Justice Department's Civil Rights Division had settled a similar complaint against the firm owned by Samuel J. LeFrak, who was an even bigger apartment operator in Brooklyn and Queens. (He owned twenty-one thousand apartments. The Trumps' holdings were reported, variously, as fourteen thousand, fifteen thousand, or sixteen thousand units.) But where LeFrak had moved quickly to negotiate a settlement, the Trumps had hired Cohn and signaled their willingness to wage a long fight.

On January 12, 1974, Cohn and Donald Trump, who was becoming the face of the family business, called the press to a conference room at the New York Hilton. (A favorite spot of publicity hounds, the hotel had recently been the site of the first cell phone call in history, which was made by an executive for a firm developing the technology.) Cohn told reporters that the federal government had failed to provide the name of a single person who had allegedly suffered discrimination by the Trumps and announced that he had filed a countersuit claiming the Trumps had suffered $100 million in damages due to the "irresponsible and baseless" claims of the civil rights office. When Donald Trump spoke, he sounded a bit like a lawyer himself as he refuted the charges in a way that left him an out should the evidence prove him wrong: "I have never, nor has anyone in my organization ever, to the best of my knowledge, discriminated or shown bias in renting our apartments."

Where Trump and the Feds disagreed, he said, was on the landlord's standards for approving or rejecting a tenant. The government's lawyers, acting on claims of would-be renters, said that black applicants with the same financial qualifications as whites who were given leases had been turned away. Donald Trump insisted this was not true and that his company only sought to exclude welfare recipients, who, he feared, would not pay rent and move out in "one or two months." Trump said that Samuel LeFrak's settlement required that he rent to applicants on welfare, and that if Trump agreed to the same type of settlement, tenants would flee his buildings and entire "communities as a whole." Although LeFrak tried to dispute this description of the arrangement, Trump was in fact correct. LeFrak had agreed that applicants who were not working but received enough in welfare to pay their rent could live in his buildings.

When asked about his organization's record, Donald estimated that seven hundred, or 4.3 percent, of his company's apartments were rented to blacks. At the time Brooklyn was 25 percent black and Queens was 13 percent. Some of the disparity between the population figures and the Trump record could be explained by location. Many Trump buildings were in white-majority communities such as Coney Island, which was 85 percent white according to the 1970 census. It was possible that few blacks sought to live in these areas. However, housing was in short supply and the rents charged at Trump properties made them affordable even for applicants on the lower rungs of the middle class. And the complaint from the Urban League presented claims of apparent discrimination.

In a different historical moment, the federal government would never have bothered to consider the racial makeup of Trump's tenants. However, after the president's landslide reelection in 1972, officials of the Nixon administration had decided to step up their enforcement of the Fair Housing Act of 1968. The act, approved by Congress in part to respond to the racial conflict across the nation, barred discrimination in housing, including a landlords' practice of "steering" applicants away from certain buildings and toward others, depending on their race. (LeFrak's firm had been accused of sending minority applicants to his buildings that were primarily occupied by blacks.) Apparently concerned about how white backlash would affect his reelection campaign, Nixon had offered only lukewarm support to the affirmative-action initiatives of his housing secretary, George Romney. But after Nixon was returned to office in a landslide victory, his administration began to focus on enforcement of the housing act and brought hundreds of complaints against landlords across the country.

Few landlord defendants responded to the Justice Department with a countersuit like the $100 million claim Roy Cohn filed on behalf of the Trumps. Cohn also complained that federal officials were "storm troopers" who had used "Gestapo-like tactics." Federal judge Edward Neaher bristled at Cohn's words, noting it was the first time he had ever heard anyone accusing the FBI of Nazi-style behavior. He dismissed the countersuit as a waste of "time and paper" and pushed the parties to negotiate. In his talks with federal lawyers Cohn attempted to bully Donna Goldstein, the young government attorney assigned to the case. The result, recalled by

J. Stanley Pottinger, who was then chief of the Civil Rights Division at the Department of Justice, showed the limits of Cohn's influence.

"I was sitting in J. Edgar Hoover's old office, which I had somehow been assigned, and my deputy Jim Turner comes in and says, 'We've got a problem. Would you see Donna Goldstein? She's quaking in her boots because she understands you're going to fire her.'"

According to Pottinger, Roy Cohn had screamed at Goldstein about a supposed error she had made in some bit of paperwork. He had said that he was a big player in the Republican Party and that he was going to call the White House and the attorney general and arrange to have her fired.

Pottinger doubted Richardson would even take a call from Cohn. "The thing about the attorney general and Nixon too, was that they really wanted to do the right thing on this issue. We were given a big budget—I had two hundred attorneys working for me—and I had gone to this meeting at the White House where [chief domestic adviser John] Ehrlichman told us, 'It's time. Go. Go. Go.'"

In the Trump case, Pottinger was confident in the evidence, which included testimony from current and former Trump workers who said they were required to report the race of those seeking apartments and had been instructed to discourage black applicants. One said that Fred Trump had told him to deny apartments to blacks who applied. "Donna told me how Cohn had threatened her. I said, 'Fuck him. Go do your job and don't worry about it.'"

With the government standing firm, Cohn began to negotiate in earnest. Eventually his clients would agree to a settlement that required a public pledge of non-discrimination. As Donald Trump would later say, "It meant nothing because we never discriminated in the first place." However the settlement also imposed a protocol on the company that was a first in New York City. For two years the Trumps would be required to supply weekly lists of vacancies to the Urban League's Open Housing Center. When vacancies opened up in buildings where fewer than 10 percent of the tenants were black or Hispanic, the center would then have three days to submit applications from minority clients who wanted those apartments. If qualified, they were to get preference.

As Donald managed the firm's dealings with the federal government, he established a template for most of the legal disputes he would face in the future. Whenever possible he would, in Roy Cohn style, go on the offensive. He would admit no wrongdoing and define a conflict to insist that he was the victim, and not the perpetrator of some immoral or illegal act. In the civil rights case, for example, he said the government had singled out the Trump Organization because as a large-scale operator it was an easy target. He also said the Feds were trying to force the company to rent to welfare recipients. Neither claim was precisely on point. The government was taking action against landlords big and small. And though regulators intended to end discrimination against welfare recipients, they weren't seeking to require Trump or anyone else to house them. They just wanted landlords to acknowledge welfare payments as income that could be used to pay rent.[9]

When he talked about welfare instead of race, Trump played to the prejudices of those who were inclined to think of assistance payments as handouts for undeserving black families. The linking of the words *welfare* and *black* had begun in the 1950s as blacks in the rural South moved to the urban North and some became eligible for welfare programs. When President Johnson declared a "war on poverty" in his 1964 State of the Union address, the American public saw a dramatic increase in national press reports on issues related to the poor. Although blacks represented about 30 percent of the welfare rolls, when national magazines published photos of recipients, most—about 75 percent in the year 1967—depicted black people. As the press also reported abuses by some recipients, welfare was symbolized, in many minds, by the image of working-age black women with children who maintained secret relationships with men who refused to care for their dependents. These "welfare queens" represented a tiny criminal element among recipients, but their existence, and attendant press accounts about them, were enough to make *welfare* a code word that communicated racist assumptions.[10]

Did Donald Trump know that as he complained about being forced to accept tenants on welfare he was using code—eventually this would be called dog-whistle language[11]—to play on racial animus? He insisted that he never intended such a thing, and complained to *The New York Times* that efforts to test the practices of real estate managers amounted to "a form of horrible harassment." But in choosing to have Cohn fight the government and claiming the Feds were trying to force him to accept welfare clients, Trump did play on stereotypes. (Cohn's own prejudices—he often used such words as *spic* and *nigger* and *fag*—have been widely reported.) When the case was finally settled, Trump agreed to a process that would make it much easier for minority applicants to move into his buildings. This type of agreement was all the federal prosecutors wanted when they first approached the Trumps, and it could have been reached without any political threats against Donna Goldstein or press conferences at the New York Hilton.

The lawsuit likely made more New Yorkers aware of the Trump name and added to Cohn's fame. Cohn understood that legal proceedings were rich with opportunities for contact with the press—lawsuits were often newsworthy—and it hardly mattered whether one was making an accusation or defending against one. As Senator McCarthy's accuser-in-chief, Cohn had discovered he could easily manipulate powerful columnists such as Walter Winchell and Westbrook Pegler, who considered themselves his teammates in a kind of game played against various witnesses. Winchell actually threatened *Washington Post* reporter Murrey Marder, who had doggedly exposed McCarthy's witch-hunt tactics. *"We're* going to get you," Winchell had muttered to Marder in a crowded elevator. Cohn and company never did "get" Marder, but the incident showed how certain members of the press identified with the man who supplied them with bits of information about suspects in Hollywood or Washington, which they then used to decorate their gossip columns and gain readers.

After his defeat in Washington, Cohn used the same techniques of friendship and leaks to favored columnists in New York City. In 1973, as Cohn helped the Trumps fight the Feds, he also aided their mutual friend Abe Beame by telling journalists at *The New York Times* that Congressman Mario Biaggi had cited his constitutional right against self-incrimination, under the Fifth Amendment, when called before a federal grand jury. Biaggi was, at the time, Beame's toughest opponent in the upcoming primary election that would determine who would represent the Democratic Party in the November mayor's race. Grand jury proceedings are supposed to be confidential, and "taking the Fifth," as the expression goes, is not to be regarded as a sign of guilt. When *The Times* went to Biaggi with the information from Cohn, Biaggi denied it. This denial backfired when other sources confirmed Cohn's leak. A spate of press reports followed, detailing investigations into Biaggi's finances and possible political corruption. Release of the grand jury testimony proved Biaggi had lied about refusing to answer questions, and his campaign was de-stroyed. In November 1973, Bcame, who had twice been city comptroller, won the mayor's job by a margin of more than forty points.[12]

◆

Beame's election, after would-be reformer John Lind-say's tumultuous eight years of struggle, turned control of the city government over to the clubhouse Democrats of Brooklyn, who had a long and mutually beneficial relationship with the Trumps. A year later, Beame's help would ensure that another Brooklyn Democrat and Trump friend, Hugh Carey, became gov-ernor of New York State. But as both men realized their great ambitions, they found themselves over-whelmed by the fiscal crisis that brought New York City, long mismanaged and lacking a coherent financial-management system, to the brink of bankruptcy.[13]

The moment many Americans recall from the crisis came when Republican President Gerald Ford refused to help the city and the New York *Daily News* an-nounced the news with a huge headline, FORD TO CITY: DROP DEAD. Although the president never ut-tered these words, they did express his sentiments as he rejected a request that the federal government guaran-tee city bond issues. Afterward, he offered lectures on fiscal responsibility and said the city needed to slash municipal spending. Many GOP officials considered big Northern cities, which were generally controlled by Democratic Party machines, to be corrupt beyond re-demption. The riots of the 1960s had only confirmed their doubts about urban America. To them, the thought of mayors in these places being forced to slash spend-ing and lay off unionized municipal workers, who al-ways voted for Democrats anyway, didn't seem like a bad idea.

Beame did enact cost-cutting measures, but he was forced to reverse some of these moves. A street protest by construction workers, for example, broke a freeze he had placed on city building projects. The construction-spending thaw brought Beame only momentary peace. Soon the city's lenders tightened the mayor's access to credit, and lawmakers in Albany, many of whom shared an anti-urban frame of mind, demanded new bridge tolls, increased mass transit fares, and even a four-day workweek for city employees to reduce payroll. As the fight over these ideas and others raged, members of the police and firefighters unions printed and distributed an ominous flyer warning tourists about the dangers posed by city layoffs. Titled "Welcome to Fear City," it advised visitors to "stay off the streets after 6 PM even in Midtown Manhattan." Sanitation workers conducted a wildcat strike that left tons of stinking garbage on the streets, and highway workers tied up traffic with roadside pickets. The backups became nightmarish when three drawbridges were raised and then their operators disappeared.

During months of argument involving city officials, financiers, and politicians in Albany, Abe Beame suffered one indignity after another as unions, bankers, and other public officials required him to meet their demands before they would help. When he signed an ordinance imposing a wage freeze on city workers, the mayor was subjected to hissing and catcalls and shouted questions: "Who is the boss? Is it the people or the banks? Who is calling the shots?" By the end of the summer of '75, state officials and lenders were calling the shots as special agencies were created to guarantee city bond payments and oversee its administration. A more-or-less final resolution to the crisis didn't come until municipal unions agreed to buy $500 million in city bonds, and President Ford, under pressure from foreign leaders who feared the ripple effects of a default, reversed his position on federal loan guarantees.

The city's wounds, as a result of the crisis, would include steep declines in public housing programs, cuts in programs that fed poor children, sweeping layoffs in the police force, and began requiring that City College students pay tuition. Add less significant indignities such as fewer school-crossing guards and reduced Staten Island ferry service, and New Yorkers found themselves living in a city where life had become a little less pleasant and a bit more challenging. Perhaps worse than the cuts was a sharp drop in housing construction, which dipped to a rate not seen since the Great Depression. In 1975 permits were granted for fewer than four thousand residences.

For Mayor Beame, who had promised to bring "new pride" to New York, the fiscal crisis brought humiliation as his powers were diminished and he appeared, in the words of one local writer, to be "a busted man." Although he would be judged among the city's worst mayors, due to his fiscal impotence, Beame was not as polarizing as some of his contemporaries. Two other prominent mayors of the 1970s, Sam Yorty of Los Angeles and Frank Rizzo of Philadelphia, distinguished themselves by rhetoric that inflamed racial animosities and contributed to violence in the streets. Compared with these men, Beame was a paragon of calm, continually seeking to soothe and placate everyone from the titans of Wall Street to the citizens who turned on their televisions to watch him struggle to explain the fiscal crisis and his plans for resolving it.

The mayor could have been excused if he had shown flashes of anger. Never a compelling personality, he had been denied the easy road to power taken by the telegenic Lindsay. Instead he had toiled inside the Democratic machine for more than thirty years, patiently serving others and awaiting his shot at the big job. When he finally got it, financial time bombs planted years before he took office began to explode. Beame was also hurt by the recession that began in 1973 and marked the end of the golden age of the American economy. Exacerbated by an embargo by oil-producing countries, which pushed prices up fourfold in two years, the recession wreaked havoc with businesses, depressed tax receipts, and threw people out of work as the national economy contracted during Beame's first year in office.[14]

◆

Watching as Mayor Beame struggled and the city was overwhelmed by a sense of crisis, Donald Trump sensed opportunity at hand. Beame had made few proposals for development in the city, but one that he favored called for a new convention center to maintain New York's status as a prime locale for big meetings. Chicago officials had recently opened a huge new meeting facility at McCormick Place and would soon expand it. An equally large convention center was planned for San Francisco. In New York, tourism had steadily declined from 1969 to 1975, but it still brought more than $1 billion into the city every year. Determined to revive the industry, Beame included a convention-center development in his 1977–78 budget and identified three possible sites. The leading contender was a Penn Central rail yard covering forty-four acres along the Hudson River between Thirtieth and Thirty-ninth Streets, and the development rights for the property were controlled by Donald Trump. The story of how he acquired them illustrates his reliance on cronyism, stubbornness, and an odd kind of charm. This formula, which called for a greater measure of style than substance, would power him through a lifetime of deal-making.

The Penn Central Midtown train yard was located partly within the notorious Hell's Kitchen, a waterfront neighborhood of docks, dives, warehouses, and cheap apartments where crime had flourished for generations. Although the repeal of Prohibition put an end to liquor smuggling, it did not put the gangs of Hell's Kitchen out of business. In the 1960s and '70s the neighborhood's dominant crime organization, an Irish American crew called the Westies, operated in alliance with the Gambino family of the Italian mob. Terrifyingly violent, the Westies were connected to more than fifty murders in ten years.[15]

Although most New Yorkers avoided Hell's Kitchen, especially after nightfall, Donald Trump was drawn to the Penn Central yard even before Beame recognized the site as a potential location for the convention center. Trump's realization was hardly a stroke of genius. New York developers had long coveted the Hell's Kitchen yard and a second West Side train facility known as the Sixtieth Street yards because they were the only large, privately held open tracts left in Manhattan. For decades they had watched freight traffic decline—from about two hundred thousand cars per year to fewer than twenty-five thousand—waiting for the moment when these properties would become available. The moment arrived in 1973, when the railroad's trustees hired a consultant named Victor Palmieri to sell its real estate to satisfy creditors in what was then the largest bankruptcy case in US history.

A lawyer who had paid his way through Stanford with a construction job in Alaska, Palmieri said he enjoyed working in crisis situations because they allowed him to cut through bureaucracy and "be a success or failure in a relatively short time." The bankruptcy court approved Palmieri's appointment, which came with a salary of $150,000 per year and the potential to make

millions of dollars in commissions on properties estimated to be worth more than $1 billion. This would be
easy money. In a bankruptcy the trustees who control a
corporation typically have little motivation to seek the
best prices as they sell assets. The money paid will not
fund future business activity or find its way to their
pockets. Instead they want to move quickly, satisfying
the barest requirements of the court overseeing the disposal of assets, and get away from the rotting corporate
corpse. Thus, Palmieri's job would be to find buyers and
make deals as quickly as possible.[16]

Politically connected at the highest levels, Palmieri
had undertaken big jobs before. In 1967–68, for example, he had helped organize and run the Kerner Commission, a historically important presidential panel that
reported on recent race riots. For the Penn Central job
he put together a team of experts in law and real estate.
Responsibility for the rail yards in Manhattan fell to
Edward "Ned" Eichler, whose family had founded a large
and innovative home-building company in the San Francisco Bay Area. Eichler Homes was known for offering
affordable, airily designed houses inspired by the sen-
sibilities of Frank Lloyd Wright. Eichler houses helped
define California modern style, and the company sold
more than eleven thousand of them, including the one
where Paul and Clara Jobs raised their adopted son, Steven. As it profited, Eichler also pursued an unan-
nounced social agenda, refusing to follow the informal
racist practices of the past and selling to all qualified
buyers. As a result, its subdivisions were integrated from
the moment they were settled. The company also mar-
keted itself with a certain fifties flair. In 1956 Eichler
built and put on display an all-steel, experimental home
with the jet-age name of the X-100. It was built with two
indoor gardens, a plastic-domed skylight, and motorized
sliding doors.[17]

Ned Eichler left the family firm after a heated dispute with his father. He then went to work for Palmieri in New York. As he settled into his office, he received a letter from Donald Trump of the Trump Organization in Brooklyn. Although Eichler didn't recognize the name, he was happy to hear from anyone with an interest in the rail yards. Though attractive as open parcels, the yards would require an enormous effort on the part of any developer, who would have to negotiate with multiple layers of bureaucracy and deal with the opposition that was sure to arise from neighborhood organizations resistant to change. The city's fiscal problems and a rapidly decelerating real estate market only added to the challenge. As Eichler scanned the industry, he saw few developers with the experience and audacity required to get the most out of such big sites in a place such as Manhattan. Even William Zeckendorf, the real estate swashbuckler, had put his campaign to emerge from a recent bankruptcy on hold and retreated to the sidelines.

After he spoke on the phone with Trump, Eichler accepted an invitation to visit Avenue Z on a late January day. There he found a young man practically bursting with ambition. At age forty-two, Eichler was fifteen years older than his host, and he considered the slim, blond-haired Trump to be remarkably boyish and outlandishly ambitious. He would describe him to the writer Gwenda Blair as "full of his own ego, wanting to make his way in the city." Eichler was impressed by the younger man's energy, even though he sometimes spoke in fatalistic terms. He recalled that Trump explained his impatience by saying he expected to die before age forty. He also told Eichler, "I'll never marry."

On a tour of the Trumps' outer-borough empire, Eichler noticed that the buildings he saw were well designed, well constructed, and well maintained. But he worried about the political complexity of building a massive apartment complex in Manhattan, and he couldn't forget that when he had asked if anyone at the Penn Central offices knew of the Trumps, no one had been able to say who they were. When he told Trump that he was worried that a company based in a humble office in Brooklyn lacked the necessary clout, Trump said the firm was up to the job. Eichler said it would help if he could go to City Hall and ask Mayor Beame to vouch for the Trumps. Trump asked, "When do you want to see him?" Eichler matched Trump's bravado, answering, "Tomorrow at two p.m." Trump said he would send a car to fetch Eichler at one thirty. Trump didn't want the man from Penn Central to be late.

At the appointed hour, Eichler walked into the mayor's office and found the Trumps, father and son, waiting with Beame and John Zuccotti of the New York City Planning Commission. After some pleasantries the mayor told Eichler, "Whatever my friends Fred and Donald want in this town, they get."

As a bit of business theater, the City Hall meeting was worthy of a Tony. It confirmed that the Trumps were so well connected that they were more likely than others to get city approval for developments on Penn Central's properties. This political power meant something to Eichler and Palmieri, whose fees and commissions—which ultimately exceeded $21 million—depended on options being converted to actual property purchases. Personally, Eichler was more taken with the obviously close relationship he saw between Donald and Fred. Where Eichler had suffered due to his father's lack of support, he noticed that Fred was unwavering in his commitment to Donald and his ambitions. The elder man's support was so complete that Eichler would recall it many years later as a key factor in his assessment of the Trumps as developers. But while Eichler felt confident in their ability to work with the city, and construct apartments, a deal to sell them the rail yards would also have to satisfy the bankruptcy court in Philadelphia, where the remains of Penn Central's assets were being sorted.

Bankruptcy judge John P. Fullam was responsible for managing the disposal of the Penn Central assets outside of the passenger and freight business that would be assumed by two federally created entities called Amtrak and Conrail. Fullam would try to get the greatest compensation possible for creditors, who were represented by a small army of attorneys including a pioneer in class-action lawsuits named David Berger. (Based in Philadelphia, Berger would eventually represent neighbors of the Three Mile Island nuclear power station after it suffered a partial meltdown.) As Eichler and Palmieri worked to submit a proposal for the rail yards to the judge, they were under pressure to maximize the amount of money that would eventually find its way to Berger's clients. The prospects for profit seemed to improve when they received an inquiry about the properties from a well-known builder and real estate operator called the Starrett Corporation.

Famous for constructing the Empire State Building in less than a year's time, Starrett was a formidable outfit. Among other projects, the firm had built the twelve thousand apartments of Parkchester in the Bronx as well as Stuyvesant Town and Peter Cooper Village, on the East Side of Manhattan. These developments were comparable to the kind of multibuilding communities that would be appropriate for the rail yards and far exceeded anything ever attempted by the Trumps. Starrett was also willing to make a deal that, under the right conditions, would pay Penn Central almost $40 million more than the maximum that might be paid by the Trumps. Starrett and the Trumps were, however, in business together in Brooklyn at an apartment complex called

Starrett City. In August of 1974 Donald visited with Robert Olnick, who was Starrett's chief executive officer, and reminded him of this relationship. Olnick then telephoned the broker who had been working for him on the Penn Central deal and told him to drop it. Before the call ended, though, he said that if the Trumps faltered, Starrett would take up the project again, under the same terms.

With Starrett out, Eichler committed to Donald Trump as the "horse" that Penn Central would ride, which meant that he would enjoy special consideration and protection. He and Trump also attempted to socialize a bit. They golfed at the exclusive Winged Foot club in Westchester County and dined with Roy Cohn at the Four Seasons restaurant. Eichler didn't find much to like in Cohn and took note when the attorney announced he had been meeting with Hugh Carey, who was running for governor, and Donald said of Carey, "He'll do anything for a developer who gives him a campaign contribution." The Trumps would donate $135,000 ($556,000 in 2015) to Carey's winning campaign. Only the candidate's brother would give more.

Reported by New York journalist Wayne Barrett, Trump's comment about Carey was the kind of unseemly statement that would make any circumspect person such as Eichler feel uneasy. Eichler had a similar reaction when Trump, just like the builders who had greased FHA bureaucrats with gifts, sent him a television set for Christmas. Eichler sent it back. "I never at any time liked Donald personally," said Eichler years later, "but that never had anything to do with whether he was the right person" to develop the Penn Central rail yards.

Certain that Donald's inexhaustible supply of energy and desire would cause buildings to bloom on the West Side yards, Eichler pressed ahead with the Trump proposal. The creditors' attorney David Berger and his associates questioned people involved with the deal and discovered that Eichler had treated the Trumps as favorites because he thought they possessed unique political connections. Berger's firm also found that the appraisal done to set a value for the sites had been based on similar land in Brooklyn and the Bronx but not Manhattan. In fact, adjacent land had recently been sold for more than six times the $4 per square foot estimated for the yards. This information was contained in a lengthy deposition sent to Judge Fullam by Berger and his associates. At roughly the same time Richard Ravitch of HRH Construction wrote judge Fullam to make an offer for the sites.

In his letter, Ravitch said that even though he had been eyeing the yards for development for almost a decade, he only learned they were for sale when the Trump deal was submitted to the court. Donald Trump doubted this was true, since Penn Central's bankruptcy was perhaps the most widely reported business event of the 1970s, and that its properties would be sold was also known. But this point hardly mattered since Ravitch followed up his letter with a proposal that was, in some ways, a better deal for the Penn Central creditors. The HRH bid, combined with David Berger's criticisms, threatened to upend the arrangement that Eichler and Trump had worked hard to complete.

Although Eichler and Palmieri wanted to complete their work and earn their commission from the Penn Central trustees, they could afford to wait for the judge to work out the issues related to the yards. Donald Trump wasn't so patient. He also recognized in David Berger the same type of roadblock his father had encountered when he tried to acquire the bankrupt Lehrenkrauss mortgage operation in 1933 and decided to try a play from the old man's book. He went to Philadelphia and, according to Wayne Barrett, "swooped into Berger's offices wearing a long, dark green cape, wrapped around his shoulders, jittery and flushed."

After Trump found Berger in a conference room, the two men retired to talk in private. When they were finished, they had agreed that Penn Central, and thus its creditors, should receive better terms, which could amount to $20 million or more should the Trump vision ever materialize. They also agreed that the railroad should pay Donald Trump to cover his time and whatever expenses he incurred as he tried to make something happen on the sites. Presumably Berger would collect a somewhat higher payment for his services from the creditors if the full amount due to them was increased. He was, after all, working for a share of the proceeds. But other than this potential gain, which would not be realized for many years, nothing in the arrangement seemed to benefit Berger in any way. (A federal prosecutor would eventually look into the matter and reach a similar conclusion.)

The turnabout stunned a young Berger associate named Edward Rubenstone, who had devoted himself to fighting for the Penn Central creditors and believed they would do better with a truly open competition for the West Side yards. For his part, Eichler marveled at Trump's resourcefulness. Later he would say, "Whatever Donald did, assuming he did anything, it was a very clever accomplishment." When he was informed of this turn of events in November 1974, Judge Fullam responded skeptically. "I am not at all satisfied from what I have heard that there has been adequate consideration given to the competing offers," he told the parties when they gathered before him in March 1975. In particular Fullam wanted to hear more from Richard Ravitch. However in the time between hearings, recently elected New York governor Hugh Carey, whom Donald Trump considered so eminently corruptible, named Ravitch to lead an investigation into the severe financial crisis at the state Urban Development Corporation. The agency had run afoul of the markets and could no longer attract bond buyers. Its commitments exceeded anticipated revenues by more than $500 million.

The UDC's trouble had been caused, at least in part, by its having operated outside the usual system of checks and balances that allowed legislators and others to oversee state agencies. It had been formed for the express purpose of allowing state officials to evade laws that required them to get voter approval, via ballot referendum, before selling bonds to raise money to finance, among other things, housing projects undertaken by private companies, including HRH. Ordinary bonds were considered secure investments because the state could not escape its commitment to pay back investors, plus interest. The type sold by the UDC was devised by the Wall Street lawyer John N. Mitchell, who called them "moral obligation" bonds and who eventually explained that "the purpose of them" was to allow the powers that be to avoid voter accountability. Though morally obliged to pay these debts, the state was not legally bound to honor them. When New York City ran into fiscal trouble, investors considered the possibility that state officials might not behave morally and stopped buying the bonds.

With Ravitch occupied with the UDC, he did not press Judge Fullam on the West Side yards. In March of 1975 the bankruptcy court in Philadelphia approved the arrangement worked out by David Berger and Donald Trump. Penn Central officials were modest in assessing the prospects, noting that if all went well, the sale would generate between $62 million and $120 million. Donald Trump, given his first-ever opportunity to

practice some major ballyhoo, said that the railroad/
creditors were in line to get $300 million from two mas-
sive projects. He said he would build twenty thousand
apartments on the uptown parcel. The smaller Hell's
Kitchen site would accommodate ten thousand housing
units or perhaps a different kind of development. Publicly Trump mentioned an industrial or shipping center,
but in private he had talked about it as the perfect spot
for a city-financed convention center. He estimated that
eventually $1 billion would be expended at the two sites,
with construction beginning in eighteen to twenty-four
months.

Thousands of laborers would be employed by the
work, said Trump, and he hoped to win state-subsidized
funding under programs to aid construction of housing
for middle-class tenants. Rents would range between
$100 and $115 per month, per room.[18]

Having used political connections and insider status
to prevail in his first big deal, Trump would have seen
all around him ample evidence that many people considered some rules to be optional. On the very day his
triumph was announced, federal prosecutors in Trenton
were selecting jurors for a trial in which developers
were charged with attempting to bribe the mayor of Fort
Lee—on the New Jersey side of the George Washington Bridge—to win approval for a $250 million project.
In New York City, two policemen were indicted for
shooting a clerk and stealing $2,000 from a grocery
store that was a front for drug sales. And in Newark a
bank officer confessed to embezzling almost $400,000
to pay gambling debts. Jeffrey Miller said he intended
to repay the money by picking winning horses at local
racetracks, but his plan didn't work out.[19]

Of course Miller and the others were the ones who
got caught and therefore represented merely the tip of
the corruption iceberg. Their alleged crimes paled in

comparison with the intersecting deceptions practiced
by the US government in its war in Vietnam and by
the Nixon administration in the Watergate scandal. The
political burglary carried out on Nixon's behalf at the
Watergate building led to the first presidential resigna-
tion in history. Various officials, including former attorney general John N. Mitchell (inventor of the moral
obligation bond) were convicted of felonies. Public trust
in institutions, as measured by opinion polls, began a
decline that would never be fully corrected. Fully
70 percent of those polled in the early 1960s said they
had faith in their political leaders. By the early 1980s
only 25 percent expressed the same sentiment.[20]

Although many felt unmoored by the events of the
seventies, young Donald Trump would consider Watergate and the lies told to justify the Vietnam War evidence of the world as it was—dangerous, corrupt, and
full of intrigue. An intensely competitive young man
who believed he was superior to others, Trump accepted
that people would seek advantages wherever they could
find them. Thanks to the advantages conferred by his
father, and Abe Beame, he had won the trust of Ned
Eichler and Victor Palmieri, who became his allies in
the bankruptcy court.

The city would actually purchase the Hell's Kitchen
site for the new convention center, paying just $12 mil-
lion, a sum that surely disappointed the Penn Central
creditors. Their take would be reduced by a commission
paid to Palmieri's firm. Trump was deprived of the big
score he would have posted if he had gotten the land and
built a commercial or residential project. However, he
did net a $500,000 sales commission, which, added to
the sum already paid to him for his time and expenses
by the Penn Central trustees, meant that he earned
$1,250,000 in payment for all of his scurryings and
machinations. His big regret would be that the city

refused his request that the convention center be named for his father, Fred. That honor would go to former US senator Jacob Javits, whose career in politics began when he worked as a volunteer in Fiorello La Guardia's campaign for mayor.

5

DONALD SAVES MIDTOWN

I saved that whole area. That area was a disaster.
—DONALD TRUMP ON THE GRAND
CENTRAL NEIGHBORHOOD

In the dismal New York real estate market of the 1970s, Victor Palmieri and Ned Eichler represented one bright spot of opportunity. The portfolio they were hired to sell for the Penn Central trustee included many valuable properties in addition to the underutilized Manhattan rail yards. Among the holdings were several prominent hotels that had passed their prime—the Barclay, the Biltmore, the Commodore, and the Roosevelt—as well as various commercial buildings and rail facilities. Penn Central owned the staid old Yale Club as well as the land beneath the ultramodern Pan Am Building (later named the MetLife Building).

An Italian developer named Renzo Zingone proposed a $40 million industrial complex for a hundred-acre Penn Central parcel in the South Bronx known as the Harlem River Yards. Zingone said he was negotiating with European firms to locate manufacturing plants on the property, which would employ as many as five thousand people. With industrial jobs leaving New York at a rate of roughly fifty thousand per year, officials voiced support for Zingone, even though he wanted the city to buy the land for him. (This approach was unusual, but not unheard of. Access to the land would be considered a form of equity by a lender, who might then advance Zingone construction loans.)[1]

Among the other players in the scramble for Penn Central's New York properties were several banks, Arab sheikhs, the Hilton hotel chain, and investors from Iran. The first of all the deals completed by Palmieri was the New York Bank for Savings' purchase of a thirty-four-story skyscraper at 230 Park Avenue. With 1 million square feet of space and a distinctive copper-and-gilt roof, the landmark building actually spans the avenue. The roadway passes through portals opened in its base, which is decorated on its north side with statuary and a gilded clock. The price paid, $26 million, would equal roughly $115 million in 2015. Considering that it was sold for more than $1 billion in 2007, it was a bargain.

Prices were declining at a rapid rate, and deals were so rare that the controversial Reverend Sun Myung Moon—widely accused of operating a religious cult—made headlines when he purchased both the two-thousand-room New Yorker Hotel and an adjacent theater complex on Thirty-fourth Street for less than $8 million. In this depressed market, most of Penn Central's properties attracted offers that were substantially lower than what the trustees expected or came with complex conditions that would have to be satisfied before any money was paid. In the first round of bidding, they didn't receive a single offer for the hulking Commodore Hotel, which rose above Grand Central Terminal from a spot on the northwest corner of Lexington Avenue and Forty-second Street.

Named for the deceased Cornelius Vanderbilt, the nineteenth-century tycoon who was not a real commodore, the hotel honored one of America's first business celebrities. Vanderbilt had risen from ferry operator to robber baron thanks to unmatched creativity and ruthlessness. His fortune, amassed first through steamship and rail lines, eventually depended most on financial engineering and legal assaults upon his competitors. The commodore prevailed in almost every scrap, and his fortune eventually grew until it exceeded the wealth of modern-day moguls Bill Gates and Warren Buffett combined. Vanderbilt's legacy—he died in 1877—included the New York Central Railroad, which built and would operate the great hotel.

The Commodore opened in 1919 with nineteen hundred rooms and amenities including en suite baths and a lobby that was the largest single room in New York City. Designed and decorated to evoke an Italian courtyard, the lobby featured an indoor waterfall and was dotted with palms rising out of urns. The ballroom was so big it could, and once did, accommodate a circus complete with elephants. Among the modern facilities available when the Commodore opened were a domestic-telegraph room, an overseas-cable office, and a lounge where stock prices were posted on giant boards attached to the walls.

Although the Commodore retained its allure for decades, competitors eventually built new hotels with larger rooms and more modern fixtures. By the 1960s, the Commodore had lost most of the business travel trade to the Americana and other competitors and served mainly conventioneers and budget-conscious tourists. Wealthier travelers preferred the Plaza, or Harry Helmsley's Park Lane. When New York City's economic woes began in the 1970s, the Commodore's managers negotiated with the hotel's unions to cut costs by eliminating certain services and laying off workers. All of New York's hotels suffered, with the overall occupancy rate dipping to 62.5 percent in 1971, which was the lowest figure in thirty years. Seven hotels closed and were converted to other uses. The Commodore rented just half of its available rooms in 1972, and its vast size became a liability. Managers began closing down entire floors to save on upkeep. Although they spent $500,000 to update the ballroom, this effort did not revive the Commodore. By the middle of the decade, many of the businesses that rented on the Commodore's main floor had departed. Some of these spaces were abandoned. Others were taken over by shops providing discount goods and services including massages and other offerings at a place called Relaxation Plus. On many weekends parts of the lobby were given over to a flea market. One industry insider said, "The value of that hotel is equal to the true land value minus the cost of demolition."[2]

Besides the decline of the Commodore, the Grand Central area suffered as the owners of the Chrysler Building, an art deco icon, were forced into foreclosure by creditors and its major tenant, Texaco, prepared to move to the suburbs. Texaco's departure would pull hundreds of workers out of the neighborhood, depriving local businesses of their spending. The owners of the famous Schrafft's restaurant, which filled much of the Chrysler Building's ground floor, decided to close before this loss materialized. A pine-paneled refuge for almost forty-five years, Schrafft's offered something for everyone in its separate dining room, soda fountain, and basement-level Men's Grill. As it ceased operation, local residents, commuting office workers, tourists, and day-trippers lost a genteel refuge in a city that seemed ever more dangerous.[3]

Though hardly as blighted as Times Square, which was overwhelmed by theaters showing pornographic movies, the area around Grand Central nevertheless also became downtrodden. In a single year, 1974–75, crime rose by 18.5 percent in Midtown South, which included the blocks around the station. Ridership on the subway lines feeding Grand Central dropped by 20 percent.

All the trouble in Midtown made Fred Trump wary of any deal involving the hotel next to Grand Central. "Buying the Commodore at a time when even the Chrysler Building is in receivership," he declared, "is like fighting for a seat on the *Titanic*." His son felt differently. Amid the worry and growing fears about the Grand Central area, Donald saw opportunity at the crumbling Commodore. As the end of the line for commuters from suburbs in Westchester County and the posher corners of Connecticut, the great railroad hall adjacent to the hotel still funneled tens of thousands of people into Midtown every day. Despite the Penn Central's troubles, the chronic traffic congestion in Manhattan gave commuters no option but the rails for getting to work. Also, Trump believed that the borough would remain the nation's preeminent business address, even if Texaco and others such as American Airlines and UPS were leaving. Big corporations were abandoning other cities including Detroit, St. Louis, and New Orleans at a greater rate. As a globally vital financial center, with a high concentration of business talent, Manhattan was destined to recover and even thrive while these other cities continued to suffer. The Chrysler Building would be rescued and renovated. New skyscrapers would rise to replace an aging stock of office buildings, and all of the executives and salespeople who came to do business would need hotel rooms, meeting rooms, and meals. A revived Commodore Hotel could supply it all and, under the right setup, turn a neat profit.[4]

The right setup would, in Trump's mind, include generous help from the government. Just as his father had benefited from federal and state programs that subsidized his apartment developments, Donald thought the taxpayers should help him make money. The project would also require a top-notch hotel operator as a partner in every stage. After failing to land the Westin chain

as a partner, Trump set his sights on Hyatt hotels, which
was owned by the wealthy Pritzker family of Chicago.
Begun in 1957, Hyatt, which had pioneered the modern
"atrium" lobby design—complete with glass elevators—
operated more than sixty hotels and motels including a
few overseas properties. The company, which had grown
rapidly from one airport location in Los Angeles, was the
only major chain without a New York presence.

As part of his campaign to woo Hyatt, Trump invited
the Pritzkers' banker Benjamin Lambert to lunch.
Trump provided transportation in his father's limousine.
As he entered the car, Lambert discovered that Trump
had propped-up drawings of a renovated Commodore
Hotel. Lambert was impressed enough by the young
man's initiative, if not his sketches, to introduce his luncheon host to the Pritzkers. But no amount of enthusiasm and boyish charm would persuade Lambert to grant
Trump's request that he sell the family on the notion that
the new Commodore would be the best hotel in Manhattan. If Trump believed this, he would have to make
the case himself. However, hype would have no bearing on the decision made by the Pritzkers and other
Hyatt executives. They were more impressed that Trump
might get substantially reduced real estate taxes from
the city, which would improve the hotel's prospects year
after year after year.

Negotiating simultaneously with Hyatt, the city, and
Penn Central, Trump used one to leverage the other. Hyatt's reputation as a hotel developer and operator would
reassure Palmieri, Ned Eichler, and their colleague John
Koskinen (a future commissioner of the Internal Revenue Service) that Trump could manage the Commodore
project. The Palmieri execs gave Trump an informal
first position on the property, based on an eventual
$10 million purchase price. But they did not sign a bind-
ing agreement to do the deal. For Trump, who didn't

have the $250,000 required to finalize his option on the property, this was not a real problem. He announced to the press that he had "an option" and a "purchase contract" for the Commodore, and no one contradicted him. When city officials asked for a copy of his agreement with Penn Central, he sent them the paperwork, minus the signatures that would have made it binding. This omission either went unnoticed or no one cared about it, because the bureaucracy continued to move forward, as if the parties had signed, and Trump had actually paid. He then used the city's cooperation to reassure Hyatt that he was bringing something of real value to their partnership.

The key to it all was the paperwork sleight of hand, which became, years later, a matter of pride for Trump. "They only asked to see *an* agreement," he would say. "They didn't say it had to be signed."

Skating along with the key details of his deal unresolved, Trump promoted it with great confidence. Here he exhibited many of the traits that social scientists would eventually ascribe to high achievers. First he set an ambitious goal. Then he focused on it relentlessly, devoting years of effort to the task and refusing to be deterred by obstacles that would have stopped someone with less confidence. Trump held a vivid image of the new hotel in his mind's eye and refused any suggestion that his tender age, his lack of experience, or the conditions of the marketplace would prevent it from becoming real. As a boy he had watched his father's developments rise from rubble-strewn earth to become solid structures of brick and steel that housed thousands of families. He had no doubt that he could do the same, and better, and that success on Forty-second Street would lead to ever bigger and better accomplishments.

In May 1975, after Hyatt executives agreed to a partnership, he summoned the press to a meeting where he and Jay Pritzker presented sketches and said they would spend $70 million to tear the Commodore down to its steel frame and construct a luxury hotel. It would have fourteen hundred rooms, an enormous ballroom, seventy thousand square feet of retail space, a Hyatt-style atrium, and a second-floor bar cantilevered over the Forty-second Street sidewalk. The entire exterior of the building would be covered in highly reflective glass. It would be open, they said, in 1978.

The renderings were made by an architect named Der Scutt, who had begun his career working with the minimalist pioneer Philip Johnson. In the late 1960s Scutt had designed the fifty-four-story building that was built on the Times Square site of the former Hotel Astor. A beaux arts masterpiece faced in brick and slate, the old Astor had welcomed guests with a lush and serene roof garden where they could dine and dance amid flowers, ferns, and vines dangling from trellises. Scutt's work on One Astor Plaza had attracted great attention because it replaced a much-loved landmark. He incorporated a large movie house and a Broadway theater in his design. But the style was brutally austere, beginning with the massive base that housed the theaters. The tower rose from the back of this structure, clad in black glass and topped by a crownlike assemblage of pointed panels made of white stone. From the New Jersey side of the Hudson River they gave the impression of a man's starched handkerchief folded into points and tucked into the front pocket.

Scutt's building offended many who had loved the old Astor and failed to see the charm of a boxy structure topped by a tilted crown. Donald Trump was not among the nostalgic. Partial to sharp angles, shiny surfaces, and uncluttered design, he admired One Astor Plaza's sleek functionality. He recognized Der Scutt as a rising star of architecture, with a bit of celebrity cachet, and recruited him for the Commodore renovation. Just as his father had enlisted Morris Lapidus to add luster to his proposal for a domed amusement park in Coney Island, Trump relied on Scutt to put a sheen on Trump's ideas for the Commodore.

The key to the whole shiny project would be a big tax break, which Trump first tried to win from the state government in Albany, where he had old Brooklyn clubhouse friends in Governor Hugh Carey and Assembly Speaker Stanley Steingut. When this approach failed, Trump turned to the city bureaucracy, where development officials helped him with a cleverly engineered scheme. Under this plan, the state's Urban Development Corporation, which had been all but shuttered when its moral-obligation bonds became unsellable, would actually own the hotel and lease it to Trump. The agency, which was tax exempt, could keep the property off the city assessment rolls. Trump and Hyatt would save more than $4 million per year.

The city bureaucrats who devised the tax break for Trump's benefit presented it as something larger—a new Business Investment Incentive Program—that could be used by other for-profit construction and redevelopment projects. The UDC's chief, Richard Ravitch (he had been appointed to the post after his investigation) pressed for modifications to make the deal better for the state. He was joined by members of the city Board of Estimate, who recognized that one especially well-connected firm—the Trump Organization—would be the prime beneficiary of the incentive program. This truth wasn't lost on other hoteliers. Mario di Genova, president of the Americana Hotel, complained that the deal was "immoral and unfair." Harry Helmsley wondered aloud whether "maybe too much is being given" to the Trumps.[5]

Upon hearing the complaints, Donald threatened to withdraw his proposal and insisted that no one else would invest in the Commodore if he walked away. This wasn't entirely true. In early 1976 the Carter hotel chain, a small regional operator, offered to renovate the hotel and help save the Grand Central neighborhood on terms more favorable to the city. The bid could not be considered by Penn Central while Donald Trump still controlled a purchase option, but this control was not legally established. Palmieri's team may have agreed to the arrangement and everyone was going along as if it were real, but Trump *still* hadn't paid the option and no papers had been signed.[6]

Critics on the Board of Estimate, as well as other hotel operators, were soothed when Trump agreed to share the hotel's annual profits with the city, up to the point where they equaled a full property-tax assessment. With this sweetener, Ravitch and the UDC also agreed to the scheme. Later, when the details showed that Trump would have many ways to adjust his accounting to limit his payments to the city, Ravitch would say he considered this decision a mistake.

With the UDC accepting its role, the clock was still running on Trump's so-called option, which supposedly came with an eighteen-month time limit. Both he and the Palmieri executives wanted to push the arrangement to completion. Together they took steps to pressure the Board of Estimate. For his part, Trump got workers at the hotel to tear down the clean-looking plywood and two-by-four studs they had used to board up the ground-floor windows of shops that had closed. They replaced these materials with dirty, salvaged scrap wood so that people who passed on the sidewalk would see that the Commodore was a mess and complain to city officials. At the same time John Koskinen suddenly announced that the Commodore, which had been open for business through all the deliberations, would close within days.

The Palmieri Company had previously told city officials that the hotel would stay open through the summer, when the nation's bicentennial celebration and the Democratic Party's presidential nominating convention would bring a flood tide of business. Yet in the first three months of the year, occupancy at the Commodore had plunged to 33 percent. At this rate, Koskinen said, the hotel would lose more money—$4.6 million for the year—if it stayed open than it would if it closed. By closing, and laying off the Commodore's five hundred employees, Koskinen would also deliver a shock to city officials, who would regret the lost jobs and fear the prospect of the huge building sitting empty beside Grand Central Terminal. The chairman of the local community board said, "It seems to me like someone's trying to force the issue."

On Tuesday, May 18, 1976, the Commodore Hotel's last guest checked out of his room. Mr. W. J. Schaap of St. Louis, Missouri, had traveled to New York to visit tourist sites with his wife and sister-in-law. He pronounced the accommodations "beautiful." On Thursday the twentieth the New York City Board of Estimate gave Donald Trump his tax break. With it, he was poised to take control of a landmark site in the nation's, if not the world's, most important city. All this, and he was not yet thirty years old.[7]

◆

Even with the equivalent to a $4-million-per-year subsidy from the taxpayers, Donald Trump had to work hard to get financing to tear down the old hotel and build a new one on its bones. Months passed as he negotiated for a loan with executives of the Equitable Life Insurance Company, who had gradually been committing more of their firm's cash to real estate. Equitable's investments reflected a big shift in the large-scale-development industry, which, up until 1970, had been dominated by individuals with the wealth required to accept personal responsibility for loans from conservative bankers. The new model allowed for "nonrecourse" lending, which would allow a builder such as Trump to borrow big sums even if he didn't have the assets to cover the loan in the event of a default. Financiers considered valuable sites to be collateral in these cases, and they charged higher interest rates for the notes, which they expected to provide a long-term stream of income. But even under this new lending model, Equitable officials vacillated as they considered Trump's application.

Trump became more frustrated as the months passed. At one point Equitable formally rejected the notion of the firm financing the entire project—at a cost of $75 million—and said they wouldn't lend more than one-third of this amount. Trump's mortgage adviser, Henry Pearce, an éminence grise in the local real estate scene, told him to fight on. He would eventually secure permanent loans—as opposed to construction financing—from both Equitable and the Bowery Savings Bank. The arrangement meant that neither institution would take on all the risk, and that the project would be subject to review by two different sets of financial overseers.

As the lenders worked slowly through their evaluation of the project and then the legal paperwork, Trump's political benefactor at City Hall faced challenges from within his own party. Leading Democrats had expected the incumbent Abe Beame, to serve a single term and make way for Percy Sutton to become New York's first black mayor. (A decorated war veteran and civil rights leader, Sutton had garnered 80 percent of the vote to become Manhattan borough president in 1965. He had held the post for twelve years.) However, Beame decided that in managing the city's fiscal crisis, and suffering the indignities that came with it, he had earned a chance to seek reelection. His choice set off a free-for-all primary against Sutton, New York secretary of state Mario Cuomo, and three members of Congress. Ethnically and religiously diverse, this group of challengers attacked Beame as an incompetent who had presided over a city in chaos. Their charges took on new meaning when a midsummer electricity blackout led to widespread looting. In a city already terrified by a serial killer who called himself Son of Sam, the blackout sealed Beame's fate as a one-termer.

The two top vote-getters in the September 1977 primary election were Mario Cuomo, who was endorsed by Beame's longtime ally Governor Carey, and Representative Edward I. Koch, who had seized upon crime as a campaign issue and balanced his liberal record with frequent statements of support for the death penalty. At campaign stops he would challenge audiences and fellow politicians with questions like "How many here are for the death penalty?"—then volunteer that he was in favor of it.

As Koch once confessed, the death-penalty stand was a political gambit that he used to distinguish himself from the other Democrats and capture support from fear-filled voters. It also helped him establish that he was bold and aggressive to the point of being obnoxious—in other words, he was a bona fide New York–style character—who was determined to define himself in a decisive way. For similar political reasons Koch, who was almost certainly gay, never answered questions about his sexual orientation and campaigned with former Miss America Bess Myerson at his side. Hugely popular, Myerson held the candidate's hand and let him speculate about her future as the "first lady" of New York City. Myerson's star power helped Koch overcome the fact that he was little known outside his congressional district. Finally, he was also aided by a well-timed editorial-page endorsement from the *New York Post*, which had been purchased in the previous year by the international media magnate Rupert Murdoch.

Murdoch's acquisition of the tabloid *Post* brought screaming, British-style sensationalism to the city. (He did not, however, import the practice of publishing a pornographic photo in every edition, as he did in his British tabloid *The Sun*.) Under Murdoch's leadership the *Post* fed New Yorkers raw-meat crime stories and celebrity confections that suggested that their city was a dystopia where the famous and fabulous could purchase power and safety but everyone else lived under the threat of random catastrophe. The 1977 blackout was, for example, 24 HOURS OF TERROR according to the *Post*. When the city's police struggled to capture the Son of Sam killer, the *Post* proclaimed, NO ONE IS SAFE.

The distorted view of the world presented by the paper would prompt Osborn Elliott, dean of the Columbia University School of Journalism to declare, "The *New York Post* is no longer merely a journalistic problem. It is a social problem—a force for evil." Elliott was expressing an industry consensus. *Times* editor A. M. Rosenthal said the *Post* practiced "mean, ugly, violent journalism." Nevertheless, as Elliott noted, Murdoch's method produced circulation gains, and his presence in New York, home of the nation's major magazines, TV news operations, and wire services, gave him outsized influence on the national scene. Others noticed and imitated Murdoch's formula of gossip and provocation, which delivered a reader's version of a sugar high, satisfying in the moment and also creating a craving for more.[8]

Koch's law-and-order posture became more of an advantage in the weeks before the November election, when every crime that made the papers gave him a chance to talk about cracking down on those who made parts of the city as dangerous as war zones. The fear that New York was out of control reached a peak during the second game of the 1977 World Series, as TV announcer Howard Cosell observed smoke outside Yankee Stadium and famously declared, "There it is, ladies and gentlemen, the Bronx is burning." His words and the images of smoke in the sky led many to wonder why anyone at all would want to be mayor of New York City and contributed to a Koch victory margin of almost 10 percent.

◆

With six weeks left in his administration, Abe Beame turned to the business of securing the future for himself and his friends. He accepted a mostly honorary part-time position in the Carter administration, named a few new judges, and appointed Deputy Mayor Stanley Friedman to a lifetime position on the Board of Water Supply. This job required a bit more engagement—Friedman would have to attend board meetings every week or two—than Beame's position on the President's Advisory Commission on Intergovernmental Relations. However, it came with a $25,000 annual salary as well as a city car and driver.

Not that Friedman would need the money. A hyperactive, cigar-chomping political operative, Friedman had accepted a six-figure offer to join Roy Cohn's law firm. But he would stay at City Hall as long as Beame was in power. He thus had good reason to be invested in the welfare of Cohn's client Donald Trump. In the final weeks of Beame's administration, Friedman worked determinedly to finalize the state and city roles in the Commodore deal so that Koch, who had campaigned with a promise to end political favoritism, wouldn't be able to stop it. In the end, Friedman steered the project through nine different regulatory agencies including the fire department, the planning board, and the Bureau of Gas and Electric to complete a stack of papers that bound the city and the state to UDC ownership of the new hotel, with a lease arrangement for Trump and the tax break. In a most unusual twist, for a period of nine months the developer would be permitted to abandon the project with no penalty if things weren't working out for him.

Rarely—if ever—had anyone with so limited a track record and no actual cash invested been entrusted with so much by the city. The parties likely had this in mind as they raced to complete the arrangements prior to Koch's inauguration. During the week before Christmas, Friedman brought lawyers for the city, Trump, and the UDC together for a marathon meeting. As the absentee mayor's proxy, he personally signed the key papers on behalf of the city government. The only detail left unresolved was the special approval required for the bar/restaurant that would hang over the sidewalk on Forty-second Street. Friedman tied up this loose end on December 29, 1977, making sure that Trump got an extraordinary long-term permit—twenty-five years instead of the normal ten—and a cut-rate price for the use of public space. Both were possible because the UDC would actually hold title to the property and, under a loose reading of the rules, qualified for the special treatment. An ordinary businessperson operating a regular enterprise would have been limited to ten years, at full freight.

No ordinary businessman, Donald Trump was connected in an almost unique way to those who held the levers of political power and therefore benefited, thanks to Cohn, Friedman, Beame, and others, from the kind of favoritism that George Washington Plunkitt savored. "Roy could fix anyone in the city," Friedman would explain to the writer Marie Brenner during lunch at 21.

Trump, who was also at the table, said of Cohn, "He's a lousy lawyer, but he's a genius."[9]

The kind of fixing that Friedman mentioned generally involved politicians who could be motivated by favors or threats. Hard-nosed bankers required collateral, which Trump did not possess. When he couldn't obtain a construction loan on his own, Trump called on his father and the Hyatt Corporation for support, and both came through for him by taking responsibility for the money provided by Manufacturers Hanover bank. (It would eventually be paid back with the more permanent loans from Equitable and the Bowery.) Without guarantees from these allies, who pledged to complete the project if Donald failed, work would not have started at the Commodore site.

When demolition began in May of 1978, the threat of blight in the area around Grand Central, which was cited to justify government favors for Trump and Hyatt, was already evaporating thanks to projects powered by ordinary, unsubsidized capitalism. On Lexington Avenue, across Forty-second Street from the Commodore, the Chrysler Building was undergoing a $23 million restoration, thanks to the Massachusetts Mutual Life Insurance Company, which had paid $34 million to take the building out of foreclosure. Mobil and Pan Am each bought the buildings where they were primary tenants, and major work had begun on seven other sites within a few blocks of Grand Central. None of these projects had involved special help from state agencies or tax breaks from the city. Each represented a clear-eyed, profit-driven decision that defied the idea that the neighborhood was doomed and that nothing could be done to save it without a government subsidy.[10]

Once Trump's deal was completed, favoritism and subsidy ceased to be matters of central concern. When architecture critic Paul Goldberger turned his attention to the changes coming at the site of the grand old hotel, he described the tortured path of the arrangement as "one of the most complicated real estate deals ever conceived," but his main interest was in the aesthetic future. He was wary of a mirrored structure rising thirty stories high in the midst of all the sober stone and concrete along Park Avenue. A Hyatt covered in reflective glass might look like a bit of Houston squeezed into the neighborhood. In early 1978 he suggested, in *The Times,* that a limestone façade "would have offered the desired new image and would have fitted in much more comfortably with the solid neighbors."[11]

As demolition crews entered the old Commodore, they made a few discoveries. In the bowels of the building they found that homeless people had broken into a boiler room and taken up residence. The rats that roamed the floors below the ground level were so big they killed the cats that were dispatched to deal with them. As walls were dismantled on upper floors, engineers discovered that much of the original steel framework, which was supposed to support the new structure, was rotted or damaged and had to be replaced. The bad steel drove up the price of the project.

Although Fred Trump tried to keep an eye on things, day-to-day decisions fell to Donald. For the first time in his life he would be responsible for the success or failure of a project, and this one was far more complex and risky than anything his father had ever attempted. With lenders looking over Donald's shoulder—a special arrangement was made to govern even the smallest payments to suppliers and contractors—he was eager to contain costs. As he tried to preserve elements of the old structure, in the hope of saving money, he ran the risk of driving up the cost due to delays and design changes. One of the key engineers on the site, Barbara Res, would recall that Donald's decisions, expressed so forcefully that no one would challenge him, contributed substantially to cost overruns. A project estimated at about $40 million would cost $70 million.

To make up for the overruns, Trump and Hyatt had to reimagine their hotel, which was originally supposed to serve the middle of the market, as a high-end destination. That way they could charge rates to cover their costs. This was accomplished through changes in design and decoration that gave the hotel a more luxurious feel. By the time the Hyatt opened, a little more than two years later, Goldberger's qualms had all but disappeared. He declared the hotel a "sleek" success in which the choice of "flashy material" was ultimately justified. He judged it better looking from the outside than both the New York Hilton and the Sheraton on Times Square. He found that the lobby of the hotel, with its brass fixtures and trademark Hyatt atrium, was "more loud than it is truly restful," but surmised that Der Scutt and Trump had wanted to evoke the energy of Manhattan and they had achieved this goal. He noted that the hotel's rooms were well furnished but did not offer the luxury of the top-of-the-line Helmsley Palace, which had recently opened just seven blocks away. However, rates at the Palace started at $140, compared with $95 at the Hyatt, and topped out at an extravagant $1,500 per day.

◆

At age seventy, Harry Helmsley had worked his way up from the bottom of his industry—he was an office boy at sixteen—to co-owner of the largest real estate management firm in the country. In the early 1970s, when he married his second wife, Leona, he said he controlled $3 billion ($17 billion in 2015) in assets. Like the Trumps, Helmsley was active in politics. He donated $48,000 to Governor Carey's first campaign. He began putting his last name on things with his purchase of 230 Park Avenue, a move that was apparently part of an effort to make the building more widely recognized. (In an earlier, but less obvious, flex of ego, the bar at the Park Lane hotel had been named Harry's.) Helmsley and Leona granted interviews to reporters in which he declared that wealth is "the only way to keep score in business" and she expressed constant devotion to her husband. Secretive about her past—she was a high school dropout who had changed her name several times— Leona made certain claims, including modeling credits, which were suspiciously impossible to confirm. She refused to talk about former husbands, her son, or her grandchildren. But she eagerly displayed her current life, which was full of privilege and glamour, including jaunts to Palm Beach in a private jet, parties with Frank Sinatra, and a Manhattan home complete with indoor swimming pool.

The Helmsleys presented Leona as not just the manager of their hotel empire, but as the queen of a realm where customers constituted her "royal family." Leona "ensures the grandeur" that guests experienced at the Palace, noted advertisements for the hotel. And lest anyone doubt that the husky-voiced Leona was determined to "lavish" them with attention, a reporter was invited to listen as she telephoned a man in California who had complained about poor service during breakfast at the Helmsley Park Lane. Solicitous in the extreme, she assured the fellow that the "pretty dining room" was so popular that the staff sometimes struggled to keep up. Next time, she assured him, service would be better. Upon ending the call she declared, "He'll be back."[12]

With these appearances in the press and plenty of paid advertisements, Harry and Leona Helmsley became famous, their comings and goings chronicled by Liz Smith, Page Six, and *People* magazine, which made them "celebrities." Historically, men and women were celebrated for heroic achievements or for leading others in a noble cause. Broad public adulation was reserved for those who represented the virtues and moral character that society prized. Joan of Arc was a celebrity in this sense. In the age of mass media a new "synthetic celebrity," as historian Barbara Goldsmith termed it, emerged. Publicity in any form was enough to make a person into a celebrity, rewarded with fawning attention, money, and power. As Goldsmith noted, the Watergate crimes of Richard Nixon and his men qualified them for celebrity to the tune of $100 million in book contracts and sales. Even those Nixon henchmen who went to prison, such as G. Gordon Liddy, would move quickly from infamy to celebrity and profit. The first of many Liddy books sold 1 million copies.[13]

As savvy synthetic celebrities, the Helmsleys promoted themselves as readily understood caricatures. He was the likable, elderly man of great wealth who could be admired because he'd made his fortune by dint of hard work. She was the beautiful, doting younger wife who looked after their shared assets with a steely resolve that eventually earned her the sobriquet Queen of Mean. But while certain negatives attached to Leona, on balance the Helmsleys benefited from all the attention, which helped them stand out in a crowded marketplace and translated into increased business for their properties and thus fatter profits.

The seemingly simple route traveled by Leona and Harry, from money to celebrity to more money, was a well-plotted journey. In Leona's case it required the careful construction of a self based on qualities she hoped to project, and omissions—she refused to reveal her age—that blurred her past. She presented this self to the world with the help of chosen, uncritical reporters who could be trusted to reveal only the aspects that would illustrate the version of Leona she had built. In this type of endeavor, sophisticated celebrities also permitted reporters carefully plotted glimpses of their flaws and foibles, which allowed them to seem "human" and therefore more appealing to the public. In New York in the 1970s gossip columnists provided this service most reliably, but the most valuable publicity came under the imprimatur of *The New York Times*. When *The Times* published a personality profile, it conferred a unique level of legitimacy on its subject. In *The Times,* Judy Klemesrud, who began at the paper working for the "women's page," revealed Leona Helmsley as a feisty yet traditional woman. During the interview Leona had, with a flourish, produced from a silver box "my best award." As Klemesrud dutifully reported, it was her marriage license.

Leona Helmsley's self-congratulating comments about her famous friends, her many talents, and her wealth—"I'm in a bad [tax] bracket now"—were presented in a matter-of-fact way that was becoming more acceptable in a society awash in marketing and promotion. The notion that one could and should construct a self and then draw attention to it was hardly limited to the rich and famous. As the writer Tom Wolfe had made clear in a seminal *New York* magazine essay titled "The Me Decade," Americans were generally enthralled by the prospect of "changing one's personality—remaking, remodeling, elevating, and polishing one's very self . . . and observing, studying, and doting on it. (Me!)" People from all walks of life were committing themselves to the kind of self-interest that permitted men to "shuck overripe wives and take on fresh ones" and encouraged women to resolve their unhappiness in affairs and threesomes. A key element in this, Wolfe noted, was to get others to pay attention to you as you accomplished your self-conscious transformation.[14]

Nowhere in America was this attention-seeking impulse more evident than in New York City, where so many people clamored for a moment of fame that success required truly outlandish efforts. The striving could be witnessed every night at clubs such as Studio 54, where movie stars, artists, athletes, and mobsters indulged in sex and drugs and preened for the attention of photographers. The rich and powerful, and those with the potential to become so, were also welcomed. Thus, Roy Cohn and Donald Trump were regulars. Drugs and debauchery were the norm, as Trump would eventually recall for writer Timothy O'Brien: "I would watch supermodels getting screwed, well-known supermodels getting screwed, on a bench in the middle of the room. There were seven of them and each one was getting screwed by a different guy. This was in the middle of the room."[15]

Although Tom Wolfe wondered if the Me Decade represented a kind of spiritual crisis, historian Christopher Lasch saw it as the mass psychological response of a society dominated by huge bureaucracies, saturated in images—advertising, TV programs, films—and subject to countless pseudo-events that were managed like theater productions. In his 1979 book, *The Culture of Narcissism,* Lasch described an America in which people accepted that one's image, whether it was transmitted on television or in a family photo album, was a vital source of identity and power. At the same time, people felt alienated by their work in large corporations and life in sprawling suburbs. Taken together, these developments made vast numbers of people feel dissatisfied and determined to relieve their anxieties through the development of an appealing image for others to see, complete with the possessions and experiences—fancy vacations captured in snapshots—others could admire. Image-making became so important in everyday life that family photos and homemade videos were typically composed and later edited to mimic the work of professionals. And if the professionals did ever appear to conduct an interview, they often discovered that their subject understood what was expected of him when the camera was focused and the reporter tilted the microphone in his direction. With the exception of, say, the on-site reporting from natural disasters, the man on the street took pains to present himself well for the viewers.

According to a theory Lasch favored, every culture socializes children in distinct ways, to meet the demands of their time and place, and therefore creates discernible types of personalities. As postwar American society divided itself into winners and losers defined by their status as consumers, the best equipped to "win" were those most driven by a need to acquire wealth and attention. He theorized that grandiosity, which sees all that is good in one's self and all that is evil in others, was the natural outgrowth of this drive and the hallmark psychopathology of the late twentieth century. Where once Americans were merely neurotic, or obsessive, they had become, in Lasch's view, dangerously self-indulgent and deluded.

Quoting research by experts in fields as varied as anthropology and business management, Lasch argued that grandiosity was epidemic. He reported that psychiatrists were seeing a broad decline in patients suffering from everyday neuroses, along with a spike in narcissism. While sometimes malignant, this trait was not necessarily a sign of mental illness. It could also be a functional response to workplaces and communities where success required the ability to make a powerful impression and manipulate others. But for those who sought to be truly important figures, it was not enough to merely succeed. "Success in our society," he wrote, "has to be ratified by publicity."

Publicity came so naturally to Donald Trump, who grew up watching his father accept plaques and present bathing beauties to the eager press, that he was able to grab more than his almost without trying. He got the attention of *New York Times* reporter Judy Klemesrud in 1976, long before he would acquire a single Manhattan property or, in the parlance of his trade, "put two bricks together."

In the summer of 1976 Klemesrud contacted Trump for one of her celebrity roundup pieces. As she once explained, these articles began with her imagining a useful question and then phoning famous people until she obtained enough replies to fill out an article. In July she included Trump in a piece intended to advise tourists on "favorite haunts" of "notable New Yorkers." Happy to be considered a notable New Yorker, Trump recommended that visitors trek to Brooklyn or Queens to take in the skyline, which was his favorite New York attraction. In the next paragraph Harry Reems, star of many pornographic movies, suggested an arcade in Chinatown where, for a quarter, anyone could see a live chicken dance.

A few months later, Klemesrud followed Donald Trump around Manhattan, sampling a day in the life of a young man with "dazzling white teeth" who "looks ever so much like Robert Redford." (Redford had recently dazzled, on-screen, as the mysterious Jay Gatsby.) Although he was chauffeured in a limousine bearing the vanity plate DJT and frequented hot spots dressed in flashy suits and matching patent-leather shoes—he chose the color maroon for his day with *The Times*— Trump insisted he was publicity shy. He also told Klemesrud that he was worth "more than $200 million" and had "probably made $14 million" on California land deals "in the last two years."

Overcoming his shyness Trump explained to the

reporter that "flair" was one of the keys to success for a young man in New York and revealed that he had graduated at the top of his class at the Wharton School. He said that though he was often mistaken for Jewish, he was actually Swedish. Even so, the National Jewish Hospital of Denver was going to honor him as a "man of the year" at an upcoming banquet at the Waldorf-Astoria.

Klemesrud, who came from small-town Iowa, wrote in a gushing style that made the big city and the people in it glow a little bit like Oz. (Hers was a view of New York and its characters that probably made readers feel that their city was a special place.) She published Trump's statements with remarkable credulity, which allowed *The Times* to present him as person worthy of precious space in its pages. She also permitted his father to declare, "Donald is the smartest person I know."

The only doubts in the article about the remarkable Mr. Trump were expressed by an anonymous banker and the architect Der Scutt, who allowed that his patron "will exaggerate for the sake of making a sale." At age forty-two, Scutt was twelve years older than Trump. He had been born near Reading, Pennsylvania, and like Trump had gone into his father's business and was attempting to outdo the old man. He had changed his name from Donald Clark to Der, which means "the" in German and obviously communicated his desire to outstrip his father. He also took up pipe smoking. He spoke of Trump as an exuberant boy rather than a malicious liar.

In toto, Klemesrud's effort yielded a picture of wealth, danger, sex, and boyish enthusiasm, as if Trump were the James Bond of real estate. Klemesrud wrote that he dated "slinky fashion" models and belonged to "the most elegant clubs." When she asked if he contemplated marriage, he responded as if a wife would be a kind of accessory or acquisition. "If I met the right woman, I might get married, but right now I have everything I need." She also let readers know that Trump's chauffeur was a New York City police officer who had been laid off due to the city's financial crisis and always carried a loaded revolver.[16]

Why would Donald Trump require an armed, police-trained driver? No explanation was offered, but readers were free to deduce that like the fictional Jay Gatsby, if not the real Robert Redford, Trump lived on the edge of violence. In fact, construction in 1970s New York *was* still under the influence of organized-crime figures, who controlled some unions as well as the price and supply of concrete citywide. That Trump might require an armed driver was plausible, which made it one of the more reliable claims in the article.[17] The $200 million fortune? Donald's father may have been worth that much, but he was not. His class rank at Wharton? Nobody knows.

Of course, no one followed up on Klemesrud's piece to determine whether it was accurate. This was a soft-focus profile, not an exposé. Nothing much would be gained by a journalist chasing down the truth about a young man who might, or might not, prove to be a significant figure. Beside, *The Times* was known as the august "gray lady" of the news business, a gospel source that defined reality for everyone else. If the paper decided Donald Trump was worthy, then he was worthy.

Within days, the article produced the result desired by anyone seeking to be a celebrity—more publicity. Trump was invited to appear on Stanley Siegel's morning talk show aired by Channel 7. An attention-getting phenomenon, Siegel was famous for provoking guests and regularly undergoing psychotherapy on the air. He one-upped Klemesrud, hyping Trump as a "real estate tycoon." (She had called him a "real estate promoter.")

An easy reference point, the term *tycoon* helped everyone understand Trump as a celebrity. That it didn't fit him didn't much matter. In a time when just about everyone sought to create an image, most people did not look behind these descriptors. Donald Trump, a military-school graduate who had painstakingly polished the brass of his uniform, was possessed of an exquisite intuition when it came to his image. He could not be expected to let anyone see past it. His father, whom Klemesrud quoted, was equally invested in promoting his son. But if she had turned to Trump's bodyguard/chauffeur, she might have heard an insight that would have disrupted the cliché picture while rendering the subject more human and more likable. Decades after he had left the man's employ, Trump's first bodyguard/chauffeur, Robert Utsey, recalled him as considerate, generous, and sincere:

The job he hired me for was posted in the police department jobs bank, which was developed for the officers that were laid off by the city. I was new, just on probation at the Forty-Third Precinct in the Bronx, so I was laid off.

I went to the Trumps' office in Brooklyn to interview. There were about seven other guys there. I waited my turn, and when he interviewed me, I told him I was the best driver in my academy class, which was true. They tested us on a course. I had the best times with the fewest mistakes. I also had a background in karate, which he liked. I got the job.

The pay was equal to a police salary, and that included overtime for nights. There were a lot of nights because he went out a lot, but I was single, so it worked out. When I got married, he came to the wedding and gave us a nice present, which he didn't have to do. When my wife was pregnant, my wife chose a doctor who wasn't in the medical plan, but he paid for it, which was about a month's salary. When the baby was born, he bought the car seat that we brought her home in.

He was a nice guy who was never anything but good to me. He expected loyalty but he was also loyal back. When I got the chance to go back to the police department, it was a difficult decision because I liked working for him. Later on, when people started saying all the negative things about him, it didn't make sense to me. The guy I knew then was a good guy.[18]

6
TOWERING TRUMP

I would say that I have never been given
the credit that I'm due.
—DONALD TRUMP

This much was certain; her first name was Ivana. After this, the facts become hazy. She was born in postwar Communist Czechoslovakia, or maybe Austria. When she got married in New York, in April 1977, her last name was recorded as Winklmayr, which she had acquired in a sham marriage to an Austrian who had agreed to it so she could get a passport. But she had also gone by her maiden name—Zelnickova—and then a Montreal newspaper article said Ivana had another husband, a Czech named George Syrovatka, who had defected during a ski meet in the West.

In addition to those about her birthplace and name, the other mysteries about the woman who, with the ministerial services of the Reverend Norman Vincent Peale, married Donald Trump at the Marble Collegiate Church were numerous. She was either a member of the Czech team sent to the 1972 Winter Olympics, or an alternate, or a good skier who had had nothing to do with the games in Sapporo. In Montreal she had been the most sought-after fashion model in the city or one of many young women who occasionally walked a runway, modeled in manufacturers' showrooms, and sometimes posed for newspaper layouts. It all depended on who was telling the tale.

The facts of Ivana Trump's early life would prove elusive to the many journalists who sought to determine them. (Among the land mines they had to avoid was the story of an auto accident in which a boyfriend was killed. The part about his death in a crash was true. The story Ivana had told about being in the car and suffering a broken back was not.) However, the self that she presented to the world—beautiful, successful, and most of all desired—would remain consistent. From the very first time she was quoted in the press (*Montreal Gazette,* 1975), Ivana offered an image of a multifaceted and accomplished woman. Modeling was just one element of her life, and one that was not so important. It was "a job to me, not a career," she said, as if she wanted to avoid the perception that she cared about her work. "I have my social life, my husband, and my home." The husband she referenced was Syrovatka, who wasn't really her husband but her live-in boyfriend. But in heavily Catholic Montreal circa 1975, it was easier and less complicated to say "husband," and besides, she had felt sort of married, until she met Donald.

It was 1976, probably. Ivana was working at a New York fashion show organized to promote the upcoming summer Olympic Games. Donald may have met her at the fashion show. He definitely saw her later, in the evening, waiting with some friends for a table at a restaurant/bar called Maxwell's Plum, which was owned by Warner LeRoy, whose grandfather Harry Warner had been one of the founders of the Warner Bros. movie studio. His father, Mervyn LeRoy, had produced *The Wizard of Oz.* Warner LeRoy liked to say that he learned the magic of showbiz illusion at age four when he visited a soundstage and skipped along the yellow brick road and right into a wall.[1]

Riotously decorated with Tiffany lamps, ceramic animals, and a stained-glass ceiling, Maxwell's Plum set a standard for décor that eventually migrated all the way to down-market national restaurant chains such as TGI Fridays. It was also a magnet for celebrities, including Warren Beatty and Barbra Streisand and for the so-called swinging singles (writer Susan Jacoby called them "swingles"), who made Maxwell's Plum so popular that even fashion models had to wait to be seated. LeRoy called his restaurant "living theater." It was the kind of place where pop stars mingled with gangsters and cocaine was consumed by so many guests that it should have been on the menu.

When he saw her at the door, Donald Trump tapped Ivana on the shoulder, which she found quite annoying, and offered to help her group jump the line. "I'm very friendly with the owner," he said. She went to report to her friends: "I have good news and bad news. The good news is we are going to get a table right away. Bad news is the guy is going to sit with us." Donald departed before the end of the meal, but he vanished with a dramatic purpose in mind. The women were delighted when the waiter told them their bill had been paid. Then, outside the restaurant, they discovered Trump behind the wheel of his Cadillac. "He took us to our hotel," recalled Ivana years later. "The next day I got three dozens of roses. And we had dinner, and we had lunch at 21 Club, and I went back to Montreal. Donald said he would come and see me on the fashion shows, which he did."

The ensuing courtship, which Donald conducted despite Ivana's relationship with George Syrovatka, led to more time in Montreal for him and a trip to New York for her, to meet Donald's parents. "He asked me to go for Christmas somewhere, so I told him that I spend Christmas on the mountains of Austria and stuff like that. I have a chalet in Slovakia. And so we went to Aspen. Donald rented [an] incredible chalet, you know, with the mirrors on the top and stuff like that. So he said, 'Can you ski?' I said, 'Yes, I can ski.' He said, 'You are good?' I said, 'I'm good.' "

On the mountain, Trump skied with the careful purpose of a novice. Ivana surprised him with a few expert moves and then whooshed past him. Long after the day became a memory she could recall every aspect of his reaction: "I disappeared. Donald was so angry, he took off his skis, his ski boots, and walked up to the restaurant. So we find his skis down the mountain with the instructor. He went foot bare up to the restaurant and said, 'I'm not going to do this shit for anybody, including Ivana.' He could not take it, that I could do something better than he did."[2]

Trump's bruised ego healed quickly. He proposed marriage on New Year's Eve. Ivana accepted. Later he gave her a three-carat diamond ring, which he had purchased at Tiffany's. In the months between the proposal and the April 9 wedding, Ivana wavered a bit, then broke up with Syrovatka and affirmed her commitment to Donald. Then he asked her to sign a prenuptial agreement.

The prenup was Roy Cohn's idea, which he raised after failing to persuade his client that marriage was not in his interest. Agreements covering the disposition of property in the event of a divorce had been illegal for most of American history. Under a legal concept called coverture, which was part of English common law, wives lost their individual rights to sign contracts and hold property when they married. State legislators and judges began to reconsider the issue in the 1960s, and by the end of that decade the prenup signed by Jacqueline Kennedy and Aristotle Onassis was widely reported in the press.

Though hardly routine, prenuptial contracts became fairly common among the richest Americans, and those who expected to one day be rich. Film stars in Hollywood sometimes used them, but outside these rarefied circles few marriages began with a contract governing a future possible divorce. In early 1977 the famous New York divorce lawyer Raoul L. Felder called prenups "a cold-blooded way to enter marriage" and said that under the pressure of contract negotiations many marriages are destroyed before they commence.

Felder's comments were made on the very day—March 18—when Ivana Winklmayr and Donald Trump met with Roy Cohn to discuss their prenuptial agreement. Ivana was represented by lawyer Lawrence Levner, whom Cohn had recommended. (Levner had worked with Cohn on previous cases.) As the little group worked its way through Cohn's draft agreement, discussing lawyerly terms in plainer English, Ivana came to understand that in a divorce she would be required to return any gift she had received from Donald. In the argument that ensued, Ivana countered with a demand for a fund of $150,000, to be deposited in an account under her name, which she would use in the event of a breakup.

With Ivana's request for cash, Donald faced a demand that he prove his public claims of great wealth—a $200 million fortune and $14 million in recent profits—with a display of real liquidity. According to documents later made public, Donald's taxable income at the time was less than $2,200 per week. He controlled a small interest in one of his father's many companies and received regular but modest payments from family-related trusts. Clearly, putting his hands on $150,000 in a matter of weeks would pose a challenge. Thus, the discussion over Ivana's demand grew so heated that she left the meeting and only returned after Donald chased her to the sidewalk and persuaded her to keep talking. However, nothing was settled.

The second negotiating session took place at Roy Cohn's town house, which housed both his residence and his place of business. As Harry Hurt III would recount in his book *Lost Tycoon,* Cohn greeted the parties dressed in nothing but a robe. Calculating as he was, Cohn's choice of wardrobe was undoubtedly intended to send a message. Like Lyndon Johnson, who famously invited reporters into the lavatory to continue conversations as he relieved himself, Cohn was demonstrating both his confidence and his power. He was so confident that he didn't need to put on pants and a shirt to conduct business. He was so powerful that no one would dare say something like "Roy, why don't you put on some clothes?" And he was so eager for attention that he would welcome any gossip or newspaper item that would result from conducting legal work while requiring the various parties to prepare themselves for a glimpse of whatever lurked beneath the robe.

Prior to the meeting, Cohn had excised the provisions in the prenup that would have required Ivana to return Donald's gifts. This concession was apparently enough to move Ivana to reduce her rainy-day-fund demand by one-third, to $100,000. A final bargain was eventually struck on March 22. It required that if the couple divorced, Donald would make annual payments to Ivana. The amount would depend on the length of their union, with a ceiling of $90,000 per year after thirty years of marriage. Although this sum would seem paltry in years to come, the package was far better than the deal offered in the original contract and showed Ivana to be a capable negotiator who understood the pressure Donald would feel as the wedding date approached. Given the truth of Donald's financial condition, and her own lawyer's connection to Cohn, it was likely the best deal she could have achieved.

On April 9 more than two hundred guests arrived for the wedding at Marble Collegiate Church. It was the Saturday before Easter, a day many Christians regard with such solemnity that flowers are removed from

churches in remembrance of Christ's entombment. At
Marble Collegiate, where cheerful optimism was practically the Eleventh Commandment, the sanctuary was
filled with white lilies, and the festive crowd included
Abe Beame, lesser politicians, and a variety of lawyers
who had served the assorted Trump entities. A few of
Ivana's friends came from Montreal. Her father, Milos,
attended as the sole representative of her family in
Czechoslovakia; the airfare was just too high for her
mother to come. Afterward, comedian Joey Adams,
whose wife, Cindy, was the main gossip columnist at the
Post, entertained at the wedding reception.

By all indications, young Mr. and Mrs. Trump were
happy. After she gave birth to their first child, Donald
Jr., on December 31—Robert Utsey chauffeured mother
and child from the hospital—the young family moved
into an eight-room Fifth Avenue apartment. The apartment was not just a home, but also a venue for publicity
seeking as the Trumps often invited the press to have a
look around. A reporter welcomed for a tour noted the
Austrian-accented English spoken by her hostess, who
had never lived in Austria. (The Olympic ski team was
again an element in her biography, only this time she
represented Austria and not Czechoslovakia.) Brand
conscious before the term was even coined, the Trumps
answered questions about the provenance of the furnishings and their own wardrobes. She favored Galanos
and Valentino. His suits came from Pierre Cardin, Yves
Saint Laurent, and Bill Blass. Donald noted that Ivana,
who had lived in Montreal for about four years, had been
the city's "number one" model for eight. Like him, she
had "flair." She would give him the nickname The Donald, which would accompany him throughout the rest
of his life.[3]

To his credit, Trump had demonstrated that he possessed, in addition to flair, the ingenuity and determi-

nation to transform the nearly derelict Commodore into an attractive, profitable, modern hotel. He had also begun the pursuit of the enormous and enormously ambitious project that would make his name known even to New Yorkers who never read the gossip columns.

◆

According to Donald Trump, the best spot for a building in any city of note was the "Tiffany location." As he told *The New York Times* in 1980, "If you go to Paris, if you go to Duluth, the best location is called 'the Tiffany location.' That is a standard real estate phrase."

If anyone actually used the phrase *Tiffany location* before Donald Trump, the evidence of it is stubbornly elusive. The jeweler didn't occupy its spot at Fifth Avenue and Fifty-seventh Street until 1940 and didn't achieve its place in popular culture until the 1950s, when Marilyn Monroe (*Gentlemen Prefer Blondes*) and Truman Capote (*Breakfast at Tiffany's*) made the store iconic. Even then it would have been hard to imagine that a real estate broker would describe an attractive parcel in Duluth, or even Paris, as a "Tiffany location." Nevertheless, the phrase sounded convincing and Trump began using it as he set his sights on the building next door to Tiffany's, which was occupied by the Bonwit Teller department store.

Like many other New York retailers, including Tiffany, Bonwit Teller had been founded on "the Ladies Mile" of Lower Manhattan in the nineteenth century and moved north as developers built more fashionable residences in Midtown. Long profitable as a high-end retailer, Bonwit thrived in the 1940s and 1950s, opening branches in the Northeast and seasonal shops in Florida. However as the company changed hands, eventually coming to lodge inside a conglomerate called

Genesco, profits became losses. The chain lost ground to competitors such as Lord & Taylor and Saks Fifth Avenue, and bargain hunters began circling its real estate holdings.

The developers' template for the Bonwit site had been cut by Aristotle Onassis, with the aid of the city's able real estate lawyers, at a Fifth Avenue address a few blocks south of Tiffany and right next to St. Patrick's Cathedral. That location had been home to the clothier Best & Co., which began in business catering to children under the name Lilliputian Bazaar. The Best store was an elegant structure covered in white marble that boasted a loyal clientele. However, it missed the youth-culture boom of the 1960s, choosing instead to cater to younger children and older women. By the time Best executives added departments for teens, younger women, and men, it was too late. The Fifth Avenue store was closed in October 1970. The Lindsay administration approved plans for Olympic Tower in the summer of 1971. Demolition began in October.

Onassis's project depended on his purchases of the "air rights" from sites next to his. Air rights govern the ultimate height that any building may reach under city zoning codes. On lots where structures squat well below these limits, owners may transfer these rights to a neighbor, allowing for the construction of a building that would otherwise far exceed the regulations. In this way, empty space would be preserved on one plot but exploited next door. Onassis purchased the air rights controlled by, among others, Cartier jewelers. Thus, with the help of Tiffany's rival, he was able to construct hundreds of condominium apartments, nineteen floors of office space, and retail shops on the ground floor. The finished building, clad in reflective glass, rose fifty-one stories, or 620 feet, above the sidewalk.

Although air-rights purchases were essential to the

Olympic Tower project, Onassis also took advantage of city regulations that allowed him to build higher in exchange for creating a building that mixed retail space, offices, and residences with a public arcade on the ground floor, which included a waterfall. Architects shielded the residents of the tower from the general public by providing them with a separate entrance and special elevators. It was the least they could do, considering prices for the condominiums would reach $650,000 ($2.7 million in 2015).

The "multiuse" plan for Olympic Tower had been encouraged by city officials, who were hoping that Fifth Avenue would retain its mix of residential and commercial spaces. Onassis also took advantage of a state tax-abatement program designed to encourage redevelopment of obsolete or underutilized real estate. The question of whether the Best & Co. site was obsolete or underutilized became moot when the store was demolished. Onassis got the tax break, which would last for ten years, and his tower site became the most densely developed piece of land in Manhattan and, quite likely, the world. At least one city official deemed it an undertaxed "monster" created by the exploitation of government policies adopted without adequate consideration of the possibility that someone might use them all at once, in the same place.

Where some saw a monster, ambitious real estate people saw a beautiful creature that generated vast profits for a man who was already one of the richest people in the world. Onassis owned fifty oil tankers, an airline, the Ionian island of Scorpios, and real estate scattered across the globe. His marriage to President John F. Kennedy's widow, Jacqueline Bouvier Kennedy, had been front-page news around the world. But the Olympic Tower, or, rather, his manipulations to wring the most profit out of the tower site, was what most impressed certain businesspeople in New York. Among them was

Donald Trump, who had actually lived in the Onassis building for a short time and thus understood it from the inside out. Determined to copy the formula, he began by looking for a downward-spiraling retailer on Fifth Avenue. One of his political connections, a political fundraiser with the unlikely name of Louise Sunshine, introduced him to a major stockholder in the firm that owned Bonwit Teller's Fifth Avenue store. Trump learned that Bonwit was in trouble and began working to acquire its site. At the same time he stalked the air rights held by the Tiffany store and considered the moves he would have to make with the new regime at City Hall.

Mayor Ed Koch's development officials had encountered Trump, and his convoluted ways, almost immediately after they moved into City Hall as they completed the city's acquisition of the Penn Central Railroad's Thirty-fourth Street yard. At the start of their discussions Trump had informed them that the option contract he had worked out with Palmieri's firm required the city to pay him a commission of $4.4 million, but he would gladly forgo it if the new facility was named the Fred C. Trump Convention Center. With the city hard-pressed to pay police officers and firefighters, $4.4 million was enough to give Koch officials pause. But then, as Deputy Mayor Peter J. Solomon later recalled, "somebody finally read the terms of the original Penn Central contract with Trump." The agreement required he be paid not $4.4 million, but rather $500,000, plus just under $90,000 for expenses. Although Solomon was impressed by Trump's chutzpah, his offer was declined.

The episode prompted questions about just why a major city landmark would be named for an outer-borough apartment developer who, except for some incidents that had cast him in a less than perfect light, wasn't a significant public figure. Donald answered that his family deserved the honor because "if it was not for me, there would be no convention center in this city." It was an impossible claim to prove, but a Trump critic agreed that he had been instrumental in the selection of the Thirty-fourth Street site, to his own benefit. "Donald Trump runs with the same clique that continues to manipulate things behind the scenes in this city," city councilman Henry J. Stern told *The New York Times*. "He had ties through his father to the Brooklyn Democratic machine that produced Hugh Carey. Roy Cohn is his lawyer. He throws around a lot of money in political campaigns."

No one quoted by the paper contested Stern's analysis. Given the $135,000 the Trumps gave to Carey (equivalent to $550,000 in 2015), Stern was right about the political money. And the ever-controversial Cohn *was* Trump's attorney. Indeed, Cohn was so important to Trump that he kept a photo of Cohn in a shadowy mobster's pose—bloodshot eyes, scarred skin, soulless expression—just to show others whom he wanted to intimidate. (When he pulled it out of a drawer for engineer Barbara Res, it reminded her of an image of Satan himself.) Cohn, in response to a call from a *Times* reporter, confirmed that Trump money flowed freely into political campaigns, but only because "it's part of the game," played by all big developers. This was easy for any reader to believe. Not so credible was Cohn's claim that his client "doesn't try to get anything for it." In the long history of American politics, few major donors, and Donald Trump was a major donor, have given money to candidates without expecting something in return from those who were elected. At the least, they expected access to the people they helped put in office, just in case a meeting with, say, the mayor of New York could help smooth the way for a real estate deal.

Cohn would have had the public believe that as a rule developers showered politicians with cash and without this watering nothing would ever be built. In fact, while men such as Donald Trump played the old-fashioned and theatrical game that Cohn described, it was hardly a requirement for those who sought building permits and zoning approvals. No political donations were associated with Olympic Tower, for example, and when Boston Properties put up a massive tower at Fifty-second Street and Lexington Avenue, the out-of-town firm had no real connections to the city's political establishment. In these and other projects, what mattered were the actual rules and regulations governing development and not personal or political favors. In the post-Watergate era of campaign-finance reform and greater public access to government records, Plunkitt-style chumminess mattered less and less each year.

Trump's success at the Commodore site gave him some credibility as he pursued his grand dream for a Fifth Avenue building. Equitable Life Insurance, one of his lenders for the Hyatt project, owned the land beneath Bonwit Teller, and when he approached company officials, they agreed to make the firm his partner in a new building on the site. By November 1978 Trump had completed talks with executives at Bonwit's parent firm to obtain a free option to buy out their lease on the land for $25 million. This arrangement gave him a six-month opportunity to negotiate, charm, and otherwise manipulate his way toward his goal. If he failed, he wouldn't be out a cent. If he succeeded, he could change the Manhattan skyline.

While his partners at Equitable watched and waited, Trump enlisted Der Scutt so as to influence the mind and heart of Tiffany's octogenarian chairman, Walter Hoving. For many years Tiffany's success had depended on Hoving's snobbery, which helped to assure customers that they were receiving the finest goods from the most reputable of merchants. (Hoving possessed such an air of superiority that a client might even feel grateful for the chance to give him his or her money.) Determined to play on the vain old man's commitment to tradition and refined elegance, Trump had Scutt sketch a hideous version of a building for the Bonwit site and presented it to Hoving to illustrate the design he might use to get the most out of the land.

Scutt's drawing allowed Trump to practice a bit of gamesmanship that would become a regular part of his repertoire. By proposing something that might seem threatening or outrageous, he staked out a position that would allow him to seem flexible and reasonable as he negotiated his way to his actual goal. In his exchange with Hoving, Trump offered a vision of an ugly building and then explained that he could build a far more beautiful structure, one more appropriate to its surroundings, if Hoving sold him Tiffany's air rights. Hoving soon gave Trump what he sought, receiving on his company's behalf the promise of $5 million and the assurance that his store would not be devalued by an ugly next-door neighbor.

The more artfully imagined skyscraper that Scutt drew for the Fifth Avenue site depended on a zigzag design that gave every residential unit views of the city in two directions. This creative approach would make the building more expensive to construct than a simple box, such as Olympic Tower, but with the views the apartments could sell at higher prices. And it would establish the building as a kind of landmark. From a distance the upper floors would look like a saw blade fashioned out of black glass. (As reported by Barrett, Scutt would eventually say that Trump had told him one of the apartments should be reserved for his personal use in the event that his marriage, which was just a few years old, ended in divorce.)[4]

Although it would look slender from afar, pedestrians would see a massive base rising from the sidewalk and the words TRUMP TOWER in gold-colored, capital letters above the entrance. Inside, on the lobby level, visitors would find a soaring atrium, an upscale shopping arcade, and water cascading down a fountain wall. Done in glossy, rose-colored marble and polished brass, the public space would suggest both solidity and glitz, something like a casino blended with a bank.

The zoning laws that would allow Trump to build a sixty-two-story tower had also permitted IBM and AT&T to build on a similar scale in the same neighborhood. All three of these massive structures would cast shadows on their neighbors and add substantially to the population in an already-crowded part of Manhattan. A mild-mannered opposition group called the New York Committee for a Balanced Building Boom pointed out these problems as it criticized the hyperdevelopment of the area. Led by a prominent stockbroker and an investment banker, the committee never generated much support. The neighborhood they sought to protect was rich and exclusive and devoid of the kind of everyman character that might attract public sympathy. Why would the average New Yorker, who rode the subway and lived in the outer boroughs, care if one millionaire cast shadows on another? Some might even appreciate new development projects that produced construction jobs while they vexed the powerful and the privileged who lived nearby.

As the tallest, and most cleverly designed, of the new giant buildings, Trump Tower promised the developing partners great returns on their investments. Nevertheless, the son whose father carefully picked up the nails dropped by his carpenters often approached the $100 million project with a penny-wise attitude. After Bonwit Teller managers ran a going-out-of-business sale and handed Trump the keys, he invited the public into the building to buy the few furnishings left behind, including venetian blinds, light bulbs, and mirrors that had been screwed into walls. When asked about the sale, Trump was able to say how much it netted—$5,000— and termed the figure "a nice little surprise."

After the Bonwit building was picked over, the demolition was done by Kaszycki & Sons of Herkimer, New York, the lowest bidder among twelve who had sought the job. It would not be an easy task. The location ruled out the use of wrecking balls or explosives. Instead the building would have to be taken apart from the inside out, with crews starting on the top floor and dumping debris down the elevator shafts. The work would be further complicated by the decorations on the Fifth Avenue side of the building—an elaborate, solid-nickel grillwork and two art deco friezes depicting half-nude women—which were artistically significant.

A Fifth Avenue art dealer judged the Bonwit sculptures to be as important as the architectural artwork at nearby Rockefeller Center and compared their value to a pair of Lalique doors that had recently sold for $200,000. Der Scutt had considered them so beautiful he wanted to include them in his design of the big public space on the ground floor of the new building. Trump had his heart set on a much more modern look and told Scutt he didn't want the Bonwit pieces to be used in his lobby. But after learning of their value, he promised to save them and donate them to the Metropolitan Museum of Art. This promise saved City Planning officials from the chore of negotiating with Trump to preserve the works.

Thomas Macari, who worked for the Trump Organization, said the grillwork would be relatively easy to remove. Set into the stone above the store entrance, it was accessible and was held together by simple bolts. The friezes were another matter. They had been carved out of the limestone fixed to the front of the building, more than fifty feet above the sidewalk. Nevertheless, Macari he was sure they could be cut away from the wall, rested on a specially built wooden platform, and lowered to the street by a crane. William Kaszycki, the Polish-immigrant founder of the demolition company, wasn't so sure. When asked whether he could pull it off, he shrugged and said, "We'll see."

Kaszycki had based his rock-bottom bid for the job on the revenue he could generate from scrap sales and his planned use of hundreds of undocumented Polish laborers who would be overseen by roughly two dozen skilled men from the House Wreckers Union Local 95. (The union local was controlled by organized-crime boss Vincent "Chin" Gigante. In 1984, two Local 95 officers would be convicted of racketeering and extortion.) The Polish Brigade, as the men were called, began dismantling the Bonwit building even before Kaszycki received a demolition permit. Laboring without the usual precautions such as hard hats, they ripped out walls and flooring until all that was left was steel, concrete, and stone.

The men of the brigade labored seven days per week, and as many as eighteen hours a day, to meet the boss's schedule. When not working, they rested in overcrowded housing supplied by Kaszycki, or on the floors of the Bonwit building itself. Their pay, which fell far below the union rate, was issued sporadically. Sometimes they were offered vodka instead of money. Complaints were answered with threats of deportation. When the city was hit by a transit strike, many of the men walked everyday from Brooklyn to Midtown Manhattan just to get to their jobs..Those who quit were replaced immediately by one of the dozens of Polish men who appeared at the job site every day looking for work.

Exhausted, and ill treated, the Polish workers were denied the pay, benefits, and other protections covering union workers. Eventually, a judge in a civil suit would find that this exploitation was aided by a "tacit agreement" between the Trump Organization and the House Wreckers Local 95, and the parties ultimately settled the case. But at the time, the Polish laborers were working at a breakneck pace while taking pains to salvage brass, copper, and steel to be sold to recyclers at pennies per pound. That Kaszycki was depending on the receipts from these sales for much of his profit indicated just how much pressure he must have felt to cut costs. He told *The New York Times* that the preservation of the artwork on the front of the building would cost at least $2,500 in extra labor, or half the amount netted by the sale of Bonwit's lightbulbs and mirrors. However, the key decision was not made by Kaszycki, but by Trump, who chose to save a little time and expense and demolish the artwork.

On Wednesday, June 4, 1980, Peter Warner looked out his Fifth Avenue office window and saw that workers armed with power tools had slashed through one of the stone friezes and begun to cut through the other. A research associate for an architectural firm, Warner had often gazed at the artwork from his twelfth-floor perch and had read that the new owner of the Bonwit site was going to save them. He was astonished as Kaszycki's men quickly cut through both panels and them pushed them off the side of the building. Warner, who felt the pieces were important artifacts of the city's history, later told *The Times* that when he saw what was happening "I really couldn't believe my eyes."

The destruction of the Bonwit friezes would never have become an issue if Trump hadn't promised to preserve them. But he had made this pledge, and when the sculptures disappeared, the press began asking questions. Calls to Donald Trump went unanswered, but a man named John Baron, who identified himself as a vice president of the Trump Organization, did speak to reporters. He explained that three different appraisers had agreed that the works were "without artistic merit" and would, if sold, fetch less than $9,000. Careful removal, crating, and transport of the panels would have cost $32,000 and delayed the demolition project at a price of $500,000 in additional expenses and lost revenues. Considering the money involved, he concluded, "The merit of these stones was not great enough to justify the effort to save them."

Ashton Hawkins of the Metropolitan Museum challenged Baron's assessment of the friezes and noted, "Their monetary value was not what we were interested in. The department of twentieth-century art was interested in having them because of their artistic merit." With the pieces reduced to rubble, the true value of the art was moot. But if Ashton Hawkins had wanted to meet with John Baron for a conversation about his appreciation of modern art, Hawkins would have encountered significant obstacles. The most challenging among them was that John Baron, at least the John Baron who spoke on behalf of the Trump Organization, did not exist.

Although he appeared from time to time in the press, John Baron (sometimes spelled *Barron*) was a name that Trump and at least one of his employees hid behind when they didn't want their identities attached to a statement. John Baron called a lawyer and threatened to bring a lawsuit against him in retaliation for claims made against Trump on behalf of members of the House Wreckers Union. Baron also responded to a rumor by saying that though "Mr. Trump enjoyed eating at the 21 Club, he has absolutely no interest in buying it." And John Baron said, "We don't know what happened to it," when reporters called to ask about the Bonwit's grill-work, which was also supposed to be preserved. In its report *The Times* noted that "repeated efforts to contact Mr. Trump over the last three days have been unsuccessful."

A handy fiction, Baron was a character out of Fred Trump's book. In his day Fred had used the name Mr. Green to hide his identity when he called certain people. The ruse was so familiar to members of the extended family that a lawyer/brother-in-law often told Donald that he wondered how soon after being issued a subpoena John Baron would take sick and die.

Outside the family, and the organization, John Baron was quoted in the press as if he were as real as the concrete structure that began to rise on Fifth Avenue soon after the last bits of the Bonwit building were trucked away. That job was overseen by an engineer named Barbara Res, who had been a key supervisor at the Commodore/Hyatt project, where she was one of just three women on the job and the only one who ever left an office to actually walk the site. In this intensely macho environment, where workers used structural columns as urinals and plastered the elevators with centerfolds, Res was subject to almost constant sexual harassment. She had performed so well, wrangling union laborers and multiple subcontractors, that Trump hired her to run the construction of the Fifth Avenue tower though she was barely thirty-one years old. This made her roughly Trump's age, which might help explain his readiness to hire her despite her lack of experience.

Built almost entirely of concrete, which meant that design changes could be incorporated more or less on the fly, Trump Tower began rising from its foundation even before the engineers' drawings for upper floors were drafted. With just two years to complete the job, Res was pressured by the schedule and Trump's competing agendas. According to Res, Trump wanted to promote his building as the finest anywhere, while also saving money wherever possible. In her 2013 book, Res wrote that Trump outfitted some of the apartments with materials and fixtures that she considered too ordinary.

Although Res was forced to scrimp on some apartment interiors, the public spaces at Trump Tower were built to impress. An unusual reddish Breccia Pernice marble became the building's signature element. Res and Ivana Trump traveled to Italy to visit the quarry and shops that would produce the stone. They made a side trip to Monte Carlo, where they visited with Ivana's jet-setter friend Verina Hixon. Although included in social outings, Res never felt completely part of the crowd she met on the Riviera. She noticed the difference most keenly while riding in the back of a Rolls-Royce that moved slowly through crowded streets. The driver noted the crowds of "pests" who didn't belong in Monte Carlo because they were not suitably rich and mused about killing them with a rifle to clear the way. As Res would later write in a self-published memoir, these comments frightened her and forced her to accept "there are people in this world who truly believe they are better."

The unpleasant, even disorienting, feelings Res occasionally experienced as she visited the world inhabited by the Trumps would be shared by others who worked for them. Although flights across the Atlantic on the Concorde and meetings with the rich and famous came with Res's job, these intoxicants were not truly hers. They were conditioned upon her performance, and this included her ability to get along with Ivana, Donald, and his father. By 1980, Fred Trump was seventy-five years old, and almost fifteen years had passed since he'd last built something himself. He did his best to present himself as active and in command. He dyed his gray hair and mustache a reddish brown, pushed his way into meetings, and attempted to boss people around. Fred Trump was especially forceful when it came to the contract for concrete work at Trump Tower, which he steered toward a company that had worked for him in the past, Dic-Underhill Concrete.

The price of concrete was higher in Manhattan than it was in any other city in the country. Much of the difference, which ranged as high as 70 percent, was caused by organized crime's dominance of every aspect of the business, which, due to geography, was surprisingly easy to control. Concrete must be delivered and poured less than two hours after its manufacture. This technical requirement, combined with Manhattan's congested streets, meant that the only reliable suppliers were the handful located within the borough or in nearby Queens.

These few operators belonged to a mob-dominated cartel that rigged bidding by dividing the work among themselves. The unions that supplied concrete workers and cement-truck drivers were also under the influence of various crime bosses. Builders who resisted the cartel suffered from arson attacks, theft of equipment and materials, and work stoppages. It was safer and ultimately cheaper to play along.[5]

Although it wasn't, as Trump claimed, the largest concrete building in the world, Trump Tower would require ninety thousand tons of the stuff at a cost of $22 million ($63 million in 2015). When he intervened in the contract decision, Fred Trump may not have known whether the cartel intended the work to go to Dic-Underhill. In fact, the mob had not controlled the concrete trade in the same way now as when Fred was still doing business. However, Res did take note of two apparent arsons on the site that suggested that someone was unhappy. The first destroyed a valuable electrical generator but didn't set back construction in any significant way. The second blaze, which occurred on January 29, 1982, was more serious.

As Res would recall, she was awakened that morning

by a five-thirty call from Ivana Trump, who told her, "The building is on fire." By the time Res had picked her way around barricades and past emergency vehicles, the fire was extinguished. A crane operator who had gone up to his cab to prepare for the day's work had been trapped as the flames consumed concrete forms near the base of the crane. As Res watched, rescue workers helped him descend safely.

One floor of the building was severely damaged by the fire. Others were affected by the water used to put it out. The incident set back construction by two months.

Although the fire brought negative publicity, Trump's arson problems and the intrigue around the concrete work was routine for New York builders in the 1980s. More unusual was a convoluted and ultimately troublesome arrangement Trump made to sell apartments to Verina Hixon, who had given Barbara Res and Ivana the grand tour of Monte Carlo. With the help of mortgages arranged by Trump himself, Hixon bought several units and began construction of elaborate interiors, including an indoor swimming pool. As this work was done, Hixon was often seen with the top man in the city's construction unions, John Cody, who gave her $500,000 to help acquire the Trump apartments.

Mob-connected and notoriously aggressive, Cody had the power to ruin a builder's project by slowing down concrete deliveries and disrupting work on any part of a job. If he was unhappy with a plumbing contractor, lift operators might refuse to carry pipes and fixtures to upper floors. A flooring specialist who bent the rules that benefited union carpenters could discover that power tools and lumber walked off the job when he wasn't looking. Cody, who had been arrested eight times and found guilty three times, counted Roy Cohn as a friend and legal adviser. Cody claimed that Trump preferred to use Cohn as an intermediary for their meetings.

Trump would one day describe Cody as "one psycho-pathic, crazy bastard . . . real scum." But when neces-sary, Trump cooperated with the man and indulged his girlfriend Hixon. Trump's working relationship with Cody came in handy for Trump when Cody gave him months of advance notice before a strike crippled build-ing projects across the city in the summer of 1982.[6]

Cody often appeared at Trump Tower to help Verina Hixon with problems that arose during the extensive outfitting of her apartments. Among the special items she added was the swimming pool, the only one in the building, which required that extra concrete be poured. Hixon's ever-changing plans brought her into frequent conflicts with Trump's people, but with Cody's aid she generally got what she wanted. (According to Hixon, Trump said, "Anything for you, John," when she and Cody asked that space reserved for a hallway be added to one of her units.) All the special treatment ended in December 1982 after Cody was convicted and impris-oned on racketeering charges. Hixon and Trump would then wage legal battles against each other for the better part of a decade. After falling behind in her mainte-nance payments to the tune of $300,000, Hixon went bankrupt and lost the apartments to her lenders.[7]

European by birth and seemingly moneyed, Hixon had been the kind of buyer Donald Trump hoped to bring to Trump Tower. He had imagined the building as a magnet for the superwealthy, including those who lived in residences scattered around the world. The rich had always sought luxury and comfort, but for the most part they had pursued these rewards with a bit of re-serve, if only to appear solidly genteel. This habit pre-vailed in the decades immediately following World War II, as the gap between the rich and the rest was nar-rowed, and discussion of one's paycheck or bank ac-count was considered bad manners. In the 1970s, as the postwar boom ended and the rich began to accumulate an ever-greater share of the world's wealth, their lifestyles and behaviors became an object of public fascination. Television gave Americans a slew of programs—*Dallas, Dynasty, Falcon Crest*—that dwelled on the operatic lives of wealthy characters, and Madison Avenue removed the working class from advertisements. From a high of 25 percent in 1970, the proportion of ads depicting working-class Americans slid to 11 percent in 1980. Blue-collar Americans became so rare on TV that the series *Roseanne,* which depicted a working-class family in the Midwest, would appear as a revelation when it debuted in 1988.

As a former actor who leased his swanky California mansion from the rich friends who owned it, President Ronald Reagan epitomized the style-over-substance ethos of the age, which the writer Kevin Phillips described as an "ostentatious celebration of wealth." In the 1950s Richard Nixon's wife, Pat, famously wore what he called a "good Republican cloth coat," but in the 1980s Nancy Reagan wore fur. Reagan's inaugural celebrations were lavish, especially when compared with the down-home style of his predecessor, Jimmy Carter, and Reagan's advisers and friends hailed from the upper reaches of the economy. In these ways, and many others, the Reagan style put an end to the 1950s notion, created in magazines such as *Photoplay,* that celebrities were like ordinary people. By the 1980s, enormous wealth, or at least a lifestyle that suggested the same, became the hallmark of real success and even moral character. President Carter, who criticized materialism as "self-indulgence and consumption," was seen as a scold who was wrong about the economy. In the Reagan formula, people could relax and allow tax cuts, increased defense spending, and big reductions in aid to the poor to magically restore the middle class. When legions of economists said the administration couldn't pull off this trick, the president offered not cogent arguments but words that made him sound like an actor delivering lines from a script. "Yes, we can," he said with great confidence, "and, yes, we will."[8]

Reagan was only loosely devoted to the truth. He continued to claim that he wrote his own speeches, even after it was shown that he did not, and he habitually offered apocrypha alongside facts, daring the listener to separate them. In time, this way of speaking would be labeled "truthiness" by the satirist Stephen Colbert. (It comes "from the gut, not from books," he would explain.) In Reagan's day it was described by journalist James Reston as a style of speaking devised "to evade the facts." With exasperation, Chief of Staff Donald Regan compared the task of answering questions about the president's statements with serving in "a shovel brigade that follows a parade" of elephants.[9]

While he produced much to shovel, the president's methods were so effective that despite his record-breaking deficits, he built a nearly unassailable reputation as a fiscal conservative. By the end of his presidency total federal debt would triple. Hourly wages fell steadily in the Reagan years as high-paying factory jobs disappeared, and laid-off workers discovered that new service jobs, when they were available, paid substantially less. Under these conditions, workingmen could not support families in the way their fathers did in the 1950s and '60s. The difference was made up, in part, by the earnings of wives and mothers who entered the workforce in greater numbers every year. Also, people borrowed more to sustain their standard of living. After a dip caused by the 1981–83 recession, credit-card debt began a rise that would continue almost uninterrupted until 2000.[10]

With all this hard work and borrowing, Americans reported feeling extraordinary stress. Yet the dream of sudden wealth, achieved in a clever way, maintained its allure. Government-run lotteries, formerly found only in New Hampshire and Puerto Rico, spread quickly across the country. For those who wanted better odds, TV pitchmen offered courses in real estate speculation, urging viewers to use OPM—other people's money—to leverage meager personal investments in properties. In 1984, one of the bestselling books in America was *Nothing Down: How to Buy Real Estate with Little or No Money Down*. Practically a clone of infomercial star Albert Lowry, author Robert G. Allen claimed that he had taught two individuals he picked out of a queue at an unemployment office enough to earn $5,000 each in ninety days. In 1987 he would admit to having his own financial problems after federal authorities placed liens on his property to recover $412,000 in unpaid taxes and penalties.[11]

While the poor and middle class labored to make it in America, Reagan's policies helped the top 1 percent notch a 74 percent increase in income during his presidency. Much of this came in the form of capital gains from investments which, thanks to Reagan reforms, were subject to much lower tax rates. The number of people with net wealth in excess of $100 million doubled in the Reagan years, and the number of billionaires tripled. These were the people who could and would plunk down $1 million or more for an apartment in Trump Tower. (Although some were priced lower, more than ninety of the apartments in the building were valued at $1 million or more.)[12]

The money that wealthy outsiders brought to New York would be essential as the city's economy moved steadily toward the business of finance and the service sector. Indeed, like all of the major cities of the Northern Rust Belt, New York was losing manufacturing jobs at a rapid rate. Under these conditions, rich people represented something like a natural resource that could be mined to support shop clerks, chauffeurs, doormen, and hairstylists. These service employees earned far less than their counterparts in manufacturing, but the trend was inexorable. Well-paying middle-class jobs were disappearing as wealth and income were being concentrated in the upper reaches of society. Under these conditions it was far better to live and work in New York, where the rich crowded the table and many more crumbs fell to the floor.[13]

In the more Darwinian economy, Donald Trump's eager pursuit of those who could afford to spend huge sums on part-time residences was a wise business strategy. The sale of a $2 million apartment involved roughly the same amount of time and effort as the sale of a $100,000 one. In fact, high-end sales might require less work because the buyers often just wrote checks to complete a purchase. But wealth didn't necessarily make Trump's customers sophisticated and worldly. Many still responded to marketing pitches that appealed to their vanity or insecurities. With this in mind, Trump circulated the rumor that Charles, the Prince of Wales, and his wife, Diana, were weighing a purchase at Trump Tower. Since Buckingham Palace refused comment on rumors about the couple, no one in authority would refute it. Trump flattered his would-be customers by saying Trump Tower was built for "the best people in the world," and he rarely missed a chance to borrow credibility in his marketing efforts. Visitors to the office that sold Trump Tower apartments were treated to a slide show—images of the building and its environs—accompanied by a recording of Frank Sinatra singing.

The sales brochure for the apartments promised that Trump Tower (not 1600 Pennsylvania Avenue) was "the world's most prestigious address" and encouraged readers to "imagine life within" a bronze colored skyscraper that was securely isolated from the outside world. After reminding would-be buyers that Astors, Whitneys, and Vanderbilts once haunted the neighborhood, the pitch noted that residents would enter Trump Tower from a doorway that was "totally inaccessible to the public" and would be greeted by an attentive staff. Every residence, the copywriter concluded, was "a diamond in the sky." According to Trump, the building was sixty-eight stories tall. However, the American Institute of Architects, which judged Trump Tower to be one of the ten ugliest buildings in New York, also reported it was just fifty-eight stories tall.[14]

Barbara Res would estimate that roughly half of the apartments in the tower were bought by foreigners. Many others were purchased by corporations, pop stars, and Hollywood celebrities. Among them were Michael Jackson, Steven Spielberg, and Johnny Carson, whom Trump had once admired but came to dislike. Carson was, Trump would recall, an imperious and impatient man who could be "a very mean, very nasty guy." These qualities came into stark relief when Carson, who had recently taken possession of his apartment, called Trump on the phone. According to Trump, Carson said, "Donald, you have two fucking men who work in the building who stole my coat."[15]

The garment was an expensive topcoat made out of the hair of a camel-like Andean animal called a vicuña. Produced in minute quantities, vicuña wool was so rare that, but for a political scandal of the 1950s, most Americans would never have heard of it. However, when President Eisenhower's chief of staff was forced to resign after accepting a vicuña coat as a gift, just about everyone came to associate the words *vicuña coat* with extravagance.

Carson's vicuña coat had, he insisted, disappeared after two maintenance men worked in his apartment, and he wanted Trump to do something about it. Trump tracked down the men and listened to their denials. He called Carson and said the workers, two fellows from Queens, "don't wear vicuña coats" and "they'd be run out of their neighborhoods if they ever did." Not satisfied, Carson demanded the men be fired. As he would later explain, Trump concluded that he "had no choice" because an important man had issued an ultimatum. Trump summoned the men back to his office and said, "Fellas, he said you stole it, you're fired." The workers left the building severed from their jobs. Months later Carson would discover the coat in the back of a closet. He telephoned Trump to report the find with chagrin, if not regret, for his demand that the workers be dismissed. "But I fired two fuckin' guys for you" was Trump's reply.

That he fired two workers on the basis of a celebrity's false accusation remained fresh in Donald's mind almost twenty years later. But when he spoke of it, he seemed certain that he had done the right thing; it would have been a mistake to stand up to Carson and defend his workers. Celebrities were worth the trouble because their presence drew buyers who willingly paid, in the case of Trump Tower, as much as $10 million for their homes. However, these buyers didn't always profit from the deals they made. Carson complained loudly to his accountant when he lost money on the sale of his apartment in 1989.

Trump, on the other hand, gained immeasurably from his associations with Carson, Spielberg, and a host of other famous people, including the King of Pop, who bought apartments at Trump Tower. Besides their money, he also basked in their reflected glow. After Trump Tower was sold-out, he would start claiming that his name, attached to any project, instantly made it more valuable. (Sometimes he quantified this "Trump effect," saying it added 25 percent, 50 percent, or even 100 percent to the overall worth of a development.) With the power of fame ever present in his mind, he also redoubled his commitment to cultivating it.

◆

7
CELEBRITY DONALD

*I have always gotten much more publicity
than anybody else.*
—DONALD TRUMP

Surrounded by stacked file folders and piles of three-ring binders, Wayne Barrett was lost in concentration as he sat at the table in a small government conference room and pored over memos and documents. The jangling sound of the phone he had pushed to the edge of the table startled him almost as much as the explanation shouted out by a secretary in a nearby office: "It's for you!" Barrett, who hadn't told anyone he was going to be working at the offices of the New York State Urban Development Corporation, reached for the receiver.

"Hello?"

"Wayne, it's Donald." The tone was eager, familiar, and arrogant. The caller didn't say his last name—Trump—which Barrett found strange since he had never encountered the man until this moment. "I hear you've been going around town asking a lot of negative questions about me. When are you going to talk to me?"

"I'm circling," said Barrett. Then he agreed to get together with Donald Trump in a month's time. It would be the first of three interviews with Trump that Barrett would recall quite vividly after more than forty years of interviewing people as a journalist and an author.[1]

In late 1978, when this call took place, Barrett was five years into a career at the alternative weekly *The*

Village Voice, where he would become a fixture of New York journalism. A skeptic when it came to the powerful, he lived in the impoverished and rough-edged Brownsville section of Brooklyn, where he had worked as a teacher and as an advocate for tenants who lived in slum housing. His devotion to their cause came with a convert's level of enthusiasm because he had begun life in a conservative family in conservative Lynchburg, Virginia, where he had been a cochair of his state's Youth for Goldwater group during the Arizona senator's losing campaign for the presidency.

Although his views began to change during his college years in Philadelphia, Barrett became a lifelong liberal after attending the Columbia University Graduate School of Journalism and covering Robert F. Kennedy's presidential campaign. Kennedy's concern for the poor and his commitment to civil rights would inspire Barrett's journalism as he focused on election campaigns, government affairs, and other aspects of civic life. He had turned his attention to Trump as the young developer demonstrated his ability to convert his political connections into profit.

One of Barrett's interviews with Trump occurred at the office on Avenue Z in Brooklyn, where Fred still managed his apartment buildings. The other two were done at Olympic Tower, where Donald and Ivana were living at the time. Barrett didn't own a suit, but he did add a necktie to his wardrobe for these visits. His wife, who window-shopped on Fifth Avenue during one of these sessions, quizzed him about the furnishings, but Barrett didn't have much to report. He was so concerned with getting answers to his questions that he had made little note of the art on the walls or the furniture in the rooms. Other writers would report on the dark-colored marble Ivana had chosen for the floor, the tables covered in goatskin, and the hammock hung hear a window overlooking the city.[2]

At their first encounter, Trump made sure that Barrett understood that he was friendly with officials at the top of the company that owned *The Village Voice*. Somehow, without Barrett's telling him, Trump knew that the reporter lived in Brownsville, which he called "an awfully tough neighborhood." He volunteered to help Barrett relocate to an apartment in a less tough place. Barrett declined, explaining that he had lived in Brownsville for a decade and was committed to the neighborhood and its improvement. "So we do the same thing," replied Trump. "We're both rebuilding neighborhoods."

In his time with Trump, Barrett sought answers to many vexing questions. He wanted to know about the Trump family's thirty-year relationship with Abe Beame and the Democratic Party establishment in Brooklyn. He asked if Donald Trump knew why the attorney representing Penn Central's creditors had suddenly dropped his objections to the Commodore Hotel sale. And how, asked Barrett, did Trump square his claim that the Trump Organization owned as many as twenty-two thousand apartments with legal documents that put the number at twelve thousand? Barrett also pressed for details on the racial-discrimination complaints made against the Trump Organization, which Trump had contested in the press and in the countersuit filed by Roy Cohn.

Trump had questions of his own for Barrett: "What do people say about me? Do they say I'm loyal? Do they say I work hard?" When Trump felt less happy about Barrett's project, he asked if the reporter was aware of his willingness to sue journalists: "I've sued twice for libel. Roy Cohn's been my attorney both times. I've won once and the other case is pending. It's cost me one hundred thousand dollars, but it's worth it. I've broken one writer. You and I've been friends and all, but if your story damages my reputation, I'll sue."

Barrett never learned the names of the writers Trump had supposedly sued, nor did he find any press coverage of libel actions the developer had initiated. But a threat, backed up with a done-it-before claim, could give a reporter pause. Barrett may have paused, but he was not deterred. In early January 1979 he published a series of articles that showed Trump's political connections and revealed him to be a clever young man who was surpassing the example set by his father. Nothing Barrett described would count as illegal, but his articles established Donald Trump's ambition as so enormous that it left little room for other traits. Barrett wrote:

> After getting to know him, I realized that his deals are his life. He once told me, "I won't make a deal just to make a profit. It has to have its own excitement. Its own flair." Another Manhattan developer said it differently. "Trump won't do a deal unless there's something extra—a kind of moral larceny—in it. He's not satisfied with a profit. He has to take something more. Otherwise there's no thrill."[3]

As the first full accounting of the Trump phenomenon, Barrett's articles would become touchstones for many who followed him in the effort to explain Donald's success. Trump was unhappy with the pieces and would eventually describe Barrett's work as "vicious" and claim, despite all their meetings having been recorded on tape, that "every quote had been changed or taken wildly out of context." Trump did not sue, however.

If reporters made mistakes as they dealt with Trump, it may have been because whenever Trump spoke to the press, he addressed so many old and new claims that even the best fact-checker would have been hard-pressed to sort them all out. In one interview Donald revised his defense of the destruction of the Bonwit artwork, saying that it would have cost him not $32,000, but $500,000 to save it. The $32,000 figure had been offered by his alter ego John Baron, which meant that, as far as the public was concerned, Trump wasn't contradicting himself. In 1983, press estimates of Fred Trump's fortune would shrink it from the $200 million reported in 1976, to just $40 million, which made Donald's accomplishments seem far more impressive. A year later, as *The Times* caught up with Fred Trump, he was credited with controlling $1 billion in assets and the family remained Swedish, and not German. (In this article *The Times* demoted Ivana from Olympic team member to "alternate.")[4]

Any effort made to resolve the confusion over Trump's public image would be overwhelmed by the volume of the publicity that attended the man's movements. A perfect example of this dynamic arose around the critic Ada Louise Huxtable's assessment of Trump Tower. When she saw the drawings for the yet-to-be-constructed building, she said that Der Scutt had envisioned a "dramatically handsome" design. When it was actually built, however, Huxtable was obviously disappointed by the execution. She pronounced Trump Tower "a monumentally undistinguished" structure that was marred by a "dull and ordinary exterior." Its interior, clad in the rosy marble so carefully selected in Italy, evoked "posh ladies' powder-room décor."

No one who had paid close attention to Huxtable's views could be confused about her opinion of the finished Trump Tower, which was consistent with her long-term concern over the ultratall buildings that had begun to crowd the sky in New York. As she observed, lawyers and developers had exploited the bonuses made possible in the zoning rules to produce a type of building that "romanticizes power and the urban condition and celebrates leverage and cash flow. Its less romantic side effects are greed and chaos writ monstrously large." A prime example could be seen in Midtown where, she noted, "Der Scutt has created the gigantic Trump Tower, a soaring, faceted form that is also guaranteed to destroy the scale and ambience of Fifth Avenue." But even as the nation's most respected architecture critic inveighed against his creation, Trump sought to exploit her credentials. To her dismay, the phrase "dramatically handsome design," which she wrote to describe Der Scutt's *drawings* of the building, were put on display in the Trump Tower atrium. Neither she, nor her publisher, granted permission for this use, but nothing in copyright law prevented it.[5]

From the moment it opened, the public space in Trump Tower was populated, in great measure, by tourists and curiosity seekers who wanted to see what all the fuss was about. As they entered the building, they were met by attendants who were dressed like British grenadiers, with scarlet coats and tall, fur-covered busby hats. Visitors to the public lobby heard live music played on a grand piano and saw streams of water cascading down a marble wall. The polished red-and-pink stone that stretched in every direction was not so much welcoming as intimidating, and the brass fixtures, which Trump hoped would shine like the buckle on his NYMA uniform, seemed industrial in scale. Escalators carried shoppers to the high-price retailers on the upper levels of the lobby. The owners of these shops, who paid some of the highest rents in the world, often struggled to make a profit. Within a decade, exclusive stores such as Buccellati, Lina Lee, Martha, and Charles Jourdan would be gone. In their place would come modest retailers such as Tower Records and Dooney & Bourke. The gawkers who passed through the spinning doors were far more

likely to spend $50 at Nike than $500 at Galeries La-
fayette.

As the landlord, Donald Trump wasn't much concerned about turnover among the retailers in the verti-
cal shopping mall, as long as the rent was paid. As of
1986 Trump said that the office and retail floors generated $17 million per year. All of the business done in
these spaces was hidden from the view of Trump Tower
residents, who came and went via a doorway and small
lobby space on Fifty-sixth Street. With no piano player,
fountain wall, or grenadiers, the residential lobby was
so dimly lit that on sunny days residents would have to
pause to let their eyes adjust to the darkness once they
stepped inside.

The sale of the tower condominiums, which report-
edly brought $277 million, paid off the $190 million
cost of the building, with plenty left over for Trump and
his partner, Equitable. Trump also sought a tax abatement similar to the one granted to Aristotle Onassis under the state law intended to aid the development of
residences on underutilized properties. But the Olympic Tower arrangement was approved under a different
mayor, at a time when New York City was in economic
distress. Trump sought his abatement at a time when
New York had rebounded and the feisty Ed Koch occupied the mayor's office. Dozens of new skyscrapers
were begun in Manhattan during the early Koch years,
and the city's credit rating improved steadily. Under
these conditions, the mayor didn't feel the need to cater
to developers.[6]

Koch was one of the few figures in New York whose
personality and ambition could rival Donald Trump's.
Aggressive and egocentric, he presented himself as the
embodiment of a certain kind of New Yorker, one who,
not unlike Trump, often spoke without thinking and
pushed himself to the front of every line. He saw the

developer's bid for a tax break as a self-interested attempt to add to the already outsize profit he had realized by manipulating the zoning regulations to maximize the size of his tower. To then seek multi-million-dollar reductions in taxes for a building that would house some of the wealthiest people in the world seemed outrageous. Besides, in the year when Bonwit Teller ceased operating on Fifth Avenue, the store generated revenues of $30 million. In Koch's view, this showed that the site did not qualify as underutilized and therefore eligible for subsidy.

Trump's lawyers presented evidence that in the 1970s, Bonwit had sometimes used just 60 percent of its floor space. This record persuaded the state's highest court that Trump could not be denied the abatement. But while he netted roughly $50 million in tax reductions, Trump also acquired an enemy in Mayor Koch. Given Trump's involvement in businesses that brought him into regular contact with city government, alienating the mayor was not a good idea.

Rich with profits from the sale of condos in his new tower, Trump found himself on the wrong side of the political game when he invested in the local franchise— the New Jersey Generals—of the upstart United States Football League. By most measures, the team was a perfect fit for someone with his competitive drive and hunger for public attention. More than any other form of entertainment, sports, especially football, benefited from a torrent of free publicity. Every daily paper in the country, save for *The Wall Street Journal,* devoted pages of newsprint—not to mention reporters' salaries and expenses—to sports. Local TV newscasts always came with a sports report, and games were a staple for the major networks. In 1979 a fledgling all-sports network called ESPN began operating from a base in Connecticut. Radio stations beamed sports-talk shows across the country, and soon some, including WNBC in New York, would adopt an all-sports format. (WNBC became WFAN.)

With the mass media devoted to sports, even team owners could become celebrities, if they so chose. Donald Trump's friend George Steinbrenner, who owned the Yankees and frequented Le Club, was a prime example. He used the press to make himself so recognized that a beer company put him in a commercial.

Steinbrenner had come along as professional teams were becoming vastly more valuable, thanks to the money paid for the rights to broadcast their games. Organized to appeal to television programmers, the USFL began playing in 1983 with a dozen teams with owners who were wealthy enough to lose money while the league developed. Trump bought the Generals prior to the 1984 season for $9 million and soon began agitating for a stadium to be built for his team with the aid of the City and the State of New York. Mayor Koch opposed him, and the idea died along with the league in 1985. Their relationship warmed a bit as Trump's father donated $25,000 to the mayor's 1985 reelection campaign. But eventually Koch and Donald Trump descended into the kind of name-calling nastiness more common to a playground than the corridors of power.[7]

The nadir was reached when Trump sought yet another tax abatement for a development on the West Side of Manhattan. It would have included a new home for the NBC television network, which was contemplating a move from Rockefeller Center to nearby New Jersey. In New York, and many other locales, big companies often threatened to leave for cheaper pastures in order to get some sort of accommodation from a landlord or local authorities. In NBC's case, however, a move from the center of media, culture, and finance seemed unlikely. Nevertheless, Trump seized upon the notion to promote a vast complex of commercial and residential buildings between Fifty-ninth and Seventy-second Streets—he called it Television City—with NBC its centerpiece. Koch responded by offering the network financial incentives to stay in the city no matter where it located its facilities. The network could even remain at Rockefeller Center and use the money to renovate.

"The city under Ed Koch is a disaster," Trump said as Koch announced his decision.

"If Donald Trump is squealing like a stuck pig," replied Koch, "I must have done something right." Trump called the mayor a "moron," and Koch taunted him with "Piggy, piggy, piggy."

The Koch-Trump feud was encouraged by the local press, especially the tabloid *Post,* which had previously given both men ample attention. Koch had been supported by the *Post* in the past, but in this battle the paper generally sided with Trump. Eventually the mayor's administration was swept by scandals, including the exposure of Cultural Affairs Commissioner Bess Myerson's attempt to bribe a judge, and a flurry of indictments and resignations immobilized City Hall.

New York magazine noted that Trump was included in some conversations about the next man or woman who might occupy Gracie Mansion once the current mayor's term ended, but no Trump-for-mayor bandwagon ever got rolling. However, his merely being mentioned in the same breath as potential aspirants such as future mayors David Dinkins and Rudolph Giuliani showed that he had become a significant figure. He was neither a politician, like Dinkins, nor a public official like Giuliani, who was US Attorney for the Southern District of New York and therefore the federal government's chief prosecutor in Manhattan. Trump wasn't even the most successful builder in the city. However, he was one of the most famous rich men in America, and this made him worthy of consideration.

Trump had become remarkably famous thanks to new kinds of mass media that seemed all but invented to lavish attention on men like him as they expanded the ranks and the very definition of celebrity. On television, this so-called celebrity journalism was pioneered by the program called *Entertainment Tonight,* which debuted in 1981. Designed to look like an evening news show, *Entertainment Tonight* functioned mainly as a window on the lives of the famous and those who would be famous. One of this show's original presenters, the British-born Robin Leach, developed a variation on the form, which he called *Lifestyles of the Rich and Famous.* Leach, who left school short of college to become a Fleet Street reporter, believed, "The audience demand for this kind of program is insatiable." In an accent that surely led many viewers to consider him both worldly and sophisticated, Leach talked of "champagne wishes and caviar dreams" and dressed in blue-blazer chic. His producers promised that he was America's foremost showbusiness reporter, who "travels the world nonstop in the circles of the elite."

(It's worth noting that while Leach's audience understood without thinking that his program would focus on the consumption habits of the rich and famous—their homes, possessions, travels, hobbies, etc.—the word *lifestyle* was actually quite new. When first used by psychologist Alfred Adler in 1929, *lifestyle* referred to strategies people used to avoid dealing with problems or uncomfortable situations. The word was repurposed in the 1960s to mean something akin to "way of living." In 1967 a new magazine called *Avant Garde* promised to explore the "life-style" of the "mad mod scene," and the journalist Gloria Steinem used the hyphenated version of the word in an article for *The New York Times*.[8] Within a decade, advertisers and consumers understood the term as a catchall that suggested social class, taste, and apparent wealth. This last factor loomed largest, and the appearance of wealth rather its actuality mattered most. No one knew if your expensive car came with a big monthly loan payment or if your fancy house was rented. Far more important was the impression one made driving around town, or stepping out of the front door.)

In 1983 millions of people tuned in to see the first episodes of *Lifestyles of the Rich and Famous,* which were presented as two-hour specials. Among those Leach selected to reveal in these first shows were Princess Diana, the actress/singing star Cher, the romance writer Barbara Cartland, and a single businessperson, Donald Trump. Cher displayed her shoe collection. Trump showed off his weekend-retreat estate in Greenwich, Connecticut, and didn't correct Leach when the host said it was worth three times the $3.7 million Trump had recently paid for it. Leach would book him for a return engagement.

While Robin Leach represented the lowest common denominator in the media, Trump also attracted attention from the higher end too. A big profile in the Sunday magazine of *The New York Times* permitted him to brag at length—"I have credibility"—and allowed his father to declare his son's success was his birthright. Ivana described her husband as boyishly charming, which he could be, and business associates praised his judgment. The praise was balanced by a few reflections on Trump's huckster qualities, but the overall picture was of a brilliant, exuberant, successful young man. The most telling note came from Trump himself, who reflected on his accomplishments and acquisitions and mused, " . . . but what does it mean?" The reflection lasted but a moment, and then Trump was on to another topic.[9]

A month after his appearance in the *Times* magazine, Trump landed on the cover of *GQ,* which selected his face for an issue devoted to the theme "success." For the first time, thanks to writer Graydon Carter, Ivana was denied the title of "Olympian" as her athletic exploits were reported to have been accomplished as a member of an unspecified "Czech ski team." Carter was also probably the first to suggest, in a national publication, that "a lot of people just don't like Donald Trump very much."

As he spoke about owning this and that, Trump could seem like a gleeful kid shuffling deeds and pastel-colored currency while plotting his triumph in a game of Monopoly. Carter noted that Trump had reneged on his promise to save the Bonwit artwork and described the aggressive tactics he used to clear tenants out of a building he'd bought on Central Park South. Frustrated that under rent-control laws the tenants paid below-market prices for their apartments, Trump did what he could to make them feel uncomfortable. He threatened to offer vacant apartments to the homeless and gave the building an ominous appearance by covering the windows of vacant spaces with metal sheeting. The *GQ* writer also let Trump express himself at his most grandiose. In one of these moments Trump claimed to own an entire block on Central Park South, which he didn't, and in another he proposed to build both the tallest skyscraper on the planet and a domed football stadium in the Bronx.

The supertower and stadium were fantasies that would never materialize, but his enthusiasm was a little infectious. During a ride with Carter in Trump's chauffeur-driven stretch limo, Trump's exuberance was so great that a reader could readily imagine a little boy who is desperate for approval and has never been told that bragging is obnoxious. "A coach maker did this for me," he said of the car. "It's wild, isn't it? We have the wet bar, the whole thing. The whole caboodle. Look, it's got a TV and a radio." He told Carter that Trump Tower "glows" at night because he insisted on using "real bronze" on the exterior. "I'm a first-class sort of person," Trump added. "I only go first-class."[10]

After *GQ,* Trump's face also appeared on the covers of *Time, Newsweek, Business Week, Fortune, Manhattan Inc.,* and *New York.* (He had many of these covers framed and displayed on a brag wall in his office.) The blizzard of publicity made his name synonymous with wealth and ambition, and it became common for people to refer to an especially assertive or braggadocious man as "the Donald Trump of" one thing or another. When these references to Trump-like men appeared in the press, the real Trump was sure to find out. The pile of clippings Trump reviewed every morning was so substantial that he could only glance at most of them. Nevertheless, he wanted to keep tabs. This effort was aided by his executive assistant, Norma Foerderer, who would serve Trump for decades as his charming but forbidding guardian and a gatekeeper. She screened every call from an enthusiast with a business proposition and every request from a journalist seeking an interview. Foerderer would also soothe the boss's ego when it was bruised and rein it in when it was careening out of control. As much a nanny as a corporate functionary, Foerderer was not so different from other assistants who served executives, celebrities, and public officials by keeping their schedules, monitoring their moods, and even managing their personal bank accounts. These indispensable women (almost all were female) handled more intimate matters in their employers' lives than their physicians and seemed to provide the gravity that kept them from spinning out of control.[11]

Press appearances were apparently a form of ego sustenance for Donald, and Foerderer kept a store of videotapes—each depicting a Trump milestone—on hand for his instant gratification. She also managed the supply of new material that poured in from around the world. The most valuable of these trophies were mentions in *People* magazine, which enjoyed the largest readership of any glossy weekly in America and was the most important arbiter of celebrity in the world. Brief and breezy, *People* articles necessarily deployed stereotype and caricature, but the magazine's early judgments about a person's essential traits often turned out to be accurate. Strong leaders acted decisively. Temperamental actors behaved abysmally. In some cases a kind of confirmation bias was at work, as observers noticed what they were expected to see. In other instances the anointed celebrity might have unconsciously lived up (or down) to his billing. Either way, the words in *People* were often confirmed later by a subject's behavior in ways that made them seem accurate.

In the fall of 1981 *People* declared Donald Trump a billionaire even before he claimed the title for himself. The magazine amplified the rumor that he had started about Prince Charles and Princess Diana's buying a Trump Tower condo to suggest they were considering "a 24-room, $5 million spread." *People* also reported that, according to one close friend, Trump hoped to head up his own TV network. To the magazine's credit, its hagiography was balanced by references to Trump's self-promotional excesses and to his destruction of the Bonwit artwork. Writer Lee Wohlfert-Wihlborg made efficient use of Trump's own words to provide her readers with a fleeting glimpse of his psyche. "Man is the most vicious of all animals, and life is a series of battles ending in victory or defeat," he told her. "You just can't let people make a sucker out of you."

As Trump spoke of life as a series of conflicts, waged by vicious creatures, he was offering, in his vernacular, a view that the seventeenth-century philosopher Thomas Hobbes had ominously described as the "war of all against all." Hobbes saw, in legally organized human communities, a way to avoid the chaos of constant and universal conflict among men. Trump saw, in his world, no moral agreement but, rather, vicious combatants engaged in a struggle without end.[12]

People did not note the echoes of Hobbes in Trump's statement. Missing too from the article was any reference to a life-shaping event that had occurred inside the Trump family less than two months prior. On September 26, 1981, Donald's older brother, Fred, died of a sudden and massive heart attack. Just forty-three years old, Freddy was the divorced father of a son and daughter. Having washed out as a pilot and then as a fishing-boat captain, he had moved into his parents' home and worked on a maintenance crew for Trump apartment buildings. Physically wasted by the effects of alcohol, his drinking had contributed so substantially to his death that Donald considered it the real cause. "Fred Trump" was listed among the names of the dead reported in *The Times* on September 29, and three notes of condolence were published by friends and business associates of the family. No formal obituary appeared in the paper. Freddy was buried in a family plot in a Lutheran cemetery in Queens.

In time Donald Trump would count his brother's death as a formative and even defining episode in his life. On one level it was puzzling because Fred was a Trump man, with many of the gifts that should have made him a success of the sort the family prized. "He was such an amazing guy," said Donald many years later. "The best personality and the best-looking guy you'll ever see."

What was the cause of Fred's addiction? Most experts would credit both nature—a genetic predisposition— and the type of nurture Fred experienced as a child. In Donald's view, "Our family environment, the competitiveness, was a negative for Fred." However, Donald also seemed to blame his brother for letting others take advantage of him. He was, in other words, a sucker. "Freddy just wasn't a killer," said Donald, and he didn't defend himself, which was "a fatal mistake." Fred's death had taught Donald "to keep my guard up, one hundred percent."[13]

8
DONALD IN SUCKERLAND

*To me a gambler is someone who plays
the slot machines. I prefer to own slot machines.
It's very good business being the house.*
—DONALD TRUMP

In a world of winners and loser, suckers and deceivers, casinos represent a diabolical version of paradise. Built on a monumental scale, they exert a magnetic pull, beckoning the curious and the deluded. The deceptions begin with marketing campaigns that show not the retirees who prop themselves on canes before the slot machines, but handsome men at felt-covered tables flanked by beautiful women in low-cut dresses, their mouths agape in ecstasy. Once the pilgrim arrives in this land, he discovers the campy architecture—fake Tuscany, fake Old West, fake Havana—that makes the casino seem like a playhouse for grown-ups. Inside waits a delirium of flashing lights and carnival sounds that establish that this is "fun" and "entertainment." No one hides that casinos exist to persuade suckers that losing their hard-earned dollars is nevertheless glamorous and exciting. So it was natural that Donald Trump, who looked good in a tuxedo, had long desired to own one.

Big-time gambling came to the East Coast after New Jersey voters approved gaming in crumbling, crime-ridden Atlantic City in a 1976 referendum. The campaign for the proposition was backed by casino operators and developers. Approval set off a land rush as both speculators and would-be operators sought property that would accommodate large casinos and parking lots for the customers' cars. The first to open was the Resorts Casino Hotel, which had formerly been the Chalfonte-Haddon Hotel. The Las Vegas–based owner immediately began to chalk up profits of $4.2 million per week. Soon other Vegas names arrived, including Caesars, Bally's, Sands, and Tropicana. By 1984, taxes levied on casinos would supply 7 percent of the state government's revenues. In the same period, Gamblers Anonymous in New Jersey recorded a tripling of its membership, and a clinic would be opened to offer gambling addicts care twenty-four hours a day.[1]

Well aware of organized crime's history in Las Vegas, New Jersey officials screened applicants for casino licenses for any connections to unsavory characters, but their decisions seemed inconsistent at best. Resorts was granted a license despite evidence that one of its consultants passed more than $400,000 to the president of the Bahamas, where the firm operated a casino. After spending $320 million on a hotel/casino complex, the well-regarded Hilton corporation was denied a license when gaming commissioners determined the company had not resolved questions about the alleged destruction of sensitive legal documents and reports of criminal activity at its San Francisco hotel. (Many observers believed the commissioners were bothered more by Hilton's failure to properly kowtow to them.) The denial infuriated the company's head William Barron Hilton, who had long cultivated an image of propriety. Hilton had been actively courted by New Jersey's top officials, who encouraged his firm's investment. Bally's and Caesars were put under similar pressure, but received licenses after they changed their management teams.[2]

The challenge of the license review made casinos more difficult to develop than ordinary projects, and would-be operators relied on local advisers and lawyers to guide them successfully. With this kind of help, Donald Trump found his way to a group of landowners who would lease him prime property close to the Depression-era Atlantic City Convention Hall. The hall, which looked like a giant cement Quonset hut, was best known for hosting the annual Miss America beauty pageant. The land included a parcel controlled by locals who were suspected of mob connections. Although Trump first intended to lease this land, he had to buy the others out to satisfy state officials, who wouldn't license a casino dependent on a relationship with such questionable characters. He also gained control of several smaller adjacent properties but couldn't come to terms with a landowner named Vera Coking, whose three-story Sea Shell Guest House sat smack in the middle of the site.

The land beneath the Sea Shell House would have been perfect for parking the limousines that would bring high rollers to the planned Trump Plaza. Her lawyers set the value of her land in the range of $2 million. Coking liked her property and was content to remain in it until she received her price. (Prior to Trump, Coking had turned away Bob Guccione, publisher of *Penthouse* magazine, who also dreamed of opening a casino in Atlantic City. Her obstinacy was one of the obstacles that eventually defeated the project, leaving the porno king with the rusting skeleton of a building and a battered bank account.) In Coking's long negotiations with Trump, the press reported that she had rejected an offer in the millions that also came with a free hotel room, and room service, for the rest of her life. This wasn't true. Nor was it true that Vera Coking died in the midst of the talks. As of 2015 she was still very much alive. What *was* true was that Coking seemed almost supernaturally resistant to Donald Trump's salesmanship. She even called him "a cockroach, a maggot, and a crumb."[3]

Atlantic City, which occupied several barrier islands, had been a place of real estate booms and busts ever since its founding in 1853 by speculators who bought up beachfront lots and then sold them at a 900 percent profit when the railroad arrived. Casinos were supposed to revive the local economy after its latest bust, but they had brought more of the same speculation. A few property owners did get rich, but the big winners had anticipated the casino referendum and, in some cases, used political connections to profit. Atlantic City's mayor would go to prison after he got caught helping organized-crime figures play this game.

In some prime Atlantic City development areas entire blocks of houses were demolished, but casino projects stalled and the land became overgrown and desolate. Other neighborhoods remained downtrodden and dangerous as escalating land prices made them too expensive for anyone who might want to carry out ordinary rehabilitation or construction projects. All, it seemed, were looking to make a killing and were willing to wait until they got their price. As 20 percent of the housing stock was torn down, middle-class residents couldn't find decent homes, and the local school district was unable to afford land for a new high school. Many of the jobs in the casinos went to people who lived on the mainland and commuted. In sum, after gambling arrived, life in Atlantic City was worse for many of the people who lived there. They tended to remain in the ranks of the poor, bypassed by the rivers of cash that built the casinos, paid executives, and rewarded casino owners.[4]

In March of 1982 Trump obtained his gaming license. In May he began construction, working around the Sea Shell Guest House. The money for this work came from the same line of credit his father had helped to arrange for the Commodore project. Despite *People* magazine's having anointed him a billionaire, the state's Division of Gaming Enforcement concluded that Trump's own bank accounts held less than $400,000.[5]

The DGE report pointed to one of the key elements of Trump's business strategy. Whatever he gained in profit with successful projects such as the Hyatt or Trump Tower, he used to start new endeavors with vast amounts of additional borrowing. In the 1990s, one former Trump executive told the writer Harry Hurt III that "it was all a shell game" in which Trump shifted small amounts of cash among a number of corporate entities to qualify for loans to develop new enterprises. Lenders, especially those who had done business for years with Donald's father, felt confident based on Fred Trump's record. They also understood the Trump methods.

Donald also worked hard to acquire real estate at bargain prices. In 1985, for example, he would buy two Manhattan properties—the St. Moritz Hotel and the New York Foundling Hospital building—for a combined $114 million. Lenders mortgaged them for $134 million, and the extra $20 million was Trump's to use as he saw fit. Unlike a homeowner who buys his house with a mortgage, Trump was not personally responsible for anything that might go wrong in these deals. Donald's reputation might take a hit in the event of a big failure, but his personal assets were protected.[6]

A third Trump strategy involved recruiting deep-pocketed partners who were willing to backstop projects that he had devised and advanced through various stages of permits and development. His salesmanship and his ability to exploit his political connections, which were often cemented as he gave campaign money to candidates and incumbents, brought real value to these partnerships. Relationships were his stock-in-trade, and he knew how to convert them to profit.

In Atlantic City, where Trump lacked the kind of deep relationships that he exploited in New York, he struggled to gain his footing. With its historical connection to organized crime and exploitation of addicts, gambling was still regarded as a shady business. Donald was aware of this darker aspect of the trade and would eventually note that for "four or five percent" of his customers, overspending was a problem. "There's no question about it." Trump, who took great risks in his businesses and his personal life, drew the line when it came to wagering in a casino: "I've never gambled in my life."

Despite the profit potential inherent in a business based on legally stacked odds, traditional lenders were generally reluctant to back casino projects. For one thing, few financial experts understood the business. For another, this highly competitive industry was dependent on unpredictable fads and fashions. As Trump looked for financing, he found little support among New York lenders and began scouring the country for construction money. In Los Angeles he visited with Michael Milken. Before being imprisoned for violating securities laws, Milken was the undisputed leader of a new approach to finance that encouraged investors to accept greater risk to obtain higher interest payments on bonds that were openly described as "junk." Trump went to see Milken after he had recently sold $160 million in bonds to help Las Vegas gambling mogul Steve Wynn build the Golden Nugget in New Jersey.

Milken offered to help Trump, but the two men never came to terms. Some smaller banks came through with loans, but even when pooled together, they failed to meet Trump's needs. Then, executives with Holiday Inn came to him with a proposal to operate one of their Harrah's casinos at his Atlantic City development. Harrah's, the hotel chain's gambling arm, was already in business in Atlantic City, but at a marina location that was less desirable than Trump's spot next to the Convention Hall. Negotiations produced a proposal for a $50 million investment by Holiday Inn, which would arrange for construction financing and manage the casino after Trump built it. With no money invested, Donald would share 50 percent of any profits.

The Holiday Inn board convened in Atlantic City to check out the development site and their would-be partner. Donald arranged for extra equipment to be on-site during a tour of the property, and only one of his visitors seemed to notice that the earthmovers that were crabbing around in the sand seemed to be moving the same pile of earth from one spot to another. Trump offered enough of an explanation to avoid real concern, and by the end of the day the board members had approved the partnership.

The showmanship and schmoozing that soothed the Holiday Inn board was a perfect example of the Trump style, which depended on the goodwill that most people, even experienced businesspeople, bring to their encounters with potential partners. As social animals, human beings naturally seek agreement and depend on others to act in good faith. Most of us are so inclined toward this attitude, which includes the tendency to fill in the gaps in our understanding with benign assumptions, that magicians and con artists rely on it as they practice their deceptions. Trump had a way of talking—sharing supposed secrets, offering praise, extending sympathies—that created a synthetic form of friendship. Under these conditions, people had trouble asking hard questions. If Trump said something like "You and I know what we're talking about," they would nod and allow a conversation to continue for fear of seeming rude or stupid. In this way, he got the benefit of the doubt.

As the casino neared completion, Donald gave his wife, Ivana, much of the responsibility for the look of the interior spaces, and she devoted as much time as she could to creating an environment that would dazzle the suckers. As of early 1984 Ivana was mother to three children—Donald Jr., a daughter named Ivanka, and a newborn son named Eric—and she was busy at home. Nevertheless she made frequent trips to the casino site and picked out every bit of decoration, which she submitted to her husband for his final approval.[7]

Harrah's at Trump Plaza opened in late spring 1984, with a bar called Trumps and a restaurant called Ivana's. Technical problems plagued the slot machines for several days, depriving the partners of millions of dollars in revenues. Business was further disrupted when the fire alarms mysteriously went off "ten million times," as one of Harrah's executives told *The Wall Street Journal*. After these snafus were corrected, the place still underperformed, earning less than half the profit envisioned for the first full year. This result was especially disappointing compared with the 1984 performance of the other nine casinos in the city, which reported winning 8.4 percent more than the previous year.

The partners disagreed on the source of the problems at the casino. Trump's side thought that Harrah's managers had aimed low and alienated the high-roller clientele he wanted to attract. Harrah's managers believed they knew better than a New York developer who had never run a casino. They also felt let down when Trump failed to build a much-needed parking garage to serve gamblers who drove to Atlantic City from Philadelphia and greater New York City. One outside analyst concluded that gamblers were confused by the cobranding of the place, with the names Trump and Harrah's appearing together and separately on various signs and in advertisements. For Donald, who was keen to make the name Trump into a brand that added value to everything he might undertake, this confusion was worse than counterproductive. It was a threat to his plan for the future.[8]

Unhappy with his partners in Atlantic City, Trump approached Barron Hilton to discuss the hugely expensive and unlicensed casino Hilton had built in the marina district, almost next to Harrah's original Atlantic City location. Hilton was, in Trump's estimation, a member of "the Lucky Sperm Club. He was born wealthy and bred to be an aristocrat." Trump offered this assessment in 1987 without a hint that he realized that he himself had been lavished with attention and benefited from the small fortune invested in his private education as the chauffeured child of one of the richest men in America. Few spermatozoa ever had it better.[9]

In his first conversation with Hilton, Trump made no progress. Then Steve Wynn offered to buy 25 percent of Hilton and made noise about eventually taking control of the company. Like Trump, Wynn was a bold and aggressive businessman. One of his first big deals was to buy a lot next to Caesars Palace in Las Vegas for $1 million and quickly sell it to Caesars for $2 million. But unlike Trump, Wynn had not been born to great wealth. His parents ran bingo parlors in Maryland, and their main contribution to his success had been $25,000 in backing for his first foray in business. He also cultivated a friendly public image, which he described as "smooth and easy." Donald Trump may have been smooth, but he was not easy.[10]

With Wynn stalking his company, Barron Hilton began raising money to defend against him. Hilton couldn't know whether Wynn was actually intending to seize control of the firm or practicing a "greenmail" strategy that would lead to some kind of ransom payment that would stop his pursuit. One of the nation's most prominent lawyers, Edward Bennett Williams, likened this practice to the "protection" rackets developed by gangsters, who threaten their victims with harm if they don't fork over regular cash payments. "You know, they'll say, 'You're ripe for a takeover.' That's the way the gangsters used to do it," said Williams. Insider trading was also aided by greenmail because once the threat was made, the stock price of a targeted company invariably rose. Friends who were tipped off in advance could buy low, wait for the greenmailer to make his move, and then sell as the target company's stock reached a peak.[11]

Greenmail was just one of several tactics that were used in the go-go Reagan years by predatory capitalists. These corporate raiders, among them Carl Icahn and T. Boone Pickens, raised huge sums of money to buy shares in companies they deemed poorly managed or undervalued. If they succeeded, the debt could be shifted to the acquired company. In some cases this burden led to bankruptcy. In others, a company would be split into pieces and sold. A raider might also squeeze money out of a newly acquired firm by selling additional shares of stock. Although raiders might destroy part or all of a company, depriving workers of employment and communities of bedrock businesses, they almost always made money themselves.[12]

In the case of Hilton, financial analysts speculated that Wynn could buy the entire company and sell off everything but the gambling houses. Divested one at a time, or even in big chunks, the regular hotels might well have attracted enough money to cover the cost of the entire buyout. Wynn would thus get Hilton's casinos free of charge. He might even make substantially more than his payment for the Hilton stock. Since virtually all of the dollars involved would be borrowed, his risk would be nil. Of course, if he were successful,

Barron Hilton and other stockholders would lose control of the firm, and the properties would probably be loaded with new debt. But the extra operating costs could always be covered by squeezing employees and raising room rates. And if some once-solvent Hilton hotels failed, it would be someone else's problem.

As the man whose name marked the Hilton empire, Barron Hilton was the one most concerned about defending against Wynn's overtures. He quickly revised his views on Donald Trump, recasting him as a kind of white knight. Trump abandoned his usual buy-low policy and agreed to pay Hilton the full $320 million asking price for the Atlantic City property. Financing would eventually come through the investment firm Bear Stearns, with bonds issued at a 14 percent annual rate of interest. The property would be christened Trump Castle. To no one's surprise, Holiday Inn sued Trump for putting his name on a casino that would compete directly with the one that Harrah's was running at Trump Plaza.

Although another businessman might have been chastened by all the debt, and the Holiday Inn suit, Donald moved decisively. He paid $73 million to acquire Harrah's half of the Trump Plaza partnership, which ended both their relationship and the pending lawsuit. Trump had reason to believe he might improve things at his original casino site. Harrah's record at this location, reported quarterly by the New Jersey Casino Control Commission, had never been good. In 1985, the Trump casino had lost money while Harrah's marina location had made more than $10 million in profit. Things improved a little for the Trump facility in the first quarter in 1986, but Harrah's at the marina still outperformed it, earning almost $6 million compared with a profit of less than $1 million for the Trump operation.

With the consolidation of his position in Atlantic

City, Trump entered a new phase in his financial life. Clearly intrigued by the corporate takeover scene, he turned the tables on Holiday Inns by acquiring more than 2.5 percent of the firm's stock and then announcing the purchase. When he bought the stock, it was selling for about $62 per share, but Wall Street analysts believed that its assets, if broken up and sold, were worth perhaps as much as $100 per share. The difference could mean as much as $500 million to someone who gained control of the firm and disassembled it. Trump issued a public notice of his purchase long before he acquired so many shares that securities regulations would have required it. This, and other factors, made it unlikely that he was interested in actually acquiring the firm. "He isn't a corporate raider," explained an official at Bear Stearns.

However, the suggestion that a takeover might occur helped push Holiday Inn's stock past $71. It also led the executives at Holiday Inn to mortgage their firm for more than $2 billion. By burdening the corporation with debt, the Holiday Inn board was following a "poison pill" strategy, which wiped out much of the value that a raider might reap by a sale of the firm's many assets. Trump sold his shares and bragged that he made $35 million on the price run-up. Later, in a report he was required to make to the State of New Jersey, he noted that his actual profit was less than $13 million, which was, nevertheless, a significant sum.[13]

Trump, who later said, "The New York Stock Exchange happens to be the biggest casino in the world," next played the raider game by targeting the casino/manufacturing firm Bally's with what *The Wall Street Journal* called a "greenmailing" scheme via the purchase of 9.9 percent of the company's stock. In Bally's poison-pill defense, it purchased the Golden Nugget casino in Atlantic City for $440 million. After making

Bally's toxic to Trump's takeover attempt, the company then paid him $84 million for his shares. The deal netted him $24 million. Bally's was left with a huge amount of new debt, and Trump moved on to his next target, Resorts International, which owned the existing Resorts casino and a yet-to-be-completed Atlantic City casino called the Taj Mahal.

Resorts International's founder had died in April 1986. In March 1987 Trump matched a previous offer for the firm and pledged to complete the Atlantic City construction project. Originally estimated to cost $185 million, the projected cost of the Taj, as it was known, had ballooned to more than $500 million. As he made his move on Resorts, Trump focused on the company's Class B shares, which cost roughly four times the price of the Class A stock, but came with one hundred votes per share. The special status of the shares allowed Trump to grab 88 percent of the possible stockholder votes while paying just 12 percent of the company's value. No wonder he considered the stock market a casino.[14]

As Resorts' Class A shareholders learned of Trump's maneuvers, a few raised an alarm. His most vocal critics were outraged by his $22-per-share offer. (At this figure Trump would pay a total of $125 million to complete his takeover.) Then, just days before Trump was to complete his purchase of Resorts and make it a privately held company, Merv Griffin announced he would pay $35 for every Class A share outstanding. The two men then sued each other.

Griffin was an unlikely challenger to Trump's claim on Resorts. He was nineteen years older and known not as a businessman but as an entertainer. After more than a decade of success as a big-band singer, Griffin had hosted game shows and substituted for Jack Paar on the *Tonight* show. In 1965 his syndicated talk program—

The Merv Griffin Show—began a run that would last until 1986. Though soft-spoken, Griffin was unafraid of controversy. When young Donald Trump was still apprenticing at his father's office, Griffin was giving a platform to outspoken opponents of America's involvement in the Vietnam War. In an earnest voice he coaxed the political agitator Abbie Hoffman and the philosopher/pacifist Bertrand Russell to share views that challenged widely held assumptions about American policy. Thanks to Griffin's afternoon broadcasts, millions of homemakers and their children also got their first glimpse of social provocateurs such as Dick Gregory and George Carlin.

As the mild-mannered Griffin quietly courted controversy, he also proved himself to be an astute businessman. When he developed the concept for the game show *Jeopardy,* he made certain to retain ownership and formed a production company to control it. He followed its success with other game shows, such as *Wheel of Fortune,* which was sold as a kind of franchise to broadcasters around the world. In 1986 Griffin sold his production company for $250 million. He brought this money to the battle for Resorts International.[15]

With Donald Trump claiming to be a billionaire, Griffin's $250 million made him the little guy in the contest for Resorts. But he was more than rich enough to pay lawyers to work on the various lawsuits and securities filings that arose in the competition with Trump. As he analyzed the situation, Griffin believed that he and his competitor wanted very different things. Trump obviously coveted the Taj, as it would give him both the maximum number of casinos permitted per New Jersey state license (three) and the biggest gambling hall in Atlantic City and, perhaps, the world. Griffin, who was an entertainer by nature and not a developer, preferred the pieces of Resorts that were intact and operating, namely the existing casino on the Atlantic City boardwalk and the four hotels plus a casino in the Bahamas.

With the two men desiring different parts of Resorts, the basis for a compromise seemed quite evident. Nevertheless, Trump chose to wage both a legal battle and a war of words. He started by accusing Griffin of making a "wholly illusory" offer intended to create excitement around Resorts stock and cause a spike in its price. (This is exactly what had happened to Holiday Inn stock when Trump had announced his purchase of its stock.) When Griffin then filed official papers with the Securities and Exchange Commission to formalize his bid, Trump called the move "feeble" and "futile." Trump's language, which was obviously intended to belittle his opponent, also betrayed his frustration. Although he controlled 88 percent of the stockholder votes, the final decision on the sale rested with the company's board of directors, and he could be stalemated there if the three independent members felt obligated to accept Griffin's bid for the Class A shares. Since it was 50 percent higher than Trump's offer, they might decide, as fiduciaries, that they had no choice.

For his part, Griffin said nothing about Trump but, after reviewing a new appraisal of Resorts, raised his bid to more than $45 per share, or $295 million. Like a poker player pushing a huge stack of chips toward the center of the table, Griffin made his offer so big that it couldn't be ignored. Trump didn't react immediately, but eventually signaled that he might not be willing to match Griffin dollar for dollar. On March 26, 1988, Trump announced that he had purchased the venerable Plaza Hotel, on Fifth Avenue at Fifty-ninth Street, for a reported $407 million. As was his custom, he added to this figure when he went to his lenders, borrowing a total of

$425 million, which gave him some extra millions to play with after he paid the seller, Robert M. Bass.

Having acquired the Plaza along with the rest of the Westin Hotel chain, Bass and his partners had doubts about whether the hotel could generate a profit after servicing its $300 million debt. They recovered almost a third of what was paid for the entire Westin chain by selling one hotel to Donald Trump. His prospects at the Plaza couldn't have been any better, considering he had piled roughly $125 million in debt on top of its previous burden. However Trump quickly sold other assets to net roughly $100 million, which gave him a bit of breathing room.[16]

The Plaza gave Donald Trump far more than a hotel with French-château lines. This building was quintessentially New York. Having welcomed guests for more than eighty years, the hotel was as beloved by locals and visitors as Grand Central Terminal and the main public library, which were built in the same period. The first entry in the hotel's guest book read, "Mr. and Mrs. Alfred G. Vanderbilt and servant." Home to the fictional Eloise of the famous children's book series by Kay Thompson, the Plaza was declared to be a National Historic Landmark in 1986. The hotel has appeared as a backdrop in countless films and TV programs. The Plaza's famous Persian Room had featured performances by a range of divas as diverse as Eartha Kitt, Liza Minnelli, and Peggy Lee, and its ballroom had been the scene of Truman Capote's famous Black and White Ball of 1966.

Trump seemed cognizant of the building's significance, but he regarded it in terms that were markedly self-referential. In a paid advertisement he leaned heavily on the word *I* to trumpet the Plaza deal: "I haven't purchased a building, I have purchased a masterpiece— the *Mona Lisa*. For the first time in my life I have knowingly made a deal that was not economic—for I can never justify the price I paid, no matter how successful the Plaza becomes. What I have done, however, is give New York the opportunity to have a hotel that transcends all others! I am committed to making the Plaza New York's single great hotel, perhaps the greatest hotel in the world."[17]

In these four sentences—fewer than one hundred words—Trump framed a deal that was driven by his ambition and commercial desires as an act of civic generosity. He was giving New York "the opportunity" to, well, be the location of a luxury hotel that was already firmly planted in its soil. As carefully constructed as any of his buildings, the ad also set the conditions by which the deal might be evaluated, in a way that made Trump's defeat impossible. He had "knowingly" paid a price that did not make sense from a business perspective. However, the Plaza was the *Mona Lisa* of hotels, and therefore he was to be admired for his largesse. And if, by some chance, the Plaza proved profitable, then he had overcome stupendous odds and worked a financial miracle.

Within days of his purchase of the Plaza, Trump agreed to negotiate with his rival in the tussle over Resorts International. Forgoing the usual businessman posturing over location and ground rules, Griffin readily agreed to travel to New York and meet at Trump Tower. He arrived in the middle of a spring afternoon and was whisked by elevator to the twenty-sixth floor. Trump led him to his private office, where the windows offered a commanding view of Central Park. Trump pointed to the Plaza and reminded Griffin that he had just completed his purchase of the eight-hundred-room icon. Griffin quipped, "That's how many rooms you're going to need to house all the lawyers it will take to fight me."

As Nina Easton later recounted in the *Los Angeles*

Times, Griffin asked Trump what he wanted out of Resorts International. Trump answered that he wanted the Taj, and the steel pier that was part of the site. Griffin asked, "Is that all?" Trump answered, "Yes." In this brief moment the feud was ended and the basic outlines of an arrangement were settled. By the end of the day attorneys for the two men had hammered out the finer details of the deal over a table in the bar at the Helmsley Hotel, where Griffin was staying. According to the agreement, Griffin would take control of Resorts International, break it up, and sell to Trump the parts he wanted at an agreed-upon price. In the arrangement announced on April 15, 1988, Trump received the bonus of several helicopters that were in the Resorts portfolio. Griffin got some seaplanes—Grumman Mallards—that Resorts operated under the name Chalk's International Airlines to bring tourists to the Bahamas. (Founded in 1917, Chalk's was the oldest operating air service in the United States.)

Both Griffin and Trump believed that their names carried real weight with the public and, thus, added value to their enterprises. Griffin, known to be genial and fun-loving, had broader fame, but he was less inclined to exploit it. Trump put his last name on just about everything he touched, save the venerable Plaza. By the summer of 1988, the list included the Trump casinos in Atlantic City as well as a roster of substantial buildings in New York, including Trump Tower, Trump Plaza, and Trump Park. However, the name was beginning to signify more than just the wealth, opulence, and excitement he hoped it would evoke. It also stood for an unseemly level of self-regard and exaggeration.

Trump's reputation had suffered first in 1980, when he destroyed the Bonwit artwork, but the negative publicity was short-lived. The conflict over his plans for the fifteen-story apartment building at 100 Central Park

South went on for years, and during much of it Trump seemed to behave like a bully. One judge found that Trump had filed a "spurious and unnecessary lawsuit" in an effort to "harass" one tenant with the goal of forcing him to leave. Trump was ordered to refund part of the man's rent. In other cases Trump was found to have made attempts at "intimidation" and to have acted "in bad faith." For three years in a row, his managers had refused to allow a Christmas tree in the building's lobby. This caused the *Times* columnist Sidney H. Schanburg to brand him "Donald Humbug." *New York* magazine's Tony Schwartz would describe Trump's performance in the project as a "fugue of failure."[18]

The tenants at 100 Central Park South proved worthy adversaries for Trump. They formed an association, hired a bulldog attorney, and tied him up in legal proceedings until he resembled Gulliver at the mercy of the Lilliputians. Evidence presented at a state proceeding revealed that the managers Trump hired for the building had promised to more or less drive out the tenants within a year. As repairs and cleaning were suspended, the roof began to leak and apartment ceilings collapsed. The common areas became filthy. Lobby staff stopped accepting packages. Doormen ceased opening the door and hailing cabs. One building maintenance man testified that he had been asked to report to managers what he knew about the financial conditions and sexual habits of the people in the building. As reported by writer Wayne Barrett, Trump disputed the maintenance worker's account. Moreover, Trump's representative told the press that "the charges of harassment [were] fabrications and a well-organized attempt by the tenants to take advantage of his prominence."

Hardly powerless, the tenants went to the local media with anecdotes about the fifteen elderly women who lived in the building and the poorest residents who would be hard-pressed to find affordable apartments anywhere in Manhattan. The tenants also enjoyed help from the Koch administration, which went to court charging Trump with "egregious attempts to harass and evict without due process of law." The suit allowed the mayor, who was seeking reelection, to pose as a defender of the little-guy tenants against a developer whom Koch was happy to paint as callous and greedy. Years of fighting produced a stalemate that thwarted Trump's effort to convert the building to condominiums. The war ended when he agreed to maintain 100 Central Park South as an apartment building and make substantial renovations, while the tenants dropped all their complaints against him.[19]

For Trump, who sought to win at every turn, the 100 Central Park South episode was a remarkable setback and a public relations mess. It was even more painful as it came after another big defeat—the collapse of the United States Football League. The USFL had struggled since its inception. Trump had persuaded his fellow owners to switch from a spring/summer season to the fall, when they would compete for attention against the well-entrenched NFL and college teams. He also pushed for the league to file a lawsuit against the NFL, with charges that the older league had violated antitrust laws. The suit alleged $567 million in damages and could have produced, with punitive provisions, a $1.7 billion verdict. In the summer of 1986 a jury found the NFL *had* sought to operate an illegal monopoly but the USFL owners were not much harmed. The panel awarded the plaintiffs a symbolic $1 in damages. By then the league was defunct.[20]

In another time, Donald Trump might have been able to fashion better outcomes in these conflicts with the help of Roy Cohn, who was a remarkably inventive legal combatant. However, in 1986 Cohn was too besieged himself to help anyone else. First, he was under attack from the state bar, which had stripped him of his right to practice law. He had not exhausted his appeals, but after many close escapes Cohn appeared to be out of moves. Even worse, he had been quite ill for more than a year, and nothing doctors prescribed helped for long.

Having kept his sexual identity a secret for so long, Cohn had been unable to tell his friends that he had contracted HIV/AIDS, which had reached epidemic proportions in the New York gay community. In this era, when antigay prejudice was extremely common, many men lived such closeted lives. However, the HIV/AIDS crisis had also led many men to come out, as an act of self-determination and solidarity. At age fifty-nine Cohn remained so committed to his ruse that he even maintained his relationships with men such as Senator Jesse Helms, a racist and a homophobe who opposed research into the epidemic.

Roy Cohn fooled many people, including his friend Barbara Walters, with the claim that he had liver cancer. In moments when he felt better, he spoke with his characteristic bombast and venom. As Donald Trump took his business to other law firms, Cohn felt his former protégé had abandoned him in his hour of need. Writer Wayne Barrett reported that Cohn said, "I can't believe he's doing this to me. Donald pisses ice water."[21]

Some of Cohn's close friends never forgave Trump, believing he had abandoned the mentor who had schooled him in the ways of success. For their part, the two men reconciled in Cohn's final year. Cohn took the initiative, telephoning Trump to ask if he could provide a place to live for a former lover, Russell Eldridge, who was also dying of AIDS. According to Barrett and writer Nicholas von Hoffman, Cohn was poised to have the line disconnected if Trump asked what was ailing Cohn's sick friend. Trump did not. Instead he provided a room at the Barbizon Hotel, which he had acquired. When hotels bills were sent to Cohn, he threw them away. Eventually the hotel staff became distressed to have someone dying in their midst and calls went out to Cohn, asking him to remove Eldridge from the premises. He did not comply with their requests, which didn't seem to bother Donald. He called Cohn several times to offer him encouragement and invited him to a dinner party in Palm Beach in early March 1986. The event was held at Mar-a-Lago, the former estate of Marjorie Merriweather Post, which Trump had recently purchased. Cohn attended.

Cohn's commitment to his constructed reality was so steadfast that he maintained it even as he was obviously dying. In the spring of 1986 he spoke to Donald Trump about submitting to an interview with the fierce Mike Wallace of the TV news program *60 Minutes*. Trump would recall that he advised against it: "I said, 'Roy, don't do it,' because it was obvious that he was sick. It was obvious at that time that he had AIDS. I said, 'Don't do it, Roy. You're making a big mistake. . . . Nothing good is happening for you now.'"

Cohn sat for the interview anyway. When the program was aired, he appeared gaunt and near death as he looked at Wallace and told him, and millions of people in the *60 Minutes* audience, "I do not have AIDS." In June, when New York's highest court upheld Cohn's disbarment for conduct it found "reprehensible" and "unethical" and "unprofessional," reporters repeated the liver-cancer deception. Staff at his office said Cohn was unavailable because he was boating, but when TV reporter Gabe Pressman dialed Cohn's home number, he reached Cohn, who said of his disbarment, "I could care less."

In July, Cohn was admitted at an inpatient clinic at the National Institutes of Health outside Washington,

DC. Beds at NIH were hard to come by, especially those devoted to the care of patients with HIV/AIDS, but Roy was a good friend of President and Nancy Reagan's, and while he could no longer call in favors at City Hall, he had lots of chits in the nation's capital. Cohn's last weeks would eventually be revealed in grueling detail by the writer Nicholas von Hoffman in the book *Citizen Cohn* and by actor Al Pacino in the television version of playwright Tony Kushner's *Angels in America*. Cohn died at six o'clock in the morning on August 2, 1986. NIH officials reported the official cause of death was "cardio-pulmonary arrest" linked to "dementia" and "underlying" infections caused by AIDS.

On August 4, 1986, Donald Trump attended a private memorial service for Cohn, where those who knew him well said their good-byes. Once one of Cohn's close friends and a longtime client, Trump stayed in the back of the room and was not among the many who offered their remembrances. On that same day, *Playgirl* magazine, which enjoyed an avid readership among gay men, announced that Trump was one of the "ten sexiest men in America." The honor was noted in newspapers across the country, where editors surely delighted in the opportunity to add a dash of sexiness to the news mix. In the twelve years since *Playgirl*'s debut, *sexy* had become one of the words most frequently used by magazine headline writers, who promised readers sexy people doing sexy things in sexy places. Sexy was typically a narrow construct. With some exceptions, women were required to be young, thin, and fair. They were also supposed to present themselves as both available and unattainable. Physical appearance also mattered for men. Over the years, *Playgirl*'s lists of the sexiest men had been dominated by lean, handsome entertainers and athletes. Among those honored with Trump, not one was short and bald. However, a man who lacked the look of an Adonis could be hailed as sexy if he possessed, in abundance, the qualities most associated with a contemporary definition of success: money, fame, and social status.

In 1980s America, the men most widely regarded as successful were not team players but solo performers who either achieved something notable or gained wide notoriety. Performers of any sort—actors, artists, athletes, entertainers, even newscasters—could be sexy. Sexy too were some politicians who posed as daring iconoclasts, even if they actually played the same games as everyone else. Businessmen could qualify as sexy if they cultivated an image as extreme individualists who resembled the mythic heroes of the West.

Donald Trump circa 1986 was just modestly famous. However, by adding his name to that year's list of the "sexiest," alongside actor Bruce Willis, musician Rubén Blades, and pro athlete William Perry, *Playgirl* added greatly to his status. *People* had made him nationally known, while *Lifestyles of the Rich and Famous* had confirmed his wealth. Now he owned the third quality—sexiness—that completed the trifecta of celebrity in the media age. At age forty, this man who craved wealth and attention was also an object to be desired by everyone who was attracted to the American male. (Since a great many *Playgirl* readers were gay men, this included them too.) The power in this status was substantial. So too was the risk, especially for a man who said he loved his wife and children and craved the approval of his parents, who had each married once and remained together for their entire lives.[22]

9

LUCK RUNS OUT

Well, I loved women. But I was never a drinker. I was
never a drug guy, and I was never a cigarette guy.
—DONALD TRUMP

Like Donald Trump, Marla Maples was officially sexy. Her bona fides were established in the beauty pageant circuit, which included an event where she had almost captured the title of Miss Hawaiian Tropic International 1985. Sponsored by a tanning-lotion company, the contest required the competitors to smile brightly as they paraded in bikinis. On her pageant application Maples wrote, "I hope to become successful as a screen actress and some day do Broadway."

Some young women had found wealth, fame, and celebrity through pageants, which serve a screening function for industries that saw commercial value in young women who were approachably sexy. In the media age, the demand was great, but so was the supply. The vast number of hopefuls suppressed market values and worsened the odds of financial success, even for those who won the most coveted pageant titles. Countless Shirley Cothrans (Miss America) and Christiane Fichtners (Miss USA) captured crowns and little else. Contestants also had to consider the possible pitfalls associated with pageants in the era of media excess. Vanessa Williams, Miss America 1984, was forced to resign when photos of her nude, which were made before she won the pageant, were published in *Penthouse* magazine. In time, the public would become almost inured to this kind of incident, as nude photos of celebrities were published with such frequency that it seemed as if every young woman in America had chosen, at one time or another, to be photographed or filmed in the altogether and no one could be trusted to keep these images private.

Williams, Cothran, and Fichtner provided cautionary examples, but dreamers could always focus on Lee Meriwether, who went from Miss America 1955 to a career in television and film, and Bess Myerson, who had won the same tiara in 1945 and became a successful celebrity who helped make Ed Koch mayor of New York. Marla Maples had them in mind as she competed in her last pageant and made plans to move to New York City. Although she had been an honors student in high school and was doing well at the University of Georgia, she left before completing her degree. She had been to the city just once before, with her parents. The family had stayed at the Waldorf-Astoria.[1]

In Manhattan, Maples would be fortunate to find an inexpensive apartment, which she decorated with images of that icon of tragic beauty Marilyn Monroe. Like Monroe, Maples's power resided in the kind of wholesome sexiness that one writer would say made her "a 13-year-old boy's ideal woman. Pretty and sexy, yet safe, somehow. The centerfold next door."

Although this kind of allure conferred some power, Maples found it could also be dangerous, especially when less-than-mature men regarded her as an object they might control. From a young age Maples seemed to attract men who became possessive and even obsessed. Her very first romantic relationship was with a handsome and engaging young man who could behave in frightening ways. Once, a disagreement led to a shove, and then Maples's hand went through a glass table top. She went to the hospital for stitches. Years later she would say she wished she had learned more from this incident, but at the time she was quite naïve and all-too trusting

As she poured herself into her career Maples attended auditions and casting calls and took acting classes at HB Studios where many prominent performers—Jason Robards, Al Pacino, Barbra Streisand, Anne Bancroft, Robert De Niro—had learned the craft. She accepted some requests for dates but in a city filled with appealing men she was selective. In August 1985 she was introduced to Donald Trump, by Jerry Argovitz, who had been a Hawaiian Tropic pageant judge. He took her to Trump's office where she appreciated the view of Central Park and admired the framed magazine covers on the wall. In the months to come Maples would run into Trump at a tennis tournament and on the sidewalk on Madison Avenue. She also saw him at a charity event she attended with Argovitz.

Although Argovitz and Maples saw each other off and on, no romance developed between them. Amid casting calls and meetings with agents, she met a former police officer named Thomas Fitzsimmons, who was trying to become an actor and writer and had a project that might include a part for her. Though an aspiring star Fitzsimmons was mainly a security man for the rich and famous. Licensed to carry a gun, he carried it often. After Maples was mugged she appreciated his toughness and the way he made her feel safe. He often accompanied her when she went out, saying she needed to be protected. The two became romantically involved.

Well-muscled and ruggedly handsome, Fitzsimmons had the physical attributes to match his ambitions. His pet project was a film script—called *Blue Gemini*—which was about twin brothers who were officers in the New York Police Department. Instead of just pitching his script to producers and directors, Fitzsimmons decided to create a few minutes of film, which would serve as a sample, or "trailer," to show potential backers. Fitzsimmons relied on friends to serve as cast and crew for his trailer. Marla Maples got an on-camera role. A veteran New York press agent named Chuck Jones served as unpaid publicist.

A Marine Corps veteran who had worked as a combat reporter in Vietnam, Jones had come to New York after being discharged. He landed with an industrial paper called *FilmTV Daily*. When the paper went out of business in 1970, Jones used his experience and many contacts to become a press agent. Representing entertainers such as Lionel Hampton and Jack Lemmon, Jones arranged for interviews and kept reporters and gossip columnists supplied with items that reflected well on his clients. Jones was so well connected to photographers, writers, and editors, who felt indebted because of the access he provided, that he could almost guarantee a client favorable treatment in the New York media. Much like politicians and donors, these journalists played a continuous game, trading tips and favors without keeping score in any serious way. It was enough that everyone except the public was in on the action and eager to keep things going.

Outgoing and reliable, Jones had developed so many credits in various favor banks that he often used them to help friends who couldn't pay his fees. When Tom Fitzsimmons asked him to help with *Blue Gemini,* Jones was able to get him attention. The tabloid press reported on the film shoot as if it were a feature-length movie beginning production in the city. Other than providing him a moment of excitement, the publicity didn't do much for Fitzsimmons, whose script never found backers. Marla Maples, however, discovered in Jones someone who seemed eager to help her advance her career.

◆

At the time when he met Marla Maples, Donald Trump's fame was approaching a peak, thanks in part to a tussle with Mayor Koch over the ice-skating rink in Central Park. Named for the Wollman family, which had donated the funds to establish it, the rink had opened in 1949 and operated every winter until it was closed in 1980 for rehabilitation work that was supposed to be finished in 1982. The job had been complicated when city officials decided the rink should double as a pond in the summer and should employ a new type of refrigeration technology using Freon gas. More difficult to install than an old-fashioned brine-based system, a Freon setup would be less expensive to operate and was expected to save taxpayers money over the long run. But problems plagued the project and the rink remained closed. In May of 1986 Trump wrote Koch a letter in which he offered to rescue the mayor from "the greatest embarrassment" of his administration by building and then operating the rink. The mayor released the letter to the press along with his own letter, which accepted Trump's offer to build the rink but declined his request to run it because the city intended to keep admission fees low. Koch concluded snidely, "With bated breath, I await your reply."

Koch considered Trump's "Dear Ed" letter to be excessively self-promoting, especially the part that noted Trump's own accomplishments and promised to finish the job before winter. Koch thought New Yorkers would agree. However, the mayor miscalculated. Editorial writers at three local papers said that Trump was right. Koch wound up giving Trump what he asked for, and the developer relied on HRH Construction to fulfill his promise with the help of no-interest financing from his friends at Chase Manhattan Bank. Managers at HRH would say that they renovated the rink at cost because

Trump promised the firm a great deal of work in the event that he got to develop the old Penn Central rail yards on the Upper West Side, which he still controlled.

Trump would claim that he found a Canadian company, Cimco, to design the rink, but the firm had been brought into the picture well before he wrote to the mayor. Trump added a bit of insult to Koch's injury by hiring a city official named Tony Gliedman to oversee the rink. Gliedman had been the housing commissioner who opposed the tax abatement for Trump Tower. During that disagreement, Gliedman reported that Trump had threatened and berated him. Now, as his employee, Gliedman made Trump look good, shepherding the rink renovation to completion sooner than expected.[2]

As Gliedman showed, Trump had an eye for talent and was happy to recruit people who had shown their abilities by opposing him. Inside his organization they were paid well and enjoyed a level of autonomy equal to the pressure he placed on them. Success depended, at least in part, upon showing dedication and toughness the boss could respect. As Louise Sunshine told Harry Berkowitz of the *Washington Post*, "He finds talented people, and he brings out the best in them and also the worst. You become very single-minded. All the rest of your life falls away. He totally absorbs you."[3]

Although many New Yorkers gave Donald Trump credit for the renovation of Wollman Rink, Mayor Koch rejected his request to have the facility named in his honor. This decision was, in part, the product of the terrible relationship between these two men. In his memoir, *Citizen Koch,* the mayor called Trump a "blowhard" and a "supreme egotistical lightweight." The feelings were mutual. Evaluating the mayor many years later, Trump said that Koch was "a cheerleader his first term. After that he became a very angry man. He had many scandals and much corruption. Ed Koch was a highly overrated mayor, and his last term was a disaster, and he left a very angry person."

The spectacle that was Trump versus Koch was an almost-endless source of entertainment for newspaper readers in New York. They were well-matched when it came to ego. Trump desired to reshape the city's skyline and make his name a widely recognized emblem of success and power. Koch was one of only three mayors in city history to be elected to three full terms and so craved the public's approval that he habitually shouted to people on the street, "How'm I doin'?" Both men loved the gamesmanship of politics, but as a private businessman Trump was not accountable to the public. Koch was expected to meet a certain standard of decorum, which made him more vulnerable to public opinion. When Koch called Trump a "lightweight," Trump, true to his punch-back-harder style, declared the mayor "a piece of garbage."[4]

As he fought with Trump, Koch suffered repeated scandals as officials in his administration were either subjected to criminal charges or forced to resign after abusing their offices. The scandals were so numerous that when the City Hall press corps held its annual charity roast, the musical program was titled *Greedlock,* a play on the term *gridlock.* In one of the more biting numbers, a reporter who played the mayor sang, "I'm not indicted! And I'm so delighted!"[5]

The most famous of Koch's fallen allies was Bess Myerson, who was indicted for attempting to influence a judge by hiring her daughter. Myerson would eventually be acquitted at trial, but the scandal was just one indicator of the decay in the Koch administration. Donald Trump would make much of the mayor's problems, and in a book he wrote he called attention to the sins of individuals such as Myerson. Conspicuously absent

from Trump's litany, however, was ...
who was convicted and imprisoned for ...
back scheme at the city's parking bur...
was, of course, Roy Cohn's law partner and ...
furiously in the last days of the Beame regin... ...nal-
ize the sweet deal Trump got when he turned the old
Commodore into the Grand Hyatt. Friedman's relationship with Trump was raised at his trial by federal prosecutor Rudolph Giuliani, himself a future mayor.[6]

Trump, Cohn, Koch, Giuliani: these were men so
ever present in city affairs one could be forgiven for
thinking that New York was like a small town where the
same few people held sway over all local business, finance, development, and politics. This was hardly true.
Among developers, Trump was just one of many who
were putting up grand new projects in Manhattan. The
Cohn law practice was overshadowed by dozens of
bigger and more powerful legal firms. And a host of
political figures often bested the likes of Giuliani and
Koch. However, in the competition for the public's attention, no one surpassed Trump. In 1987 alone, his name
appeared in the local papers more than a thousand
times. Radio and TV programs added to his fame, and
then there was the book.

In the summer of 1987, Random House prepared to
publish *Trump: The Art of the Deal,* which he produced
with such considerable aid from the professional writer
Tony Schwartz that Trump gave his collaborator credit
on the cover. The title reflected Trump's belief that clever
negotiation, in the pursuit of profit, should be recognized
as a creative endeavor equivalent to the efforts of a
painter or a poet. The "deal," as he put it, involved per-
suading someone to sell him a property, hiring the right
architect to design a new development, obtaining government approvals, and then contracting with the builder
who would make the thing real. If this was art, then it

, a kind of performance art that depended on his ability to manipulate, schmooze, and cajole. It was also, by implication, a talent that millions of other people could also claim. The salesperson who got you to add rustproofing to your order for a new car or the waiter who talked you into purchasing an appetizer were practicing the art of the deal. Granted, their art would not benefit others in the way that a great artist's may, but it *was* a kind of creativity.

Knowing the book would require massive amounts of publicity to satisfy his desire for sales, Trump planned to exploit his many contacts in the press, especially those at various TV networks. He also raised his own profile by dabbling in politics. In early July he met with Roger Stone, a longtime friend of Roy Cohn's, to discuss Stone's proposal for a challenge to New York Governor Mario Cuomo. Stone, who worked in the shadowy corners of right-wing politics, got his start in the Nixon campaign of 1972. In that race he made campaign contributions to GOP representative Pete McCloskey under the false name "Jason Rainier" and the "Young Socialist Alliance." McCloskey was challenging Nixon in the New Hampshire primary. Stone alerted the press to the donation as proof that McCloskey was linked to the wrong kind of supporters. In 1987 Trump wasn't interested in running for office, but he did like Stone's proposal for an "open letter" kind of newspaper ad to attract attention.[7]

In early September, Trump spent more than $90,000 to purchase full-page advertisements in *The Times, The Boston Globe,* and *The Washington Post*. The headline of the ad announced, "There's nothing wrong with America's Foreign Defense policy that a little backbone can't cure." In the text, which was addressed "To the American people," Trump questioned America's defense commitments in Europe and Asia and argued that the United States "should stop paying to defend countries that can afford to defend themselves." He added, "Make Japan, Saudi Arabia and others pay for the protection we extend as allies. Let's help our farmers, our sick, our homeless . . . " His closing was a rallying call: "Let's not let our great country be laughed at anymore." Trump did not speak to the first reporters who phoned after the ad appeared, but then he changed his mind. He told them that he had no intention of running for office but had paid to spread his message because "I'm tired of watching the United States get ripped off by other countries."[8]

Considering that Trump's criticism constituted an attack on their beloved Ronald Reagan, the ad would have drawn howls of protest if Republican partisans believed Trump were a serious political figure. None did, and so none responded. His comments did spur press attention worth far more than $90,000 to someone about to publish a book. After the ads ran, newspapers across the country published items about the flamboyant New York businessman's political interests. Then Trump's executive assistant, Norma Foerderer, received a phone call from Michael Dunbar, a Republican activist in Portsmouth, New Hampshire. He said he wanted to meet "Mr. Trump" to talk politics.

Home to the first party primaries in the nation, New Hampshire played such an outsize role in presidential politics that a minor figure such as Michael Dunbar wielded remarkable influence. Days after he made his phone inquiry, Dunbar was at Trump Tower, where he was pleased to discover that his favorite noncandidate "didn't treat me like I was a rube from New Hampshire at all." Although he forgot to ask if Trump might want to run for president, Dunbar went back to the Granite State and ordered some new stationery with *Draft Trump* printed in red at the top. He collected donations and went to the leaders of the local Rotary Club to propose they invite his man to speak. They agreed and arranged to have him visit before Thanksgiving.[9]

Trump flew to New Hampshire in October, landing in his black helicopter at an airstrip in the seaside town of Hampton. Dunbar was waiting with a rented limousine, which sped north on US Route 1 to a roadside restaurant called Yoken's. Marked by a kitschy neon sign depicting a spouting whale and the words *Thar she blows!,* Yoken's provided the space and the food for the Rotary Club's regular meetings. Hundreds of Rotarians and their friends packed the place along with several reporters. More than one would describe Trump's forty-minute performance as more comedy than policy. President Reagan's budget deficit should be addressed through a kind of tax levied on the nation's allies, he said. "We're being ripped off and decimated by many foreign nations who are supposedly our allies. Why can't we have a share of their money? I don't mean you demand it. But I tell you what, folks, we can ask in such a way that they're going to give it to us—if the right person's asking." America's trade imbalance with Japan should be approached with a tougher negotiating stance, continued Trump. "The Japanese, when they negotiate with us, they have long faces. But when the negotiations are over, it is my belief—I've never seen this—they laugh like hell."

Without rimshots from a drummer, some of Trump's lines missed their mark, but he kept on delivering them. The White House needed a tough guy, he said, because the world was filled with difficult adversaries. "You think [Soviet leader Mikhail] Gorbachev is tough? Think of this character Khomeini," he said of Ayatollah Ruhollah Khomeini of Iran. "I mean this son of a bitch is something like nobody's ever seen. He makes

Gorbachev look like a baby. And Gorbachev is one tough cookie." Then Trump turned sober, even a bit apocalyptic, adding, "If the right man doesn't get into office, you're going to see a catastrophe in this country in the next four years like you're never going to believe, and then you'll be begging for the right man." The crowd greeted Trump enthusiastically. One woman told a *New York Times* reporter that he possessed the "aphrodisiac" that is power. Another noted that he had drawn a far bigger crowd than real politicians, including Senator Robert Dole and Congressman Jack Kemp.[10]

Anyone who listened closely would have concluded that Trump was not a real candidate. "I'm not here because I'm running for president," he said. "I'm here because I'm tired of our country being kicked around and I want to get my ideas across." He was also there, at the Portsmouth Rotary Club meeting, to give a camera crew from the ABC TV program *20/20* something exciting to film. (The title of the program referred to perfect eyesight, not insight, and the program was known for offering little more than glimpses into the lives of its celebrity subjects.) Weeks later *20/20* host Barbara Walters, who moved in Trump's social circle, gave him the Judy Klemesrud treatment before a national audience of about a million people. Her narration began, "Look, up in the sky! It's a bird! It's a plane! No, it's superbuilder Donald Trump's ten-million-dollar French Aérospatiale helicopter, heading for the Sixtieth Street heliport to pick up the brash forty-one-year-old billionaire businessman and whisk us off to check up on part of his ever-expanding empire."[11]

Walters's homage, which was titled "The Man Who Has Everything," was wealth pornography that titillated viewers with images of valuable real estate and a cooing narration that explained that "the Trumps are treated like American royalty" wherever they go. The display of the family's gilded lifestyle was an advertisement for a man who was becoming a human brand. His residences, yacht, aircraft, and limousines were billboards that urged people to buy whatever he was selling, from swanky apartments to hardcover books, and join him in luxury. Though he often said he related best to "the construction workers and the cab rivers," Trump understood what Barbara Walters meant by "American royalty." The country may have been founded in rebellion against the crown, but the people still needed princes and princesses, kings and queens, if only for aspirational entertainment. In the United States, where money had replaced inherited titles as the pathway to aristocracy, everyday citizens could thrill to the possibility that they might grow rich and join the elite. This hope made it easier for people to admire Trump, even when he said obnoxious things. He was, by virtue of his money, entitled, and anyone who achieved as much would be entitled too.

Entitled American royals possessed no power to govern directly, but their wealth allowed them to buy the lawyers, lobbyists, politicians, and other functionaries who would help them impose their will on others. They also enjoyed the attention of various courtiers, who fluffed their egos with a chorus of assent. In Trump's case, many of the most important voices of support emanated from the mass media, and they often assured readers, listeners, and viewers that they could have faith in the superior qualities of leading executives, entrepreneurs, and investors. This superiority justified the growing gap between the super-rich and everyone else.

The distraction provided by reports on the lifestyles of the rich and famous helped divert attention from how the middle class as it was known in the fifties and sixties was rapidly disappearing. Stabilized for thirty years, income inequality began to increase sharply in 1980 as

ABOVE: Always an aspiring showman, Fred Trump wielded an ax as bathing beauties posed in the bucket of an earth-mover at the site of his development in Coney Island. *(Charles Frattini/NY Daily News Archive via Getty Images)*

RIGHT: As he sought to create the image of a dashing young man about town, Donald Trump acquired a Cadillac and outfitted it with vanity plates bearing his initials. *Chester Higgins Jr./The New York Times/Redux*

Trump's first mentor, other than his father, was the notorious lawyer Roy Cohn who got his start as counsel to the pugnacious, red-baiting Senator Joseph McCarthy. *Ron Galella, Ltd./WireImage/Getty Images*

Trump's first wife, Ivana, is mother to his three eldest children, Donald Jr., Ivanka, and Eric. © *Norman Parkinson Ltd./ Courtesy Norman Parkinson Archive/Corbis*

Donald and Ivana pose with the staff at the famous Mar-a-Lago estate in Palm Beach. *Ted Thai/ The* LIFE *Picture Collection/ Getty Images*

As Trump's first book, *Trump: The Art of the Deal*, was published, Barbara Walters, shown here aboard the mogul's helicopter, presented him to a national TV audience. *© ABC/Courtesy: Everett Collection*

Fred and Donald together at the *Art of the Deal* book party.
Ron Galella/ WireImage /Getty Images

Marla Maples was a contestant
in swimsuit beauty contests
who came to New York to seek
fortune and fame as an actress
and model. *Liaison/ Getty Images*

After Donald Trump's affair with Marla Maples became known, New York gossip columnist Liz Smith, shown here with Ivana after luncheon, helped make her a symbol of a woman who had been wronged.
Ron Galella, Ltd./ WireImage

Satirists, comedians, and cartoonists have long had a field day with Trump controversies. Here he gets the *Bloom County* treatment from Berkeley Breathed.

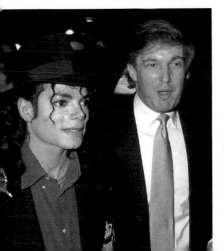

Michael Jackson kept an apartment in Trump Tower and appeared here with Trump at his Taj Mahal casino in Atlantic City.
Photo by Ron Galella/WireImage / Getty Images

ABOVE: In early 2004 Trump was guest host on *Saturday Night Live*. He joined members of the cast in a mock advertisement for Donald Trump's House of Wings.
Mary Ellen Matthews/ © April 3, 2004 NBCUniversal/Getty Images

MIDDLE: Among the many Trump products sold over the years is a doll that can, with the pull of a string, repeat catch phrases coined by the man himself.
Spencer Platt/Getty Images

LEFT: Trump's third wife is the former Melania Knauss, a Slovenian-born model who is twenty-four years younger than her husband. *AP Photo/ Stuart Ramson*

Trump's grown children, Donald Jr., Eric, and Ivanka, work in his businesses.
© *Michael Filonow/ Corbis Outline*

Michael Forbes, who battled Trump's golf course development near Aberdeen, was named Top Scot in a 2012 vote by his countrymen. *Jeff J Mitchell/Getty Images*

ABOVE: After dabbling in politics for years, Trump finally took the leap, announcing he would seek the 2016 Republican nomination for president. *James Messerschmidt/Polaris/Newscom*

RIGHT: Trump's candidacy was greeted with derision by his hometown paper, the *Daily News*. *NY Daily News via Getty Images*

the richest Americans seized more of the wealth generated by the economy and workers barely kept up with inflation. Tax rates levied on capital gains from investments were slashed, and salaries of chief executive officers in American corporations rose from forty-two times the average worker's pay in 1980 to a multiple of eighty-five in 1990. In the same decade the ranks of American billionaires would increase from about a dozen to almost one hundred. The number of Americans with fortunes greater than $100 million more than tripled, to twelve hundred. For these richest Americans, investments in stocks, bonds, and high-end real estate, Trump's specialty, were the surest source of wealth. In New York, where Wall Street millionaires competed with the global rich to buy choice apartments, prices rose and Trump reaped the profits.[12]

A mere millionaire, Barbara Walters was nevertheless a media queen who wielded the imprimatur of ABC News as she asked Trump, in all apparent seriousness, "If you could be appointed president, and you didn't have to run, would you like to be president?" He coyly replied that to be appointed leader of the free world might not be so appealing because he would be deprived of the satisfaction of winning an election. He concluded, "It's the hunt that I believe I love."

The 20/20 profile presented was aired on the day Trump's book went on sale. The timing was no doubt arranged as a condition of Walter's access to her glamorous subject. Other networks presumably sought this "get," as exclusive interviews were called, but Walters enjoyed real advantages in such competitions. The daughter of a showbiz impresario, her stock-in-trade was the personality profile that offered a view of the famous that was mostly celebration. She might get a subject to cry with a deft play to emotion, but as a shrewd player in the celebrity economy, she was unlikely to expose too much of the people she interviewed. No sense in risking future valuable access.

Four days after the *20/20* program aired, Phil Donahue presented Trump to the millions who watched his afternoon TV talk show. One viewer, in Saddle River, New Jersey, was so impressed by what she saw that she made sure to mention Trump's performance to her husband. A week later he signed a typed note, which was dispatched directly to Trump Tower:

> Dear Donald
> I did not see the program, but Mrs. Nixon told me you were Great on the Donahue show.
> As you can imagine, she is an expert on politics and she predicts that whenever you decide to run for office you will be a winner!
> With warm regards,
>
> > Sincerely
> > RMN[13]

When it was reviewed, the Trump book was generally found to be readable and charming. Framed as a "week in the life" story, it was also, in the words of Christopher Lehmann-Haupt, "a display of the author's not inconsiderable ego." In its pages Trump pointed to the personal qualities that had allowed him to become wealthy beyond anyone's dreams, and he portrayed himself as a deal-maker without equal. He even tried to sell his readers on the notion that money wasn't important to him. "I don't do it for the money" was the opening line of the text. "I've got enough, much more than I'll ever need." It was an implausible, if not impossible, claim. But as Lehmann-Haupt would also note, in most of the book Trump managed to blow his own horn without sounding too many sour notes. Yes, he bragged, but he also copped to many of his flaws (he selected the ones that were essentially harmless) and charmed with heartfelt passages about his family and business associates. The result was, the reviewer noted, "like a fairy tale," but also a book that entertained and inspired.

Trump: The Art of the Deal would spend months on various bestseller lists and reveal its putative author as a champion promoter. In the book he wrote, "A little hyperbole never hurts. I call it truthful hyperbole. It's an innocent form of exaggeration and a very effective form of promotion." In his effort to sell his memoir Trump's hype included so many exaggerated claims that tracking them was almost impossible. But he did not have to hype the party he threw for himself at Trump Tower. Thousands of people streamed through the lobby of the building as twenty violinists played and boxing promoter Don King, clad in a floor-length mink, repeatedly shouted, as Donald and Ivana circulated, "Here's the king and the queen!" In his remarks Trump was generous in praising his publisher and his collaborator, Tony Schwartz, and in pledging his royalties to charity. Schwartz said he would hold on to his share.

Schwartz and Trump represented the top end of an emerging genre of professionally aided autobiographies. Begun with auto executive Lee Iacocca's 1984 bestseller, *Iacocca,* these books were of limited value to the public record and rarely offered much insight. Of his work for Trump, Schwartz would say, "There was nothing I wrote that on its face was false. But there's a lot open to interpretation." This was a kind way to describe the mythmaking in a book that reiterated the claim that Ivana Trump was an Olympic skier and inflated the cost of saving the Bonwit Teller friezes, which Trump had chosen to destroy, to hundreds of thousands of dollars. But like society-page reporters, reviewers are not fact-checkers, and celebrity memoirs are not intended to present unvarnished truth, but a glossy version of reality. This is best done with carefully crafted revelations about flaws and foibles that are either inconsequential or have been overcome.

Missing from the personal revelations in the *Art of the Deal* was any indication that Donald Trump was vulnerable to the allure of beautiful women, though he truly was. Eventually he would admit this weakness, and to the trouble it caused him. But he wouldn't have to correct anything he wrote about his family attachments. Trump was a genuinely loving father who often conducted business while his children played on the floor of his office. He also valued the stability of marriage as it was represented in his parents' lives. As Fred Trump had demonstrated the workings of power to his son, he had also shown him that the support of a wife and family—through illness, loss, achievements, and scandals—was essential to his success.[14]

◆

Almost unnoticed in the crush of people at the Trump book party were Tom Fitzsimmons and Marla Maples, who attended at the insistence of her publicist Chuck Jones. In his version of the story, he did his best to introduce Maples to people who might help her find work as an actress and even took her to California for the Daytime Emmy Awards show, where the people in soap operas, talk programs, and game shows competed for recognition. He hoped she might attract some attention and, perhaps, some work. He also pressured her to attend the book event and a party celebrating the reopening of the famous Rainbow Room five floors below the top of the RCA Building at Rockefeller Center.[15]

Closed for two years while restorers worked on everything from the floor to the colored lights, the Rainbow Room had been a cherished part of New York since it opened in 1934 as a supper-and-dancing club for the rich. Over the years it had evolved from a formal and exclusive setting where Astors might bump into Roosevelts, into a place where anybody who could pay was welcomed. The guest list for the party that marked the reopening reflected the shifting social scene. The great doyenne Brooke Astor was in attendance, but so were many whose celebrity came as the result of their talents as politicians, entertainers, and businesspeople. As the party buzzed, Mayor Koch lectured the wandering cigarette sellers, who were dressed in pink pillbox hats, on the evils of smoking. Leona Helmsley gazed out the window and asked, "How do you like my husband's buildings?" Donald Trump swanned into the room with Ivana at his side, scanned the renovated space, and said, to no one in particular, "Nice job."[16]

Standing to the side of the stage, where Lionel Hampton conducted his orchestra, Jones and Maples eyed the crowd. Jones took notice when the Trumps entered and made sure that Maples noticed too. (Later she would wonder if Jones hoped she would give him access to Trump.) The scene was an elegant blur of men in tuxedos and women in gowns. At a long buffet table the guests selected from boneless quail on watercress, scallops in their shells, and striped bass with lobster mousse.

As Maples would recall it, Trump's longtime aide Norma Foerderer telephoned her after the Rainbow Room event to say that her boss, a married man with three children, was inviting her to lunch at the St. Regis Hotel. After several more phone calls, she accepted. The date was set for December 19.

Lunch lasted five hours. In that time Maples and Trump would discuss, among other topics, his business, his family, her family, and their views on religion. Although she felt as comfortable as if she were sitting with a longtime friend, Maples continued to call him

"Mr. Trump." He introduced her to people who happened by their table and, in the most important part of their conversation, insisted that his marriage was all but over.

In time, much of America would study the details of Donald Trump's romantic life, thanks to the tabloid press. But Maples would say their long lunch at the St. Regis marked a moment when her relationship with Trump was entirely private and not well defined. She said that she had told him she would not enter into a relationship with a man whose marriage might be saved. According to Maples, he replied that a divorce was inevitable. In fact, a couple of years would pass before Donald and Ivana's relationship would end. The pages of Maples' datebook, which Jones took and copied, include a note that declares, "I don't want to be only something that keeps the boredom away!"

Considering the frenzied quality of Donald Trump's activities, it would be difficult to imagine the man was ever bored. While he operated high-profile commercial buildings and hotels, he was also laboring to develop new projects. In addition, he was having trouble digesting the deals he had made to acquire the Taj Mahal and the Plaza Hotel, where he had put Ivana in charge. Nevertheless, he soon began to pursue the purchase of Eastern Airline's shuttle, which linked New York City to both Washington and Boston. He was keenly interested in the shuttle's cash flow, which would be substantial considering that many flights were packed full of travelers paying the maximum walk-up fare.

After years of losses—the deficit was more than $180 million in 1987—in the airline's overall operations, which spanned the nation and included routes to the Caribbean and South America, Eastern's managers needed cash. The one part of the company that made money, the shuttle possessed valuable gates at three busy airports, where airlines had great difficulty adding flights because of the lack of spaces to dock more arriving planes. Although he knew so little about airlines that he had considered his deceased brother's work as a pilot comparable to driving a bus, Trump did see that the gates were like coveted bits of real estate. LaGuardia, Logan, and National Airports were unlikely to build any more of them, so their value would only increase over time.

Negotiating directly with Frank Lorenzo, the chief of the holding company that owned Eastern, Trump quickly accepted that the price for the shuttle would be in excess of $300 million. The price, and the prospect of her husband's managing an airline in addition to his other businesses, bothered Ivana Trump. She had noticed that her husband was having trouble sleeping at night and couldn't imagine how he would handle the additional burden. Ivana was also concerned that profits from the Trump gambling operations, which she helped to manage, were going to be wasted on the purchase. But as she raised her concerns, the negotiations went forward, and the deal was eventually completed for $365 million.

When his purchase was announced at a press conference at the Plaza Hotel, Trump also revealed that he would call the service the Trump Shuttle. Soon all the planes were painted with the name TRUMP in gold, and the interiors were outfitted with wood veneers, leather seats, and gold-colored restroom fixtures. All of this was done with portions of $380 million in debt ($365 for the Eastern assets, $15 million to revamp the equipment), which was arranged by Citibank and then divided among some twenty banks. To cover the obligation, let alone generate positive cash flow, Trump would need to

capture at least 60 percent of the Boston–New York–
Washington business, which meant thrashing the rival
Pan Am shuttle.[17]

◆

With an airline, casinos, real estate, and hotels,
Donald Trump had no need for distractions, but
he continued to have one in Marla Maples. He also saw
certain elements of the press turn against him in ways
that would have wounded almost anyone. A new magazine called *Spy,* which was founded by Graydon Carter,
Thomas Phillips, and Kurt Andersen, targeted him regularly. *Spy* was comparable to Tom Wolfe's landmark
novel *Bonfire of the Vanities* in the way that it skewered
New York society and the financial elite. Wolfe's book
viewed the greed and narcissism of the age with an unblinking eye. Its main character was a wealthy, self-
described "Master of the Universe" who could have
been modeled after Donald Trump. For its part, *Spy* was
a monthly accounting of the poseurs, the pretenders, and
the naked emperors of 1980s New York.

In early 1988, the editors of *Spy* commissioned an article about Ivana Trump, which prompted a letter from
Trump attorneys who threatened "rapid and major" litigation in the event of an inaccurate or defamatory piece.
In October 1988, the magazine's Joe Queenan made
Donald Trump one of several case studies in a column
that asked, "Why do good things happen to bad people?" Seeking answers, Queenan phoned Rabbi Harold
Kushner, author of *When Bad Things Happen to Good
People,* who said that Trump was either an honest, driven
businessman or an "evil person" who will "trip himself up at some point." On the following page readers
were treated to a photo essay titled "The Unglamor-
ous World of Mr. Trump."

In response to *Spy* and later articles that Carter published in other magazines, Trump took to attaching the word *sleazebag* to Graydon Carter's name every time he uttered it. He also told gossip columnist Liz Smith of the *Daily News* that he believed the magazine was in financial trouble. Smith reported to her readers that she had chided the "handsome mogul, of whom I am very fond," for speaking ill of others. In the circular way that comments can become newsworthy when they relate to the press, *Spy*'s editors then recycled the item in their own pages. Thus, idle chatter at a party became fodder for public consumption in not one publication but two. This was the risk anyone takes with the press. A stray comment gets published, then republished, and pretty soon you find yourself in a conflict with people who use ink by the barrel.

Trump was not afraid to splash some ink around when he thought the moment demanded it. He had happily invested in the big print ads that announced his purchase of the Plaza and his views on foreign policy. He was so skilled at obtaining free publicity that he could command press attention almost at will. In early 1989 journalists from *Time* spent hours with him to produce a cover story that was filled with cringe-worthy quotes from the man himself. Writer Otto Friedrich began with Trump's claim that Britain's Queen Elizabeth, who was last in America in 1983, asked to use his helicopter when she "is over in this country" because it is the safest to fly. Trump further asserted, "No one has done more in New York than me," and that the Eastern shuttle was "the single greatest franchise in the world."

Along with his more outlandish claims, Trump offered pithy explanations for his business success and explained how his approach to real estate differed from his father's: "It's much easier to sell an apartment to Johnny Carson or Steven Spielberg for four million dollars than it is to collect a couple of dollars of rent in

Brooklyn." (He didn't mention that Carson had recently sold his apartment and was angry that he had lost money on his investment.)[18]

Friedrich quoted Trump as he confessed that he possessed something like a con man's talent for persuasion. "I can sit down with the most sophisticated people in the arts in New York and get along fabulously with them. If I want to, I can convince them that I know as much about something as they do, and I don't." Asked how he managed this trick, Trump said, "It's a feeling, an aura that you create." In another bit of reflection Trump revealed himself to be defended even against self-evaluation: "When you start studying yourself too deeply, you start seeing things that maybe you don't want to see. And if there's a rhyme and reason, people can figure you out, and once they can figure you out, you're in big trouble."

Born in Boston and educated at Harvard, the *Time* writer Friedrich was a New Englander with an old-fashioned moral sense that obviously guided his consideration of Donald Trump. His profile included a complaint from a designer who said Trump took two years to pay his fees and an anecdote from Der Scutt about an awful display of temper. As he recalled it, Trump ruined his expensive shoes when he kicked a chair across a conference room after being informed that a project was behind schedule. "He always has to have his way," said Scutt. Friedrich concluded that Trump could become his generation's Howard Hughes, "living alone in a single room."

The Hughes reference may have stung Trump (even though he admired the reclusive billionaire), but it did not deflect him from the overarching project of his lifetime—the construction of his public image. In a subsequent interview with the *Chicago Tribune,* he and Ivana offered a version of him that was warmer and more sympathetic. "He's the people's billionaire," she insisted. He confessed, "I have a feeling of guilt about my living so well. I don't need three hundred rooms. I'm not even interested in boats." But even as he strained to strike a populist note, the man who demanded and won tens of millions of dollars in tax breaks had to complain about the rent-control program that made it possible for thousands of less-than-rich people to live in Manhattan: "The rent-control laws are incorrect, and the big losers are the people of New York, because the city is getting such a tiny tax revenue."[19]

In April 1989, Trump saw another opportunity to speak his mind when a young woman who was white and an investment banker was raped and beaten until she became unconscious while out for a jog in Central Park. As media reports shocked the city and the victim struggled for survival, police mounted an intense investigation that ended with the apprehension of five black youths between the ages of fourteen and sixteen who were then interrogated for many hours. The five implicated themselves, but would later recant, saying they had been pressured into making false statements. Editorial writers at the tabloid *Post* urged readers to "channel your outrage" by demanding lawmakers reinstate the death penalty. Donald Trump bought full-page advertisements in the city's four big daily papers to proclaim, BRING BACK THE DEATH PENALTY. BRING BACK OUR POLICE!

Although he avoided naming the accused in the jogger case, Trump's reference to "roving bands of wild criminals" left no doubt about why he had paid for the ads. Newspaper accounts had described "wolf pack" gangs marauding in the park. (The press reported, erroneously, that the slang term for this kind of spree was *wilding*.) Trump also took a swipe at his nemesis Mayor Koch, who had said that New Yorkers should not indulge in hatred and rancor as they considered the attack. "I don't think so," wrote Trump. "I want to hate these muggers and murderers. They should be forced to suffer and when they kill they should be executed for their crimes."

Not one of the accused was linked to DNA evidence discovered by investigators, but all five would be convicted and begin their prison terms in less than eighteen months. The crime would remain one of the most notorious in generations. Trump's expression of outrage, which echoed the feelings of many, would reinforce his status as a figure who occupied a unique place in the public arena. His instincts were populist and generally conservative. With the exception of his frequent references to his own Ivy League education, he almost always favored a stubbornly anti-intellectual type of common sense that played to the grievances of the kind of white men represented by the TV character Archie Bunker, who, like Trump, came from Queens and offered his opinions with chin-jutting pride.

Donald displayed his inner Archie in the summer of 1989 when he told TV interviewer Bryant Gumbel, "A well-educated black has a tremendous advantage over a well-educated white in terms of the job market. I've said on one occasion, even about myself, if I were starting off today, I would love to be a well-educated black because I believe they have an actual advantage." In the universe of "well-educated black" men, some *had* gained from affirmative action programs, but only the most superficial view of the landscape would lead someone to agree with Trump. On the program, filmmaker Spike Lee called Trump's statement "garbage" because it reeked of racial ignorance. But it sounded like tell-it-like-it-is honesty to many who would insist that they were decent people who were not at all racist because, like Archie, they could be respectful to all sorts of individual people. To them, Trump and his wealth—which was supposedly the product of bold entrepreneurial effort and not book learning—represented what was good about America, and they welcomed his frank talk.[20]

The Trump approach was consistent with a long tradition of divisive and extreme rhetoric in American politics. Trump's provocative statements invariably attracted the attention of the news media, especially the tabloid press, where his style was tailor-made for headline writers. Of course, on rare occasions Trump would have preferred to be left alone. One of those arose when *Spy* finally produced its article about Ivana. The magazine's cover that month featured a more-or-less life-size photo of her cropped to show her eyes, nose, teeth, and painted lips in a garish light. Though factually accurate, the article was by turns mocking, hilarious, and cruel. It was illustrated with images of Ivana as a Barbie doll and filled with damning anecdotes and quotes. ("She would scream at the top of her lungs and really lose her temper big-time," said one source.) Writer Jonathan Van Meter also dissected the distortions in accounts of Ivana's past and asserted she was as ambitious and controlling as her husband.[21]

Spy's withering portrait of Ivana hit the newsstands at a moment when both she and her husband were especially vulnerable. So many rumors of infidelity swirled around Donald Trump, who made no secret of his interest in beautiful women, that one gossip columnist published a barely veiled hint about his relationship with Marla Maples. When Ivana's friends suggested her husband was betraying her, she turned them away. After he complained about her appearance, she flew to the West Coast for plastic surgery. She returned looking younger, but so surgically altered that she was almost unrecognizable. For Donald, the stress at home was substantial, but it was one of many problems of his own making. As he acquired the Eastern shuttle and devoted extra millions to give it the gilded Trump brand, he also added expensive upgrades to the Taj Mahal, which he had wrested from Merv Griffin at a cost of more than $270 million. To pay for the pricey construction of the casino, Trump turned to Merrill Lynch to sell $675 million in junk bonds. The high interest rate on the bonds would further burden the casino operation.[22]

With so much of his corporate borrowing done at high rates of interest, Trump needed everything to go right, especially with his airline and his giant new casino. Under Eastern, the shuttle routes were profitable. However Trump had burdened the operation with so much debt in acquiring it, he had to do better than the previous owner. With upgraded airplanes, better service, and splashy promotions, he did attract more passengers than Eastern, but he failed to break even in revenue.

As the airline racked up losses, Trump faced self-inflicted problems at the Taj construction site, where upgrades that he ordered helped push the cost of the project past $1 billion. The casino became a mishmash of minarets, striped domes, and flashing signs. The entrance was guarded by life-size statues of Indian elephants. Inside awaited more than one hundred gaming tables and three thousand slot machines. Given his debt-driven operating costs, Trump needed these tables and one-armed bandits to produce more than $1 million per day. The odds of this happening were not good.

Long before the Taj was even finished, an industry analyst named Marvin Roffman had warned that Atlantic City already had too many gambling halls and revenues were not keeping up with inflation. Seven of the city's twelve casinos lost money in 1988. The troubles continued in 1989, with Merv Griffin putting Resorts International into bankruptcy and the Atlantic casino closing. Atlantic City's mayor and more than a dozen of his associates were arrested on corruption charges. Unemployment and blight continued to plague most of the city as outsiders took most of the casino jobs and profits were delivered to distant investors. "Atlantic City used to be a dump," Roffman told the *Los Angeles Times*. "Now it's a dump with casinos." Six months later Roffman would describe the whole Atlantic City gambling business as a "house of cards."

Roffman spoke as the local casino operators reeled from the effects of a fatal helicopter crash that killed three of the top executives in the Trump gambling empire. Stephen F. Hyde, Mark Estess, and Jonathan Benanav had been in Manhattan on business and were returning to Atlantic City. Witnesses said that the helicopter's tail rotor broke off before the copter plunged into woods along the Garden State Parkway. The pilot, Robert Kent, and copilot, Lawrence Diener, also died. As chief operating officer for all of Trump's gambling businesses, "Hyde was the most important ingredient in Donald Trump's success in Atlantic City," said Roffman. Hyde's death, devastating to family, friends, and colleagues, was also a loss for the companies he served. No one else in the organization could match his experience, or talent.[23]

Within the Trump organization talk circulated of possible sabotage, which seemed plausible to those who knew that the boss received the occasional death threat. John O'Donnell, another Trump casino executive, would report this concern and take issue with Trump's claim that he had considered taking the flight but changed his mind. In O'Donnell's tell-all book—titled *Trumped!*—he also recounted the effort made to prevent a face-to-face meeting of Marla Maples and Ivana Trump when they attended the funeral services. Maples had become a regular presence at the Trump casino hotels and often showed up with friends or family. O'Donnell would describe her as a charming woman who became accustomed to first-class treatment. In his telling, many Trump employees were aware of her status, but she and Donald would take pains to avoid flaunting their relationship. They did not sit together at shows, and when he left her messages, he told desk clerks to tell Marla that "the Baron" had called.

With turmoil in his personal life and the loss of three key executives, Trump was more embattled than ever. Investors rendered their verdict on the condition of his Taj Mahal casino, pushing the value of its bonds down by 70 percent. Trump could take some comfort in that this downgrade was, at least in part, a reflection of a larger market trend. Nearly all the undersecured, high-interest junk bonds issued in the go-go 1980s dropped in value during this time. This included the debt issued in takeover actions such as the Kohlberg Kravis Roberts acquisition of RJR Nabisco for $25 billion. The enormous RJR Nabisco deal, accomplished with just $15 million of the buyers' own cash, became the iconic example of a practice that allowed financial engineers to earn hundreds of millions of dollars by loading debt onto a company before selling its parts. It was all a matter of paperwork, accomplished in KKR's case by a firm with just eighty-five employees and twenty partners. KKR's owners, who were relatively anonymous, made vastly more money than world-famous actors, athletes, and artists. "Henry Kravis would make $400 Million! Without lifting anything heavy!" wrote financial journalist Adam Smith.[24]

In dollar terms, Donald Trump's bonds represented a tiny fraction of the vast pool of junk-bond debt that frightened many investment experts, but he had made himself such a visible figure that reporters invariably threw him into their stories about troubled companies. Similarly, when they considered Trump, they quoted

Marvin Roffman, who was the man to call for critical analysis of gambling in Atlantic City.

Roffman was so respected on Wall Street that Donald Trump sought to win him over. He invited the analyst to come to Atlantic City for a tour, to be conducted by his brother Robert. But on the day Roffman arrived, Neil Barsky of *The Wall Street Journal* published an article in which financial analyst Kaye Handley predicted, "Somebody will probably lose money on the Taj Mahal, but it might not be Donald Trump." Roffman's quote in the same article was more biting and more specific: "When this property opens, [Mr. Trump] will have had so much free publicity he will break every record in the books in April, June and July. But once the cold winds blow from October to February, it won't make it. The market just isn't there."

With his words preceding him, Roffman encountered an infuriated Robert Trump at the door of the Taj. In a burst of temper, Robert shouted, "You're no fucking good," and barred Roffman from the property. Coming from the more reserved Robert, this angry display revealed the pressure that accompanied the debut of the Taj at a moment when the Atlantic City casino market was going sour. It was also consistent with Donald Trump's way of speaking when he was unhappy, and it suggested a family trait that may have been handed down by their tough-talking father. Donald Trump saw a world inhabited by winners and losers, allies and enemies. When displeased, he would indulge in tirades spiced with expletives. Employees, rivals, critics, and associates would become, in his words, "stupid," "dumb," "losers," or "wimps."[25]

On the day when his brother kept Roffman away from the Taj, Donald Trump wrote to the analyst's employer, Janney Montgomery Scott, to say, "I am now planning to institute a major lawsuit against your firm unless Mr. Roffman makes a major public apology or is dismissed." The letter began one of the strangest episodes in the annals of finance. Roffman's boss curtailed his duties, demanded the return of a bonus, and then asked Trump for input on the wording of an apology. Roffman then signed a letter that said, among other things, "Unquestionably, the Taj's opening will be the grandest and most successful the city has ever seen." Immediately regretting his decision, Roffman sent another letter stating, "I retract the [previous] letter and direct that you not use it for any purpose." When he went to work the next day, he was dismissed.

With securities firms laying off thousands of employees amid a market downturn, Roffman's employment prospects were dim, and he felt besieged as Trump criticized him in the press. Trump described Roffman as "a mediocre man with no talent" and even claimed to have intervened to save Roffman's job when his bosses considered dismissing him months earlier. Incensed, Roffman said, "He's a liar." Clearly David to Trump's Goliath, Roffman enjoyed a few moments as a cause célèbre as financial industry watchdogs sided with him. But it would take nearly a year for him to win his arbitration case against his employer and receive a $750,000 judgment. His suit against Trump would take even longer to resolve and resulted in a confidential settlement.[26]

Amid the furor over Trump's battle with Marvin Roffman, the Taj Mahal opened in April 1990 with a smiling Donald Trump touching a magic lamp like the one of Arabian (not Indian) legend to prompt a light show and fireworks display. The most famous celebrity guest at the gala was, ironically enough, Merv Griffin. As Marvin Roffman had predicted, the Taj did well and then it did poorly. *Forbes* cut its estimate of Trump's worth to $500 million and speculated that his businesses were losing $3 million every month. Although Trump argued with the *Forbes* account, it was affirmed in an independent audit, which said that if he sold his assets in an orderly way, he might net half a billion dollars. In an immediate fire sale, the report added, he could wind up almost $300 million in the hole.

The raw numbers explained why construction contractors were complaining about unpaid bills totaling more than $30 million. Trump said they were attempting to overcharge him. When Neil Barsky came to interview him for *The Wall Street Journal,* Trump made a show out of displaying a collection of Barksy's articles and complained that he was spreading rumors about Trump's cash-flow problems. He threatened to sue. Then he confirmed that he was intending to sell the Trump Shuttle.

On June 4, Barsky published a stunning report on Trump's debt problems, layoffs at the Taj Mahal and Trump Shuttle, and his failed attempts to raise cash through the sale of properties or refinancing. (One offer, which lenders rejected, included stakes in the Grant Hyatt and the Plaza.) Barsky noted that much of the trouble stemmed from lenders' having accepted Trump's assertion that by adding his name to a casino, hotel, or airline he could raise its inherent value. This wasn't true for the shuttle, which had lost $85 million under the Trump name, and it wasn't true of the Taj, which was also losing money. Many of his possessions, including a yacht called the *Trump Princess* and a Boeing 727, had also declined in value. Publicly Trump disputed bankers who said his net worth might be zero. Privately he admitted they were right, telling Marla as they passed a homeless man on the street that the poor fellow enjoyed a higher net worth than his own. He would later make much of the fact that Marla supported him during this time.

The anxieties Trump shared in private were not

shared in public. Instead, he expressed great confidence in his abilities and shifted blame to others. He criticized the casino executives who had perished in the helicopter crash, blaming them for much of his troubles in Atlantic City. While one source told *The Times,* "People are hiding under their desks," to avoid becoming Trump's targets, he insisted that his team was functioning well: "People want to work for me. Trump does well with management." The same article noted that he had promptly fired a casino executive who was hospitalized for exhaustion after the chaotic opening of the gambling floor at the Taj Mahal.[27]

Trump's detractors savored his struggles. *Late Show* host David Letterman made Trump the subject of the his nightly, satirical Top 10 list, which was titled "Top Ten Signs That Trump Is in Trouble." Among the "signs" was that Trump had "asked his advisers how they thought a 'battling billionaire' character would go over on the pro wrestling circuit." After years of drama and stress, John O'Donnell would leave Trump's employ in 1990. When the onetime president of the Trump Plaza Hotel published his tell-all book about his former boss, he presented a picture of an imperious and possibly prejudiced man who seemed indifferent to others. In *Trumped!,* O'Donnell wrote that his former boss had said, "I've got black accountants at Trump Castle and at Trump Plaza. Black guys counting my money! I hate it. The only kind of people I want counting my money are short guys that wear yarmulkes every day." O'Donnell also reported on a race horse named Alibi, which Trump had promised to purchase and rename D. J. Trump. Impatient for an account of Alibi's performance, Trump supposedly pressured trainers to run him even though they were worried he might have caught a virus. The horse ran and, as the trainer feared, got sick. Veterinarians had to amputate Alibi's front hooves to save his life. The hooves would grow back, but Alibi, whose bloodline included the famous Native Dancer, would never be fit to race. According to O'Donnell, when the weeping trainer called with the sad news, the purchase was canceled.

Drawn from his years spent working for the man, many of O'Donnell's anecdotes about Trump were repeated in the press. O'Donnell admitted that Trump considered him a "disgruntled former employee." When interviewed by Mark Bowden for *Playboy* after the book came out, Trump called O'Donnell "a fucking loser." He said that he had only met with him a handful of times, but also allowed that "The stuff O'Donnell wrote about me is probably true."

Although Trump would say that O'Donnell "needs the money, so he uses my name to sell some books," in fact the former head of Trump Plaza landed a top job with Merv Griffin Resorts. (In his first year as chief operating officer, O'Donnell would help the Resorts Casino Hotel achieve the greatest revenue gains in Atlantic City) During this time Trump lost other key personnel at his casino. In New York his chief counsel and his leading real estate sales executive resigned. He would also lose his chief financial adviser, engineer Barbara Res, and Tony Gliedman, who had been instrumental in the Central Park skating-rink project.[28]

◆

The Taj Mahal went bankrupt in January 1991. Under an agreement with creditors Trump gave up a substantial portion of the casino's ownership, but he would be allowed to net a bit more than $1 million per year in exchange for leaving his name on the building. Soon he would give up control of the Trump Shuttle to his lender, Citibank. The planes would be operated by USAir, which showed no interest in keeping the Trump name. According to the arrangement made between the bank and the airline, USAir would be permitted to top any bid for the shuttle when it came up for sale. The airline would purchase the operation in its entirety in 1997.

As USAir relieved him of responsibility for the shuttle, Trump and his lenders, including dozens of banks, undertook complex negotiations to salvage what they could from his companies and avoid bankruptcy court. This course only made sense to those who knew that under US bankruptcy laws a debtor who owed billions was a greater threat to his lenders than they were to him. If Trump used the courts, he could tie up his assets for years and escape most, if not all, of the debt. If his creditors stayed in business with him, they stood a chance of receiving more of what they were owed, while avoiding the enormous legal fees that accompany such bankruptcy cases. This reality exasperated some of those who held Trump casino bonds. In one creditors' conference call, bondholder Randolph Goodman challenged the idea that the courts would leave Trump in charge of a bankrupted casino: "We would be stuck with the worst guy in town?" The answer came from a lawyer who worked for all the bondholders: "If it were possible to throw the bums out on the basis of their past performance, the standard in bankruptcy would be the immediate appointment of a trustee. But in virtually every case that goes to bankruptcy court, management is left in place."[29]

Trump grasped the power in his position after the lender who held the mortgage on his yacht not only accepted that Trump had stopped making payments, but took responsibility for the vessel's upkeep and insurance, at a cost of $500,000 per month. In time Trump was able to reduce his obligations by $750 million and hold on to many of his properties, including the West

Side rail yards and Mar-a-Lago. Others had used the peculiar dynamics of bankruptcy to similar effect, preserving substantial fortunes while escaping the stigma of personal bankruptcy, but few considered it a great accomplishment. Ever the showman, and an optimist, Trump saw in this outcome a public relations advantage. "If I had filed a personal bankruptcy, I don't feel that my comeback story would have been nearly as good a story," Trump said. "It would have been always a tarnished story."

Spinning the tale like a gifted advertising man, Trump said that bankers "love me because I'm good and I'm honest," and "through cooperation rather than conflict, everybody has come out much better." This assessment was true from the perspective of the various bank officers. They had been paid well as they approved Trump's borrowing and would remain well employed because Trump would be responsible if things didn't work out. One former member of Trump's executive team told writer Harry Hurt, "We had all these assets but we never had any money in hand. That's why we had to keep doing more deals." The deals, which typically included extra money for operating or upgrading a new property, provided the cash fuel that kept the juggernaut rolling.[30]

Not everyone felt so sanguine. Lawrence Lambert, speaking for the investors who held Trump bonds, said, "I think it's morally reprehensible what he gets away with." No one spoke for the millions of depositors and stockholders whose investments in various banks were diminished by the losses these firms accepted to square their accounts with Trump. Likewise, no one could place a value on the loss of public confidence caused by the spectacle of a tycoon walking away from obligations totaling more than half a billion dollars when ordinary American householders were ruined because they couldn't repay consumer debts of a few thousand dollars. In time, the phenomenon that spared Trump would be understood by the general public as "too big to fail." However many ordinary Americans would forever be puzzled when lenders gave troubled borrowers more money.

Less opaque, thanks to Neil Barsky of *The Wall Street Journal,* was the maneuver Trump used to avoid defaulting on the bonds floated to support another of his casinos, Trump Castle. As Barsky reported in January 1991, Fred Trump had sent an attorney to the casino with a $3.5 million check, which was used to purchase gambling chips that were never used. Essentially a loan, from father to son, the money inflated the Castle's balance sheet and helped the casino make its bond payment. Truly clever, this arrangement meant that the senior Trump could get back his money at any moment by simply redeeming the chips. None of his son's other creditors could do the same.[31]

As Donald Trump's creditors accepted losses, advanced him new loans, and permitted him to keep substantial assets, he escaped the humiliation of personal bankruptcy and put himself in a position to continue the deal-making game. However, he could not evade the shame that accompanied the slow-motion destruction of his marriage, which began when Jerry Argovitz brought Marla Maples to his office. Out of his first encounters with her—on the sidewalk, at the Rainbow Room, at the book party—he developed a relationship that doomed Donald Trump's marriage and revealed the dreadful side of the business of celebrity.

◆

Despite the rumors and the direct questions from friends such as the *Post*'s gossip columnist Cindy Adams, Ivana Trump had worked to keep her family together. For his part, Donald Trump vacillated between discretion and loose talk. While he relied on "the Baron" to hide his calls to Marla, he couldn't help but brag about her beauty to those he wanted to impress. At age twenty-four, Marla was fourteen years younger than Ivana, the mother of three children who, while still beautiful, was approaching her forties and had endured all the stress of accompanying her husband through more than a decade of striving. Marla regarded Donald as the "king" his father had said he would be, and she was enchanted by all that she encountered in his realm. She did not dwell on the possibility that her dream could become a nightmare.

The incident that led to the cascade of scandal depended on such a mundane intervention—Ivana picked up an extension to listen to her husband on the phone—that Hollywood writers have abandoned it as a device to drive their plots. Ivana acted as a worried spouse, not as a character in a script. She heard a male voice on the call noting, in the crudest terms, that "Marla" was sexy. When the call ended, Ivana confronted her husband. He told her that Marla was a woman who had been pursuing him for two years, but he was not involved with her.

This tense exchange occurred in the lovely setting of a recently opened luxury hotel called the Little Nell, in Aspen, Colorado. The Trumps had arrived two days after Christmas, when Aspen was crawling with celebrities. (Among those who regularly spent time there were the actor Jack Nicholson, the singer Prince, and the ubiquitous Barbara Walters.) In the winter of 1989–90 the locals were debating a possible ban on the wearing of fur, which had been proposed by animal rights activists. The transient rich were engaged in their usual party-hopping, posing for the paparazzi, and displaying their elegant skiwear.

Two days after the telephone incident, Ivana confronted Marla at a slope-side lunch spot. As later reported in print, Ivana had noticed Marla and realized she was the woman mentioned in the phone call she had heard. According to *People* magazine, she said, "You bitch, leave my husband alone," and then chased after her husband, who had put on his skis and taken off down the mountain. The magazine reported, "Fascinated observers swear they saw her whip in front of Donald and then ski backwards down the slopes, wagging her finger in his face."

The confluence of events that brought Ivana, Donald, and Marla together in that moment was so remarkable that it would appear to have been planned. Marla would marvel at the many witnesses, including journalists, who happened to be present during the episode on the mountainside, which she thought was quite unusual and wondered if she was set up. She said nothing of this at the time. She also said nothing about the ring, a sign of commitment, that Donald had already given her.

Donald tried to smooth things over with Ivana, but the weeks that followed the incident in Aspen were strained. It didn't help that when he appeared in an article in the March issue of *Playboy* magazine—which was published in early February—he refused to answer when interviewer Glenn Plaskin asked, "What is marriage to you? Is it monogamous?" In the same question-and-answer session Trump observed that every successful person, including Mother Teresa and Jesus Christ, was driven by ego. "Far greater egos than you will ever understand." He also acknowledged his publicity seeking: "The show is Trump, and it is sold-out performances everywhere."

Trump's ego, which depended on status and the attention of others, made it all but impossible for him to let go of a beautiful woman such as Marla who expressed so much interest in him. His makeup also made it difficult for him to recognize his vulnerability. He decided to travel to Tokyo to see heavyweight boxer Mike Tyson fight Buster Douglas and, perhaps, to sell some real estate to wealthy locals who presumably didn't know or didn't care that he had used Japanese businessmen as straw men in his speech before the Portsmouth Rotary Club. As Trump departed, Ivana spoke to the *Daily News* columnist Liz Smith about her marriage. Having heard many rumors about Donald and gotten wind of Ivana's run-in with Marla in Aspen, Smith was not entirely surprised. (In 1988 the *Post* had reported that Marla was involved with "one of New York's biggest business tycoons, a married man." The paper subsequently reported that Maples "supposedly goes around to all the stores in Trump Tower saying, 'Charge it to Donald.' ") Nevertheless, Smith was disappointed by what she heard from Ivana. Donald had always been, in Smith's mind, a rambunctious boy whose sins could be forgiven because he was good at heart. Her article, "Love on the Rocks," appeared in the Sunday, February 11, edition of the *Daily News*. It announced that the Trumps were separating and touched off a media frenzy that surprised even the man who collected newspaper clippings by the hundreds.

In the torrent of reports that followed the Liz Smith icebreaker, reporters rehashed all the rumors about actresses, models, and socialites Donald Trump supposedly knew in the carnal sense and speculated that he and Ivana were locked in a conflict over her work as manager of the Plaza. In the nation's most competitive press market, the Trump breakup was irresistible to editors. Smith and the *News* generally stood by Ivana, while the competing *Post,* and its columnist Cindy Adams, gave a little more leeway to Donald and painted his wife as eager to fleece her husband in divorce proceedings. Generally more down-market, the *Post* was also the first to name Marla Maples and publish her photo.

Feeling as if she had been caught in a publicity meat grinder, Marla lodged protests with various reporters but they seemed uninterested in what she had to say and inured to her anguish. At the same time, Ivana Trump transformed herself from a symbol of aggressive ambition into the ultimate example of the middle-aged woman wronged by a her husband. Finally Maples escaped the city, and the press, for the Hamptons and then Guatemala where she stayed with a friend who was in the Peace Corps. Her former boyfriend Tom Fitzsimmons was hounded by reporters and, he later said, he turned down a six figure offer to tell all he knew to a national tabloid. Marla's family in Georgia was hounded by reporters who, at various points, hid in ditches near their homes and walked into their kitchens. One media company even put a $1,000 reward in the *Dalton (Ga.) Daily Citizen,* the newspaper in Maples's hometown, for any information locals might share. Many came forward, including some who didn't know her at all.

On Valentine's Day, photographers and TV news crews, tipped off by an item in Liz Smith's column, crowded the sidewalk in front of La Grenouille, the posh Manhattan restaurant, as Ivana arrived for a long-planned lunch. For two hours, Ivana and a dozen women who were friends and family dined on lamb chops and shared conversation that occasionally brought tears to Ivana's eyes. Among the attendees were her mother-in-law, two sisters in-law, and Georgette Mosbacher, whose husband was the US secretary of commerce. When the meal was finished, Liz Smith and Barbara Walters, would escort Ivana from the restaurant to her waiting car. "Take him for all he's worth!" shouted one onlooker as the photographers jostled for position. Another yelled, "Get the money!"[33]

In time Hillary Clinton would widely be regarded as the most wronged woman in America, but in February 1990, Ivana attracted such enormous sympathy that *Spy* magazine's portrait of her as temperamental, self-interested, and materialistic was all but erased. In its stead appeared the image of a woman who had supported her husband, even when others found him insufferable, and had been terribly wronged. She won the publicity war because her husband was painted as a cad, and because Liz Smith was the best ally anyone could hope to recruit in a battle of headlines.

Born in 1923, Smith had been raised in Fort Worth, Texas, where she learned about glamour at the Tivoli movie house, which was flanked by a hamburger joint playfully named Rockyfellers. Captivated by celluloid glimpses of glamour, she arrived in New York in 1949 as a "stage-struck out of towner" and found work as a writer at a movie fan magazine called *Modern Screen.* By 1990 she was one of the most powerful gossip columnists in the country, but she retained her out-of-towner charm, which no doubt felt reassuring to many of the people she interviewed. Her kindness showed when she declined to use tidbits that would harm those she considered innocent. On television Smith's engaging smile and warm Texas accent inspired trust and confidence. She was the friend, sister, or aunt you could rely on.

The *Post*'s Cindy Adams, in contrast, was more like the mean girls everyone knew in high school. When offered a quip about how Donald feared that Ivana would become like Leona Helmsley, who had recently been convicted of tax fraud, Adams printed it. Cindy became Donald's conduit to the public and a sympathetic ear.

Although he was taken aback by the level of press attention his marriage troubles received, he remained faithful to his belief in the value of publicity and would tell *Newsweek* that the scandal had been "great for business." Though his father complained that "it's going to give me a stroke," Donald fed fuel to the tabloid fire and contributed to the speculation about dalliances with beautiful, famous women. He even told a reporter for the *News* that his wife still loved him. "Ivana doesn't want the money," he insisted. "She wants Donald." (Trump often referred to himself by name, a nickname such as The Trumpster, or by his own initials—DT—as if he were reporting on the activities of a separate person.)[34]

The storm in the press reached its howling worst when the front page of the *Post* screamed, "Marla Boast to Pals About Donald: 'Best Sex I've Ever Had.'" The source for the story was a woman who claimed to have attended an acting class with Maples. A distressed Marla insisted the anonymous claim was false, and Chuck Jones, who became her spokesman during the scandal, would refute it. However nothing they said would save her acting career, which was being destroyed by the negative publicity. *Playboy* came with an offer of $2 million for her to pose nude, which she rejected. Maples also refused to lend her name to a brand of lingerie called The Other Woman but finally did agree to endorse a brand of jeans called No Excuses. The company's previous high-profile model had been Donna Rice, who was the "other woman" in the scandal that ended presidential candidate Gary Hart's political career. Maples would receive $500,000 and use half that sum to help her family financially and she required the company to match her donations to an environmental advocacy group. Later Maples would note that her charity work was mostly ignored by the press and she cringed at the memory of a TV commercial that was "sad and laughable because they focused on my body in the jeans and spoke over my speech about the environment."

The No Excuses ad helped sell millions of dollars' worth of jeans and confirmed the commercial power of tabloid fame. In the weeks when the scandal blazed hottest, that a woman who looked like Marla Maples found Donald Trump attractive confirmed that he possessed true sex appeal. Maples had the kind of wholesome, youthful good looks that Trump and most American men preferred. He definitely favored her over the gaunt and overly decorated women of high society, whom writer Tom Wolfe had dubbed "social X-Rays."

In the most trenchant published analysis of the whole affair, *New York* magazine writer John Taylor reviewed the roles played by each of the participants. Taylor and his sources described Donald Trump as a remarkably buoyant man who could delight in headlines that would have made others distraught. In Taylor's view Trump may have resented Ivana's visibility and chafed at the restrictions imposed by his marriage vows. Although Taylor quoted Trump's kind words for his wife, and his pledge to "always treat Ivana great," these statements could not be accepted at face value because they came from a man who publicly justified his use of "truthful hyperbole."

The Ivana Trump whom Taylor revealed sought and enjoyed the acceptance of high society, which her husband disdained, while striving to please him even to the point of undergoing plastic surgery. Her suffering was the suffering of every woman who approached midlife only to be thrown over by her husband for a younger woman. Her pain was exacerbated by a media circus that found even President George H. W. Bush using her marriage as a punch line. "I am here in New York where one of the great contests of 1990 will take place," joked the president at a campaign rally. "But I'm not here to talk about the Trumps!" Ivana also had to endure nastiness from those who saw an opportunity to settle scores. Alfred Winklmayr, who had momentarily been married to Ivana when she sought to leave Czechoslovakia, surfaced to sell his story to a tabloid. He snidely commented, "I can't help but think she's finally getting what's coming to her."

In Taylor's reporting, Marla Maples represented all the interlopers who possess the power that comes with beauty. She clearly served Donald Trump's ego, and given his beliefs about publicity, she aided his bottom line. But based on the account in *New York* magazine, it was difficult to imagine things working out well for her. Sources quoted by Taylor insisted that Marla was not sufficiently "classy" (whatever that meant) to hold Trump's interest, and Donald seemed so certain that as a woman aged a man might be justified in looking elsewhere that Maples had good reason to fear the clock and the calendar.

Marla dreaded dealing with the press, which, in its Murdochian form, had a voracious appetite for scandal. This was new in American journalism. For generations journalists had ignored the sexual transgressions of major public figures under a sort of gentleman's agreement. The Gary Hart–Donna Rice scandal of 1987 ended this agreement and announced a new era in which salacious stories, expressed at sufficient volume, would find their way into mainstream media. Journalists would say this new practice revealed truths that should not be hidden and served some public purpose. This Taylor dismissed as a fig leaf that couldn't obscure the real value of the story, which was the entertainment of the masses.[35]

As a married couple's breakup became entertainment, the Trump children paid a price. Aged six, eight, and twelve, they had not asked for the life in the spotlight that their father and mother had cultivated. Their parents did try to shield them, but they could not put the children in a protective bubble. Ivana confessed to Liz Smith that her daughter and son were "wrecks." She said that Donny had confronted his father with real anger, shouting, "You just love your money!" Ivanka had been crying, and Eric feared his mother would be exiled. Decades later, middle child Ivanka would readily recall how she felt when a classmate brought a tabloid to her school and how snide remarks circulated among her classmates. The Internet would forever be populated by accounts of her parents' troubles.

The Trump kids were on Liz Smith's mind when she paused in the midst of the blitz to say she regretted the fire she had started. "I want to let this go," she told an interviewer from *The New York Times*. "But I have my bosses, two sets, editors at the newspaper and producers at the television station. They want this to go on." The story was so big that it was picked up by the very untabloid *Washington Post*. As the international press began to report on the ongoing drama, it became clear that reconciliation would not be possible. Ivana's lawyer hired a team of investigators to document his client's contribution to the Trump fortune. Donald briefly barred his estranged wife from her office at the Plaza.[36]

The war of the Trumps continued for months, with the two sides trading leaks to the press. In one moment the *Post* reported that Donald was rejecting Marla for good. In another the *News* revealed that she had stayed at Trump Tower for almost six weeks. Ivana's first legal move involved a challenge to the nuptial agreement that supposedly governed their divorce. The legal papers she filed quoted her husband's praise, in his book, for all her work on his various projects. They also said that when she signed the agreement, in 1987, Donald intended to betray her. She followed the lawsuit with a cover story in *Vanity Fair*, complete with glamorous photos of her at Mar-a-Lago, and several public appearances where she seemed to be enjoying her independence. Donald briefly retreated from public view while his lenders worked out the agreement that would allow him to escape personal bankruptcy in exchange for accepting temporary supervision of most of his financial affairs.[37]

Confronted with Ivana's demands, Trump hired a divorce lawyer named Jay Goldberg who had described himself as a "killer" who could "rip the skin off a body." As Goldberg and Ivana's lawyer Michael Kennedy dueled with subpoenas, Donald began to appear in public with Marla Maples and introduced her to his parents. When *Vanity Fair* offered Marla the opportunity to be photographed for the November issue, she agreed. After she was dressed and posed with her hair and makeup arranged just-so, the result was a series of pictures that resembled those of Ivana published in the magazine's May issue. As any subscriber may have noticed, the spreads invited snide, side-by-side comparisons of the two women. Although Marla was a willing participant, she regretted the decision when she saw the result, which practically screamed "this is the other woman."[38]

Given the game she had joined, Marla didn't engender much public sympathy as she explained that Ivana "wants a billion, but we just don't have it." In fact, Donald Trump did not have anywhere near $1 billion to give his soon-to-be-ex-wife. He would insist he couldn't pay her more than $1.5 million, let alone the many millions called for in their nuptial contract. When Ivana told the court she believed that her husband had been involved with other women, he reminded her that the most recent nuptial agreement, completed in 1987, did not require his "continuing love and affection." Their previous agreements had included this term.[39]

When a judge finally granted Ivana Trump's petition

for divorce on the grounds of "cruel and inhuman treatment," she mentioned Marla Maples by name. In the negotiations for the financial settlement Ivana's lawyers concluded that once various loans and obligations were considered, he may not have been worth more than $100 million. Ivana accepted a $10 million check upfront plus $650,000 a year in support for herself and the three Trump children. Thirteen months had passed since Liz Smith announced the crisis in the marriage. In that time, Donald had been dealt a crushing defeat in Atlantic City, and his supposed great fortune had been revealed to be an illusion.

Years later Trump would explain, "Learning how to win is a very important thing. Very few people understand how to win, very few people." But just as winning begat winning, defeats could cascade. "You can be tough and ruthless and all that stuff, and if you lose a lot, nobody's going to follow you because you're looked at as a loser."

Having suffered some losses, Trump would set out to prove he was resilient. With all that he had attempted, and gained, and lost, he was still just forty-four years old. He remained one of the most recognized men in America, and few, if any, knew better how to transform recognition into cash.

10
TRUMP THE SPECTACLE

I am the creator of my own comic book,
and I love living in it.
—DONALD TRUMP

Donald Trump never went bankrupt. He would frequently and energetically assert this in the years after he sought the shelter of the court for his Taj Mahal casino. The filing was made by a Trump *corporation,* not Trump the *man,* and he would describe this action as a sensible business move, devoid of shame, that gave him powerful leverage in his negotiations with creditors. "You have to be strong enough *not* to pay," Trump would eventually explain, adding that the people he owed could rage with frustration but would eventually have to accept that his companies were not going to meet their obligations.[1]

At the time, lots of prominent businesspeople were using the courts to get out of corporate debt. In the year Trump's Taj Mahal went bankrupt, so did United Press International, Bloomingdale's, and Piper Aircraft. But while many well-known firms went under in the recession of 1990–91, none were associated with an owner who even approached Donald Trump's level of fame and notoriety. "The show is Trump," he said in a moment of candor that revealed his life to be a moneymaking construct. Having made his personality synonymous with his business, Trump's troubles, including his marital problems, invariably affected his brand. This problem was widely discussed in the business press by experts in marketing and advertising. Renee Frengut, of the firm Market Insights, noted that people who became disillusioned with a celebrity "are not very forgiving." Noted advertising expert Jerry Della Femina said that he would like to hire Ivana Trump, and not Donald, to promote his clients.

Remarkably, Trump continued to enjoy a life of luxury, retaining his many residences, including his home atop Trump Tower and his mansion in Palm Beach. His budget for personal expenses, approved by his creditors, was $450,000—per month. At home he was attended by servants. On the road he traveled with bodyguards. Any reasonable person would conclude that this material ease proved Trump was a success or, as he would say it, a "winner." But in his frenzied sprint through life, he had continually sought to raise the bar in his own game, suggesting to the world that a successful man's trophies must be ever more glittering and impressive, lest he be judged a failure. First he welcomed a writer from *The Times* to describe his luxury apartment in Olympic Tower. Then he brought Robin Leach to his mansion in the country, so it could be seen by the millions who tuned in to *Lifestyles of the Rich and Famous*. His private airplane had to be a converted commercial jet. His Palm Beach home had to be Mar-a-Lago. His yacht had to be almost three hundred feet long. The woman at his side had to be beautiful in a way that everyone would admire.

Arriving at a time when wealth was being redefined—the real rich claimed not millions, but billions, in assets—Trump was not alone in his ambitions. In general, the rich men and women of his generation indulged at a level not seen since the medicine of the Great Depression quelled the fever of the twenties. In his prime, Fred Trump was among the richest men in America, yet he lived among doctors, lawyers, and accountants. He rarely traveled, except for vacations in Florida, and was careful about expenses. In 1955, when *Fortune* published a study on the subject, this far-from-ostentatious life was the norm for top executives across the nation, who remembered the excesses of the Roaring Twenties and refused to repeat them. Don Mitchell, president of Sylvania Electric, lived in an eleven-room house in Summit, New Jersey, and commuted by train to Manhattan. D. A. Hulcy, president of Lone Star Gas, counted a small lakeside cottage as his main indulgence.[2]

The top executives profiled by *Fortune* in 1955 enjoyed far more luxuries than the typical workers in their firms, but the gap that separated them was much smaller than the one that existed in 1990 between the wealthiest and everyone else. And in the top echelon, Trump was alone when it came to flaunting his power and possessions. In this way he came to symbolize changes that disturbed those who defined success along the lines of the traditional American Dream, which included a stable family life, a secure home, and a place in one's community. Trump's definition of a good life was a cartoonish fantasy, which he promoted with the help of media figures such as Robin Leach and Barbara Walters.

As he thrived, others also began to display their wealth in excessive ways. Real estate magnate Gerald Guterman marked his son's bar mitzvah with a $500,000 cruise for several hundred guests. Gayfryd Steinberg lavished $1 million on her investor husband's fiftieth birthday celebration in the Hamptons. Malcolm Forbes spent more than $2 million on his seventieth birthday party in Tangier, where the entertainment included an authentic cavalry charge. In the precincts occupied by the Gutermans, Steinbergs, and Forbeses, vast sums were also spent on parties for wives and mistresses, and on plastic surgery to make wives look more like mistresses.[3] As the lives of ultra-upper-income Americans became more extreme, middle-class Americans struggled to maintain their standard of living. Wages stagnated, debt rose, and high-paying manufacturing jobs continued to disappear. Beginning in 1984, personal bankruptcy rates had reached new levels every single year. In 1991, the year when the Taj went bankrupt, so did approximately nine hundred thousand individuals. Unlike Trump and others who used bankruptcy as a financial tool, ordinary people could not hide behind corporate entities or demand better terms from their creditors. Ordinary people who filed for bankruptcy suffered financial ruin as they lost their homes, their cars, and everything else of monetary value. In the late eighties and early nineties foreclosures and evictions spiked in suburban New York City, and homeless shelters filled to overflowing in Oregon. In the Midwest public-health experts blamed economic stress for a sharp spike in suicides by farmers. On both coasts, economists noted the development of a "dual" society in which the few thrived as the many struggled.[4]

In this environment, many people delighted in the troubles of men such as Ivan Boesky and Michael Milken, two fraudsters whose crimes revealed the underside of financial engineering. Boesky had inspired filmmaker Oliver Stone's Gordon Gekko when he told business-school graduates at the University of California, "Greed is all right, by the way. I want you to know that. I think greed is healthy. You can be greedy and still feel good about yourself." Boesky later paid a $100 million fine and served prison time for his violations of federal law. Milken, who was born a month after Trump and also attended Wharton, supported many greenmailing assaults and was, for more than a decade, one of the most adept and creative practitioners of the junk-bond trade. After Ivan Boesky implicated him in various crimes, Milken pleaded guilty, paid a $200 million fine, and also went to prison.[5]

Famous as they were, Milken and Boesky were not as well-known as Trump, whose face, voice, and unique hairstyle were recognized by almost everyone in America. Much of the Trump image was manufactured, by him, through the repetition of not-fully-accurate anecdotes, which he told in a consistent way. The holes in these stories made Trump vulnerable to those who considered him arrogant and overreaching. Skeptics took delight in his continued struggles even after the Taj reorganization and the sale of his yacht, the *Trump Princess,* to a member of the Saudi royal family. Trump was forced to put his two other casinos—Trump Castle and Trump Plaza—into bankruptcy in March of 1992.

For a man who openly confessed that "image means a great deal to me," the ridicule and occasional pity that accompanied Trump's losses must have seemed all the more painful. The cartoonist Berkeley Breathed installed Trump's brain in the skull of a scoundrel cat in his comic strip *Bloom County.* A fake think tank called the Boring Institute named Trump the most boring celebrity of the year, and an entrepreneurial jokester began selling a game called Chump, which required players to compete over who could lose the most money. In Hollywood, movie executives began talking about Trump as the archetype for a new type of villain. In Boston, Malcolm Forbes provided the funding for some Harvard students to present a fake Marla Maples at a press conference as an April Fools' joke. Everyone, it seemed, had an opinion about Donald and Marla. Jeff Bulmer, a Vietnam vet, a helicopter pilot for Trump based in Manhattan, told a reporter, "I knew about Marla Maples before anyone else. She's a gold digger."

Despite the furor, Marla and Donald stayed together. When he appeared on the CNN, Trump lashed out at the media. "The press is very dishonest," he told interviewer Larry King. "I've been quoted in various articles where I never spoke to people, where they just make up a quote. Donald Trump said this, and he said that. . . . They go with lies to an extent that I've never seen before. They make up stories. . . . I'd love to grab some of those guys, I really would."[6]

Trump seemed sincere in his outrage, but his own lifelong pursuit of press attention had set the stage for his current troubles. This fact limited any sympathy others might feel for him. Marla Maples faced a similar problem since her own career aspirations practically required that she speak with reporters.

In April, Maples reluctantly agreed to appear on the ABC TV news program *PrimeTime Live* where she would be interviewed by Diane Sawyer. A one-time aide in the Nixon White House, Sawyer was persistent in her pursuit of a scoop. Her team had joined the media horde that had besieged Maples and her family. In deciding to submit to one high-profile interview, Maples hoped she might satisfy the demands of the press and ease the pressure on herself and her family.

Sawyer, who was a worthy rival to Barbara Walters, had a way of establishing an almost instant emotional rapport with her subjects. This skill allowed her to ask deeply personal questions, and get answers. When she asked Maples if she loved Donald Trump, her subject answered, "I can't lie about it. You know I do." However, when Sawyer asked if she and Trump had ever discussed marriage Maples said, "No. He's, he's a friend. You know? He has a family, and that's number one to him, I know."

Maples, who had lost ten pounds due to the stress of events swirling around her, appeared wearing a peach-colored suit and a silver necklace. Speaking in a soft voice she said Trump supported her decision to be interviewed because " . . . he has a lot of sympathy for how we've been besieged by this. And I think he wants to see me come out looking okay." When she addressed the breakup of the Trump marriage, Maples kept herself out of the equation. "I believe that that's a very sad and very serious thing between two people, and I would've only hoped that it could have stayed more private." She also expressed some distress over the publicity that had attended the scandal that she had touched off, which was an odd claim for anyone to make while appearing on a TV program that regularly drew more than nine million viewers. As Norma Foerderer predicted, ABC benefited immensely as it captured five million more viewers than usual for *PrimeTime Live*. It was the biggest-ever audience for the program, which had long lagged behind its competitors.[7]

But for the scandal, Marla Maples would never have heard from anyone at ABC. Nor would she have received *Time* magazine's invitation to attend the 1990 Washington Correspondents Dinner. But there she was, a week after the *PrimeTime* broadcast, causing a bigger stir than any of the assorted senators, movie stars, and administration figures including President and First Lady Barbara Bush, who would complain that she didn't get to meet Ms. Maples. At *Time*'s pre-dinner reception, photographers pushed aside Supreme Court Justice Antonin Scalia in the rush to take her picture. During the banquet itself, the comedian Dennis Miller, who was chosen to entertain the crowd, quipped that Marla "should have asked Diane Sawyer if Mike Nichols was the best sex she's ever had."

In her star turn, Marla Maples proved far more adept than Ivana Trump had ever been, playing her role with the same kind of ease that Donald usually brought to the stage. Maples would later say that she had dreamed that a life with Trump would allow her to practice philanthropy and somehow contribute to the greater good. She saw in him the reincarnation of a former monarch. He was "a king . . . a ruler of the world, as he sees it." Maples hoped she could cultivate the benevolent side of the man for humanitarian work and soothe "the little boy that still wants attention." At least that was her dream.

Donald spent the spring and summer of 1990 dealing with the troubles of his business empire and preparing for the publication of his second book. To promote the sales of the book Trump agreed to press interviews, including a session with Barbara Walters, whom he told, "I'm not going to let my guard down." Walters managed to get him to say, "I make mistakes," but he fessed up to little else. Trump also agreed to cooperate with writer Marie Brenner for an article published in *Vanity Fair*. Thinking better of the idea, he called editor Tina Brown to complain before the piece was actually published. When it did appear, Brenner's story presented him as a reeling, desperate man. In one passage she quoted a Trump attorney saying, "Donald is a believer in the big-lie theory. If you say something again and again, people will believe you." In another passage Brenner recalled that a remorseful news reporter had told at her, "He was always a phony, and we filled our papers with him!"[8]

Trump responded by writing Brown: "It was only at your request that I agreed to do the interview with Marie Brenner. Prior to your call, I was adamant about not doing it. It is indeed unfortunate that you, based on our friendship, prevailed upon me." He called the piece "a fabrication and a disgrace" and added, "*Vanity Fair* has libeled me." Days after the magazine article was published, Trump's book appeared in stores. Coauthored with journalist Charles Leerhsen, *Trump: Surviving at the Top* was liberally salted with attacks on those

Donald perceived to be his enemies, especially those in and around the practice of journalism.

Having participated vigorously in the tabloid battle of the headlines during his marital crisis, Trump now complained that "the publicity dehumanizes you." He criticized *Time* magazine, the cartoonist/satirist Garry Trudeau, and the writer Wayne Barrett. Of Liz Smith, he wrote that she "used to kiss my ass so much that it was downright embarrassing." Trump's most pointed assault was against publisher Malcolm Forbes, whom he described as a kind of shakedown artist who favored those who advertised in his magazine. He wrote that Forbes had screamed at him when staff at the Plaza Hotel wouldn't allow his two underage male companions to drink at the bar. He also characterized Forbes as a hypocrite because he lived openly as a homosexual but insisted that others keep his orientation secret. Long the subject of gossip, Forbes's sexual identity has been dissected by many press outlets, and they generally agreed that besides having a long marriage and fathering three children, he also had male sexual partners.

The *Boston Globe*'s Mark Feeney called the attack on Forbes a bit of "smarminess worthy of Richard Nixon." Only the most informed readers would know that Trump's view of Forbes was affected by Trump's own long-standing complaints about where he ranked in the annual *Forbes* magazine list of wealthy individuals.[9]

When Trump turned to the subject of fame and its effects, he wrote from a unique perspective. Fame, which was part of his business plan, had contributed substantially to his successes even as it exacted a price. It is, he wrote, "a kind of drug, one that is way too powerful for most people to handle." *Trump: Surviving at the Top* was filled with firsthand reports on the bizarre behavior of fame-addled celebrities. Trump described Frank Sinatra as screaming to a bodyguard when he was approached by a fan, shouting "Get this bum out of here!" Trump devoted a full page to Howard Hughes, whose eccentricities became pathologies in the years prior to his death. In his youth, the sandy-haired Hughes could have passed as Trump's brother. Like Donald, Hughes was linked to many beautiful women and operated a gambling business. He was also famously germophobic, a trait that Trump confessed he too possessed. "I'm constantly washing my hands, and it wouldn't bother me if I never had to shake hands with a well-meaning stranger again."

Trump's seemingly frank statements about his contamination anxiety and his angst over his financial struggles—"My life is shit," he declared—gave the impression of a man who was willing to reveal himself. But all he copped to were a few missteps and quirks and forgivable sins such as working too hard. Sprinkled into a text that was otherwise an exercise in name-dropping and chest-thumping, these confessions revealed nothing meaningful about the man. The book was savaged in *The Times* by the prominent journalist Michael Lewis, who observed, "He's not exposing himself so much as he is shopping for new identities." Lewis found the book to be "a strained, sloppy exercise in facade restoration." Trump's businesses were crippled, Lewis wrote, "Yet he still insists, like a captured tyrant, that he is in charge."[10]

◆

Trump's second book coincided, roughly, with a flurry of works from writers who attempted to sound an alarm about 1980s-style excess. *Barbarians at the Gate,* by Bryan Burrough and John Helyar, painted a picture of breathtaking avarice and ego as it told the story of the $25 billion takeover of RJR Nabisco. In *The Politics of Rich and Poor,* former Republican Party strategist Kevin Phillips showed how a new Gilded Age had begun. Others reported that the portion of national income going to the richest 1 percent had risen from 8.1 percent to 14.7 percent, and that salaries for Wall Street's top earners had increased 1,000 percent in ten years. Earl Shorris, author of *A Nation of Salesmen,* named Donald Trump specifically as he decried the crass "subversion" of American culture by those who believed that anything, from the admiration of the masses to the policies of Washington, could be bought and sold.[11]

On television, the celebration of wealth offered by Robin Leach on *Lifestyles of the Rich and Famous* was challenged by those with a more critical eye. ABC joined with the Public Broadcasting Service to present a new series called *The New Explorers,* which reported on the lives of those who helped the super-rich spend their money. In Beverly Hills and Manhattan, the program's producers revealed the lives of caterers who were asked to deliver environmentally sound meals and florists challenged to outdo themselves with every assignment. Personal trainers also got plenty of attention, with the cameras entering an oak-paneled workout room to capture Marla Maples and Donald Trump learning the best way to perform jumping jacks.[12]

Trump was an easy target for anyone who was distressed by the rise of tabloid culture and gold-plated materialism. He also mystified those who sought to measure his achievements. His many complex business dealings were conducted in private, which made it almost impossible for anyone to know which bold proposals were moving forward and which had been abandoned. Was he still planning to build the world's tallest building on the West Side? How about Television City? A New Yorker needed a scorecard to keep track. Trump's personal life was another matter. A married man's dalliance with a much younger woman, who fit everyone's idea of a blond bombshell/home wrecker, fit into a narrative understood by all. A photo of Marla Maples on the front page of a tabloid was enough to shame Donald Trump in the eyes of the world. To make matters worse, even mainstream publications such as *The Washington Post* and *The New York Times,* having added gossip columns and *People*-magazine-type features to their menus, gleefully attended to the smarmier aspects of the lives of the rich and famous.

Unlike the reserved society types of yore, who strove to present themselves as better than the unwashed masses, the new celebrities willingly offered the public a pageant of shamelessness. In early 1991, for example, Trump and Maples were among hundreds who donned tuxedos and gowns for a ballroom party to honor Joey Adams, comedian husband of the gossip columnist Cindy Adams. The swells included Sydney Biddle Barrows, who was best known as a madam for high-end prostitutes, and Yankees owner George Steinbrenner, whose criminal record (illegal campaign donations to Richard Nixon) had been wiped clean by Ronald Reagan in the last days of his presidency. Imelda Marcos, kleptocrat wife of the deposed dictator of the Philippines, sang "Happy Birthday" to the eighty-year-old Adams. Cindy Adams used her finger to remove lipstick from the teeth of Bess Myerson, who had recently pleaded guilty to shoplifting. A comic named Pat Cooper brayed, "Marla, ya picked another loser!"[13]

For Maples, who was just a few years removed from Cohutta, Georgia, the concoction of crass and class displayed at Joey Adams's party blended into the blur that was life with Donald Trump. "I was caught up in the drama," she would recall many years later. "I was so caught up in that. I couldn't get out. . . . I didn't know how to get out, and like he'd say, 'Well, I wasn't stopping you.' But the truth was it felt like I was swimming against the current every day. I felt completely smothered and I didn't know how to get out."

Others seemed to thrive on controversy and notoriety. In the new economy of celebrity, famous people who behaved abysmally could overcome almost any disgrace—and continue to make money based on their fame—if they remained in the spotlight long enough for the public to move on to a new scandal. This required an exceedingly thick skin, but few people ever rose to such prominence without developing quite a few calluses. Those who would be famous had to show they were tough enough to suffer derision and indignity and keep on flashing their perfect smiles. As Trump observed, modern fame was like a drug, and addicts will do almost anything to get a fix. This included feeding the maw of the publicity machine yourself to remain relevant.

In June 1991 Donald Trump scheduled a big public celebration of his birthday, and the Taj Mahal's first full year in business, for the last weekend of the month. (The resort was operating under the supervision of the federal bankruptcy court.) He and Marla planned to serve as hosts. He told *Newsday* that he had begun asking women he wanted to date to visit his doctor's office for an HIV test. "It's one of the worst times in the history of the world to be dating," said Trump with characteristic grandiosity. The test was "one way to be careful," he explained. "There are lots of ways. I'm saying take all of those ways and double them." The same article noted that Trump, who had said he was commencing a search for the "right woman," was dating the European model Carla Bruni, future wife of French president Nicolas Sarkozy. According to the paper, Trump regarded his relationship with Bruni as "just the first in what he expects to be a long, hard search for 'the right woman.'" Marla was hopeful that he would someday return to her and told *Newsday*, "If a miracle happens and Donald finds God—I'm there."[14]

Any woman with the slightest romantic connection to Trump would rightly feel hurt, angered, even humiliated, by his comments. Bruni didn't respond publicly, but according to writer Harry Hurt, she complained loudly to Trump, who couldn't believe she wasn't delighted by the publicity. When a writer for *People* magazine called Trump's office, she spoke to a man who identified himself as John Miller but sounded an awful lot like Trump and noted that "important beautiful women call him [Trump] all the time." Among them, he said, were actress Kim Basinger and the pop superstar Madonna. Turning sympathetic, he added, "Competitively it's tough. It was tough for Marla, it will be tough for Carla." Upon hearing a recording of the "Miller" interview, Maples said it was in fact Donald. She said she felt "shocked and devastated."

All of Marla's reaction to Trump's stunt was reported in print, along with her sad observation that "I came into this for love, and I hope he finds happiness." However, by the time the magazine hit the newsstands, Trump and Maples had conducted a semipublic reconciliation that was too strange for fiction. The episode began with Maples baring her wounds to the TV talk-show host Kathie Lee Gifford and her husband, the former football star Frank Gifford, during a visit to their home. Kathie Lee had a few things in common with Maples. Like Maples, she was married to a much older man. She also craved attention. Descended from a family of snake handlers, Kathie Lee Gifford was trained in theater at Oral Roberts University and had worked hard to become a celebrity. Her conservative religion, burning ambition, and theatricality made her a comforting presence for Maples. Kathie Lee lent an ear to Marla until Donald arrived at the house.

Putting his salesmanship skills to work, Trump implored Maples to come back to him, promising marriage and an enormous diamond ring.[15] Marla employed a specific logic to get to the point where she could renew the relationship. As she told *People* magazine writer Karen Schneider, she believed that on a subconscious level Trump had deployed Carla Bruni, Kim Basinger, and Madonna "to push me farther away from him." He was, in this analysis, like a little boy who does something bad to test his mother's love. At the same time, said Maples, "John Miller" had moved her to realize "I could be happy alone." Brief as her alone time may have been, it was enough to make her certain that she could love Trump, not out of desperation, but "out of choice." This kind of reasoning reflected New Age psychospiritual thinking, which blended various religious principles with concepts of popular psychology. Among the popular maxims of the New Age movement is the saying "If you love something, set it free. If it comes back, it is yours. If it doesn't, it never was."

On the day after his reconciliation with Marla, Trump telephoned the studio of Kathie Lee Gifford's TV show to report that Maples had accepted his marriage proposal. Technicians at *Live with Regis and Kathie Lee* arranged for the call to be broadcast to millions of viewers, who heard the distinctive voice of The Donald say he was "indeed" engaged to Maples and "Marla's a very special girl." In the afternoon, Trump and Maples played golf with Frank Gifford and William Fugazy, a well-known New York businessman. (One of Roy Cohn's major clients, Fugazy would eventually plead guilty to committing perjury in a bankruptcy proceeding. Like George Steinbrenner he would receive a presidential pardon.) While on the course, Trump was met by a messenger who delivered the big ring he had promised to give Marla. He promptly gave it to her, thus sealing the engagement in front of prominent witnesses.[16]

The televised announcement delivered big doses of publicity for both Trump and Maples. Members of the celebrity press would continue to follow the couple like eager puppies, reporting breathlessly on, among other matters, her consideration of a prenuptial agreement and his apparent struggle to remain committed. Ten weeks after he gave her the ring, the *Daily News* trumpeted, HERE WE GO AGAIN . . . TRUMP DUMPS MARLA. Amid the turmoil, Maples's acting career got a boost with a guest spot on a television comedy called *Designing Women,* as she appeared as herself with the show's fictional characters. Trump attempted a more serious pose, traveling to Capitol Hill to tell a congressional committee that he thought they should raise taxes on the rich. Reagan tax cuts that had reduced the maximum rate to 31 percent ought to be abandoned, he said. A top rate of 50 or 60 percent would be better for the country.

Coupled with a previous statement suggesting that illicit drugs should be decriminalized, Trump's tax comments placed him left of center on the political spectrum, but they gained him little press coverage. The press and public were far more interested in the spectacle that was his personal life, and those who made a living by ridiculing public figures had a field day with him. Often Trump couldn't resist responding. When New York radio host Don Imus declared Trump had "fat, grandmotherly arms," Trump announced he would no longer advertise on Imus's program. Imus, who like Trump, thrived on attention, gleefully replied, "We want only advertisers who can pay their bills." In the spring of 1992, Ivana Trump traveled the country giving interviews and talks at bookstores to promote her romance novel, *For Love*

Alone. She also got a spot on Oprah Winfrey's hugely popular talk show, where she was greeted as a stand-in for every woman ever wronged by a man.[17]

In the same summer of 1992, Marla Maples was offered the role of Florenz Ziegfeld's mistress in a Broadway play called *The Will Rogers Follies.* She prepared by taking acting lessons, which wasn't easy considering she was one of the most recognized women in New York. Later she recalled, "Donald would say, 'Take the limo.' . . . I would get out two blocks away from where I had to go just to not be seen in a limo because I was embarrassed that I'm working with other struggling actors and I just didn't want to show up" in a limousine. Marla also worked with famous voice coach David Sorin Collyer, whose clients had included Bette Midler and Paul Simon.[18]

The Will Rogers Follies was presented at the Palace Theatre, where Rogers himself had performed his vaudeville act. On Maple's first night, Kathie Lee and her husband were in the audience along with scores of friendly celebrities. The reviews were mostly favorable, but Marla's previously established fame was as much of an attraction as her singing and dancing.

In the year to come, Donald and Marla would set, and miss, several wedding dates. In October 1992, after the *Daily News* announced, SPLITSVILLE—NEW YORK'S FUN COUPLE CALLS IT QUITS . . . AGAIN, Maples and Trump each made a point of flaunting their happy comings and goings for the tabloid press. Trump even invited a camera crew from the TV program *Entertainment Tonight* to film him with a gaggle of fashion models at a party he threw at Mar-a-Lago. In November, Marla was absent when he invited a big crowd of people to the ballroom at the Taj Mahal, where they were serenaded by entertainers who impersonated Marilyn Monroe and Elvis Presley.

Under most circumstances, Elvis and Marilyn impersonators would be enough to mark an event as certifiably odd. In this case, the attendees were treated to much more strangeness. At each of the tables in the ballroom the partygoers found Trump's head on a stick, or rather, a life-size photo of Trump's head on a stick, and a camera they could use to capture themselves as The Donald for posterity. As the ballroom was filled with the rousing theme music from the movie *Rocky,* an announcer bellowed, "Let's hear it for the king!"—and Trump burst through a large paper screen. He emerged wearing big red boxing gloves and a red robe draped over a tuxedo. Then, as if this weren't sufficiently awkward, Trump casino executive Nick Ribis offered the crowd a paean to his boss in the style of Muhammad Ali:

> *He was tough and resilient*
> *and he had no fear.*
> *He made the comeback of the year.*
> *Against all odds, his opponents*
> *buckled with a thump.*
> *The winner was, Donald J. Trump.*[19]

In the post-Boesky, post-Milken moment, Trump was one of the few business figures still strutting as if it were 1985. Was it true he had made "the comeback of the year" and become, once again, a "winner"? Given that no reliable data could be had, the claim could only be regarded as hype. But in time it would appear that with a variety of maneuvers, including the sale of assets, Trump *had* reduced his personal debt by hundreds of millions of dollars. Like the good behavior that gets a prisoner closer to freedom, his accomplishment wasn't so much a victory over his "opponents," whoever they were, as a sign that he had accepted reality. His businesses continued to bob in a pool of red ink, but the lenders who held this debt were, like wise prison guards, hoping to see him get out from behind bars as soon as possible. If he profited, so would they.

The general public, including those who gambled at Trump casinos and shopped at Trump Tower, weren't required to determine whether claims about a comeback were accurate. He was, for them, like a character in a soap opera. Depending on a viewer's perspective, he could be a hero, a villain, a king, or a clown. For the convenience of the audience, he offered a never-ending monologue to support the variety of narratives. He was reflexively tough on crime, as his response to the Central Park "wilding" showed, but wanted to legalize street drugs. He often wore a tuxedo and owned the most impressive mansion in Palm Beach, but regularly complained about high-society phonies. In his business life, Trump could favor women executives such as Barbara Res, but he often spoke about women in the most sexist terms.

By saying almost everything, Trump created a record that allowed him to appeal to various kinds of people depending on what he hoped to achieve. He also developed a set of anecdotes and claims that he offered as filler in conversations and interviews. These generally focused on his possessions—homes, aircraft, commercial buildings—or his superior qualities as businessman, athlete, or evaluator of human beings. Like many monarchs, his proclamations did not necessarily rely on established facts. He deployed all of these rhetorical techniques as journalists buzzed around him in the early 1990s. In a single article by Julie Baumgold, published in *New York* two days after the comeback party he threw for himself, Donald offered vintage Trump:

On his reputation: People do not know "how smart I am."

On Marla: "I'm the greatest star maker."

On the dangers of asbestos: "One of the great cons is asbestos. There's nothing wrong except the mob has a strong lobby in Albany . . . because they have dumps and control the trucks."

On Barbara Walters: "A disloyal lady."[20]

In almost every case, Trump's opinions depended on how a person, place, or thing reflected on him. Walters could be a steadfast friend to the likes of Roy Cohn, whom many considered unworthy of such kindness, but after she asked Trump some tough questions, she became categorically "disloyal." Asbestos was "harmless" despite all the science that proved it caused lung disease and cancer. As he offered opinions with a smirk, a scowl, a grin, or a poker face, Trump dared the world to guess when he was serious and when he was not.

No one was more challenged by the puzzle of Trump than Marla Maples. Despite his proposal, they remained unmarried through her pregnancy and the arrival of their daughter, Tiffany. Finally, after consulting those he trusted on how a marriage might affect his business, Donald went forward with the plans for a wedding. A guest list was compiled, and invitations were sent. Donald and Marla were to be married on Monday, December 20, 1993, a week after the planned introduction of Maples's new line of fashionable maternity clothes.

Just days before the ceremony, Maples was confronted with a prenuptial contract. As she later reported, her fiancé informed her that he would cancel the wedding if she didn't sign. "I refused to read it because I felt it was sealing our fate," she would tell a reporter. "Prenuptial agreements contradict the marriage vows. If you expect someone to sign one, you're not expecting the marriage to work." If she *had* read the contract, Maples would have seen that she would receive far less in a divorce than the settlement Ivana got. Donald would justify it by saying, "I built this empire and I did it by myself." Marla signed.[21]

Years later Trump would elaborate on women and prenuptial agreements in a book called *Trump: The Art of the Comeback*. In this book he allowed, "There are basically three types of women and reactions" to a proposed prenup. One type refuses to sign a contract "on principle." She should be abandoned. The second type won't sign because she intends to exploit "the poor unsuspecting sucker she's got in her grasp." The third type signs but quickly seeks divorce to get "a fat check for very little work." Although he would acknowledge that his views might appall those who "lead a more normal life than I do," he would insist, "People are really vicious, and no place are they more vicious than in their relationships with the opposite sex."

Marla and Trump's wedding ceremony and celebration were held at the Plaza, which had, like other Trump properties, gone through a bankruptcy that left him with far less equity in hand. The bride wore a white dress designed by Carolina Herrera, whose previous clients included Caroline Kennedy and Kate Capshaw, wife of Steven Spielberg. Maples felt uneasy amid the splendor, especially wearing a $250,000 diamond tiara borrowed for the night from a Manhattan jeweler. She would recall that her mother and stepfather told her, "You should just enjoy it. People love to see people living big." She did smile and pose for the cameras, but would later insist, "It didn't feel right to me."

Although she found much to worry about in the Trump way of life, Maples at least felt good about the man she was to marry. The groom was not as certain. "I was bored when she was walking down the aisle," he would tell writer Timothy O'Brien. "I kept thinking, 'What the hell am I doing here?' " For him the getting was everything. The having, not so much. Shortly after the wedding he would tell ABC TV correspondent Nancy Collins, "I've really given a lot of women great opportunity. Unfortunately after they're a star, the fun is over for me. It's like a creative process. It's almost like creating a building. It's pretty sad."[22]

No sadness was apparent as the Reverend Arthur Caliandro, successor to Norman Vincent Peale at the Marble Collegiate Church, consecrated the Trump-Maples union in a ceremony that resembled nothing as much as it did the coronation of Queen Elizabeth, which had captivated Donald Trump's mother when he was just seven years old. The nine hundred guests included Liza Minnelli, Robin Leach, Saudi arms dealer Adnan Khashoggi, the entertainer Rosie O'Donnell, and athlete-turned-media-star O. J. Simpson. A generous-hearted Liz Smith described the wedding as "part of the pageant of New York." A less generous Amy Pagnozzi of the *Daily News* declared it "tacky. Overblown. Depraved in its conception." The Trumps honeymooned at a ski resort not far from where Ivana was vacationing with her three children, who did not attend the wedding. Norman Vincent Peale died while the couple was away.[23]

I I
NEW TRUMP

*I always say you can learn from your mistakes, but
it's much better to learn from other people's mistakes
because you can learn from other people's
mistakes without having to make the mistakes.
Learning how to win is a very important thing. Very
few people understand how to win. Very few people.*

— DONALD TRUMP

Marla Maples dreamed of stardom, built on her performance in *The Will Rogers Follies,* and a happy family life with her daughter, Tiffany, and her husband, Donald. She also hoped that over time she could win him over to certain causes. She believed that a big measure of his money should go toward making the world a better place. This belief was mainly a spiritual concern, based on her sense that something unseen was at work in her life with her new husband. She would recall it this way: "I thought, 'My, gosh. Can you imagine what we could do with his ability to do business and with my heart and passions?' I really felt that there must be something bigger in the picture going on than I could understand. . . . I thought we were really supposed to do some great things together."[1]

The greatness Marla Maples imagined would depend on her husband's efforts to recover his fortune and his developing a strong commitment to the common good. A bettor would get long odds if he or she wagered on Donald Trump's devoting himself to humanitarian or spiritual causes. This man reflexively put his own interests first. How else could one explain his effort to overturn a law that allowed impoverished Indian tribes to operate casinos? His suit alleged that he was the victim of unlawful discrimination because, like laws granting special tax breaks for developers, the Indian gaming law benefited only a "very limited class of citizens."[2]

Trump's court challenge failed, but he would continue to attack his Indian competitors. In 1993 he got into a shouting match with California representative George Miller at a congressional hearing as he insisted that tribal casinos were courting "the biggest scandal since Al Capone." He yelled, "Organized crime is rampant on Indian reservations. People know it; people talk about it. It's going to blow." Trump also said of the tribal representatives at the meeting, "They don't look like Indians to me, and they don't look like Indians to Indians." After the hearing an Indian leader accused Trump of "economic racism." An official of the FBI refuted Trump's charge, which came as New Jersey congressman Robert Torricelli proposed legislation that would protect Trump's casinos from Indian competition. The proposal was never made law and Torricelli would leave politics amid a scandal over campaign donations from a Chinese businessman.[3]

In this time period Trump also moved to restore his personal finances and his control over his businesses. He turned to his siblings for a $10 million loan, pledging his share of their father's estate as collateral. Trump also began pursuing new deals in real estate and laid the groundwork to recover his equity in the three casinos he had built.[4] Under proper management, casino gambling is *supposed* to be a sure thing for the house, returning steady revenues. Proper management required putting limits on debt and operating expenses, including promotional events and the freebies offered to high rollers, known in the industry as whales. When the famous whale Akio Kashiwagi visited Trump Plaza in 1990, the casino hired a Japanese chef for him. The secretive Kashiwagi, who said his wealth came from real estate, bet $200,000 per hand at the baccarat tables and won $6 million. Killer whales were not the only problem affecting the casino. In 1989, Trump Plaza lost $800,000 on performances by the Rolling Stones, who did not sell out the hall and did not draw people who added to the money wagered on the casino floor. But while losses on promotions mattered, all casinos suffered these kinds of setbacks. What mattered far more was the burden of the debt piled onto Trump's Atlantic City operations.[5]

As he sought to manage the debts on his various holdings, Trump turned Mar-a-Lago into a membership club, reserving only part of it for his own use as a residence. He sold a controlling interest in the iconic Plaza Hotel to Saudi prince Al-Waleed bin Talal. Just forty years old, the prince was younger and much richer than Trump. *His* personal jet was a Boeing 747, and his homes were *actual* palaces. His previous investments in debt-strapped American enterprises had included $800 million poured into Citicorp and a $338 million investment in Disney.[6]

The Plaza was an ideal investment for a Saudi prince who coveted premier properties and had the cash to buy them when their owners were in distress. More ordinary investors, whom Trump would court with new bond and stock offerings, could be more difficult to entice. As he implemented his recovery plan, Trump tried to sell bonds that would be paid from the revenues of the Taj Mahal but failed to attract enough interest. Then he notified the federal Securities and Exchange Commission that he intended to sell $295 million in securities to finance the Trump Plaza Hotel and Casino, which was considered the best of his properties in Atlantic City. Although he had to hike the interest rate to 15.5 percent, which qualified them as junk bonds, these did sell. Trump also floated a stock offering, which was given his initials—DJT—for a ticker symbol. It sold for $14 per share. This debut price was at the bottom edge of the range expected by investment analysts. Nevertheless, both offerings—the bonds and the stock—were judged a success on Wall Street, and they allowed Trump to retire $88 million in debt.[7]

At first the investors who bought Trump stock were rewarded with a price increase of more than 50 percent as an improving economy brought droves of East Coast gamblers to Atlantic City. By November 1995 his three casinos ranked at the top of the market in profits. On Wall Street, brokers eyed Trump's new winning streak like gamblers drawn to a poker player who has won a big pile of chips. Some, such as the managers of Putnam Securities in Boston, expected the streak to continue and pledged to back him. Others, including Jerry Paul of Invesco Trust, were skittish. "I don't think you want to spend too much time holding Trump paper," he told *The Wall Street Journal*.[8]

Anyone who held Trump stock for more than eighteen months would lose big. After peaking at $35.50 in the middle of 1996, it plummeted to below its initial price of $14 by the end of the year. The big drop happened after shareholders approved Trump's plan to have the publicly traded firm—DJT—purchase his third casino, Trump Castle. Stockholders took note of the price paid for the property, and the payments being made to make good on the 15.5 percent bonds, and began selling. By early 1997 Trump stock had fallen below $10. By by this time, Donald Trump had worked diligently to accomplish the comeback he had announced years earlier by punching through a paper screen. His personal finances had stabilized and improved as many of his investors lost.

A new, successful Donald Trump was created through ventures he formed with wealthy partners who, unlike individual stockholders and bond investors, possessed the kind of financial power that he respected. In Manhattan he negotiated with a new group opposed to his plans for the old Penn Central yard. Called Westpride, it included historian Robert Caro, former mayor John Lindsay, and the novelist E. L. Doctorow. The members of Westpride developed their own plan for the site, which would be less ambitious but also less expensive to build. Trump privately agreed to work with the new plan, which would include fewer apartments and a park covering more than twenty acres. As the arrangement was announced, Trump said, "All you folks have persuaded me to really do what was right." In fact, he was responding to both a new political reality and the financial pressure associated with the huge loan payments he had to make just to hold on to the property.[9]

When the City of New York finally approved the development, which would be called Riverside South, it instantly increased the value of the land. However, by the time this happened, Trump lacked the financial strength to proceed on his own. In the summer of 1994 he relinquished control of the property to five Hong Kong businessmen, who formed a partnership called Hudson Waterfront Associates. They would pay Trump a salary to lead the development, and he stood to earn a share of eventual profits, but his partners, who said they had built much bigger projects elsewhere, would make all the biggest decisions.

As so often happens with large-scale urban developments, Riverside South would change in many ways as construction began in 1997 and continued for more than a decade. The elevated highway remained. The buildings that were constructed were taller and less attractive than the structures many West Siders expected. They also blocked river views enjoyed by thousands who lived to the east. Though attractive to those who bought and rented the units, the new community was resented by those who believed its cookie-cutter buildings blighted their neighborhood with shadows and traffic. Others just didn't like Trump and recoiled at the idea that he might profit from the project. In fact, Trump's financial gain was not nearly as great as it would have been if he had been able to proceed on his own. However, his success at Riverside South, which came to be known as Trump Place, was one of two projects that confirmed that he was back. The second involved the dramatic overhaul of the Gulf+Western Building, which had stood on Columbus Circle since 1969.

An unwieldy conglomerate best known for its Paramount motion picture division, Gulf+Western had made everything from aluminum to zinc. Beginning in the 1980s the company went through a long period of restructuring, and many of its divisions were sold. By the 1990s the smaller firm, which was operating as Paramount, was acquired by Viacom. As Paramount left the building on Columbus Circle, its owner, the General Electric Pension Trust, took control of the property. Forty-four stories high, the skyscraper had been designed and constructed to flex when buffeted by winds. Although it was perfectly safe, the movement could be unnerving to those who did business in the building or dined at its rooftop restaurant. The swaying caused problems for rental agents, but the building's height was extremely valuable. Modern regulations would not permit such a large building on the site. However, if demolition crews could strip the building to its skeleton, and steelworkers could reinforce the steel to reduce the swaying, the structure could be turned into a profitable, high-end condominium.

In his weakened financial condition Trump could not buy the Gulf + Western tower and rebuild it on his own. But as he had shown at Riverside South, he could function well as a partner and a manager. At Columbus Circle he would be a minority partner with GE and a firm called Galbreath and Company in what became Trump International Hotel and Tower. Blessed with a desirable location and views, the building was popular with those who could afford the high prices. However its shiny black design, which evoked the Darth Vader character in *Star Wars*, left critics such as James Polshek of Columbia University dismayed. Dean of the school's architecture program, Polshek said that Trump had taken a building that was "nothing" and turned it into "less than nothing." On the West Side, added Polshek, Trump's Riverside South was "grotesquely banal" and an architectural "embarrassment." Writer Elizabeth Kolbert quoted another architect who described Trump's collection of Manhattan buildings as a "trail of tears." She also explained that the term Trumpification had come to represent urban developments that were "big, shiny and self-absorbed," not unlike the man himself. "I can't think of anything that he's done that has any lasting urban or esthetic value," said architecture critic Carter Wiseman.[10]

But where the aesthetically oriented found banality, Trump's partners saw profits. When Japanese hotelier Hideki Yokoi purchased the Empire State Building for $42 million, his daughter brought Trump in as a partner. Everything about this deal was complicated. First, the skyscraper's previous owner had refused to sell to Yokoi because he'd made his bid from prison, where he was serving a sentence as a result of a fire at his Tokyo hotel, which had killed thirty-three people. Yokoi then used a front man to purchase the skyscraper. He got it for an extraordinarily low price because it was burdened by an onerous lease, which gave Harry Helmsley and his partners the right to rent out the entire building in exchange for an annual payment of just $1.9 million. With tenants paying a combined $80 million annually, it was a good deal for the Helmsley-Spear management company, and it would only get better because it actually called for their rent to decrease over time. The contract, signed in 1961, would not expire until 2075.

After operating expenses, which included upkeep on the building, Helmsley-Spear still made far greater profits than whoever might own the property. For Yokoi and Trump, who had little say in how the place was run, the Empire State Building was a passive investment, like a savings bond paying less than 5 percent interest. To solve the problem of the lease, Trump turned to one of his favorite business tools—the lawsuit. In court he alleged that Helmsley-Spear had broken the terms of its contract in more than one hundred different ways. The litigation continued after Harry Helmsley died in 1997 and his interest was inherited by his wife, Leona. Trump carried on a public feud with Leona Helmsley, who had been imprisoned from 1992 to 1994 after her conviction on federal tax-evasion charges. He called her "vicious," "horrible," and "a living nightmare." She called him "sick" and a "skunk" and declared, "I wouldn't believe Donald Trump if his tongue was notarized." After seven years and untold sums spent in legal costs, Trump and Yokoi gave up and sold the building to a group headed by local real estate investor Peter Malkin.[11]

How much did Trump earn from his effort and his interest in the Empire State Building? Speculation in the press ran as high as $6,250,000, but his arrangement with Hideki Yokoi was private. Whatever his profit may have been, it also included the bragging rights that came with having a stake in one of the best-known landmarks in the world. This allure had attracted Yokoi, and it surely motivated Donald Trump. Early in his partnership with Yokoi, Trump invited a journalist from the BBC to accompany him on a tour of his properties and noted that he owned the Empire State Building. Reporter Selina Scott was duly impressed, until she examined the claim more closely and discovered that he was just a *part* owner, and the property, minus the leasing rights, was not an impressive holding for a big-time real estate man.

When she met Trump, Scott was one of Britain's most-recognized TV journalists. She had cohosted the BBC's morning show for more than a decade and had worked for several British networks. Her piece on Trump was to be aired as part of a series on prominent people around the world. She began her research believing "he was a regular guy, obviously good at making money," but came to regard him as a man who had "gotten his own way by treating people appallingly." Scott was especially put off by Trump's behavior with women.[12]

With blond hair and blue eyes, Scott was the sort of beautiful woman who seemed to catch Trump's eye. (She was once voted the sexiest woman on television in Great Britain.) Her producer Ted Brocklebank would recall that she was charming, especially with powerful men. "She came over as very innocent and flickered her eyelashes," he said. With Trump the flickering came with some banter about eligible men in America. During a flight to Palm Beach on Trump's jet, he flirted back. When they then sat for a formal interview, Scott asked tough questions about Trump's comments about Barbara Walters and others. She also pressed him about his true wealth. She later discovered a camera problem had left her with no usable tape. To her amazement, Trump agreed to another session. However, he did not provide Scott and her crew with a plane ride back to New York.

Scott returned to Great Britain persuaded of Trump's abilities. "He can be effusive," she eventually concluded. "He's been trained to turn on the charm." But she and Brocklebank were both disturbed by the aggressive, hypercompetitive elements of the man's personality and struggled to explain them. They had visited with Trump's mother, who had been born in 1912, hoping to detect the source of his ambition and attention-seeking. She relaxed enough with them to marvel at the fate that had brought her from a poor Scottish household to a life that found her making the rounds of her husband's developments, in a Rolls-Royce, to collect the coins tenants used to pay for washing and drying their clothes.

Scott concluded that as a mother who had known true hardship in her childhood Mrs. Trump had spoiled her son. "He was Mummy's boy," said Scott, "and terribly spoiled as a child. He had everything he wanted and never had much taken away from him." Trump reminded Scott of bullies she had known in her school days: "I came across embryonic Donald Trumps. Usually people lose that trait of saying, 'I want it. You give it to me, or I will smash you.'" Trump, she said, had not lost that trait.

When Scott and Brocklebank assembled their film, they made biting use of the song "It Ain't Necessarily So" from the opera *Porgy and Bess*. The program was peppered "from beginning to end with assertions on his part that didn't stand up," said Brocklebank. Trump responded quite angrily after the report was aired. In letters to Scott, which she made public, he described her as "very sleazy," "unattractive," "obnoxious," and "boring." He also wrote, "Selina, you have little talent and, from what I have seen, even fewer viewers. You are no longer 'hot'; perhaps that is the curse of dishonesty. You would, obviously, go to any lengths to try to restore your faded image, but guess what—the public is aware and apparently much brighter than you. They aren't tuning in! I hope you are able to solve your problems before it is too late."[13]

The public conflict led executives at Scott's network, ITV, to shelve the film after it was aired just once. Plans to distribute it for broadcast in other countries were also scrapped. Scott continued working in television full-time for a few more years, but then cut back her broadcasting work to start a textile business. She would report that Trump continued sending her occasional angry letters for a decade. She also said that after her broadcast, Princess Diana, whom she considered a friend, phoned to ask her about Trump because he had sent Diana many bouquets of flowers. (Diana's unhappiness in her marriage was widely known, but she was not yet officially divorced.) Scott recalled that in her conversation with the princess "I told her to just bin the lot."

In 1997, eight weeks after Diana's death in a car crash, Trump would tell interviewer Stone Phillips and a national TV audience in America that he regretted that he had never asked the princess for a date. When Phillips asked Trump if he thought he would have received a yes, he answered, "I think so, yeah. I always have a shot."[14]

As he mused about missing the opportunity to date a recently deceased mother of two young boys, the unseemly quality of Trump's remarks was moderated, a bit, by his being almost single again. Early in the year he and Marla had confirmed they were going to divorce. When she spoke to the press, Maples sounded more sad than angry. She described her husband as a man obsessed with business to such a degree that he was emotionally detached from loved ones, including his four children. "I absolutely wish he could have been more present in all of their lives," Maples said. "I would have loved to have seen him be the kind of dad that would take us all to Disney World and sit around the dinner table without having to have the financial news on. My big argument was 'At this table is what's going on in the world. It's about your family. It's about the people who love you. That's what's going on in the world.' "[15]

The other side of the story emerged in the pages of Donald Trump's third book, *Trump: The Art of the Comeback,* which included separate chapters on the women in his life and "The Art of the Prenup." In these pages, Trump depicted women as sexually voracious "killers" who traded on their beauty to dominate men. In one passage he puzzled over his track record: "I don't know why, but I seem to bring out either the best or the worst in women." In another he offered a possible answer: "Part of the problem I've had with women has been in comparing them with my incredible mother, Mary Trump." Prenups were, he wrote, an unfortunate necessity for people of great wealth, and if Marla hadn't read the one she signed, he recalled, it was reviewed by her attorney. He also declared that if he ever fell in love again, he hoped it would be with a "no-maintenance" woman.

The end of Donald Trump's second marriage did not produce the same drama as the public saw in the divorce of Donald and Ivana. Nevertheless, Marla did challenge the prenup, which provided for a onetime payment of $2 million and ongoing support. Before a judge, and the court of public opinion, she argued that her husband had promised her more, although he didn't put it in writing. But after eighteen months of legal maneuvers, and the start of a new romance with writer Norman Mailer's son Michael, she accepted the original deal. Donald withheld $1.5 million for a few days when Marla told a British paper she would divulge "what he's really like" if he pursued a campaign for president. Lawyers intervened. Trump concluded that Marla was just angling for attention and the check was delivered.

◆

Although the Trump/Maples marriage didn't work out, they maintained a shared interest in their daughter and would occasionally come together to deal with echoes of the past. One that continued to reverberate for years involved a bizarre criminal case involving the publicity agent Chuck Jones.

In the mid-1990s Jones was arrested on charges of stealing various personal items, including more than forty shoes, from Maples's apartment. (When investigators found he possessed an unlicensed firearm, he was also charged with this crime.) In his defense Jones made much of the fact that he was often permitted to enter the apartment when his client was not present and for a time it seemed the charges would be dropped. Maples actually participated in talks to head the case off before it went to court. However, the agreement that would have saved Jones from trial eventually fell apart and he was subjected to prosecution.

In the annals of New York crime, Chuck Jones would become the object of much ridicule as he was convicted of stealing from Maples to satisfy a fetish. However the conviction was overturned on a technicality and Jones was released after serving just a few months of a term that could have run for nearly five years. Despite his good luck, Jones couldn't stay out of trouble. When he sent out photos purportedly showing Maples and Trump in intimate circumstances and was promptly arrested for aggravated harassment.

In 1999, after Trump and Maples were no longer married, Jones was tried again on the original burglary charges. It was a sign of his poor judgment that he represented himself in court. The picture of Jones that emerged during the proceedings was of a man who was obsessed with his client and unable to leave her alone. Some of the evidence made it seem that he could even be dangerous. He was convicted and this time there would be no technicalities to save him from prison.

Remarkably, Jones's obsession was so powerful that even a federal prison term couldn't squelch it. As late as 2012 he would send her harassing e-mails and land in court again. This time a plea deal would net him a six months' sentence. Jones would forever be remembered as the publicist who stalked—and terrified—a client. Those who knew him to be a charming and intelligent man could only wonder at his fate. Those who knew him only from what they learned from the press would consider him a sad if not pathetic figure.[16]

12
CANDIDATE TRUMP

Mostly driven by ego, some driven by greed,
most driven by both.
—DONALD TRUMP ON THE MOTIVATIONS
OF POLITICIANS

For six years Donald Trump failed to make the *Forbes* magazine list of America's four hundred richest people. Limited by the data available, and because some people prefer to keep their wealth private, the list has never been a perfect representation of the richest slice of America. But no other source had kept a running tally of individual fortunes for so long, which meant that the publication of the list was widely anticipated and announced in the press around the world. For some among the four hundred, the publication became an annual rite of affirmation. It demonstrated to one's peers, and the entire world, just how well you measured up. This explained why Donald Trump regularly contacted the magazine's editors to say that he should be included when he was not, or that his fortune was bigger than they reported.

Trump's exile ended in 1996, when *Forbes* pegged his net worth at $450 million, which made him number 373. Nevertheless, he called the editors to complain that his worth was much bigger: "I've got that much in stock market assets alone." In 1997 he returned to the billionaires' club—$1.4 billion—and almost cracked the top 100. Still he wasn't satisfied: "The real number is

$3.7 billion." The pattern continued for the next couple of years. In 1999 he said the *Forbes* estimate of $1.6 billion was off by almost $3 billion. "We love Donald," said the *Forbes* editors. "He returns our calls. He usually pays for lunch. He even estimates his own net worth ($4.5 billion). But no matter how hard we try, we just can't prove it."

Forbes struggled with Trump's score because much of his wealth was privately held and not subject to independent audits to confirm the balance between his assets and his liabilities. Also, any measure of Trump's wealth depended on estimates of the value of his real estate holdings. Unlike stocks and bonds, which are traded at posted prices, buildings and vacant land are not plastered with price tags. Their value depends on what a buyer will pay, and no one can predict the figure until a purchase is made. Still, the editors at *Forbes* knew that by concentrating on the highest end of the market, in one of the world's most expensive cities, Trump had made a wise bet. With every year Manhattan attracted more of the world's wealthiest people, who sought to live in luxury apartments. This demand ratcheted up the value of real estate, which motivated developers, who purchased properties that once served middle-class New Yorkers and turned them into expensive housing. Manhattan's gentrification was aided by city officials, who envisioned greater tax revenues with each new development. As this process took hold, the share of affordable, rent-controlled apartments declined, which sent the poor and the middle class to the outer boroughs. Those who criticized this trend noted that incoming whites were pushing black and Hispanic residents out and Manhattan was starting to resemble a high-rise suburb. For Trump, who only had to maintain his properties to see them increase in value, this gentrification brought almost magical returns on his investments as, every year, the borough of Manhattan became more exclusive.[1]

The value of Trump's real estate was subject to interpretation. However, the performance of Trump Hotels and Casino Resorts, which included all of his gambling properties and required active day-to-day management in a highly competitive market, was plain to see in its stock price. Every year, as Trump's fortunes rose, the stockholders in his public company suffered. In September 1999, as Donald Trump claimed he was vastly more wealthy than others recognized, a share of the stock traded under the man's initials could be had for a mere $4.44.

All casino stocks declined in value in the same period, but DJT was hit especially hard as the company failed to meet Trump's predictions for big revenue gains.

Trump's performance when it came to running a public company led to talk about how his name, which supposedly boosted the value of real estate, had the opposite effect on stocks. This "Donald discount" meant that traders shaved the price to compensate for the difference between his hype and his results. In March of 1997, Steve Ruggiero, an analyst for Chase securities, said "[t]he biggest problem is they aren't forthcoming with all the analysts . . . It raises suspicions." Suspicion may also have been fueled by occasional reports of improprieties committed by Trump the man, and his companies. In early 1998, the casino operation paid a $477,000 fine to the US Treasury for failing to submit timely reports on currency transactions, as required by regulations that were intended to prevent money laundering by criminals. In 2000, Trump and his associates would pay $250,000 to settled the State of New York's claim that they failed to disclose that they had secretly financed advertisements against the development of casinos in the Catskill Mountains region. A full $50,000 of this fine was paid by Trump Hotels and Casino Resorts. The agreement provided that there was no admission of wrongdoing on Trump's part.[2]

Among the associates who were also fined in the connection with this scheme was Roy Cohn acolyte Roger Stone, who once summed up his methods in a conversation with *New Yorker* writer Jeffrey Toobin by saying, "Attack, attack, attack—never defend" and "Admit nothing, deny everything, launch counterattack." In general, Stone's attacks were intended to persuade voters that the GOP, which was traditionally the party of big business and the country-club set, was actually the anti-elite party of the working class. To do this he played on many Americans' discomfort with intellectuals (the elites Stone opposed) and their appreciation for those who succeeded in the economic marketplace. In this calculus wealth equaled virtue, and thus anyone who defended business or proved himself a success as an entrepreneur was worthy of support. This formula produced what writer Thomas Frank called "market populism," which melded aspects of pop culture, patriotism, and pro-business ideology into a belief system that blamed most of the country's problems on government and intellectuals, especially those who could be called politically liberal. At GOP rallies and on Fox News network programs, the enemy sometimes included labor unions and anyone else who might oppose those who would amass enormous fortunes as businesspeople or financiers. Millions of Americans embraced this view, including many who were themselves falling out of the middle class as wealth became ever more concentrated at the top.[3]

Although Stone was able to articulate market populism and design campaigns to exploit it, Donald Trump understood it viscerally. Eager to identify with those who were wary of social and intellectual elites, he talked about how he preferred meat and potatoes to haute cuisine and disdained high-society events. Always ready to push the bounds of propriety, Trump also pandered to the prejudices that arise out of fear.

When he said, "If I were starting off today, I would love to be a well-educated black because they have an actual advantage," Trump touched directly on the insecurities of whites who were struggling to keep up in a Darwinian economy. In 1989, when he made this remark, few white men would choose to be black. Some did, however, resent both affirmative action programs, which were created to redress historical discrimination, and school integration efforts that affected their families while exempting those who could afford to send their children to private school. Trump cut through the complexities of these issues, appealing to white grievance and forgoing a sophisticated understanding of race in his time.[4]

But while Trump occasionally promoted his views on race and social class, he constantly dwelled on his own success. He would confess that he had struggled in some aspects of his personal life, but would also draw attention to the many beautiful women he had known as proof that he was an impressive man. In another place or time, this kind of talk would be dismissed as crass and self-defeating. But in Trump's time, self-promotion had become an acceptable if not essential part of everyday life. With the advent of the Internet and then social networking sites such as Facebook, individuals in all walks of life developed sophisticated, brochure-ready versions of themselves based on flattering pictures, tales of their impressive exploits, and reports on their latest purchases. Sizing up the end of the twentieth-century, an NBC TV executive with a doctorate in sociology said that superficiality had triumphed over substance. "All the stuff our parents told us didn't come true," said

Rosalyn Weinman, PhD. "No one cares if you're good. People only care if you're good-looking and rich."[5]

Having won the attention of the press and public as a rich and good-looking man, Donald Trump continually sought to keep it. To stay good-looking he battled against middle-age weight gain, wore a uniform of expensive suits, and devoted great effort to keeping his hair. "The worst thing a man can do is let himself go bald," he had once told casino executive Mark Estess. "Never let yourself go bald." As he said this, Trump gave Estess a tube of cream that supposedly stopped the progress of hair loss. The cream was just one part of the Trump campaign against baldness. In his book *Lost Tycoon,* writer Harry Hurt described a surgical procedure that had closed the bald spot on the back of Trump's head.[6]

Trump denied he underwent surgery for hair loss, but beginning around 1990 his coif became the subject of frequent speculation in the press. Once a helmet of brown, it became an extravagant complex of reddish-gold swirls and parts that included swooping strands that moved from one side of his head to the other, and others that went from back to front. All this effort led *Time* magazine to consult a stylist and publish a diagrammed account of how it was done. Presented under the headline "The Secret to Donald Trump's Hair," the graphic showed how a man's hair, grown long in the back, could be combed forward, then swept back and fixed with spray. Captions warned, "Don't confuse this with a classic side-part comb over," and referenced the dramatic styles of cartoon character Wilma Flintstone and real-life talk-show host Conan O'Brien, whose unruly, red waves resembled breaking surf.

Trump was a good sport about the hair commentary. On occasion he would invite an interviewer to examine his head to see if it was real. But the media's fascination with Trump's hair didn't revolve around the question of whether it was real. What was significant was what it said about his audacious vanity. In his mind, going bald was a greater shame than the confection atop his head. In time, his hair would become such a distinguishing feature that costume makers would sell Trump wigs for Halloween.

As a man who craved attention, Trump was unable to change his hairstyle because it got him noticed, and there was almost nothing he wouldn't do for attention. In 1999 he went so far as to renounce his membership in the Republican Party and engage in an extended flirtation with the Reform Party of the United States of America, which was preparing to field a candidate in the 2000 presidential election. As Trump began his political whirl, he turned to Roger Stone, the onetime dirty trickster, to direct what was called an "exploratory" committee. These organizations allowed anyone who thought he or she might want to run to act like a candidate and solicit the attention of the press and public, without committing to a process that could be won or lost on the basis of actual votes. Exploratory activities were like the pitches thrown by a fastballer warming up for the game. Fans might ooh and aah at the sound of the ball popping into the catcher's mitt, but it didn't count until the umpire cried, "Play ball!"

One could have said that Reform Party process was basically an exhibition that would amount to little more than an outlet for the frustrations of those who believed, more as a matter of faith than fact, that Bill Clinton had won election as president because his GOP opponents were insufficiently conservative. A legacy of businessman Ross Perot's failed 1992 and 1996 presidential campaigns, the Reform Party was so small and disorganized that it stood no chance of winning a national election. Perot's showings had, however, qualified it for more than $12 million in federal aid in the 2000 campaign. This money was a lure for consultants, who would enjoy a bit of cash flow if they were hired to conduct polls, craft strategies, or develop campaign advertisements. But no independent political expert would give the party any chance of playing more than a spoiler's role in the 2000 presidential race.

The party's one real claim to success had been the election of former pro wrestler Jesse "the Body" Ventura as governor of Minnesota in 1998. Yet Ventura's election was more a matter of his celebrity than his Reform Party affiliation, which he underscored when he left the group during his first year in office. Some in the Reform Party hoped to woo him back, but as the 2000 election approached, the Body declined to seek its presidential nomination. His decision left the field open to others, including the longtime Republican activist Patrick Buchanan, who claimed a "peasant army" would support him. Like Roger Stone, Buchanan was a Nixon alumnus with rather extreme views. His inflammatory comments about the Holocaust, for example, had earned him the label "unrepentant bigot" from the Jewish Anti-Defamation League.

Buchanan, who had mounted two previous failed attempts to win the GOP nomination, framed his campaign for the Reform Party nod as a matter of principle, saying that he represented the true conservatism that the Republicans had abandoned. Anti-abortion and isolationist in his foreign policy, Buchanan was driven by his desire to get a hearing for his ideas, some of which were consistent with those Perot had advanced as the Reform Party's first standard-bearer. With his campaign, Buchanan got what he wanted as voters attended his speeches, reporters wrote articles about his views, and TV producers invited him to appear on national programs such as *Meet the Press, Face the Nation,* and *Fox News Sunday.*

Trump received the same kind of attention after he joined the party in the fall of 1999 and said he was considering a run for the Reform Party nomination. His views were less refined and detailed than those offered by Buchanan, who had spent decades in politics. Trump also expressed some ideas that would have appealed to mainstream Americans but were anathema to many Reform Party stalwarts. For example, Trump said the Republicans had "moved too far toward the extreme right" and that he was capable of capturing more than the "really staunch-right wacko vote" by reaching middle-of-the-road Americans. But the core of the Reform Party was "staunch right," and Trump would never win the party's nomination by veering left. He did make himself more visible with every appearance in the press, where his audience could be rewarded with outrageous statements:

On Buchanan: "He's a Hitler lover; I guess he's an anti-Semite. He doesn't like the blacks, he doesn't like the gays."

On Cuba: Fidel Castro is "a killer and should be treated as such."

On his ideal running mate: Oprah Winfrey because "she's popular, she's brilliant, she's a wonderful woman."

On candidates who are proud of their humble backgrounds: "They're losers. Who the hell wants to have a person like this for president?"

In the amalgamation that was his platform, Trump included items from the left side of the political menu, including a big, onetime tax on the rich to trim the federal deficit, a policy to allow gay soldiers in the military, and universal employer-based health insurance with subsidies for the poor. Reports on his campaign tended to dwell more on the idea of his candidacy rather than on the ideas he would advocate. Quoted as Trump's campaign manager, Roger Stone made much of how

Trump possessed a list of 6.5 million names and addresses, thanks to the record keeping at his casinos and hotels. Stone also celebrated that his man came in second to George W. Bush in a poll of voter preferences.

The survey was cited by Trump as evidence of a groundswell of support, which, he said, prompted him to form a campaign committee to advise him on a run. He did not make public the names of those who would advise him, and the poll, which was conducted by the less-than-authoritative *National Enquirer* tabloid, surveyed just one hundred people in a land of 280 million. Nevertheless, Trump said that he believed he had "huge" public support. He also noted that he enjoyed two great advantages over other candidates: first, he was extremely well-known, and second, he was extremely rich, which meant he could pay for his own campaign and forgo the effort and obligations that come with soliciting donations.

In 2000 *Forbes* estimated Trump's wealth at $1.7 billion, which made him the 167th richest man in America. The magazine explained that Trump believed he was worth "more than $5 billion" but "back on earth" his fortune was "considerably less." Trump's view of his political capital was similarly inflated. Though he claimed to enjoy broad voter support, a Quinnipiac University poll found that roughly nine out of ten New Yorkers, the people who knew him best, didn't think they would vote for him.[7]

With his scattershot platform and talk, candidate Trump evoked not a serious leader but the main character from the movie *Bulworth,* which premiered the year before his flirtation with the Reform Party. As played by Warren Beatty, suicidal Senator Jay Bulworth careened around his state seeking votes with outspoken abandon, gathering more support with every outrageous statement. His profane, and even racist remarks, were taken as evidence of his sincerity by voters, who had been subject to so much political manipulation that they found his efforts to repel them absolutely magnetic.

Although the fictional Jay Bulworth intended to lose by being offensive and inconsistent, the real Donald Trump hoped to gain as he veered from left to right and denigrated other candidates. ("He's got a bad way about him," said Trump of former senator Bill Bradley, who was often mentioned as a presidential contender.) Trump would have had to be delusional to believe he had any more of a chance to be elected than the comedian Pat Paulsen, who had received 921 votes in the 1996 New Hampshire Democratic presidential primary. However, unlike Paulsen, Trump never let on that his campaign was a joke. Instead he presented himself as a serious candidate whose business success qualified him for the highest office in the world. In this way, the Trump-for-president folly may have been the first true pseudocampaign in the history of the presidency, a determined effort to exploit the political process by a man whose real purpose was profit. Susan Tolchin, a public-policy professor at George Mason University, suggested that the performance was actually a duet that included Buchanan. While they weren't serious political figures, Tolchin said they could not be entirely dismissed: "I think people are taking them seriously. They are entertainers, a very important part of society today."

As an entertainer Trump was such a game performer that he had pushed himself forward as a candidate less than three weeks after his father's death. Fred C. Trump died after suffering from Alzheimer's disease for six years. He was dispatched with a prominent obituary in *The New York Times,* which called him a "postwar master builder of housing for the middle class."

The paper also noted that Fred had been "overshadowed in recent years by his son Donald."

Donald was not interviewed and quoted at the time of his father's death, but at the end of the year he did offer a comment, albeit a self-referential one, for the annual roundup of obituaries, which *The Times* published to mark the passing of notable men and women: "I had friends whose fathers were very successful, and the fathers were jealous of the sons' success and tried to hurt them, keep them down, because they wanted to be the king. My father was the exact opposite. He used to carry around articles." Maryanne Trump pointed to her father's caution and humility. Noting he had never put his name on any of his previous projects, she said her father had to be coaxed to have a sign that announced TRUMP VILLAGE posted on the big complex he built in Brighton Beach.

As the Reform Party convention drew near, Trump attacked Governor George W. Bush of Texas as inexperienced. He said that he was offering voters a businessman's "eye for the bottom line," which was an odd kind of offer, given that his Trump Hotels and Casino Resorts operation was about to post a loss of $34.5 million for the last quarter of 1999. Trump also derided his most likely opponents, Al Gore and Bush, as "Ivy League contenders" without a hint of embarrassment about his diploma from Penn, which was an Ivy League school. He announced that if elected president, he would appoint himself to the post of international trade representative, which would permit him to be addressed as either Mr. President or Mr. Ambassador or, perhaps, Mr. President Ambassador.

Political veterans such as Dick Morris observed that Trump was publishing a new book, *The America We Deserve,* which might get a boost in sales from the author/candidate's appearances on TV talk shows such as *Larry King Live* (CNN), *The Early Show* (CBS), and the *Tonight* show (NBC), which invited him to talk politics.

Many of his ideas were dismissed as unworkable. For example, a onetime tax on the rich was labeled "harebrained" by economist and securities analyst David Jones, who said it could cause a stock-market collapse. (A former IRS commissioner called it "wacky, constitutionally.") A few of Trump's proposals did show he was both forward-looking and ideologically flexible. Among them was a project to develop and stockpile treatments in anticipation of future pandemics or the use of release of biological agents by terrorists.

Always unconventional, Trump didn't deliver stump speeches to political audiences. It appeared that he made just one traditional campaign-style foray, which brought him to South Florida to speak to Cuban Americans for a day. Otherwise he traveled the country via private jet and pocketed $100,000 per appearance for the business advice he dispensed at seminars, where he shared the stage with Tony Robbins, a janitor turned self-help guru. Robbins, who in recent years had legal troubles that cost him more than $870,000, organized the Results 2000 speaking tour for himself, Trump, and others he called "the masters of our time." But while Robbins advertised these events as "seminars," for which attendees paid as much as $229 apiece for tickets, the Trump exploratory committee described them as "speeches." On the day of the Results 2000 event in Hartford, Connecticut, a Trump aide told a reporter for the *New York Daily News* that while others expended great amounts on their campaigns, "Trump is *making* money running for president."

When Trump arrived for the Results 2000 event in St. Louis, a reporter for the *Post-Dispatch* newspaper dutifully noted the big private jet with TRUMP emblazoned on it and informed her readers that the man would be speaking at the nineteen-thousand-seat arena where the local pro hockey team played its games. The crowd heard roughly thirty minutes of Donald's business advice, much of which could be found in his books, including "Donald's Rules of Success," which included "think big" and "be paranoid." Tony Robbins offered Norman Vincent Peale updated for a new century. Where Peale emphasized the power of positive thinking, Robbins stressed the use of "trigger" phrases such as "Step up!" and "I'll do it" to provoke the mind's power. "We're not talking confidence," said Robbins, "we're talking certainty. It's a different level." As Trump dwelled on money, Robbins emphasized power. The word *power* appeared on many of the products he offered for sale, including a book called *Unlimited Power* and an audio set called *Unleash the Power Within*.

Headliners Robbins and Trump were joined by different costars in each city. In St. Louis the crowd heard from retired US Army general Norman Schwarzkopf, who led US and allied forces in America's first Gulf War in 1990. Widely regarded as a military hero, Schwarzkopf had accepted $5 million for his memoirs and was spending much of his retirement giving well-paid, inspirational speeches to audiences who greeted him with enthusiasm. At the St. Louis event, however, the biggest cheers were reserved for Dick Vermeil, whose honors had been earned in the American sport most closely resembling warfare—football. Vermeil's St. Louis Cardinals had won the Super Bowl days before the seminar.

After his St. Louis speech, Trump stayed in character as a politician until the middle of February, when he went on television to announce that he was ending his campaign because "the Reform Party is a total mess." The other side of the story came from Reform Party stalwarts who complained that his campaign had never been serious. They believed that he ran to get people to buy his books, purchase tickets to hear him speak, and drop their cash at his gambling halls. "Donald Trump came in, promoted his hotels, he promoted his book, he promoted himself at our expense, and I think he understands fully that we've ended the possibilities for such abuse of our party," said Patrick Choate, a Reform Party leader.[8]

Trump would admit that his political gambol had been good for his business interests. For example, without his supposed candidacy he would not have drawn press to an airport hangar in St. Louis when he jetted into town to address a crowd of people who had bought tickets to hear him speak about life, business, and the secrets of success.

Not one to leave the measure of his success to anyone else, Trump published an accounting of his experience days after he took himself out of contention. His self-portrait was of a man who was thwarted by the rules and stymied by those in the Reform Party who were so extreme they believed a conspiracy of the powerful ran the country. Trump also took a swipe at Al Gore because he appeared to be tired as he trudged through snowy New Hampshire seeking votes. In contrast, Trump said, "I had enormous fun thinking about a presidential candidacy and count it as one of my great life experiences."[9]

It is hard to argue with the idea that *thinking* about running for president was more fun than actually doing it, although some candidates—Bill Clinton, Ronald Reagan, Hubert Humphrey—had made campaigning look quite joyous. Trump said that his presidential flirtation "doesn't compare with completing one of the great skyscrapers of Manhattan," but he wouldn't rule out a reprise in 2004. That year he did stay on the sidelines, but he occasionally heckled President Bush for his economic policy, and the war in Iraq, which Trump doubted would produce a stable democracy. The war had been the centerpiece of Bush's response to the attacks on

America by the Islamic terror group al-Qaeda on September 11, 2001. Trump said that if he were president, Osama bin Laden, who led the terrorist group and remained at large, "would have been caught long ago."[10]

Trump's comments about Bush and bin Laden were published in July 2004 by *Esquire* magazine and repeated by the press across the country. Weeks later, stock-exchange officials halted trading of shares in Trump Hotels and Casino Resorts as word spread that the company was going to file for bankruptcy. Under the company's reorganization plan, the stockholders' share of the firm's value would decline from more than 40 percent to less than 5 percent. Investors who had put money into Trump bonds would fare better, suffering just a single-digit loss.

Rumors of the company's demise had circulated for two years. Analysts blamed competition from new casinos in Atlantic City and nearby states where lawmakers had approved gambling to generate tax revenues. Upkeep had been neglected to the point where, as *The Wall Street Journal* noted, "Trump's casinos have been running down." In the reorganization plan Trump was given a $2 million annual salary, plus expenses, to continue running the firm. He received, as well, a minority stake in the Miss Universe pageant, which the firm owned with the NBC television network, and a three-acre piece of Atlantic City real estate valued at $7.5 million. When shareholders sued, Trump paid them $17.5 million and agreed that the lot would be auctioned and the proceeds distributed to them.[11]

Remarkably, Trump's personal net worth, as estimated by *Forbes,* actually increased as his casino/hotel company stumbled and declined. In 2003, he was estimated to have a fortune of $2.5 billion, which made him number 71 in the United States. In 2005 the figure would be $2.7 billion, which made him number 83. How could

Trump fall a dozen spots even as he gained $200 million? For the very rich, the new millennium had brought astounding increases in their net worth. As of 2005, more than twenty Americans held assets valued at greater than $10 billion. During this period the income gap between the top 1 percent and every other American had grown wider, upward mobility had decreased, and the median net worth for American families, minus the value of their homes, had remained essentially unchanged since the 1980s at about $20,000. Wages had barely risen during this same period, and job security in the private sector had declined. Traditional company-paid pensions almost disappeared, replaced by savings plans that workers were supposed to fund and manage themselves with the aid of Wall Street. (According to free-market wisdom, those who invested in corrupt companies such as Enron, which went bust in spectacular fashion, had only themselves to blame for their losses.)[12]

For those Americans who sought advice to help them cope, Trump offered two new books, *Trump: How to Get Rich* and *Trump: Think Like a Billionaire*. Both books were heavy on photos and recycled bits that would be familiar to an avid reader of his oeuvre. *Think Like a Billionaire* promoted Trump-branded products such as his signature cuff links and items offered by companies that had done business with Trump. As he recommended American Express cards, he noted that the company rented space in one of his buildings. He boosted McDonald's hamburgers as one of the two best burgers available with the reminder "I did a major ad for them." The best books? "I have two: *The Art of the Deal* and *How to Get Rich,* both by Donald J. Trump."

Trump's titles competed with a shelf-ful of popular financial self-help books such as *Who Moved My Cheese?* and *Secrets of the Millionaire Mind,* which exhorted readers to shape their lives with entrepreneurial creativity even as they struggled to stay employed and pay their bills. Napoleon Hills for twenty-first-century, the authors of these books prescribed constant self-reinvention and relentless positive thinking as the keys to continued employment in a global economy that pitted the workers of the world against each other. One of these books was actually titled *We Got Fired! . . . And It's the Best Thing That Ever Happened to Us.*

In the moments when they weren't working, researching retirement funds, or reinventing themselves, middle-class Americans could find entertainment on an exploding number of TV channels brought to them via satellite dishes or coaxial cables. Television viewing had, by the year 2000, almost conquered the American consciousness, becoming by far the most popular activity for people of all ages. Scientists had found many ways to study the medium's role in a host of serious problems, from obesity to violence, but measuring its effects on social consciousness was trickier. However the experts generally agreed that while television and, more recently, the Internet, reflected society, they also shaped it.

The images and messages people absorbed as they viewed omnipresent video screens changed their expectations in the real world. The polished skin, teeth, hair, and physiques presented by even minor media figures led to spikes in eating disorders and plastic surgery as viewers sought to copy what they saw. As art imitated life, and then life imitated art, a self-reinforcing cycle was established. To attract attention, the media were required to present provocative people and behaviors. When viewers imitated what they saw, extremes in style, behavior, and even the human body became normalized. Thus the stakes were raised, and soon the media provided even more extreme offerings to keep the public watching.

Similarly, the values of entertainment leaked into

many other human realms, changing what was expected of people. For example, when teachers appeared on TV, even on news programs, they were generally entertaining, which put pressure on real teachers to be entertaining too. (For a thorough analysis see Neil Postman's *Amusing Ourselves to Death*.) The value of performance had become so widely accepted that business experts spoke of an entire economy dependent on the performance abilities of executives and workers. Michael J. Wolf, of Booz Allen Hamilton consultants, noted that many "celebrity executives" such as Richard Branson and Steve Jobs had become characters who made consumers feel good about what they sold. Wolf advised his clients to "incorporate entertainment into their products and services in order to stand out in the marketplace."[13]

Inevitably, the mad scramble to entertain led to a new media genre dependent on the idea that everything human could be reduced to entertainment and sold as a commodity. "Reality television" promised glimpses of what appeared to be spontaneous, unscripted events, which audience members could observe like voyeurs. The programs were supposedly filmed in a less formal style that resembled documentaries and, instead of actors, presented supposedly ordinary people. Theoretically these shows could deliver glimpses of what people craved as they sat isolated in the glow of their screens: authentic humans in genuine interactions. In practice, producers selected telegenic people who represented recognizable types, then put them in carefully plotted scenarios and recorded hours of video to produce just minutes of carefully contrived programming. Audiences were sufficiently entertained to watch in great numbers, but only an insider would be able to identify what was real in each episode and what was not.

Appropriately enough, one of the biggest stars in all of reality TV would be one of the most puzzling real-life characters in the land, a man who was cosmetically buffed and synthetically coiffed, and willing to say and do whatever was required to attract attention. Courageously extreme, he understood that in the media age, the frontier that might challenge a man or woman was found, not in the wilderness, but in the media. The boundary of this wilderness was marked by propriety, which was an elastic concept. Every day people pushed at the limits that were formed by shared ideas about fairness, kindness, and what makes a person obnoxious. At times they suffered rejection, but such setbacks were usually temporary, and eventually the boundary would be moved. Comedian George Carlin's "seven dirty words," which were long-barred from the public airwaves, lost their power due to common use. Greed became good.

In the case of Donald Trump, social frontiersman, the public—his customers—encountered a man who, in the words of Tony Robbins, exuded confidence at "a different level." Trump was willing to say and do almost anything to satisfy his craving for attention. But he also possessed a sixth sense that kept him from going too far. This talent was no doubt honed as he tested the rules imposed by his father, his teachers, his military-school superiors, and every other authority figure he encountered in life. His presidential exploratory committee provided a case in point. As a vehicle for seeking publicity, it made a mockery of national politics. Yet Trump had to know that a great many Americans view politics as so hopelessly corrupt that mockery is in order. By confining himself to the Reform Party, Trump limited himself to a sideshow status, never threatening to disrupt the main contests waged by Republicans and Democrats. The talk-show hosts and political reporters who gave Trump their attention benefited from his quips, comments, and star power. They were themselves entertainers and needed the material Trump brought them.

Two weeks after Trump announced the end of a campaign that never actually began, he accepted a phone call from Vice President Al Gore, who would face George Bush in the general election. Gore wanted Trump's backing, and the billionaire said he was open to the idea. He never did supply what Gore sought, and as the election season progressed toward the autumn of hanging chads, Trump faded from the national political conversation. He had, however, achieved an important goal, establishing himself as a worthy source of commentary on the electoral game despite the fact that he had never formally run for office.

I 3
TRUMP THE TV SHOW

If somebody's going to do a show on me, why would
I say, "No, I don't want it"?
—DONALD TRUMP

Mark Burnett was extreme, even by Trump standards.[1] When he served in the military, the real
military, he led a British commando unit in the war his
country fought against Argentina in 1982. More than
900 lost their lives, among them 256 British citizens, as
the United Kingdom maintained its control over the isolated and sparsely populated Falkland Islands. After
his military service the adventurous Burnett visited Los
Angeles as a tourist and found a job as a nanny in Beverly Hills. He then became a businessman, selling
T-shirts, insurance, and credit cards. By 1995 he had figured out the value of attention-seeking and turned an
outdoor competition he dubbed Eco-Challenge into a
show for broadcast on USA Network, a cable-TV outlet.

Though far more exotic, *Eco-Challenge* resembled
the pioneering British program *Now Get Out of That*
(1981–1984), which had allowed viewers to watch the
exploits of two teams plunked down in the wilderness
who raced to complete a variety of difficult tasks—
building a raft to cross a lake was one—that were only
modestly dangerous. Thus began the modern era of reality programming. Variations included a Dutch show
called *Big Brother,* which focused on students sharing
an apartment, and *Expedition Robinson*, broadcast in

Sweden, which marooned people in completely isolated and uninhabited places, except for a TV production crew. The first two winners of *Expedition Robinson* became instant celebrities. One parlayed her victory into a long and lucrative television career.

Cheaper to produce than dramatic series that depended on the creativity of actors, directors, and writers, *Expedition Robinson* was such a big and profitable hit in Sweden that networks across Europe lined up to pay the producers to license the format, and soon versions of the show were airing in Switzerland, Austria, and Germany. Mark Burnett arranged to get the American license and began trying to sell it to networks. After NBC declined, he persuaded CBS to put it on under a new name—*Survivor*. The network also bought the rights to the Orwellian *Big Brother,* which confined a group of strangers in a specially built house equipped with cameras that revealed every moment of their lives. The two shows represented an attempt by CBS to catch rival ABC, which had established the live game show *Who Wants to Be a Millionaire* as a valuable hit.[2]

Lord of the Flies in a tiki-bar setting, *Survivor* followed format of the Swedish original as it exploited the worst in human nature in the cause of entertainment and profit. To start, Burnett selected sixteen contestants who, based on their eagerness to participate, were already desperate for attention. Beauty and youth were also weighted heavily in the selection of the contestants, whose bodies would become ever-more exposed as their clothing suffered the ravages of a castaway's life on a Malaysian island. In re-creating as entertainment the dangers faced by real explorers of centuries past, *Survivor* was a product of its time. The contestants would lose a bit of weight and acquire a patina of grime, but all of this was showbiz, as the crews that recorded every scene were also authorized to summon rescuers at any moment. Within hours, and perhaps minutes, the woman in revealing rags or the man with the two-month beard could be carrying his plate to a hotel buffet table. Lewis and Clark, or Stanley and Livingstone, would be amazed.

In *Survivor*'s first season, which was in the summer of 2000, the participants set a template of double-dealing and outrageous behavior. The winner, Richard Hatch, spent much of the show naked as he orchestrated voting alliances to advance himself. But with Hatch's private bits obscured by blurred video and his imprisonment for tax evasion still in the distant future, the program was hardly the kind of depraved display that could be seen on the Fox network's *Who Wants to Marry a Multi-Millionaire?* On that program, which debuted before *Survivor,* the millionaire in question wasn't a wealthy motivational speaker, as he claimed. Rick Rockwell was, instead, a modestly successful comedian who lived in a house with a discarded toilet in its yard. Darva Conger, the telegenically slim and blond "winner," who married Rockwell on camera, quickly divorced him, sold her engagement ring, and posed nude for *Playboy*.

In contrast to *Who Wants to Marry a Multi-Millionaire?* and successor shows that found men or women groveling to be chosen on *The Bachelor* or *The Bachelorette, Survivor* was mainly good-natured camp. With a cast filled with exhibitionists determined to serve a massive audience of voyeurs, *Survivor* was perfect for the attention-getting age. Advertisers, who were offered opportunities to insert their products in the show, clamored to buy commercials and made the program profitable even before it first aired. The show was so widely watched that rival network NBC invited winners to appear on its morning program *Today,* where they were hailed as if they had won something real, say an Olympic medal, and not a game contrived to sell Budweiser beer, which was an original sponsor. Burnett proved to be a deft promoter as he sold both the program and himself. His celebrity led to talk-show appearances and gave him the standing to publish a self-help book—*Dare to Succeed: How to Survive and Thrive in the Game of Life*. He appeared on the cover wearing a black fedora that made him look like the fictional explorer Indiana Jones.

As a silver-screen hero, Jones found adventure as he sought archaeological treasures. Burnett sought treasure as he manufactured adventure. In May 2002 he rented Wollman Rink and turned it into a TV set decorated with beach sand and trees to film the final episode of the fourth competition. Comic/actor/celebrity Rosie O'Donnell was enlisted as host, and an audience of two thousand cheered, moaned, and gasped until a thirty-six-year-old woman from Oregon named Vecepia Towery won. (Towery would be rewarded with $1 million and subsequently give birth on another reality program.) Among those in the audience were assorted journalists and TV producers whose reports would broaden *Survivor*'s reach to take in those who didn't watch the actual program, as well as an admiring Donald Trump. When Mark Burnett stood before the audience to thank them for their attendance, he offered his gratitude to Trump for allowing *Survivor* to use the rink site for the finale. (The space actually belonged to the City of New York.) The two met for the first time after the program. Burnett would recall that Trump said, "I'd love to work with you at some point."[3]

Among New York real estate developers, only one could have been possessed of the chutzpah to offer himself as a partner to a network-television producer. If he felt that his life was a performance, Donald Trump had starred in his own reality show since before Burnett was born. At book signings and paid speaking engagements

Trump had delivered entire monologues for audiences of varying sizes until he was consistently the buoyant and daring man he intended to be, even if the daring things he said were as calculated as the words in a script. He dressed in expensive suits, monogrammed shirts, silk ties, and gold accessories, all of which reflected choices a Hollywood wardrobe specialist might make for an actor cast in the role of "executive." Like many a performer, he did whatever was required to maintain a body that appeared fit, a smooth complexion, a smile that would please any cosmetic dentist, and his trademark glowing hair.

With the effort and expense Trump devoted to his appearance, he managed to conform to media-driven ideals that grew more extreme every year. During his lifetime—which coincided with the age of video— plastic surgery, cosmetic dentistry, and other interventions had gradually changed expectations of what women and men were supposed to look like. As cosmetic advances were embraced by the rich and famous and later by the upper middle class, they became as firmly associated with status, and therefore as desirable, as a fancy sports car or a huge diamond ring. Trump always had the right look, which meant he was always ready for the cameras, even when high-definition technology made every pore visible on-screen.[4]

Mark Burnett recognized Trump's star qualities, but was busy making *Survivor* and adjusting to the demands of wealth and fame. Having joined the armed forces after high school, Burnett was a self-taught mogul who needed to pour great effort into learning how to deliver the programs he promised and manage a production company with hundreds of employees. As Burnett succeeded in television, his marriage fell apart. He would later recall standing in the Amazon jungle talking on a satellite phone with his then ten-year-old son, James, who told him, "Dad, I forgot what you look like.' " Said Burnett, "I thought, 'I really, really have to do something in the city. I have to shoot something that will keep me at home.' "

Months earlier, Burnett had watched a British documentary about a series of candidates all vying for a job at a top company. He thought this could make for a successful reality show. After he spoke with his son, Burnett noticed what looked to him like warring ant colonies on the ground. The sight reminded him of people swarming past each other on the sidewalks of Manhattan. He imagined a program that would pit teams of ants, or rather people, against each other in pursuit of a plum position. Trump came to mind as the ideal host for the program, which would reward the winner with a one-year job in the Trump organization at a six-figure salary.

In 2002, the US economy was reeling from the effects of the 9/11 attacks and the so-called dot-com bust, which saw high-tech companies lose billions of dollars in value and dozens of well-known firms—Pets.com, Razorfish, WorldCom—disappear, taking thousands of jobs with them. According to a historic index of economic attitudes, Americans were pessimistic about their prospects and discouraged about the future. Jobs were of particular concern, and pollsters identified a "leading indicator" that pointed toward a very real problem. In the first decade of the twenty-first century the percentage of adults who were employed full-time would drop from 58 to 41 percent while median wages increased by less than 1 percent. Many corporations were paring direct employment and relying on contract workers, who were paid less and enjoyed little security. In the hotel industry, for example, direct employment would fall to 20 percent of the workforce.[5]

Amid the gloom about jobs, a TV series that dramatized the anxiety many people felt and offered a happy ending that included a high-paying apprenticeship with a glamorous businessman would be ideal entertainment. The competitors on the show could be selected so as to give different segments of the audience contestants to root for and, just as important, against. As the host, Trump could bluster and bully as convincingly as any actor, and his shiny lifestyle—wealth, fame, a jet with his name on it—represented success to millions.

When Burnett returned to the United States in December 2002, the New York press was buzzing with news of a court proceeding in which a state judge was considering evidence that exonerated all five teenagers—now men—convicted in the notorious Central Park Jogger rape of 1989. DNA tests had confirmed that a convicted murderer/rapist named Matias Reyes, who would eventually confess, committed the attack alone. The supposed confessions of the teenagers who were imprisoned for the crime resulted from manipulative techniques deployed during excessively long and grueling interrogations. Countervailing evidence had been ignored as loud voices like Trump's howled for convictions. Reyes said he came forward out of conscience, but the journalists who interviewed him, including the writer Sarah Burns, said he was motivated by the modern, all-American desire for attention. Two reporters who wrote about Reyes's confession noted that Donald Trump had inserted himself into the case with his full-page newspaper advertisements about "roving bands of wild criminals" who "should be forced to suffer." His role was otherwise ignored in the press as the district attorney requested that the men be released, and the judge ordered it.[6]

While the city and the nation reconsidered one of the most notorious criminal cases in memory, Mark Burnett arranged to meet Donald Trump at his office to do some business. As he sat with Trump, Burnett described a program he had decided to call *The Apprentice*. Contestants, who would be called candidates, would be drawn from applicants whose experience or education in real estate, hospitality, promotion, or sales would make them qualified to work in one of Trump's varied businesses. As on *Survivor,* the competitors would be grouped into teams, which would be assigned tasks. Trump would judge their performances, and the weaker participants would be "fired," until eventually only the winner remained.

Although everything about the show suited Trump's desires to be noticed and enriched, he wasn't sure he would have enough time to star in a TV program. Burnett then offered to record it at Trump Tower and promised that Trump wouldn't have to devote more than three or four hours to each episode. Reassured, Trump agreed to work with Burnett for half the profit. After his many long negotiations with executives in the television business, Burnett was all but amazed that he and Trump established the outlines of their partnership in a single session. "Afterwards some of his representatives had different ideas, and he just said, 'No, I've made a deal. We shook hands. It's over,'" recalled Burnett years later. "We have never had a bad word or any issues between lawyers. If something comes up, me and him get on the phone and solve everything, one-on-one."

With reality television more popular than reality itself, NBC executives who regretted that they had passed on *Survivor* promptly bought *The Apprentice*. The network's president, Jeffrey Zucker, who had been criticized in the press for falling behind his competitors, rushed to announce the show was coming as soon as contracts were signed. On April 1, 2003, Zucker joined Trump and Burnett backstage at the *Today* show, on which they would reveal their plans and explain how hopefuls could audition to become candidates. As they discussed the points they hoped to make, the three men realized they hadn't settled on all the elements of the game they would present. In a few minutes of conversation they decided that at the end of each episode the contestants would come before Trump and a board of advisers to be judged on their performances in the day's assigned task. They also determined that the contestants would be sworn to secrecy and live and work together during their quest.[7]

More than 215,000 people applied to be among the first 16 contestants on the show, which wouldn't be broadcast until January 2004. Taking over a vacant floor in Trump Tower, Burnett built a set that looked like a corporate boardroom, but was illuminated by stage lights and ringed with TV cameras set behind two-way mirrors. The chair where Trump would sit was placed on a platform, so he could literally look down on those around him. Burnett built living quarters for the players on the same floor, although on the broadcasts they would be seen entering elevators to suggest they were "going up" to meet Trump and his panel of business experts.

Trump and Burnett made the show in hopes of earning many millions of dollars per year, but this was not a point they emphasized when they discussed it publicly. In dozens of press interviews Trump talked about the educational aspects of the show. "I think there's a whole beautiful picture to be painted about business, American business, how beautiful it is, but also how vicious and tough it is," he told *The New York Times*. "You meet some wonderful people, but you also meet some treacherous, disgusting people that are worse than any snake in the jungle."

The hype reached a crescendo on the day before the premiere broadcast. Burnett and Trump sat together for a day, fielding questions from various entertainment-news reporters. During a break, Trump invited Burnett and public relations man James Dowd up to his apartment in Trump Tower. Dowd and Burnett would recall that in his kitchen Trump opened up the refrigerator to discover it was almost empty. He removed a package of bologna and three Cokes. He took out the bologna, slice by slice, rolled it up, and ate it. When he offered the package to his guests, they joined him, rolling up the pink meat and sliding it into their mouths.

The bologna moment was the kind of thing that won the affection and loyalty of Trump's inner circle and served as a counterpoint to his fits of anger. (Among those fits Dowd recalled were a rant about the ice cubes in his drink and the firing of a driver who wasn't on time.) Trump sought to bond over guy talk, said Dowd, "almost to the point of annoyance. The man talks and talks and talks—about sports, or women. The amount of conversation about sex and women is endless. But he also wants to hear what's going on with you. 'It looks like you lost weight, how's it going?' Nobody knows that about him. The image he's created is so egotistical and not friendly, and he really is the opposite in many ways."

Years after he won the first *Apprentice* contest, Bill Rancic would recall most vividly an encounter he witnessed between Trump and a boy of perhaps ten who had terminal cancer. The boy was a fan of the program and wanted to be "fired" by Trump. A charity called the Make-A-Wish Foundation, arranged a meeting, and the boy got dressed in a suit and tie and rolled a suitcase into the boardroom set of *The Apprentice*. (The show requires that contestants who are dismissed be filmed departing with a wheeled suitcase.) As Rancic would tell the story, Trump shook the boy's hand, listened to his request, but couldn't bring himself to utter his signature line "You're fired." Instead he gave the boy a check for several thousand dollars and said, "Go and have the time of your life."[8]

The reserved Trump who couldn't fulfill a boy's dream to be fired was nowhere to be seen on edited broadcasts of *The Apprentice*. Instead, viewers who tuned in got a nonstop display of his ego. The show opened with the cliché of film shot from an aircraft approaching Manhattan over water. Next came views of skyscrapers, the bustle of Times Square, images of traders on the floor of the New York Stock Exchange, and the patriotic majesty of the Statue of Liberty. The narration was provided in Donald Trump's nasally New Yorkese: "New York. My city. Where the wheels of the global economy never stop turning. A concrete metropolis of unparalleled strength and purpose that drives the business world. Manhattan is a tough place. *This* island is the real jungle. If you're not careful, it can chew you up and spit you out."

To make the specter of failure clear, Burnett exploited the image of a homeless man sleeping on a bench. Next Trump said, "But if you work hard, you can really hit it big, and I mean *really* big."

The image of success Burnett chose for his viewers was a picture of Trump's sprawling mansion, well outside the urban jungle. Then, suddenly, Trump appeared in one of his expensive suits, riding in the back of a black stretch limo and speaking directly into the camera. "My name is Donald Trump, and I'm the largest real estate developer in New York. I own buildings all over the place. Model agencies, the Miss Universe pageant, jetliners, golf courses, casinos, and private resorts like Mar-a-Lago—one of the most spectacular estates anywhere in the world. But it wasn't always so easy. About thirteen years ago, I was seriously in trouble. I was billions of dollars in debt. But I fought back, and I won. Big league. I used my brain, I used my negotiating skills, and I worked it all out. Now my company's bigger than it ever was, and stronger than it ever was, and I'm having more fun than I ever had.

"I've mastered the art of the deal and have turned the name Trump into the highest-quality brand, and as the master, I want to pass along some of my knowledge to somebody else." As music swelled, Trump in the limo gazed at the audience and said, "I'm looking for the apprentice."

By some measure—height, perhaps—Donald Trump may have been the "largest real estate developer in New York," but many builders could reasonably claim to have accomplished more. The company controlled by Jerry Speyer, to cite one example, owned $10.5 billion in real estate. Trump was by far, though, the most successful real estate showman in America, and by the end of the first episode of *The Apprentice* he was a genuine TV star. In that first broadcast, contestants were called to meet Trump at the New York Stock Exchange. There, standing on the balcony where the bell is rung to announce the start of each day of trading, Trump gave them their first task: to sell lemonade on the streets of Manhattan. The members of the team that made the most money would receive a special prize. The losing team would come to the boardroom, where one of them would be fired.[9]

With music and drama and moments of levity, the show cut back and forth between the two teams, which were divided by gender, as they argued about how and where to buy supplies and set up their lemonade stands. The cameras caught individual players' wild ideas to generate more revenue, from one male contestant's attempt to convince a wealthy buyer to spend $1,000 for a single cup of Trump-branded beverage, to the women's decision to use sex appeal and dole out kisses to drum up business. During the day Trump flew over the teams in his helicopter and dismissed the men's location near Fulton Fish Market as "stinky."

While the first contest would be broadcast over thirteen weeks, it was all shot in just over a month. The grueling schedule would bring out the worst in the contestants, which was something Burnett had learned with *Survivor*. In the first episode of *The Apprentice*, the kissing women prevailed, selling $1,200 worth of lemonade in a single day by hawking their wares at five bucks a cup. As a reward, Trump gave them a tour of his apartment. "The nicest apartment in New York City," he said. "I show this apartment to very few people. Presidents. Kings. And they walk in, they look around, and they really can't believe what they're seeing." The team walked in through the gold-colored doors. He turned on a fountain. They gazed out the window at the Plaza Hotel and Central Park.

As the women breathed the rarefied air of the Trump Tower penthouse, the men on the losing team negotiated to see who would be sacrificed in the pretend boardroom where Trump would preside in his elevated chair. The contestants quickly ganged up on Sam, a wild-eyed entrepreneur who'd tried to sell Trump lemonade for $1,000 a cup. "Every one of these guys thinks that you're not so hot," Trump said to Sam when the boardroom season turned to the question of who would be fired. Sam then stood and made an impassioned plea, claiming that he had what it took to work for Trump's company. His passion saved him. Trump turned his focus to a contestant named David, who had both an MD and an MBA, but who had faded into the background during the contest. Polite, self-effacing, and cooperative, he was, in a way, an anti-Trump. Trump told David that he had failed to "step up" during the competition and said, "You're fired."

More than 20 million Americans watched that first

episode, and in its first season *The Apprentice* became a moneymaking machine for NBC, Burnett, and Trump. Much of the credit went to Trump's name and performance, which included a hand gesture he called "the Cobra" which he used as he fired losing contestants. The Cobra accented the public humiliation that was often part of the reality show dynamic. (Worse was the dismissive "You *are* the weakest link, goodbye!" that host Anne Robinson chirped on her program.) Although Trump's personality would carry *The Apprentice* through many seasons, the most compelling person presented during the show's first season was a female contestant named Omarosa Manigault-Stallworth. After just a few episodes Manigault-Stallworth's first name became synonymous with aggression in the minds of many viewers. ("The woman America loves to hate" was how *Jet* magazine put it.) At the start of the contest Manigault-Stallworth was actually the victim of a teammate's manipulations, but she lost the favor of the audience when she announced, "I didn't come here to make friends," and stalked out of a team meeting.

In time Manigault-Stallworth would reveal that Burnett's cameras focused on her only when she was saying something outrageous or critical. Her efforts at cooperation and collaboration were ignored. With some of the press speculating about racial stereotypes, she became a caricature of an angry black woman, even though she wasn't any more aggressive than the other contestants. Most of them were rude or hypercompetitive at times. The turmoil ended for Manigault-Stallworth when the producers urged her to barge into a meeting and defend herself. Trump quickly fired her. In the attention economy, all publicity is good publicity, and Manigault-Stallworth would capitalize on her fame. Like Trump, who could make money with an image that was quite obnoxious, she rode the negative racial and sexist stereotypes to success as public speaker, author, and "personality."[10]

The idea that someone might be a "personality" and that this might be a way to make money harkened back at least to Oscar Wilde's 1882 tour of America. Wilde delivered more than a hundred talks to crowds of as many as two thousand people, each of whom paid to catch a glimpse of a man who had yet to establish himself as an author but was nevertheless a stylish sensation. Trump has done much the same thing as Wilde, cultivating attention long before he had built his first building, and with the help of *The Apprentice,* the same process became available to the sixteen men and women who were selected from among thousands to be on the show each season. The first winner, the twenty-three-year-old, recent college graduate Bill Rancic, would work with Trump for a year as a real estate executive and then become a TV host and paid spokesman for a drug called Rogaine, which helped him avoid the one thing his boss said executives should fight with all means necessary, going bald.

With more than 27 million people watching the finale, *The Apprentice* provided Donald Trump with publicity so valuable it would be impossible to calculate its worth. Besides the program itself, which often featured products such as Trump Ice bottled water, he benefited from weekly press accounts of the action on the show, which was covered as if it were a major league sport. Seeking to exploit the ink and airtime, he put his name on a number of consumer items, including a fragrance, men's suits, and a Visa credit card. He starred in a commercial for Verizon cell phone services, agreed to provide brief daily commentaries to a radio network, and accepted an invitation to host the comedy show *Saturday Night Live.* He performed gamely, but not so well that he was ever invited back.

If *Saturday Night Live* proved that Trump was not a versatile entertainer, it didn't dim his prospects as a TV entrepreneur. He and Burnett would create a version of their original program that featured the doyenne of domesticity, Martha Stewart, in the boss's chair. Born to a middle-class, Polish American family in Jersey City, the former Martha Kostyra had been a fashion model as a teenager and acquired the English-sounding name Martha Stewart when she married Andrew Stewart. He became an executive in the book business, and through him she made the connections to publish a hugely successful, ghostwritten volume called *Entertaining*. After seven more books and a divorce, she was the editor of her own magazine and the host of a daytime TV show. She was so rich she considered buying the giant department store chain Kmart. Then, in 2004, she was convicted of conspiracy, obstruction of justice, and making false statements in connection with the investigation into federal charges that she used inside information to avoid losing a little less than $50,000 in stock. Her sentence—five months prison time and five months of confinement at her home—was the minimum permitted under the law. Soon after her release from prison and return to her afternoon program, Trump and Burnett offered her a version of *The Apprentice* of her own. (In its second season the original had lost 25 percent of its audience. Nevertheless, it was still a success.)

Regarded by many as the victim of overzealous prosecutors, Stewart possessed the kind of notoriety that could draw an audience. Also, like Trump, she was temperamental and prone to occasional arrogance. The trouble was that the "Bad Martha" who could have drawn Trump's fans with displays of steely temper conflicted with the "Good Martha" image that she had used to sell herself, with great success, as an arbiter or taste and manners. On her version of *The Apprentice* she was too kind to win big ratings. Instead of telling the dismissed players that they were "fired," she said they "didn't fit in" and sent them condolence notes. "I'm sorry that you are the first to go," she wrote to the first dismissed contestant. "Not to fail, but rather not to fully succeed."

Having grown accustomed to treachery and tantrums, reality-show fans weren't moved by the Martha Stewart version of *The Apprentice*. At less than 4 million, Stewart's initial audience was small. Trump had seen his own viewership shrink for two straight seasons, which reduced the price of commercials on the show to $350,000 per minute, which was half the rate charged by the top program, *American Idol*. But even as some TV critics announced that viewers were becoming bored with the whole reality genre, Trump voiced his displeasure with his spin-off. During a radio interview he said, "I never thought it was a good idea," and complained that Stewart's failure was affecting his program. She then revealed that she had been told that she might replace Trump on his own program and actually fire him on TV.

When her show was canceled, Stewart said good-bye to her viewers by declaring that the experience had taught her that "I really cannot be destroyed." Among the contestants who appeared on her show, three would return to television. One of these, Bethenny Frankel, would become a star of sorts on *Real Housewives of New York City*, a reality show that presented the excesses and dramas of a group of wealthy women. Frankel would cash in on her fame, developing books and a brand of low-calorie alcoholic drinks called Skinnygirl that she eventually sold for $100 million.

After Martha Stewart's *Apprentice* was canceled, she and Trump continued to spar in the press, and each gained free publicity over months of squabbling. She called his criticism "mean-spirited and reckless." In a letter that was made public he wrote, "Your performance was terrible," and he said the show had been "a mistake for everybody—especially NBC," the network that carried it. The note ended with a threat: "P.S. Be careful or I will do a syndicated daytime show, perhaps called 'The Boardroom,' and further destroy the meager ratings you already have!" Soon afterward he considered Stewart's claim that she might have replaced him and asked, "What moron would think you're going to fire the guy with the number one show on television?"

The Apprentice was the top-rated program for one week, when the finale of the first season aired. It was never "number one" in any year, or season. In the spring of 2004, when *The Apprentice* peaked, the final episode of the TV series *Friends* was seen by twice as many people. *The Apprentice* would do well on some nights, but never approached the status Trump suggested. He would continue to make his claim even as the audience shrank to 7.5 million in its sixth season, and he demanded that his press man, Jim Dowd, promote *The Apprentice* as the top-rated show on the air. "He felt that I wasn't telling the story that the show was number one, when it was [actually] number seventy-three," recalled Dowd. He added that reporters literally laughed at him when, on Trump's instructions, he demanded they publish "corrections" of articles that did not describe *The Apprentice* as the top program on TV.

Although *The Apprentice* was never the kind of smash Trump said it was, he did keep it going by changing the cast—his adult children Ivanka and Donald joined the show's panel of experts—and then he allowed the network to shift the premise of the show from a contest among applicants who auditioned to one waged by low-ranking celebrities including, in the first season, a softball pitcher named Jennie Finch and (the now-divorced) Omarosa Manigault, who had managed her fame so successfully that producers believed she would draw viewers. Charities would get the $250,000 first prize, and participants would receive the attention that is the stuff of celebrity, but no pay.

Almost every celebrity who participated in the contest would express gratitude with the exception of the magician, TV host, and author Penn Jillette, who described the contest as "venal people clawing at stupid, soulless [stuff] in front of the modern-day Scrooge McDuck in order to stay famous." A television veteran, Jillette complained of hours of taping while "Donald Trump just does what he wants, which is mostly pontificating to people who are sucking up to him." But Jillette also saw a kind of public service in a program that revealed the desperate if not pathological yearning for attention that is often the dark side of fame. As Jillette told one interviewer, "*Celebrity Apprentice* is more honest in that creepy kind of way that the guy who admits he's racist is more honest."[11]

◆

While Donald Trump was firing people in a fake boardroom, the business press was warning of troubles in his real casinos, and auditors were compiling data to support their concern. In March 2004 the auditors at Ernst & Young declared that Trump Hotels and Casino Resorts might not be able to continue "as a going concern." With newer casinos such as the Borgata providing tough competition, the company, with $1.8 billion in debt, lost $3.39 per share in 2003. New or upgraded facilities could have helped the Trump casinos lure more gamblers, but with 80 percent of the firm's revenues going to repay debt, executives had no money to spend on such improvements. Remarkably, the Trump company had lost investors' money for every one of the eight years it had existed.

When the Trump company went bankrupt, just months after *The Apprentice* 2004 finale, its stock was worth thirty-cents per share. Financial writer David Pauly of Bloomberg News offered a caustic assessment: "All Trump, 58, can teach anybody about managing, if Trump Hotels is a guide, is this: Sell more bonds than you could ever possibly pay back, let the competition eat your lunch, live the good life as chief executive—and then go bankrupt."[12]

With stockholders already wiped out, the bankruptcy arrangement called for bondholders to forgive $544 million in debt, and Trump agreed to reduce his ownership stake from 47 percent to 30 percent. He would, however, remain head of the company and be paid $2 million per year. Considering his claim that his first profit-sharing check for *The Apprentice* exceeded $10 million, Trump would see no change in his way of life and no reason to admit he had been defeated in any way. By his lifestyles-of-the-rich-and-famous standard, he was a big success, even though, as David Segal of the *Washington Post* noted, "The people who know the least about business admire him the most, and those who know the most about business admire him the least."[13]

Trump didn't need Wall Streeters and business leaders. They weren't important when it came to the size of the audience for *The Apprentice,* and they weren't the folks who pumped coins into the slot machines at his casinos. Nor were they going to buy a ticket to learn Trump's methods at the Los Angeles Convention Center.

◆

Advertisements for the big lecture appeared on billboards and bus stop benches in early April 2005. On radio and TV, the event's organizers promised, "One weekend can make you a millionaire." Besides Trump's talk, the offerings included lectures with titles including "The Lazy Way to Create Real Estate Wealth" and "How to 'Quick Turn' Real Estate in Los Angeles with No Money, No Credit or Risk." The other featured speakers included Russell Simmons, who got rich producing rap-music recordings, and the exhortationist Tony Robbins.

As Trump appeared at the Los Angeles Convention Center and collected his $1 million fee, local house prices had more than doubled to a median of $550,000 in five years. At this level just 41 percent of people in the Los Angeles metropolitan region could afford a home. To keep business going, some lenders had begun offering interest-only loans, which reduced buyers' monthly payments but extended their debts month by month. More cautious mortgage lenders, who feared the bubble of price inflation was about to burst, began raising the rates they charged for conventional loans.

In April 2005 anyone in Los Angeles who followed Trump's advice and invested in local real estate would have been well advised to sell or "flip" his or her property as soon as possible. In roughly a year's time the price run-up would end, and the value of all but the most expensive properties would decline precipitously. As the real estate crisis moved to other states, the national foreclosure rate doubled, and millions of people were swept out of their homes. In California, Nevada, and Florida, housing developments that had been started in the boom time began to look like ghost towns as buyers disappeared and builders boarded up windows and doors. By this time Trump had cashed his $1 million paycheck from the lecture in Los Angeles and two more earned from offering the same message in Chicago and New York. In 2006, after the slide began, he would publish yet another you-can-get-rich book. This one was coauthored by Robert Kiyosaki, who had put out fifteen previous financial-advice books. Best known for his *Rich*

Dad Poor Dad advice books, Kiyosaki also sold seminars to the public. Eventually one of his firms, Rich Global LLC, would go bankrupt after a court ordered the firm to pay $23.6 million to a creditor.

The book Trump published with Kiyosaki, titled *Why We Want You to Be Rich,* was not part of Trump's main occupation, which he stressed was still developer/builder. However, among the four hundred Americans listed by *Forbes* on its 2005 "richest" list, only Trump delivered paid lectures, sold self-help books, and appeared on a TV series. Why a man ranked eighty-third wealthiest in America would do such things was one of the questions that motivated writer Timothy O'Brien in his study of Trump for his book *TrumpNation.* As a reporter for *The New York Times,* O'Brien had been among the first to signal that another Trump bankruptcy was coming in Atlantic City. But despite O'Brien's articles, which reported claims that Trump's casinos hadn't made money for almost a decade, Trump hosted O'Brien in his office and at his home and even drove him around South Florida, explaining how he could denigrate the writer in the press if he didn't like O'Brien's book.[14]

O'Brien notes near the end of his book that Trump explained to him how he had established a reputation that allowed him to make outlandish statements and have them disseminated. He was always good copy, especially for reporters and editors who didn't worry about fact-checking, and he had devoted countless hours to keeping his name in the press. Having supplied many journalists with juicy stories, even some that reflected poorly on him, Trump had banked favors that he could redeem. Certain that homosexuality would reflect poorly on the journalist, Trump imagined telling reporters, "He [O'Brien] loves men." Then, raising the ante to criminal behavior, he added, "He loves boys." O'Brien's description of Trump's implied threat, complete with profanity, included quotes of Trump adding, "Oh, fuck, I can say that. Nobody else can. . . . I am the only guy who can fight back on an even plane."

When the book finally appeared, one of Trump's lawyers wrote to the publisher, Warner Books, demanding it be taken out of bookstores. He also demanded an apology and a retraction because *TrumpNation* "contains out-and-out defamatory falsehoods concerning Mr. Trump, his business and his family." The publisher stood behind O'Brien, and Trump's lawyer filed a lawsuit in a New Jersey state court claiming his client, Trump, had been damaged to the tune of $5 billion because O'Brien had written that Trump "was not remotely close to being a billionaire," and that his "net worth was somewhere between $150 million and $250 million." O'Brien also noted that when he mentioned these estimates to the man himself, Trump dismissed both the data and the sources. "You can go ahead and speak to guys who have four-hundred-pound wives at home who are jealous of me, but the guys who really know me know I'm a great builder."[15]

In measuring Trump's wealth and declaring it far short of his claims, which ranged as high as $9 billion, O'Brien had hit a nerve. But in responding so aggressively, Trump stepped into an arena he could not control. He won the first round, when the trial judge ruled that O'Brien had to reveal his sources. (Trump's lawyers said that when named, they would be added to the suit as defendants.) Then an appeals court overturned the decision and found that O'Brien was protected under the First Amendment to the Constitution. Trump could have dropped matters and avoided the one hazard the case held for him: a sworn deposition. He chose to proceed.

In December 2007 Trump arrived at a law office at 1633 Broadway, just a few blocks from Trump Tower. He was accompanied by three New York attorneys and one from New Jersey. Seven lawyers appeared on behalf of O'Brien and Warner Books, including Andrew J. Ceresney and Mary Jo White. Before entering private practice, Ceresney had been a federal prosecutor. White had been the first woman US Attorney in New York City and had prosecuted both the mobster John Gotti and the bombers who attacked the World Trade Center in 1993.

In his deposition Trump cited other people, including an executive in his company, an outside lawyer, and two of O'Brien's former colleagues, to suggest the writer was a "nut job" and "a rude, arrogant person who refused to acknowledge what he was being told." Trump said O'Brien wasn't interested in documents he had been shown because he was more concerned with flirting with a Trump executive who was on hand. Trump put it, "He was trying to make it with Michelle Lokey."

Time and again Trump addressed O'Brien's character, calling him a "bad guy" and "a very sick person" and "a maniac trying to destroy me." He reiterated the point about Ms. Lokey—"He was sexually harassing her"—and suggested that O'Brien had harassed other women. Trump told an anecdote about O'Brien's asking him to sign a book for his mother. When informed that O'Brien's mother had been dead for many years, he said that perhaps the request had been for someone else. After defense lawyers played an audio recording for Trump in which he threatened to tell the press that O'Brien had "been sued for sexual harassment, he's been this, he's been that," Trump agreed that he believed "in getting even."

Trump's interrogators presented press accounts published long before *TrumpNation* in which his claims about his wealth were cast into doubt. Confronted with five articles in national publications, each of which made the same suggestions that O'Brien had made, Trump re-

THE TRUTH ABOUT TRUMP

minded the attorneys that he had shared volumes of financial information and devoted extensive amounts of his time to O'Brien. The others weren't given the same attention. It seemed, according to the deposition, that Trump felt personally betrayed because the writer did not accept what he had been told. Also, Trump was keenly aware that a book such as *TrumpNation* would stand as a record long after individual articles in magazines and newspapers passed from readers' minds.

The confusion that swirled around estimates of Trump's wealth was evident as various publications and recordings of conversations were presented to show that Trump and his associates had, themselves, offered estimates ranging from $3 billion to $9 billion. He explained the wide swings as a function of market conditions, and his own sense of the value of his name. This brand valuation—he estimated it was worth $6 billion—could depend, he said, on "my own feeling toward myself, about myself. It can change when somebody writes a vicious article like O'Brien. I mean, I didn't feel so great about myself when I read that article. I would have said that—after reading that article I would have said that that psychologically hurt me."

Here was the heart of the matter. Donald Trump's sense of well-being was affected by media accounts of his wealth, and O'Brien's skepticism—in his book and reports based on it—hurt Trump personally. He also seemed offended by the suggestion that he was extreme in his efforts at self-promotion. When asked if he exaggerated, he said, "I think everybody does. Who wouldn't?" In an echo of Norman Vincent Peale he added, "I like to be as positive as I can with respect to my properties." He explained that he was so inclined to look on the bright side of things that he regarded his 30 percent interest in the West Side yards development as *50* percent. Why? Because "if the seventy percent owner puts up all of the money, I really own more than thirty percent. And I have always felt I own fifty percent, from that standpoint."

No competent accountant or attorney would review a partnership arrangement and agree that a 30 percent stake was equal to 50 percent. But Trump seemed absolutely sincere as he made this argument. In his mind, he owned the equivalent of a 50 percent share and he expected others to accept his view. When he said he couldn't remember the details of various projects, including whether he owned 100 percent of a development in Waikiki, he struck a convincing note when he said, "I believe it is owned by me. I have many different companies." Here he sounded much like his father, who explained to state investigators, decades ago, "I've got forty-three corporations I'm sole stockholder in. These things escape my mind sometimes."

The difference in 2007 was that defense attorneys had documents to fact-check Trump's claims. They presented the agreement governing his involvement in the Waikiki property, which showed he had licensed his name to the hotel and would manage it in exchange for fees, but held no equity. In his mind, however, it was "such a strong licensing agreement that it's a form of ownership."

When the deposition was made public by the court, the editors of *The Wall Street Journal* reported it on the paper's front page. Included was a Deutsche Bank estimate of Trump's wealth. The bank put the figure as $788 million. The story also included an exchange Trump had with attorney Andrew Ceresney about a golf course Trump had purchased and operated in Bedminster, New Jersey. (Trump had entered the golf industry in 1999, with the development of a layout in West Palm Beach.)

After Trump presented statements showing that the Bedminster course had an operating loss of $4.6 million in 2005, Ceresney asked if Trump had reassessed his investment. He said he believed he would ultimately make $120 million on the course.[16]

O'Brien's side argued that Trump had failed to support his claim that he had lost money because of the book and couldn't show that the author had acted with malice, which is required to prove a journalist has committed libel against a public figure. The judge agreed, dismissing the suit. Ever combative, Trump promised to fight on with an appeal, declaring O'Brien guilty of "gross negligence, lack of professionalism, and bias." The writer and the publisher, who likely spent more defending the case than was generated by the book's sales, both used the word "gratified" when they answered questions about the decision. Trump's lawyers made noises about continuing the litigation but then dropped it. Their client, who used lawsuits to demonstrate he was always willing to stand up for himself, had already moved on to an even more public feud, which brought him far more publicity.[17]

◆

The dispute began when the entertainer Rosie O'Donnell, who had attended the Trump/Maples nuptials, called him a "snake-oil salesman" on the national TV chat show *The View,* which O'Donnell cohosted. Miss USA, Tara Conner, a former bikini model, had gotten into trouble with drugs and alcohol. Trump, who owned the Miss USA pageant, very publicly gave Tara Conner "a second chance" when she announced she would enter a rehabilitation center. Others had criticized Trump for publicity-seeking in this case, but O'Donnell did it before a huge audience. "He's the moral authority," O'Donnell said, after she tossed her hair to one side to mock his. "Left the first wife—had an affair. Left the second wife—had an affair. . . . But he's the moral compass for twenty-year-olds in America. Donald, sit and spin, my friend!"

In response, Trump told *People* that O'Donnell was a "loser" and promised to sue her, adding, "I look forward to taking lots of money from my nice fat little Rosie." In an interview with the *New York Daily News* he said, "When I saw the tape, I said, 'You'd better be careful or I'll send one of my friends over to take your girlfriend!' I imagine it would be pretty easy to take her girlfriend away, considering how Rosie looks." (One of a handful of openly gay celebrities, O'Donnell and her partner, Kelli Carpenter, maintained a household that included four children.)

Considering himself the injured party, Trump held true to his policy of "hitting back ten times harder" whenever he felt attacked. He suggested that O'Donnell was interested in a romantic relationship with Ms. Conner and reported that Barbara Walters, another member of the panel on *The View,* "cannot stand Rosie O'Donnell." He said that O'Donnell would hurt the program, which Walters had created, and complained, "I'm worth billions of dollars, and I have to listen to this fat slob?"

In fact, *The View* had enjoyed a 13 percent increase in its audience since O'Donnell had brought her outspoken style, which was not entirely unlike Trump's, to the panel. Although she said she would resist continuing the spat, she could not. After Trump called her "a stone-cold loser," she posted a statement on her Web site declaring, "The emperor has no clothes," and saying, "The comb-over goes ballistic." On the feud went. Barbara Walters felt compelled to announce that she had never complained about O'Donnell and was glad she had hired her. Gallup got into the act with a poll of a thousand

Americans who were asked to choose sides. The result was a 41–28 Trump victory.

Soon Ivana would explain to the press that it was all about publicity, and the fight ended without lawyers or judges getting involved. With Rosie on board, the ratings for *The View* stayed high.[18] Trump didn't get a similar payoff. *The Apprentice* returned to the airwaves in the midst of the spat. His audience fell by six hundred thousand viewers compared with its previous debut episode.

Two years later, the Miss USA Pageant would cause a bit more controversy for Trump as seminude photos of Miss California USA Carrie Prejean circulated on the World Wide Web. In May of 2009 Trump stood behind Prejean, saying, "We've reviewed the pictures carefully. . . . We've made a determination that the pictures taken were acceptable. Some were risqué, but we are in the twenty-first century." Weeks later Trump did fire Prejean, citing her nonperformance of certain duties.

In November of 2009, Prejean published a quickie book in which she claimed that Trump had reviewed Miss USA contestants to screen out those he found less attractive. She wrote that many of the women found this exercise "humiliating" and cried when they realized that, as Trump divided the group in two, they had lost the competition before it began. "Even those of us who were among the chosen couldn't feel very good about it—it was as though we had been stripped bare, she wrote." Trump denied he had put the contestants through the inspection Prejean described, and her accusation was quickly obscured as the press reported that pageant officials had learned that Prejean had made an explicit video when she was younger.

So-called "sex tape" scandals had become so de rigueur for celebrities that, in some cases, it seemed those involved had arranged for themselves to be filmed and revealed so they could become more famous. In Prejean's case the video was more an emblem of hypocrisy, and she quickly settled a legal battle she was waging against pageant officials, who had financed her breast-implant surgery and wanted the money back.

14
"THE BEAUTY OF ME"

I've been very successful and people are starting to find out I've been much more successful than people even admit. People are starting to figure that out. Much more successful. You're not covering economics or finances, I guess, but I'm much richer than people understand.
—DONALD TRUMP

At five feet eleven inches, Melania Knauss was thin enough to satisfy the modern standard for fashion models, which meant that three of her wouldn't push the needle on a scale to the four-hundred mark.

An immigrant from Slovenia, Knauss had made her debut as Trump's romantic partner in 1998, when he was not quite divorced from Marla Maples. Knauss was twenty-eight years old. He was fifty-two. The two were present at a gala marking the completed renovation of Grand Central Terminal. A month later the *Daily News* reported that Knauss—"Donald Trump's latest model"—had been hired to appear in ads for BMW cars.

Although Knauss matched the previous Mrs. Trumps when it came to beauty, she was different in one essential way. She wasn't much interested in being his partner outside of marriage. Ivana had run the Plaza. Marla had hoped to push him into active philanthropy, which she would help direct. Knauss had no such ambitions. As a friend said, "For Melania it's never, 'Ask what The

Donald can do for you.' It's 'Ask what you can do for The Donald.'"

On the day they became engaged. Donald gave Melania a $1.5 million ring, which he had obtained at half price because the jeweler, Graff, appreciated the value of the publicity that came with selling a diamond to Trump. The wedding, which took place on January 22, 2005, came in the couple's seventh year together. Among the 350 guests who attended the ceremony at a Palm Beach church and the reception at Mar-a-Lago were many present and former public officials and celebrities, including Hillary Clinton, Oprah Winfrey, Shaquille O'Neal, and Rudy Giuliani. A press agent, and the man who whitened the groom's teeth, were also in attendance.

According to Tina Brown, herself a celebrity, at least a few of the guests had attended in hopes of witnessing Trump's trademark "over-the-topness." Except for the decorations placed on the reception tables—six-foot-tall candelabra draped in flowers—they were disappointed. Trump: The Wedding III was a mostly elegant affair. He even declined an offer to broadcast the event on TV.[1]

In marriage, Melania Trump would continue to work a bit as a model, and devoted herself to her son, who would be born in 2006 and named Barron William. His name recalled the "John Baron" whom Trump invented to say certain things to the press, and the famous William Barron Hilton, whom Trump had once described as a product of the Lucky Sperm Club. In the years since Trump had issued this judgment, the holdings managed by Mr. Hilton had grown to include twenty-eight hundred hotels worth $26 billion. He had also won Trump's esteem.

In many ways, Hilton could be seen as a quieter and more successful version of Donald Trump. Like Trump, he had purchased a landmark property from Penn Central at fire-sale prices. Hilton's $35 million investment in the Waldorf-Astoria would one day be valued at $1 billion. Like Trump, Hilton had gone into the casino business, although none of his casinos went bankrupt. Hilton had thrived with a conservative financial strategy. Beginning in the 1970s, for example, his company entered into a variety of arrangements that put the Hilton name and management to work for investors who owned hotel buildings. Trump followed the same strategy, but went beyond hotels to put his name on a remarkable variety of products and services.

In the first decade of the twenty-first century, Americans could buy a home with a Trump loan, dine on Trump steaks, and book travel at a Web site called GoTrump.com. For the true Trump loyalists he offered a Trump University, which, promotional materials promised, "will deliver the experience, knowledge, and wisdom of Donald Trump himself." The mortgage, steak, and travel endeavors were short-lived, but after it was formed in 2005, Trump U persisted for years. Students paid for access to a Web site where they could see videos and read articles about such topics as salesmanship and coping with failure. They could also learn what Trump thought about the pop singer Britney Spears, who, he wrote, "has seen better days. She performed four or five years ago at the Trump Taj Mahal and she was great. Now it seems as if everything's slipping away from her. Britney, don't let that happen. Don't let it slip away. Keep your head on straight."

Trump U's offerings varied widely in price and content and included "retreats" covering subjects such as "wealth preservation" and "creative financing" at $5,000 each. Students could also purchase one-on-one instruction with a Trump U mentor and even a Gold Elite program, which would include the mentoring plus five retreats—a $50,000 value—for just $34,995.

Although he generally didn't appear at classes in

person, Trump's face was on the cover of the book, called Trump 101, that was handed out as a pimary text for students and his name was on every piece of paper in sight. At one seminar, the room was decorated with a life-size cardboard cutout of Trump, dressed in one of his fine suits, and students were encouraged to have their photos taken standing next to it. It was the next best thing to an actual photo with the man himself.[2]

Trump U received little press coverage in its early days, but in 2008 the Tampa Bay Times reported on instructor James Harris's free presentation in Florida. The event was preceded by advertisements trumpeting, "Unheard of Real Estate Market Factors Have Created A PERFECT STORM of Profit Opportunity!" (In fact at the time Tampa real estate prices were plunging and wouldn't hit bottom for another four years). In the ballroom of a Marriott hotel Harris offered personal testimony of how real estate transformed him from a teen who slept on the New York City subways into a successful man.

Despite the exciting prospect of a PERFECT STORM, he advised his students to buy low and sell high and to content themselves with modest gains. At the end of his talk Harris noted that he could only share so much information in a single session and then explained that Trump U was offering far more at an upcoming three-day seminar that cost $1,495.

"There are three groups of people," Harris told the students. "People who make things happen, people who wait for things to happen, and people who wonder, 'What happened?' Which one are you?" He also said, "There are gonna-bes and wannabes. And I want to talk to the gonna-bes when we're done."[3]

Two years after the Tampa Bay Times feature, the Daily News in New York reported that complaints were being voiced by Trump U students around the country.

In 2010, a group of students filed a lawsuit against Trump and Trump U in a California Court. Attorneys general in six states reported they had received complaints about the company. Among them were seven students who said they were pressured to use all the credit available on their bank cards to buy Trump University's offerings. Others complained of internships that never materialized and of promised connections to powerful contacts that were never made. That same year, under pressure from the State of New York, which required accreditation for any institution offering itself as a "university" to state residents, Trump U changed its name to the Trump Entrepreneur Initiative.

In court, Trump and Trump U denied the allegations and mounted a vigorous defense. In his public comments about the controversy, Trump stressed the high number of participants who said they had a good experience—he said 98 percent fell into this category—and he told the *Daily News*, "There are plenty of people who went to Harvard and did very poorly, and there are plenty of people who went to Trump University and did very well."

In the summer of 2013 New York Attorney General Eric Schneiderman sued Trump and Trump U for $40 million, alleging that the university defrauded students. The court papers alleged a number of deceptive practices, including claiming that prospective students would be taught by successful real estate "experts" who were "handpicked" by Donald Trump. In fact, Schneiderman alleged, none of the instructors had been "handpicked" and some were actually bankrupt real estate entrepreneurs. In a press release Schneiderman said, "Mr. Trump uses his celebrity status and personally appeared in commercials making false promises to convince people to spend tens of thousands of dollars they couldn't afford for lessons they never got."

Included in the court papers was a Trump University

document, prepared for its staff in Texas, which served as a kind of playbook. As reported by the *Atlantic Monthly,* this document encouraged them to use free lectures to "Sell, Sell, Sell!" the fee-based Trump U programs. The playbook instructed staff to observe those in attendance for changes in body language that might indicate they were becoming receptive and outlined the duties of workers identified as sales coordinators. These people were to be armed with "objection rebuttals" for those who resisted a sale pitch. The *Atlantic* article detailed how the playbook addressed everything at the lectures from the room temperature ("no more than sixty-eight degrees") to the space between the chairs ("bringing attendees out of their comfort zone"). The "Minimum Sales Goal" per seminar was $72,500. This goal would be reached, in part, by channeling people past a sales table as they left the conference room. The playbook further advised Trump U staff to avoid reporters because they "are rarely on your side and they are not sympathetic," and they were advised that "If a district attorney arrives on the scene, contact the appropriate media spokesperson immediately."[4]

Besides fighting back in court, Trump responded to the New York AG's lawsuit by developing a Web site—98percentapproval.com—where his defense was made in documents and videos that stressed the high ratings students gave Trump U in the surveys they filled out at the end of their seminars. The Web site also presented tabloid-style news articles that depicted the attorney general as a "dirty" political "hit man" with allegedly corrupt ties. Trump also went on Fox News to call the attorney general a "lightweight" who was "respected by nobody." Then he suggested that Schneiderman had, perhaps, acted at the behest of President Barack Obama.

After saying, "I'm not a very paranoid person," Trump added, "When he meets with the president and then files a suit, like, twenty-four hours later, I think yes, I think I've been targeted. And I think it's a big problem and I think people ought to look into it."

A channel surfer who landed on Trump's words might have been puzzled by the suggestion that the president of the United States had Donald Trump in mind when he met with the attorney general for the State of New York. Eric Schneiderman said he and Obama had "more important stuff to talk about than Donald Trump." But among those who depended on the highly partisan Fox cable-TV channel to inform their political views, Trump's words rang with a familiar tone. In many of their minds, Donald Trump had good reason to worry about a conspiracy. He was one of a handful of people leading an effort to determine whether the president was a foreigner who had somehow concealed that he was born in Kenya and was therefore ineligible to hold the highest office in the land. In time, great numbers of people joined him to challenge the first black president's legitimacy. They were called the birthers.

◆

The idea that Barack Obama was not whom he seemed to be can be traced at least as far back as 2004 and a lawyer named Andrew Martin. Early in his career Martin had been denied permission to practice in Illinois under a state Supreme Court ruling that he lacked "responsibility, candor, fairness, self-restraint, objectivity and respect for the judicial system." (The court cited the US Selective Service, which had found he suffered from "well documented ideation with a paranoid flavor and a grandiose character.") Martin had been a perennial losing candidate for office and once registered to campaign under the banner of the Congressional Campaign to Exterminate Jew Power in America. In 2004 he had given the press a statement claiming

Obama was not a Christian but "a Muslim who has concealed his religion."

Coming in the aftermath of the 9/11 attacks by Islamic terrorists who had killed thousands of Americans, Martin's charge seemed designed to play on fear and prejudice to harm Obama, but it was not widely published. This was probably because the year before, Martin had claimed he knew the whereabouts of fallen Iraqi dictator Saddam Hussein when a vast American army in Iraq was unable to locate him. Eventually Martin would explain that he had promoted his theory about Obama in part "to put some sizzle on the plate" of one of his failing political campaigns.[5]

Martin's explanation did not diminish the power of his claim. Loose on the Internet, his theories resonated with those who hated Obama and did not trust mainstream sources of information. As an unlimited resource for connection, the World Wide Web has made it easy for isolated paranoid people to come together and reinforce their beliefs. The process is usually marked by a language of suspicion, as participants insist they are only "raising questions" that deserve a hearing. With this rhetorical trick, doubts can be raised about settled issues, such as evolution, by fringe figures demanding fair treatment. The discussion arising from Andrew Martin's claims was laced with insinuations that Obama could not be trusted, and the suggestion that he deserved to be investigated. In 2008 supporters of Hillary Clinton, who was then running against Obama for the Democratic Party's presidential nomination, circulated an e-mail that said, in part, "Barack Obama's mother was living in Kenya with his Arab-African father late in her pregnancy. She was not allowed to travel by plane then, so Barack Obama was born there and his mother then took him to Hawaii to register his birth."

Suddenly bipartisan, the rumor mongering had escalated grown to include a challenge to Obama's status as a US citizen qualified to run for president. At one campaign event a voter publicly challenged Republican candidate John McCain to demand Obama present proof of his citizenship. McCain refused and then pointedly rebuked a woman who insisted his opponent was secretly "Arab."

After the election, groups including ResistNet Tea Party paid for an ad in the *Chicago Tribune* that said that if the president-elect failed to meet certain demands, he should be considered a "usurper" not deserving "support from the People." In 2009 Mark Williams of the group Tea Party Express included the claim that Obama was "improbably a native-born citizen" in a published attack on the president, which also compared him with Hitler. From talk-radio hosts, members of Congress, and Tea Party activists came a chorus of suspicion that Obama was not truly and properly American. These rumors would persist and reverberate on Fox News and in other right-wing media outlets throughout his presidency. By February 2011, 51 percent of Republicans surveyed by Public Policy Polling said they believed the president was foreign-born and therefore ineligible for the office he held.[6]

"Questions" about Obama's birth, and his claim to Americanness, circulated with the power of a Joe McCarthy/Roy Cohn Red Scare smear. Just as Roy Cohn used doctored photos in the McCarthy era, birther Orly Taitz presented a faked Kenyan birth certificate to bolster the Obama-as-foreigner meme. Like McCarthy and Cohn, Obama's antagonists said they were merely seeking answers to questions, while ignoring the evidence. That evidence included a copy of his "certificate of live birth" issued by the State of Hawaii and made public during the campaign, and contemporaneous announcements published in Honolulu newspapers. Any sophisticated consideration of the birther campaign had to consider that Obama was the first black president, and the first with a Muslim parent. Racial prejudice and religious fear lurked in the background of the birther movement. Hence the cartoon, circulated online, that showed the Obama family as chimps above the caption "Now you know why—No birth certificate!"[7]

As a man who craved attention and often made bold statements to get it, Donald Trump was drawn to the birther cause as he once again dabbled in presidential politics. His previous flirtations—1987, 1999—had coincided with the publication of Trump books. This time he had an entire backlist of titles and a TV show to promote. In early 2011 Michael Cohen, an aide to Trump, explained that his boss was "seriously considering" a campaign because "he's disgusted with how the country is being run." A number of prominent Republicans had expressed an interest in challenging Obama, and Trump edged toward the scrum when he accepted an invitation to speak at the February 2011 gathering called CPAC, or the Conservative Political Action Conference.

At CPAC, Trump was introduced via the strains of a hit song called "For the Love of Money." (Its lyrics include "For the love of money, people don't care who they hurt or beat.") In his remarks he delivered the same economic jingoism he had offered in Portsmouth, New Hampshire, in 1987, before the publication of his first book. During that exercise he had railed against the oil producers of OPEC (the Organization of Petroleum Exporting Countries) and the Republican president Reagan's trade policies. He had also speculated that Japanese businessmen secretly "laugh like hell" over their advantages. More than twenty years later, Japan was in its second decade of economic stagnation, which rendered Japanese businessmen inadequate as bogeymen. Instead Trump replaced Japan with China and "the Mexicans," who "cannot believe what they are getting away with." He predicted "seven-dollar, and eight-dollar, and nine-dollar" per gallon gasoline, "which believe me, a year or two from now you are going to be paying" because "we have nobody who calls up OPEC and says that price better get lower and it better get lower fast."

The audience at CPAC greeted Trump's policy thoughts warmly, but his main topic was his appeal as a candidate and how his wealth was "a scorecard and acknowledgment of my abilities" and that his competitiveness—"I've beaten many people"—made him the right man to run the country. He also signaled to the birthers in the crowd who viewed Obama as foreign and unworthy, saying, "Our current president came out of nowhere. Came out of nowhere. In fact, I'll go a step further. The people that went to school with him never saw him; they don't know who he is. Crazy." In Trump's eyes, the man who bested Hillary Clinton and others in Democratic Party primaries and then defeated John McCain in the general election had failed to demonstrate he was truly capable. However, he, Trump, was qualified to be president because he had succeeded in business.[8]

Although rabid birthers and Tea Party activists (often one and the same) represented a minority in the GOP, what they lacked in numbers they made up for in zeal. For them Obama represented a national existential threat—some even considered him the biblical Antichrist—and consequently, they would turn out in large numbers for someone who shared their views. In the early stages of the Republican Party's nominating process, as candidates eyed the 2012 presidential primaries, this energy could be an advantage for the candidate who was willing to risk alienating voters, donors, and party leaders who considered birtherism an embarrassment. The risk would be too great for the likes of mainstream aspirant Mitt Romney. But someone who was more comfortable with extreme attention-seeking and less serious about actually becoming president might find the birthers/Tea Party fringe irresistible.

Donald Trump followed his CPAC performance with a birther blitz on Fox News, telling the audience of Bill O'Reilly's nighttime program that he had once believed that Obama had been born in Hawaii but added, "I've seen too many things" and "come to have doubts."

Under tough questioning from O'Reilly, who had dismissed the birther claims, Trump allowed that perhaps the president had a US birth certificate. But he added, "Now, he may have one, but there is something on that birth certificate—maybe religion, maybe it says he's a Muslim, I don't know." O'Reilly said, "You get a lot of attention raising the question, but I don't think you believe it."[9]

As the top star on Fox News, O'Reilly's opinion carried weight on the political right, but the story intrigued the network's rabid anti-Obama viewership. Despite O'Reilly's efforts to knock down Trump's argument, Trump was invited to repeat his "questions" on other Fox programs. One, a morning show, made him a regular weekly guest so that his political views could be aired.

Trump's performances on Fox brought him attention from other networks. One interviewer from ABC TV introduced her report with a winking description of the five hours she spent with "The Donald," which included a flight on his big jet, which she called "a sweet ride." Under the warm, unblinking gaze of the TV camera's eye, Trump told her that he resented the term *birthers* because it cast anyone who questioned the president's origins as an "idiot" and added, "Let me tell you I'm a really smart guy who was a really good student at the best school in the country." Trump also offered the claim, which was impossible to verify, that he had $600 million to spend on a presidential campaign. As Trump sat in a blue suit and red tie, with an impressionist painting behind him, the sound of jet engines hummed in the background. "Part of the beauty of me"—he opened his arms wide—"is that I'm very rich."[10]

Days later, Trump upped the ante on the birther issue, saying, "I have investigators in Hawaii. . . . They cannot believe what they're finding." In the midst of the birther frenzy, as Trump and others demanded Obama make public his birth certificate, TV hosts occasionally mentioned that Obama's "certificate of live birth" had been made public in 2008 and Hawaii state officials had repeatedly affirmed that he was born there. Despite this official documentary proof, Trump talked as if facts were being withheld. His wife, Melania, echoed him on a cable-TV talk show, adding, "It's not him [Donald] that's bringing it up. It's the media all the time, all the time."

In none of his statements did Trump offer any reliable sources, and in one case he seemed to ignore the actual record. This happened when he announced, "His grandmother in Kenya said, 'Oh, no, he was born in Kenya and I was there and I witnessed the birth.' Now, she's on tape and I think that tape's going to be produced fairly soon."

Already public, the tape in question was a recorded telephone interview of Obama's stepmother, Sarah who was in Kenya. Sarah spoke Swahili. The interviewer was an English-speaking preacher named Ron McRae. In 2005, the *Pittsburgh Post-Gazette* had described McRae as a police officer turned street preacher and a "self-proclaimed bishop" of a sect of Anabaptists. A writer for the paper had interviewed McRae because he was protesting the design of a 9/11 memorial that he thought honored Islam in its use of red maple trees. His tiny denomination, called the Anabaptist Churches Worldwide, had established a branch in Kenya in 2007. In a photo on the church Web site, McRae is shown posing in a pith helmet.

An edited version of McRae's conversation with Obama's stepmother circulated among birthers. It included McRae's question "Could I ask her about his actual birthplace? I would like to see his birthplace when I come to visit Kenya in December. Was she present when he was born in Kenya?" This was followed by the translator's voice: "She says yes she was. She was present when Obama was born."

The rest of the interview, missing from versions posted on some Internet sites, finds McRae saying, "Okay, when I come in December, I would like to go by the place, the hospital where he was born. Could you tell me where he was born? Was he born in Mombasa?" In response the translator says, "No. Obama was not born in Mombasa. He was born in America." McRae pressed Sarah on the issue, and the translator, after asking the question and waiting for the answer, replied, "Hawaii. She says he was born in Hawaii."

If Trump couldn't find the full interview online, he could have read Sarah Obama's recollections of the circumstances of her famous relative's birth in Hawaii, which were first published in the *Chicago Tribune* in 2007. This report was readily available to anyone willing to look for it. However Trump apparently relied, instead, on an author named Jerome Corsi, whose writings on politics were widely judged to be riddled with errors. Corsi had written that John McCain had received substantial support from a Muslim terrorist group and had at another time called for the impeachment of

President George W. Bush. (Among the conspiracy theories Corsi had promoted was that Bush supported a union of Canada, Mexico, and the United States that would replace the sovereign United States.)[11]

Despite his credibility problems, or perhaps because of them, Jerome Corsi was wildly popular among the millions of Americans who toyed with conspiracy theories. This audience had made two Corsi books into bestsellers and was eagerly awaiting the release of his next—*Where's the Birth Certificate?*—which was due in May 2011. Items related to the book's contents were published in the weeks prior to the book's release. Among them were reports of Obama's supposed foreign birth. On April 27 some of the steam was taken out of this publicity campaign when the White House released a "long form" birth certificate showing the president had been born at Hawaii's Kapiolani Hospital. (Most states issue both short- and long-form birth certificates. Both are accepted by authorities for most uses, but the long form generally provides more information about a child's parents. The type of information varies by jurisdiction.)

On the day after the president's long-form birth certificate was released, Trump flew to Portsmouth, New Hampshire, his helicopter landing in the fog at the local airport. He walked from the chopper to a hangar where, through the big open door, he could see reporters gathered before a small podium where microphones were arranged like a bouquet. Trump claimed credit for the release of the document, which "nobody else has been able to accomplish." With Yoken's "Thar she blows!" restaurant closed and demolished, he then went to a diner to shake hands with voters, insisting, even though he had spoken of it himself, that reports of his germophobia, were "invented by my enemies." Maggie Haberman of the Web site called *Politico* noted that

Granite Staters were quite skeptical about his candidacy, and locals were put off when Trump interrupted a meeting to take a phone call.[12]

Soon Trump went right back to spinning conspiracy theories about the president's birth. "We have to see, is it [the birth certificate] real? Is it proper? What's on it?" In classic doublespeak he added, "I'm sure, I hope it's the right deal." He wasn't sure the document was correct, only that he hoped it was. And even if the birth certificate were judged authentic, Trump added, the president should be forced to answer more questions.

"The word is, according to what I've read, that he was a terrible student when he went to Occidental [College]. Then he gets to Columbia. He then gets to Harvard . . . how do you get into Harvard if you're not a good student?" These questions could be resolved, Trump said, if the president released all his educational records. Of course he didn't promise that he wouldn't then pose a new set of queries, perhaps about Obama's golf handicap.[13]

Having made improbable claims about his own performance at Penn, where Trump had enrolled after two years at a less exclusive university, his focus on Obama's academic record seemed, at best, ill considered. At worst it stirred animosity among whites who resented affirmative action laws, which had been enacted to redress centuries of discrimination, but which they believed were unfair. Political provocateur Patrick Buchanan, who no longer imagined himself a future president, put it directly as he asked how Obama could have been admitted to Colombia and Harvard law and then "suddenly he's the editor of *Harvard Law Review*. We've never seen any grades of the guy. These are legitimate questions. . . . I think he's affirmative action all the way!"

If Obama had benefited from affirmative action admissions, the policy would have had nothing to do with his magna cum laude honors at Harvard or his position on the prestigious law review. Indeed, the rise of an African-American child from a single-parent home to the White House may have pointed to the efficacy of affirmative action. But this was not the view that Buchanan and Trump would promote. In less than subtle terms they were signaling that Obama got special treatment, couldn't have made it on his own, and was therefore illegitimate. In this line of questioning some saw a strain of racial insensitivity if not outright bigotry. David Remnick of *The New Yorker* said Trump had engaged in "a conscious form of race baiting." Bob Schieffer of CBS News said Trump had engaged in "an ugly strain of racism." These criticisms, which Trump disputed, resonated with some intellectuals, but it was the outrage of David Letterman, host of a nationally broadcast nighttime talk show, that brought it to a wider American public.

Letterman criticized Trump during an on-air chat with psychologist and talk-show host Phil McGraw. Known to the public as Dr. Phil, McGraw had once treated patients in a private practice. He then worked in a business that presented therapeutic seminars, which led to television appearances. Glib and folksy, he got his own gig starring in a syndicated show that offered case studies of people with social and psychological problems as entertainment. McGraw was, in essence, a reality-TV star like Trump, and he counted Trump as a friend. This relationship may have explained Letterman's decision to make Trump a topic of conversation. "It's all fun, it's all a circus, it's all a rodeo, until it starts to smack of racism," said Letterman. "And then it's no longer fun."

Drawn into the issue, McGraw said he didn't think Trump was a racist. He preferred to say Trump was rash:

"I don't think he always thinks everything through. I think sometimes he's a little from the hip. I don't think he has a racist bone in this body." Letterman said, "If he comes back on this show, and I'm not sure we want him back under those circumstances, but he ought to be prepared to apologize just for that kind of behavior."

After the broadcast Trump wrote to Letterman saying, "I was disappointed to hear the statements you made about me last night on your show that I was a 'racist.' In actuality, nothing could be further from the truth and there is nobody who is less of a racist than Donald Trump . . . Based upon your statements, and despite the fact that we have always done so well together, especially in your ratings, I am canceling my May 18th appearance on your show."

Months later it would be Letterman and not Trump who apologized, albeit in a convoluted way. At the start of his broadcast he said of Trump, "maybe it's not that he's a racist" but rather "a guy that says stupid things periodically to get attention" which was a quality "we have in common." It's possible "that I was wrong," Letterman continued, "that he's not a racist, because we don't want to think that of anyone, but he's just a dope. How 'bout that?"

Although Letterman did offer a kind of apology, he did not match Dr. Phil's analysis, nor did he agree with Trump's onetime bodyguard Robert Utsey, who was unequivocal in his view that Trump was without racial animus. But it's hard to agree entirely with Utsey's point of view. In his public life, beginning with his complaint about being required to rent to welfare recipients in the 1970s, Trump has exhibited what might be called insensitivity rather than bigotry. When he inserted himself into the Central Park jogger case, in which four of the accused were black and one was Hispanic, he added tension to a situation that was already fraught with racial overtones. In a TV interview he had said, "I would love to be a well-educated black because they have an actual advantage."

None of his earlier comments and actions compared with his attacks on Obama as he questioned the president's admission to Harvard and Columbia and repeatedly demanded proof of his birth in Hawaii, even after the proper record had been made public. For his part, Trump insisted that he was just asking questions about an issue that was, in his mind, unresolved. This shred-of-doubt strategy required Trump to ignore a reliable record and insult the president, but he was not alone as he flailed away. The election and reelection of America's first black president caused some on the right to become so unhinged that they circulated racist cartoons about the Obama family and made repeated attempts to demonize him as strange and different and then denied the racist undertones in such statements. An example of this dynamic arose in 2015 when former New York City mayor Rudy Giuliani declared, "He wasn't brought up the way you were brought up and I was brought up, through love of country." When confronted over this statement, he explained that it couldn't be considered racist because Obama "was brought up by a white mother."

Anyone sensitive to the nation's racial history would understand that challenging Obama's status as a native-born citizen or as a man who loves his country was beyond the pale. These statements excited the small portion of the electorate that could not accept, for racist reasons, that an African-American was president. This corner of American politics was home for people such as the federal judge who circulated a racist joke about the president's parents and an official of the California GOP who sent out a cartoon depicting the president as an ape. In these precincts people cheered the statements made by Giuliani and Trump as honest and brave and applauded when they refused to back down.

For a moment, the behavior Letterman deplored gained Trump a following, at least according to a *Wall Street Journal* poll. The survey, which was conducted in early April, found him running second to Romney among the subset of citizens who identified themselves as Republican primary voters. This result may have had something to do with his plain speaking—"China is raping this country," he said—but was more likely the product of his visibility. As a celebrity of many years running and the star of a TV show, he was much better recognized than all the other candidates. Celebrity had brought attention to Trump's political views, and it had made him the ideal foil as both comedian Seth Meyers and the president ridiculed him in a speech at the annual dinner of the White House Correspondents' Association.

Meyers got a big laugh when he looked at the table where Trump sat as a guest of the *Washington Post* and said, "Donald Trump has been saying he would run for president as a Republican, which is surprising because I thought he would be running as a joke." Unable to resist the target that was Trump's hair, Meyers said, "Donald Trump often appears on Fox, which is ironic, because a fox often appears on Donald Trump's head." Meyers advised the people seated with Trump that if they were unable to finish their meals, "don't worry, the fox will eat it." Meyers mercilessly tweaked Trump for his role in the birth-certificate uproar and made fun of him for saying, "I have a great relationship with the blacks." Meyers said this could not be true "unless the blacks are white people."

Throughout the performance, viewers watching the event on the C-SPAN TV network were treated to occasional shots of Trump, who sat grim-faced throughout the monologue. A widened view showed writer/ editor Graydon Carter, who had tormented Trump in various magazines, smiling just a few feet from Donald's right shoulder. The look on Trump's face made it seem as if he were enduring a terrible ordeal, rather than a roasting at the hands of a comedian. In contrast, President Obama smiled broadly as Meyers joked about how the Barack Obama of 2008 was so much better, and how he had aged terribly in office, adding, "Is this the change you were talking about?"

In his remarks later that night, the president also targeted Trump, which, considering the birther issue, may have brought him some personal satisfaction. He painted Trump as a conspiracy-theory extremist and then paused before adding, "All kidding aside, obviously, we all know about your credentials and breadth of experience. For example—no, seriously, just recently, in an episode of *Celebrity Apprentice*—at the steak house, the men's cooking team did not impress the judges from Omaha Steaks. And there was a lot of blame to go around. But you, Mr. Trump, recognized that the real problem was a lack of leadership. And so ultimately, you didn't blame Lil Jon or Meat Loaf. You fired Gary Busey. And these are the kind of decisions that would keep me up at night. Well handled, sir. Well handled."

The president's comments and the crowd's laughter came as elite US Navy SEALs were on an extremely risky mission that would result in the killing of terrorist leader Osama bin Laden. When Obama appeared at the White House on the day after the correspondents' dinner and revealed the death of the al-Qaeda leader, the news highlighted the grave issues a president must face and the frivolous quality of birtherism and its related "questions." Soon Republican senators John McCain and Lindsey Graham complained that Trump was a distraction who diverted attention from serious issues and

serious candidates. A poll published May 10 showed
Trump's support evaporating as he fell to last among six
likely GOP candidates, and the majority of Republican
voters said they didn't like him. Trump claimed to have
decided "in my mind" to conduct a real campaign, but
he took note of the TV schedule and said he wouldn't
make a final, formal announcement until the current run
of *The Apprentice* was completed on May 22, 2011.[14]

With executives from firms that purchased TV advertisements headed to New York for a conference on
May 16, officials at NBC told Trump to decide immediately whether he would host the next season of his
show. Required to choose between the money the network would pay him and the prospect of real political
combat and, perhaps, public service as president of the
United States, Trump took the cash. He revealed his decision not at a rally of citizens who had supported him,
but before the crowd of advertisers. After he affirmed
his commitment to them, he made sure to pound his
chest a little: "I maintain the strong conviction that if I
were to run, I would be able to win the primary and, ultimately, the general election." A week later, viewers
saw Trump anoint a country singer named John Rich
winner of *The Apprentice*. Rich prevailed over a lineup
of celebrities that included, among others, a baseball
player who had admitted using steroids, a *Playboy* centerfold model, and the winner of Mark Burnett's first
Survivor contest, Richard Hatch, who had been imprisoned for tax evasion.

The ratings for the show had improved during
Trump's political theatrics, and he did what he could
afterward to hold the spotlight. He didn't have to try
hard as would-be Republican standard-bearers seemed
unable to imagine themselves prevailing without Trump's
approval. Even Mitt Romney trekked to Trump Tower
after Donald had publicly denigrated him as a "small

business guy" who "walked away with some money from a very good company that he didn't create." Trump had also predicted that Romney was "going to lose." Yet there was Romney, sober Mormon bishop and paragon of solidity, seeking the approval of a serial fake candidate who used bankruptcy as a business strategy, spoke a profane strain of New Yorkese, and was a principal in one of the most notorious sex scandals of the twentieth century. (Trump remained, however, a teetotaler like Romney.) When Romney did eventually lose, Trump took no pleasure in being right. He logged on to his Twitter account and used the social media platform to loose a stream of despairing comments including:

"We can't let this happen. We should march on Washington and stop this travesty."

"Our nation is totally divided! Let's fight like hell and stop this great and disgusting injustice!"

"The world is laughing at us. This election is a total sham and a travesty. We are not a democracy!"

"Our country is now in serious and unprecedented trouble . . . like never before."

"Our nation is a once great nation divided! The Electoral College is a disaster for a democracy."

"Hopefully the House of Representatives can hold our country together for four more years . . . stay strong and never give up!"

In the aftermath of the tweets, the *Daily News* of New York cited a "Trump insider" as it reported that the man's three grown children, who each worked for him, had gone to him with a request that he back off Obama. A Trump spokesperson insisted that this meeting never occurred, but Donald Trump did seem to direct his ire elsewhere. He sparred with the singer Cher and then the comedian/panel-show host Bill Maher, who jokingly promised to donate $5 million to charity if Trump proved, with his birth certificate, that he was not fathered by an orangutan. Never one to be outdone, Trump directed a lawyer to send Maher a copy of Trump's birth certificate and a letter, which said, in part:

> Attached hereto is a copy of Mr. Trump's birth certificate, demonstrating that he is the son of Fred Trump, not an orangutan. . . . Please remit the $5 million to Mr. Trump immediately and he will ensure that the money be donated to the following five charities in equal amounts: Hurricane Sandy victims, The Police Athletic League, The American Cancer Society, The March of Dimes, and The Dana-Farber Cancer Institute.

Maher may well have possessed the $5 million, but a comedian's joke is a joke, and he wasn't going to give Trump what he wanted. Trump filed a legal claim against Maher, then withdrew it. He had many other battles to attend to, including his conflict with the attorney general of New York over Trump University and a fight with the first minister of Scotland, a onetime ally who had become an enemy because of a disagreement over some wind turbines.[15]

◆

15
A NOT-SO-INNOCENT ABROAD

Even the windmill stuff, it's fucking great.
Every day there's a story about Trump.
—DONALD TRUMP ON HIS BATTLES
WITH SCOTTISH OFFICIALS

Susan Munro spread birdseed on the patio outside her kitchen window, then scattered some kibble in the grass for the shy hedgehog that sometimes nosed around her garden. She was glad that the fox that once raised a litter of kits in a den on the north side of her cottage had moved on. A clever fox will push a hedgehog onto its back, and, well, it was better not to imagine such things.

Well into her fifties, Munro's blond hair was turning gray. Her face was weathered and creased, and she spoke with a tobacco rasp. But her health was good and she felt content. Munro had been born and raised in the nearby city of Aberdeen. But for decades her life had been here, at the house called Leyton Cottage. It stood at the end of a rutted dirt road. To the east lay only towering sand dunes and the sea. In every other direction stretched the vast Menie Estate, which was owned by a gentleman farmer from America named Tom Griffin. With the exception of the occasional shots fired by hunters who paid him to shoot at pheasant and partridge on the estate, Griffin was a quiet neighbor.

The isolation at Leyton Cottage was so complete that Susan Munro could recall every visitor to her door, but she would have remembered Peter Whyte even if she'd lived in the city. It's not every day that a stranger turns up to say he wants to buy your house. As she recalled it, he said, "I was here on holiday and walking along the beach. I saw your house and just had to ask if it might be available."

Paunchy, with a smooth face, blue eyes, and wavy hair in rapid retreat, Whyte spoke with a posh-school accent. Perhaps, thought Munro, he was just another victim of the real estate fever that was burning across the United Kingdom. In five years, the median price of a British home had roughly doubled. Many owners had turned their paper gains into cash by taking out new mortgages. Much of this money had been invested in more property, but if you didn't have cash, you could apply for a new type of mortgage that covered 100 percent of a purchase. Everyone was talking about real estate, and it seemed as if only the most cautious— some would say slow-witted—stayed out of the game.

Peter Whyte had the look of someone who was winning the game. But if he truly hoped to turn a profit, thought Munro, why bother with the most humble house around? Yes, it was close to the sea, but the dunes, some of which were forty feet high, made the path to it daunting. And the house itself was much too modest for this fellow. Why wouldn't he go for David and Moira Milne's place on the bluff, or Sheila and Michael Forbes's farm with its many acres? Munro didn't ask any of the questions that came to her mind. Instead she made mental notes to give her husband, John, an accurate report when he got home from work.

As Whyte departed, Munro thought, "You can't see this house from the beach. I wonder what he really wants." In the evening, the Munros agreed that their property wasn't an asset to be sold, traded, or mortgaged.

Had they not preferred to keep things private, the people who lived in the homes scattered across the

Menie Estate would have known sooner that Peter Whyte had knocked on every one of their doors. David Milne had been watching a rugby match on TV. Annoyed by the intrusion, he sent Whyte away. Sheila Forbes, a brassy woman inclined to speak her mind, told Whyte, "Fuck off," and refused to even talk to him.

When the Menie neighbors finally spoke to each other about Peter Whyte, they became suspicious. A call to Whyte's phone was answered by someone who announced, "Hobday Golf." The proprietor's full name was Neil Peter Whyte Hobday. When he came on the line, Hobday confessed that he was not a holiday visitor eager to buy a vacation home. He was, instead, a consultant to a real estate developer who had big plans for the windswept stretch of Scottish coastline where the Munros, Milneses, Forbeses, and other neighbors lived in contented isolation. Tom Griffin had already agreed to sell his Menie Estate, all eight hundred acres, and a big golf resort was being planned.

The truth about Peter Whyte spread as neighbors stopped on narrow farm roads to trade information from car to car. As spring arrived, the development became a topic of conversation at the local convenience store and at the café/gallery called Tarts and Crafts. Finally the local press announced that an American named Donald Trump planned to build five hundred houses and nearly a thousand apartments near the fairways of two golf courses. A 450-room hotel was also in the offing, with the usual restaurants and meeting rooms. The golf links would require a sprawling clubhouse—of Disney/neo-Victorian design—and then there would be the roads and parking lots and housing for four hundred staff. The development would also chew up some of the dunes, which had supposedly been set off-limits as an environmentally sensitive Site of Special Scientific Interest (SSSI).[1]

◆

Trump arrived in Aberdeen on the last Saturday in April 2006, landing at the airport in his Boeing 727. Descending from the plane to the strains of "Highland Laddie" played by a bagpiper, he was met at the airport by a bigger crowd than normally greeted the queen when she visited nearby Balmoral Castle. Boosters had already begun to promote Trump and his promised investment. The members of one organization, called the Economic Forum, had even declared that the development represented the biggest boon to Scotland since the rise of the oil industry. True to his germophobic form, Trump said, "I should *almost* kiss the earth," because he had arrived in his mother's homeland.

The American billionaire's visit to Aberdeen and the Menie Estate resembled a modern political campaign swing. Outfitted in an expensive suit and distinguished by his glowing hair, Trump's presence commanded attention even if he was merely walking to a waiting car. Trailed by aides and reporters, he was transported in a motorcade to a whirlwind of meetings and receptions attended by local bigwigs. Journalists filmed and photographed his every move and recorded what he said about the good his money would accomplish for the people of Scotland. The Aberdeen papers jumped on the bandwagon. One, the *Evening Express,* reached an immediate conclusion on the plan, telling readers, "It is crucial we embrace" Trump's project.[2]

As they viewed Trump on their televisions and read about him in the paper, the denizens of Menie Estate thought that their predicament seemed like something out of a movie. Then they realized that they had actually *seen* the movie in 1983.

In *Local Hero,* a stranger suddenly appears and tries to buy a swath of the Scottish coast on behalf of a wealthy American with a secret plan. Greed prevails and the locals scheme for windfall profits on their land until an eccentric holdout stops everything. In some ways the film foreshadowed events here in Balmedie village with uncanny accuracy, even providing a role model for those who would be heroes. In the movie, the American was a Texan named Felix Happer (Burt Lancaster), who changed his plan to accommodate the Scots. In real life, the American was a New Yorker named Donald Trump. He had already cultivated Scottish politicians in hopes of speeding his project to approval, and he didn't seem to be interested in accommodating anyone.

Donald Trump had acted as if the development game in Scotland were essentially the same as the one played in America, except for the occasional pipers in kilts. Big projects invariably run up against zoning and environmental regulations, which are the purview of elected officials. As politicians, elected officials were generally concerned with making voters happy so they could stay in office. The happiness of the voters required good jobs, good public services, low taxes, and the feeling that the future was bright. In Scotland, a shrinking population and declining revenues from North Sea oil wells shadowed the future, and First Minister Jack McConnell was eagerly seeking investments to reverse the trends. He believed that tourism and wind energy were especially prime for growth. Trump wasn't in the energy business, but he knew how to build a golf resort that might draw tourists to the windswept eastern coast of the country.[3]

McConnell and Trump had both attended the "Dressed to Kilt" fashion show in Manhattan in April 2005. The annual event brought prominent Americans of Scottish ancestry together with Scottish officials. By summer, officials of a Scottish-government economic-development agency were courting Trump in hopes he would invest in something they code-named Project X. In October, after Trump signaled he was ready to proceed, McConnell jetted back to New York for a private lunch and consultations at Trump Tower. (The first minister had been on a bit of an international spree, traveling around the world hoping to lure business investment.) The Scottish public was told that the meeting was intended as an opportunity to "discuss Trump's interest in and connection with Scotland." In McConnell's inner circle, however, it was acknowledged that he went "to discuss Mr. Trump's proposal for entry into the UK golf resort market via a project in Aberdeenshire."

A day after the Trump Tower meeting, the Scottish press reported only the cover story. Trump was quoted saying it was "possible" he would invest in Scotland and was pleased because his mother was from the Hebrides, which is "serious Scotland." McConnell said only that "one of the most successful businessmen in the world" was interested in his country. Privately, a Scottish development official wrote to a Trump aide to say, "I hope you were reassured at the highest level possible through both Jack McConnell, Scotland's First Minister, and Jack Perry, our CEO's involvement in today's meeting, that we are committed to the partnership that will deliver this project." Trump was also assured he had "a direct line into the government in Scotland."

In January 2006, Scottish officials met privately in Aberdeen with architects whom Trump had hired as he began to assemble land for his development. They agreed that the project he wanted to build might conflict with land-use plans and recognized that a proposal for development on the dunes might prompt opposition by environmental groups. But they also wanted to see the project built, and toward this end they set a strict timetable for pushing it through the local council so that Trump could start building as soon as possible. The government officials also noted that in the event that the council refused to grant Trump permission, Jack McConnell's national government could overrule the locals. This type of intervention was rare and could only be accomplished after a formal public process. But if they wanted Trump's investment, and the locals wouldn't yield, they could force it on them.

The power move would be a last resort. How would it look if the government pushed people out of their homes so that rich golfers could hack around the dunes? McConnell's government preferred that the public embrace Trump as a benefactor bearing a huge bank account, and not a developer intent on spoiling the countryside. Unfortunately this hope depended on a man who often seemed like a walking caricature of greedy self-interest. The suits. The hair. The big airplane painted with his name in huge, gold letters. It may have worked for him on his TV show, but for some in Scotland it reeked of flimflam. McConnell could do little to counteract this image. Getting too close to Trump in public might hurt him with voters. So, from a distance, McConnell announced that Trump had been named a "Global Scot."

The title—Global Scot—rang with a certain majesty. It suggested power, status, and even official privileges. In fact, it was more like an invitation to join a booster club, and not a very old one at that. Created in 2001, the Global Scot network was run by a government economic-development agency. Members were encouraged to attend lectures and social gatherings and perhaps do some business. Did this program actually make a difference for Scotland? It would be almost impossible to answer this question. But it did add a fillip to an executive's biography—"He's a Global Scot"—that might be helpful were he ever introduced to a crowd in, say, Aberdeen.[4]

◆

For a rich man who was mad for golf, the prospect of building a course in the country where the game was invented was tantalizing. Trump had already developed successful high-end golf resorts with housing in the United States, including one in Westchester County, New York, and another in Palos Verdes, California. But in Scotland, a country already endowed with many of the best courses in the world, he would need to offer something special to attract golfers who could pay the high greens fee—up to $300 per person—necessary to support a first-rate development. Something special existed in the links land in Balmedie. This had been obvious even to Tom Griffin, who had never played the game.

Griffin had considered building a course himself, but some problems had stopped him. For one thing, Aberdeen's cold, wet weather would limit play. (Even in the summertime highs average just shy of sixty-five degrees.) Then there was the legal status of the dunes. The government had designated them an SSSI because they provided natural habitat for wildlife and plants. Also, the dunes were unusual geological formations. The tides and winds moved them at a rate of several meters per year. The Menie Sand Sheet, as it was called, was one of the most impressive examples of a dynamic dune system in all of Britain. In the fifteenth century a gale that blew across the sands for nine days buried all of a nearby village except for the spire of a church.

The breezes that had shifted the sands for millennia had also made the waters offshore attractive to energy experts, who imagined windmills anchored to the seabed and power lines delivering electricity to the shore. This vision had been embraced by national leaders, who hoped that as North Sea petroleum ran out, wind power would become a new valuable commodity. Wind-power stations would be supported by engineers and industries already located in Aberdeen to serve the offshore drilling platforms. Talk of Scottish-built turbines and electricity exported to the European mainland soothed fears of post-oil job losses. But as Trump promised his own version of economic development—roughly $1.5 billion in construction, six thousand temporary jobs, and twelve hundred permanent ones—he repeatedly told Scottish officials that he didn't want his golfers to see offshore windmills. He would eventually report they had assured him this wouldn't happen.[5]

As he negotiated with politicians in private, Donald publicly proclaimed his love for Scotland. In Aberdeen he cited his mother's Scottish birth to show he was sentimental about the place and meant no harm. Unfortunately, he sometimes said she was not "Scottish" but rather "Scotch," which many locals considered a pejorative except when it was applied to whiskey or eggs. But slips of language were forgiven by those who saw the benefits of a resort that might attract the golf pilgrims who trek to Scotland to test themselves at ancient courses. Among the supporters were the officials of local business groups and journalists at the local papers, the *Express* and the *Press and Journal,* who greeted Trump and his project with great enthusiasm.

With a population of 5.2 million, which was less than that of New York City, Scotland didn't see many private investments of $1.5 billion, which explained the support Trump received from many in Aberdeen. However, he recognized the obstacles in his way. A Trump aide told the local press that the golf development would be canceled "if people want to ruin Aberdeen and Aberdeenshire [with windmills]." Trump demanded quick action to resolve land-use issues, saying, "Either this will happen very quickly or it won't happen at all." And he made sure to tie First Minister McConnell to the project, speaking of him as if he were a partner, if not the instigater of the whole project. McConnell had contacted him "many times," said Trump. "He was fantastic and did a great job in persuading us."[6]

Although Trump talked of him as an ally, the first minister's actual constituents included the people who lived at Menie and had turned away Neil Peter Whyte Hobday. Some of the residents suspected that McConnell had violated a code of conduct that barred him from doing anything that "might be seen as prejudicial" when it came to development proposals. Of course conflict over the Trump plan would be eased if he could buy out his neighbors, so when his representatives failed to persuade the holdouts, Trump went to Menie to see what he might accomplish himself.

Tom Griffin played go-between, hosting some of his neighbors and Trump at his home. The Griffin house had been built in 1835 atop a much older foundation. Made of gray stone and decorated with a circular tower, Menie House resembled a small castle and would become a hotel when Trump took over. A few neighbors showed up to discuss the planned development, but Michael Forbes was not among them. Griffin went down the farm road to talk to him and found Forbes in his yard, mending the nets he used to catch salmon off the beach. The Forbes family had controlled the rights to this catch for generations.

"He came up and said, 'Do you want to meet Donald Trump?'" recalled Forbes years later. "I said, 'Nae really.' Tom told me the fella wanted to talk to the locals, and I said that if he wanted to speak to me, he knows where I am."

Forbes was a granite block of a man, short, broad-chested, and stubbornly set in his ways. Nestled between the dunes and out of his neighbors' view, his property was very much a working farm, with hay fields and sheds, goats, fowl, and a horse. Broken machines were left where they died, to supply spare parts for those that worked. This was a matter of practicality, and since none of his neighbors could even see his property, Forbes considered his way of managing things to be no one's business. Indeed, he had purchased his land for the sole purpose of living as he pleased. He had even moved his mother to the property. Her cottage, which sat across the one-lane road from the main house, was decorated with a small sign that read PARADISE.

Although Griffin liked Forbes well enough, he considered him stubborn and emotional and not the kind of man who would go along with Trump's plans. Nevertheless he went back to Mcnic House to fetch Trump, and the famous golf architect Tom Fazio, who had come to inspect the land. The group found Forbes still in his yard. As Forbes would recall, Trump tried to engage in a little small talk. It didn't go well.

"Trump said to me, 'What's this land worth, about twenty dollars an acre?'

"I said, 'Ach, in yer dreams.'

"Then he said to me, 'We're here to build a golf course and we're going to do it.' He turned to Tom Fazio and said, 'You deal with this man. Tell him we'll give him a job for life.'"

A designer, not a developer, Fazio was not the man to negotiate a land purchase, and he did not try to talk terms. Forbes would remember telling Fazio about the salmon concession he had inherited, which controlled the fishing off the beach, and his own plans for the property. He had a grown son and two grandsons and he expected them to inherit the place. With them in mind, he couldn't imagine selling at any price. Fazio wouldn't try to talk him into it. In fact he would leave the project and let another prominent designer, Martin Hawtree, take the commission.

Forbes was not the only holdout. Several property

owners, including the Munros and the Milnes, also refused to sell under any terms. Tom Griffin, who had known each of them for about twenty years, wasn't surprised. The Milnes had poured their life savings and thousands of hours in labor into converting a bluff-top former coast-guard station into a home with incomparable views of the sea. After raising a family there, the Munros were emotionally attached to their place and also imagined leaving it for future generations, who could wander the dunes and play on the beach.[7]

◆

If some of his neighbors seemed to Griffin like immovable objects, he considered Trump a comparably irresistible force. In his own negotiations with the man, Griffin had noticed that Trump was relentless about getting what he wanted. For example, before making his final payment, Trump noted that a big electrical generator and several big blocks of stone, used to repair the house, had been left on the property. He demanded that Griffin have them trucked away or accept a reduced payment. In America at the time, Griffin considered the expense that would be required to satisfy Trump and gave in. "He beat me out of about thirty thousand or forty thousand dollars," Griffin would recall. "You might think it was a small amount for someone like him, but you could also think that he made himself tens of thousands of dollars just by making a demand most people wouldn't make." (According to published accounts, Trump paid Griffin about 6.7 million British pounds, or roughly $11.3 million, depending on the exchange rate.)

Griffin would also remember a dinner with Trump at a place called the Cock & Bull, which overlooked the Menie Estate from a spot along a highway called the A90. Throughout the meal Griffin felt as if he were dining with an actor playing a part. "It was Donald Trump, playing Donald Trump." When "the waitress came up with the bill," said Griffin, "Donald said to her, 'Usually, I get comped in these situations.'" Griffin supposed that Trump meant that businesspeople gave him freebies wherever he proposed to invest heavily in the local economy. "She went to talk to the manager, who said he would agree if Trump would pose for a picture with the staff." The staff filed out. Trump posed. The dinner was free.

Although he didn't always convert his fame to favors in such a direct and obvious way, Trump was accustomed to getting what he wanted. Concerned that the Forbes farm and other houses would ruin the vistas for golfers, he dispatched his son Donald Jr. and a Trump Organization executive, George Sorial, to make further offers. Both men dressed in expensive clothes and wore their dark hair slicked back, which reminded the recalcitrant Scots of New York mobsters. "At one point Sorial handed me a piece of paper and said, 'Have a look at this,'" said Forbes. On the paper was written an offer of £350,000. Forbes added that when he declined the offer, "Sorial said, 'We'll come back with more.' I said, 'No, you won't, because this is the last of it.'"[8]

Sorial would travel back and forth to Scotland more than a dozen times as he worked on the golf development. A lawyer by training, Sorial, like most Trump executives, wore a variety of hats. In 2007 he had been identified in *The Wall Street Journal* as managing director of Trump International Golf Resorts. Sorial lived in a Trump building, where he was on the board of apartment owners, and considered his position with Trump a kind of dream job. He confessed that like his boss he had been a somewhat unruly kid who was straightened out at an all-male school—in his case a Catholic school run by Benedictine monks, which he attended from 1982 to 1986. Sorial had ties to Scotland and the

Isle of Lewis, where he had spent many summers of his childhood visiting relatives.

As Trump and his associates tried to buy up properties, they also developed a proposal for Scottish authorities, who would have to approve the development because it deviated from existing land-use plans. At the local level, they would have to deal with committees of the Aberdeenshire Council and then the entire council itself. The key committee was headed by Martin Ford, who in style, purpose, and personality couldn't have been more different from Donald Trump.

Born and raised in the countryside of southwest England, Ford came from a family of stubborn idealists. During World War I his grandfather was one of very few conscientious objectors whose status was confirmed by government authorities. He spent the war years helping farmers produce food for the troops. Ford held a doctorate in plant ecology and, prior to his election to the council in 1999, had been a professor at the Scottish Agricultural College. Thirteen years younger than Trump, Ford was an angular, athletic-looking man with blue eyes and gray, curly hair. Although he lived in the countryside, he was so committed to environmental protection that he rode a bicycle, in all weather, sometimes logging fifty miles in a day as he served a rural district of ninety-five hundred scattered citizens. His wife, Gina, whom he had met at a conference of the Liberal Democrats, would say he was "an eccentric." Ford would say he was a man of principles.

Among Ford's principles was his commitment to the rules that governed his work as chairman of the committee that oversaw development in Aberdeenshire. He would conduct the hearings that took public comment on Trump's proposal and would guide the committee through its review of reports from professional experts—planners, economists, scientists—who would consider the effect of the project on everything from traffic and the environment to the local economy. He was required to consider the merits of the application, and not the applicant. "What matters is the land and what's being proposed for it," he explained after dealing with the issue. "Where your mother was born isn't a consideration. Highway traffic congestion *is*." Ford never referred to Trump by name, calling him instead "the applicant." He also turned away reporters who tried to get him to stake out a position on the golf development.[9]

As Ford proceeded with the review, more than thirty-five hundred people sent letters or signed petitions forwarded to the council. The ranks of those in favor exceeded those against by about one hundred and fifty names. Most of the letters, were the product of organized campaigns and made echoing arguments. Those in favor, encouraged by the Chamber of Commerce, welcomed the jobs and business activity that would come with the development. Those against, who were supported by a group called Sustainable Aberdeenshire, said Trump would not deliver what he had promised and that the environmental costs were too high. Further opposition also came from various preservation groups, including the Scottish Wildlife Trust and the Royal Society for the Protection of Birds.

As Trump's people developed the documents necessary to apply for planning exceptions, editorial writers in the local papers tried to rally reader support for him. "Seize the day," declared the *Press and Journal*. They also lampooned his opponents in cruel terms. In the eyes of the editorial writers they were "shiny-eyed saviors of a bit of sand" and "whinging, squabbling bairns [children] more worried about birds than people." They were also "no-hopers" and "misfits" and "small-minded numpties [fools]" and "buffoons in woolly jumpers." One of the papers even banished an antidevelopment group from its news pages, insisting it had no legitimate interest in the region. Members of the organization would never again be quoted by the *Press and Journal*.[10]

While the local press tilted toward Trump, journalists from outside Aberdeen began to arrive in pursuit of the story of the American billionaire intent on developing one of the last unspoiled places on the Scottish coast. Most made their way to the Menie Estate, where they found Michael and Sheila Forbes, Susie Munro, and David Milne. With each interview, Trump's local opponents grew more outspoken. Michael Forbes, who had been so shy for most of his life that he hated casual conversations, quickly became a most quotable subject for interviewers, who couldn't get enough of his thick brogue and chin-first attitude. "I wasn't against the golf course from the start, but then they just went mental because I wouldn't sell," he told *The Times* of London in the fall of 2007. "They said they'd make my life a misery and they are."

Forbes's misery included a locked gate installed across the path that he and his ancestors had used for decades to access their fishing station. He complained of security men who followed him on farm roads and Trump executives who pestered him because they wouldn't take no for an answer. When photographers asked, he obligingly dressed in his kilt or folded his tattooed arms across his chest as they clicked away. When she was interviewed, his eighty-three-year-old mother, Molly, said, "I came here to live in peace."

Confronted with a stubborn man who was unmoved by his money, Trump responded in the style he often displayed when he was frustrated. He said Forbes's farm was "disgusting" and wondered aloud whether he left machinery and supplies lying about "on purpose to try and make it look bad, so I have to pay some more money." This kind of talk only won Forbes more admirers, especially among Scots, who saw in him, and his somewhat ramshackle property, reminders of a proud, rural past. Indeed, when he spoke of his farm as a "croft" Forbes sounded a cultural note that was unmistakable to anyone with a passing acquaintance with Scottish history.

In the local language a croft was the type of small family farm once found across the country. Although a few were owned by the people who worked them, most were occupied by tenants who paid rent or gave a share of their produce to a landlord. Between 1700 and 1900 thousands of crofters were forced off their lands in government-sanctioned "clearances" that forced farmers into villages, where they often suffered abject poverty. Crofters, who eventually won some protected status, became symbols of both English oppression and Scottish resilience. According to genealogists, Donald Trump's ancestors were almost certainly driven off the land during a clearance on the Isle of Lewis. In Tong, where Trump's mother had lived as a child, displaced croft families lived, according to one account, in "human wretchedness" alongside arable land that was set aside for game preserves. A century later, Trump seemed unaware that in his battle with Michael Forbes, he occupied the villain's role in another attempt at the clearance of a croft.

By the time Martin Ford's committee began to consider Trump's application, few Scots were undecided. Michael Forbes and others who opposed the big development were likely favored by the majority of Scots. (To encourage their support Forbes had painted the words NO GOLF COURSE in giant red letters on the side of his barn.) But in Aberdeen, where any development's benefits would be felt most directly, Trump enjoyed substantial backing. He could also count on Alex Salmond, who had replaced Jack McConnell as first minister, and Trump was supported by many on the shire council.

At the end of November 2007, Martin Ford and others on the committee debated Trump's plan. As the public meeting wore on, the group seemed split right down the middle. Although the proposal was presented as an all-or-nothing proposition, projects were commonly rejected, revised, reconsidered, and approved. When the votes were tallied, Ford broke a tie and the plan was turned down. Trump didn't get what he wanted, but many of the committee members expected him to try again with a modified plan. This was how things were done.[11]

After the vote, George Sorial angrily told the press, "If you want to do big business, don't do it in the northeast of Scotland." The front-page headline of the *Aberdeen Evening Express* screamed, YOU TRAITORS, next to photos of the councilors who opposed Trump. (The pictures had been photoshopped to make them look like turnips—*neeps* in common parlance—which was not a compliment.) At his home in the country Martin Ford's phone rang with callers who shouted threats and curses. Police advised him and his wife to stay in their home behind locked doors. Councilor Debra Storr, who had voted against the Trump application, was assaulted physically on her doorstep by an angry citizen. Within days, lawyers for Trump were pressing local politicians, who were, in turn, talking about how to give him what he wanted, lest he take his money elsewhere. George Sorial demanded action within thirty days.

On the Monday after the committee vote, Alex Salmond huddled with Sorial and Neil Peter Whyte Hobday at an Aberdeen hotel called the Marcliffe. After this session, Salmond called Scotland's chief planner, James Mackinnon. Sorial and Mackinnon met the following afternoon in Edinburgh. By the end of the day, Salmond's national government would send the Aberdeenshire Council notice that it was taking over the process. Trump, who considered the committee vote to be "sad for Scotland, and certainly sad for Donald Trump," would also declare, "We didn't have anything to do" with the national government's move. In the past, Edinburgh had stepped in to halt a development approved on the local level. But as far as Martin Ford could recall, this was the first time the government had intervened to *advance* a project that had been turned down by officials closest to the people who would be affected.

Having declared Martin Ford a traitor, the *Evening Express* campaigned for him to be removed from his chairmanship, arguing, among other points, that as a "non-driver" he was somehow unqualified to consider traffic issues. The sister paper of the *Express,* the *Press and Journal,* said Ford was "one step removed from eco-warrior status" and must therefore quit or be forced out. Ford resisted but soon found himself the subject of a raging debate among his colleagues. When they voted on a proposal to replace him as chairman, twenty-nine abstained, ten supported him, and twenty-six voted to remove him. Thus a minority managed to punish him by taking away his chairman's post, which cut his $40,000-per-year salary by almost $20,000. Half-distressed and half-relieved, Ford would reflect on these events and decide he had been the victim of a level of hype and hyperbole so extreme that otherwise sober people he had known and collaborated with for many years had "gone mad" under the pressure from Trump and his allies in business, the press, and the government.[12]

With so much promised by Trump, Scottish national officials moved quickly. They announced they would convene public hearings at a convention center in Aberdeen and that Trump would be the first witness. On the day before he was to answer questions, Trump's 727 set down at the only airport on his mother's home island big enough to accommodate it. It was his first visit to his ancestors' home since he was a child of three or four. His sister Maryanne, who accompanied him on this trip, had come many times before and after her mother's death in 2000. As he stood on the tarmac, a gust of wind sent strands of his carefully constructed hair flying in different directions. Cases of his own books, including *Trump: How to Get Rich* and *Trump: Never Give Up,* were loaded into a Porsche Cayenne, the fanciest vehicle on the island, which had been borrowed for the day from a local millionaire.

Trump's carefully plotted visit included a stop at his mother's home in Tong, where one reporter noted he spent ninety-seven seconds inside. When he and his sister chatted with relatives, she charmed them with a few Gaelic phrases. He told them about his successes. Of *The Apprentice,* he said, "If you get ratings, you're king, like me. I'm a king. If you don't get ratings, you're thrown off the air like a dog." Of his career as a developer he told them, "They all want Trump because I do the highest level of work, and I'm known for that. People know that our level of work is the best, and when a project is finished, it's going to be the best, and that's why governments call me. They've a piece of land in a certain country, they call me." The great majority of Trump's business activity had been in the United States, but he was involved in projects in Canada, South Korea, Mexico, Dubai, and elsewhere. Some would come to fruition. Others would not.

In his three-hour visit, Trump also conducted a press conference, where he said he would consider funding the restoration of the island's most important landmark, Lews Castle. Built in the nineteenth century by an opium trader, the castle had been given to the local people by the same Lord Leverhulme who had been unable to fulfill his promise of bringing jobs and prosperity to the island.[13]

After his brief visit, Trump departed Lewis to defend *his* promises of jobs and prosperity in Aberdeen. The next day he sat at a witness table to face the panel that would review his project. He dressed down for the appearance, choosing a sober, striped-blue tie instead of one of his usual power reds. In prepared remarks he said he intended to build "the best golf course in the world" and that could only be accomplished, at a profit, with the accompanying homes. "Without the funding from the construction of homes," he added, "the economics are far below your acceptable return on investment."

Later, in response to a question, Trump reverted to his off-the-cuff style, saying, "Let's do it properly. Let's not do it . . . half-assed." He also insisted that a golf course, even one that would destroy some of the protected land, would be an improvement over the dunes, which might blow away in a storm. "When you walk on the site right now, it's sort of disgusting. There are bird carcasses lying all over the place. There are dead animals all over the site that have been shot. There may be some people that are into that. I am not." He later evoked the Khmer atrocities in Cambodia by describing the Menie Estate as "a killing field."

Other witnesses, including government experts, supported Trump's analysis, telling the panel that the resort and housing were, by far, the most valuable aspects of the development and could pump more than $1.5 billion into the region and produce fourteen hundred permanent jobs for people in northeast Scotland. The golf course would cost a comparative pittance—roughly $40 million—and would likely require fewer than one or two hundred workers, and many of them would enjoy only seasonal employment. Clearly, the big payoff for

Scotland, as well as Trump, came with the sprawling vacation village he had envisioned. Here the local political controversy may have helped, as it attracted worldwide press attention. It was all free publicity.

When he returned to New York, Trump played up the drama of his Scottish endeavor when he appeared on David Letterman's talk show. (With the birther bandwagon not yet rolling, he was introduced as "America's favorite cutthroat billionaire.") On TV Trump said he believed the Scottish authorities would give him permission to build as he wanted, but when quizzed on the location of the development, which was in the Scottish northeast, he sounded a bit less certain. Letterman asked if it was on the west coast of the country and Trump answered, "More or less."

As officials considered overruling the local committee and giving Trump what he wanted, the British press was filled with reports that an economic recession was at hand. Lenders stopped making mortgage loans, and big banks turned to the taxpayers for bailouts. All the years of speculation were ending in misery for those who could not make payments on homes that were worth less each month. The biggest builder in the Aberdeen area laid off more than one hundred workers. Amid the gloom, Trump's promises offered a bright spot of relief. In the fall, the Scottish government intervened to give him the permission he wanted, with some conditions covering, for the most part, the way the land was to be carved to accommodate fairways, greens, and tees. Trump expressed gratitude and then asked that the government consider forcing the holdouts to sell to him.[14]

◆

According to a letter that came to light after the fact, the idea that the government could seize Michael Forbes's croft, and the homes owned by the Milnes and the Munros, was first raised by George Sorial and Neil Hobday. In February 2009 one of Trump's lawyers, Ann Faulds, sent the Aberdeenshire Council a memo outlining the reasons that could be given for forcing the holdouts to relinquish their properties. A few weeks later she sent a formal request for the council to use its power of "compulsory purchase orders," which would force the sale of the parcels to Trump. Faulds said that Trump could cover the cost of this effort, but would want, in exchange, "to retain control of the process."

In requesting the government force people out of their homes, Trump gave his opponents the moral high ground. Michael Forbes went to the press with a catalog of complaints about local authorities helping Trump to bully Forbes off his property. First an inspector had come to determine whether Forbes was abusing his chickens, his geese, or his horse. They were all found in good condition. Next came an officer asking if Forbes possessed an illegal shotgun. He did not. Finally an official wanted to check out a rumor that Forbes was storing chemicals in an old tanker truck. He was not. All of this amounted to harassment, said Forbes, and all of it had happened *before* he learned that he might be forced to vacate his land. Forbes also reported that equipment operators on Trump's property had broken the line delivering water to his house and repairs had taken ten days.[15] During that time, his family had no water.

The threat of compulsory purchase seemed to energize opposition to the Trump project. In May 2009 homeowner David Milne showed up at a public event at which Neil Peter Whyte Hobday intended to show locals the plans for the development, where work was about to begin. Milne, who intended to share his views too, began speaking to people at the event. An incensed Hobday was caught by TV news cameras raising his voice to tell Milne, "This is not your show. Pick your own platform. Pay for it somewhere else. Invite the media and do it there. Just clear off." Milne stood firm and got to say his piece, telling the people at the event, "If this is permitted to go ahead, no one in any home, anywhere in this country, will ever be safe again. That cannot be allowed. This is supposed to be a civilized country in the twenty-first century." Ten days later Hobday resigned from the Trump project. He would land on his feet, eventually finding employment as the executive director of a posh, London-area polo club that had been founded by Queen Elizabeth II's husband, Prince Philip, Duke of Edinburgh.

After the confrontation at the Trump exhibit, an Internet group called Tripping Up Trump began a campaign against his project. More than seven thousand people joined a "landshare" scheme that divided approximately one acre of the Forbes farm into tiny plots, for which they received actual deeds. Theoretically, this action would require the authorities to issue compulsory purchase orders for every little slice of this tract, which the organizers hoped might discourage them from using this power. Councilor Martin Ford and others announced they opposed compulsory purchase, and it was never formally proposed.

Trump made public a letter in which he called Councilor Debra Storr "a national disgrace" for opposing his development plan. In September 2009 his son Donald Jr. and George Sorial went to the Forbes farm and attempted to negotiate with Forbes. Like his brother and sister, Donald Jr. was employed by the family business. He had held the title of executive vice president since joining the firm in 2001, at the age of twenty-four. His younger sister and brother held the same title. Although the three siblings had special areas of interest, no sharp lines separated them. Just as their father moved from project to project, focusing on TV in one moment and golf courses the next, they were expected to handle a variety of assignments, which would, presumably, expose them to the full range of the Trump empire.

When Donald Jr. and George Sorial met Michael Forbes, he had been infuriated by the threatened compulsory purchase order, and he greeted them with a torrent of verbal abuse. Trump Sr., who was offended by this incident, eventually replied in a venomous press release that stated, among other things, that Forbes "has always been dirty, sloppy and unkempt in his personal appearance and demeanor. He is a loser who is seriously damaging the image of both Aberdeenshire and his great country. His property is a disgusting blight on the community and an environmental hazard, with leaking oil containers, rusted shacks and abandoned vehicles dumped everywhere. It is a very poor image and representation for the world to see of Scotland."

For years to come, Trump and Forbes would trade barbs. In the main, Trump talked about the condition of the Forbes croft, suggesting its owner was somehow unworthy of respect because his property was untidy. "My mother was born in Stornoway. She was so meticulous. The Scottish people are very clean people, and yet this guy runs the property like a slum. He lives in squalor." He also complained that Forbes had agreed to sell, only to break his promise. Forbes insisted he would never sell: "There's no truth to this at all. He is a compulsive liar. The last time his son came here, I chased him off the land. He's got all these bodyguards with him, and if he keeps saying these things about me, then he will need them."

Trump did deploy security guards, who patrolled in trucks marked ESTATE SECURITY and followed residents who used the farm roads on the estate. Police were frequently called to the Trump property. In July 2010 they responded to a complaint from Trump employees about two filmmakers who had come to an office. By the time the officers arrived, Anthony Baxter and Richard Phinney had moved on to Susan Munro's house. The police followed them there and interrogated them as the camera continued to record. When the police demanded that they stop filming, Baxter refused. A tussle over the camera ensued. The police forced Baxter to the ground and took him and Phinney into custody. The episode would become a major plot point in the 2011 documentary *You've Been Trumped,* which Baxter presented at dozens of film festivals before it was aired by the BBC.

In August 2010 Trump sent a survey and fencing crew to claim a sliver of property that Michael Forbes was using. Forbes came out to argue with them, with a property map that showed the boundary. Police who had accompanied the Trump workers ordered Forbes to step back while a fence was installed. If Forbes wanted to contest this seizure, they said, he could take it up with government authorities, but they were there to satisfy the crew's request for protection. (Documents in the local land register would show that the boundary determined by Trump's men was correct.)

In October, during a tour of the construction site, a small convoy of black sport utility vehicles brought Trump and his son Donald Jr. to David Milne's house. Milne refused to meet with them and asked them to leave. Later a film crew that was present to report on the Menie project for the Golf Channel TV network captured Trump discussing Milne's house with a young woman named Sarah Malone, whom he had recently hired as "executive vice president." Malone admittedly knew nothing about golf courses, but she was so beautiful she had won a contest to become the Face of Aberdeen.

"Sarah, I want to get rid of that house," said Trump.

"It's going to create a bit of a stir, but if we're up for it, let's do it," she answered.

"Who cares, you know what, who cares? It's our property. We can do what we want. We're trying to build the greatest course in the world . . . his house is ugly."

The same camera operators recorded Trump speaking to head greenkeeper Paul O'Connor, whom he had hired away from the famous course at Carnoustie. As he gestured toward Milne's home, Trump said, "I don't know what the fucking problem is." A moment later he added, "I gotta make a change if you're not going to do it."

Eleven days after Milne turned Trump away, men working for Trump installed a fence that ran along Milne's driveway and then encircled his house. They also pounded a blue stake into the ground next to Milne's garage. Two weeks later he received a notice from Trump's representatives demanding that he tear down the garage. Next, a work crew installed a second fence, closer to Milne's home, and he received a letter demanding he pay $4,000 for it. Milne didn't comply with any of the demands. A row of Sitka spruce were planted by Trump workers along the fence line, blocking the view of the sea that had prompted Milnes and his wife, Moira, to buy their home in the first place. Next came a wall of earth twenty feet high and one hundred feet long, pushed up behind Milne's house. Still Milne refused to negotiate, and in days the greenkeeper O'Connor resigned.[16]

◆

The feud between Trump and his neighbors made for good copy in the newspapers and lively TV viewing, but it was often a torment for the holdouts. Susan Munro may have been the most affected. The construction of a parking lot near a temporary golf clubhouse flooded the road to her home, washing it out and making it impassable. Five weeks passed before it was fixed. Worse were the piles of dirt, twenty-feet high, made at the boundary of her house lot. These berms, planted with trees, spared golfers the sight of the Munro house as they parked their cars. They also deprived the Munros of vistas that they had enjoyed for decades. In winter the berms even blocked the light from the sun. When she stopped to think about it, Munro felt shocked. She said, "Living here, so far from everything, who would ever think that this bloody American could come and do this to you?"

The press reports on their plight won Munro and the others growing support at home and abroad, as newspaper readers sent letters and postcards urging them on. When Anthony Baxter's film *You've Been Trumped* was set to air on the BBC Trump's lawyers asked the network to cancel the showing because they considered it defamatory and misleading. *The Guardian* newspaper reported that Trump had called filmmaker Baxter a "stupid fool." The network refused Trump's request. The audience, estimated at 1.1 million viewers, was forty percent above the average for the Sunday night series that presented the film.

In the wake of *You've Been Trumped* Michael Forbes won the most votes in the annual "Top Scot" competition sponsored by the whisky company Glenfiddich. Forbes donned his kilt for the ceremony. Donald Trump announced that the bars and restaurants at his properties would no longer serve Glenfiddich whiskies. The award made to Forbes, Trump added, "is a terrible embarrassment to Scotland."

Trump didn't make things any easier on himself with such self-serving pronouncements. Typical was his attempt to rename the dunes "the Great Dunes of Scotland" because they were "the biggest dunes in the world." When told they weren't the biggest, Trump accepted the correction, but he wouldn't agree that he was arrogant to assume that he could suddenly rename a geological feature that had been known to the world for generations. He put it, "Arrogant would be if I called them the Donald J. Trump Special Dunes."[17]

As earthmoving machines broke the land to create the first of Trump's two planned golf courses, the housing market in Scotland and the rest of Europe remained weak, and entire developments of vacation homes in much sunnier spots, such as the coast of Spain, were abandoned. No start was made on any of the buildings Trump had promised for the Menie Estate, and he continued to complain about the wind-energy project planned for the waters just offshore. The British government was committed to the idea, and Scottish first minister Salmond had worked hard to get the European Union's approval for a wind-energy test field in the North Sea waters. Trump said that Salmond had assured him the windmills would not be built. He insisted that he was fighting not just for himself, but for the country, because windmills were a bad technology. "We have to save Scotland," he declared. "You cannot allow these industrial monstrosities." Later he compared wind-power plans to one of the most tragic events in recent history, the tragic bombing, in 1988, of a passenger jet over Lockerbie, Scotland: "Wind farms are a disaster for Scotland like Pan Am 103, an abomination, only sustained with government subsidy."

In his political war with Alex Salmond, Trump sounded like his younger self tangling with Ed Koch. He referred to Salmond as "mad Alex" and funded the efforts of a group opposed to the turbines. Citing his status as a Global Scot, he wrote to the Scottish Parliament to oppose the wind farm, which he said threatened his investment of "tens of millions of pounds." The amount Trump had spent at the Menie Estate, which was noted as a boon to the region, was actually in doubt. In 2011 Trump claimed to have already spent sixty million pounds on his way to building the most expensive course ever seen in the United Kingdom.

The mentions of big money were obviously intended to impress upon Scottish officials that Trump was both serious and capable. But considering that a recently opened course in western Scotland called Machrihanish Dunes had been built for 1.5 million pounds, the figures didn't add up. Andrew Wightman, a writer and land-use consultant in Edinburgh, looked at corporation reports and discovered that Trump had paid less than 7 million pounds for Menie Estate, all of which went to Tom Griffin in America, and spent less than 14 million to develop it. By the time these facts were made public, Trump and the press had moved on to other issues. Besides, it was easy to simply disseminate exciting claims that huge sums were being spent, but difficult to parse corporation reports and then publish the boring details.[18]

No specific accounting was available on the money Trump had paid lawyers, or on how much he had spent attacking the wind project. But as he pursued the argument about the windmills, Trump laid the groundwork for an argument that would justify him walking away from the parts of his plan that would have produced the jobs and business revenues that had seemed so tantalizing to Scottish officials. When he lost this fight, he withdrew his application to build the second course and directed his attention, and his money, elsewhere. Soon he would announce that he had purchased famous courses at Doonbeg, Ireland, and at Turnberry, Scotland.

The one course Trump completed on the Menie Estate was judged by experts to be of beautiful design, thanks to the land and Martin Hawtree, but hardly the best in the world. Instead of more than a thousand jobs, Trump had delivered perhaps two hundred, and many of them were seasonal. The planning approvals he had received for housing and a hotel would remain attached to the property. He could wait for the next economic bubble, build and sell all the homes he proposed, and escape with a big profit. Alternatively, he could sell all the acreage to someone else, who would inherit the rights to all the development that had been approved.[19]

In Balmedie, the residents he had battled so furiously were left to feel battered and confused. Pilloried in the Aberdeen papers and scorned by locals who had anticipated a golf boom, they struggled to understand why someone would swoop into their community, promise so much, accomplish so little, and cause so much upset. Jack McConnell, who had tried at the beginning to accommodate Trump, was named to the House of Lords by the queen. Alex Salmond led a failed campaign for Scottish independence and then resigned his post as first minister. Sarah Malone, the Face of Aberdeen and of Trump's development, married the editor of the local *Press and Journal,* which had backed the golf development from its inception. On the Isle of Lewis, the trust seeking to restore Lord Lever's castle had yet to receive funds from Mary Anne Trump's son, the billionaire Global Scot.

POSTSCRIPT:
UNDERSTANDING DONALD

I'm a very smart person, I could give an answer
that's perfect and everything's fine and nobody
would care about it, nobody would write about it,
or I could give an honest answer, which becomes
a big story.
—DONALD TRUMP

Meeting with Donald Trump at his office is like performing a walk-on part in a movie. Flooded with natural light from two sides, the space is as bright as a stage set. The star is an aging leading-man type whose face is so plastic-perfect that he doesn't seem to have any pores. His elaborate hairdo, glowing, swooping, and sprayed into place, announces his identity. The ultimate professional, he delivers time-worn lines so well they almost sound fresh. Think Michael Caine in one of his lesser, late-career films.

As I shake Trump's hand, I wonder, Will he reach for sanitizer? A handkerchief? Anyone else who was famous for his anxiety about germs might elicit a bit of consideration. But Trump's penchant for bombast and cruelty—he had recently declared that the elderly actress Kim Novak should "sue her plastic surgeon"—makes it hard to feel much empathy for Trump. We clasp hands and then I watch closely as he slips behind his desk and discreetly brushes his hand against the fine fabric of his expensive suit.

No other businessman in America, and perhaps the world, can turn something so small—a little fear of contamination—into a trait that a stranger has in mind upon meeting him, but then again, there is no other Donald Trump. This is what I tell him during our first meeting in his office, where a brag wall is covered in magazine covers featuring his face and heavyweight Mike Tyson's championship belt, payment for some debt, lies on the floor. "As far as I can tell, there's no one who's been on the stage as long as you and still remains in the public eye," I add. "Who else is there?"

The world is Trump's stage, and most of the players from the early years of his celebrity in New York are either faded or gone. Old enemies and friends including Ed Koch, Roy Cohn, Leona Helmsley, and George Steinbrenner are dead. Others, such as Rudy Giuliani, are sometimes visible but generally irrelevant. Meanwhile, the press clippings he receives at the start of each day attest to Trump's ongoing celebrity, and the quantity and quality of this attention is what interests me. In his wealth and fame he is truly a man for our time, the ultimate expression of certain aspects of the American spirit in the twenty-first century.

Trump says he was prepared to decline my request for a series of formal interviews, and he has only agreed to this meeting because I'm being assisted by the writer Mark D'Agostino, who is helping me with research. Mark reported on him for *People* magazine and Trump likes him, but as he says, he is only talking to us as a courtesy. We deserve to hear no in person. But this all sounds like salesmanship. *No, I couldn't possibly sell. This property means too much to me. But maybe for you, I could make an exception.*

After a bit of talk about Trump's status as a unique American figure, we agree to half a dozen interview sessions, which would give us time to march through his life in an orderly way. Trump says he'll do his best to address the past, although he much prefers to discuss the present and, whenever possible, the future. With this decision made, he eases into a monologue.

A fiend for news of all sorts, from celebrity gossip to politics, Trump criticizes Jamie Dimon of JPMorgan Chase, who had recently approved a $13 billion payment to settle federal cases related to the bank's role in the financial industry's meltdown that led to the Great Recession. Trump clearly thinks Dimon is a wimp, and he's generally disgusted by President Obama, whom he also regards as weak. In our meetings Trump often filled pauses with criticisms of Obama. Often these statements came during walks to the elevator, when the audio recorders were switched off, or they were couched as "off the record." In two instances when he spoke on the record, Trump veered from a general discussion of "success" to an evaluation of the president. In the first case he said Obama lacked the qualities of a winner and "has had so many losses and people don't even want to watch him on television." In the second he said the president was not psychologically tough. "It's all psychology. If Obama had that psychology, Russia's Vladimir Putin wouldn't be eating his lunch. He doesn't have that psychology and he never will because it's not in his DNA."

When Trump spoke about Obama, he sounded personally irritated, which may have been because the White House had ignored his offer to lead the federal response to the 2010 Gulf of Mexico oil spill because the admiral in charge "doesn't know what he's doing." Unfortunately Obama's former senior adviser David Axelrod had revealed this exchange, and Trump's offer to build a ballroom at the White House, after Donald stopped speaking to me, which made it impossible to follow up on it with him.

Although Trump's attitude toward Obama was tinged

with emotion, he was far more caustic in his remarks about the fourth estate. "There is tremendous dishonesty, tremendous dishonesty, in the press," he volunteered, naming certain journalists, including Timothy L. O'Brien and Wayne Barrett, as chief offenders. "I believed in the press. And when this guy [Barrett] wrote this way, I realized, 'Wow, we've got a different situation than I thought. This is not an honest business.' Now I've met some great reporters and writers, and I've met some really dishonest ones, I mean, some really, really dishonest reporters and writers. O'Brien would be one." Trump's most venomous words are reserved for the editor of *Vanity Fair,* whom he calls "scumbag Graydon Carter." Trump will mention the man many times, always saying the phrase in a hurry as if it were a single, indivisible word: "Scumbagraydoncarter."

Considering his lifelong dance of mutual manipulation with the press, Trump's complaints are more than a little ironic. Few have profited more from the tide of celebrity news that has swamped the public discourse. His analysis is also entirely self-referential. Writers and reporters are worthy, or not, depending on how they have responded to his various pitches. Those who make the purchase are good. Those who don't are bad. The worst make fun of him or challenge the score Trump posts—$3 billion? $5 billion? $7 billion?—as he speaks of his own riches. When the writer Timothy O'Brien said Trump wasn't as wealthy as he claimed, Trump sued. He lost, but considering the costs incurred, O'Brien's publisher lost too. In this case, he doubts we'll be meeting in court: "It'll probably be a bad book and I'll regret doing it. But, okay, I could sue you if it's bad, but I won't bother because the book won't sell. People want positive, inspiring. That's what you should write if you want a success."

After Trump issues his advice we are dispatched to

an outer office to make arrangements with Trump's chief assistant, Rhona Graff, who presides over a clutch of secretaries who are beautiful in the way of the women who play attractive secretaries on television shows and in movies. Smartly dressed and flawlessly made-up, they are both functional and decorative. Graff sets a date and time for our first session with "Mr. Trump" and agrees to help with introductions to people who know and like him. There's Trump's mentor from his days at a military academy and, of course, his grown children, who all work for him. It is hard to escape the feeling that Rhona and Mr. Trump are trying to push me into the role of dutiful pet biographer.

In the elevator Mark and I stand in stunned silence as we descend to the pink-marble lobby of Trump Tower. Over coffee we decide we are glad our subject has agreed to be interviewed, but feel less than optimistic about what this process will yield. Trump famously avoids discussing the past, resists self-analysis, and is doggedly committed to the image he has constructed. He tends to repeat reliable phrases and plays games with information. At one point he said, "You can use this, but don't say you got it from me," then shared some tidbit about a recent success. Trump's use of this technique was noted by Mark Singer in *The New Yorker* in 1997. He'll try it again with us many times. Fortunately he has abandoned others, such as posing as a "Trump spokesman" named John Baron—but his use of "off-the-record" remarks must still work because it's still in his publicity-seeking repertoire.

Trump's effort at capturing the public's attention has produced a trail of public statements that would fill many thousands of scrapbook pages. Over time he has been quoted so widely on such a variety of topics that anyone who sought to keep track would feel overwhelmed. When he discussed the "worst president," was he talking about Republican George W. Bush or Democrat Barack Obama? In fact he said it about both men. Bush was awful because he pursued the war in Iraq. Obama was awful for a host of reasons.[2]

Over the years Trump has been opposed to gay marriage and in favor of gays serving in the military. He has supported abortion rights and then opposed them.[3] More recently he has questioned the overwhelming evidence that human activity is causing the earth's climate to change—"GLOBAL WARMING bullshit has got to stop"—and he has suggested that inoculating children with multivaccine injections could cause autism, a claim without scientific support.[4] These positions, and Trump's pandering to the "birthers" as he repeatedly challenged President Obama's legitimacy, show that he is willing to say almost anything to gain attention. He promotes everything he does as the greatest, and he practically begs to be mocked when he talks about his wealth, the ratings of his TV show, *The Apprentice*, or even his own intelligence.

But it is not Trump's outrageousness that makes him worthy of interest. More important is that he has succeeded, like no one else, in converting celebrity into profit. (No matter how many billions he has, we are still talking about billions.) Somehow he has done this even as a substantial proportion of the population, arguably more than 50 percent, consider him a buffoon if not a menace. What does it say about Trump that he is so undeniably successful by the two measures that matter the most to him—money and fame? And what, pray tell, does it say about us?

◆

I went to New York Military Academy for five years, from the year before freshman."

"So eighth grade on?

"Yes."

"Whose idea was this?"

"Well, I was very rebellious and my parents thought it would be a good idea. I was very rebellious."

"How did it evidence itself?"

"I was a very rebellious kind of person. I don't like to talk about it, actually. But I was a very rebellious person and very set in my ways."

"In eighth grade?"

"I loved to fight. I always loved to fight."

"Physical fights?"

". . . All types of fights. Any kind of fight, I loved it, including physical, and I was always the best athlete. Something that nobody knew about me."[5]

In fact, just about everyone who ever interviewed Trump had surely heard about his athletic prowess. His past exploits on the playing fields and more recent ones on various golf courses are often on his mind. Trump says that if we want to understand him we should speak to Theodore Dobias, his coach and "drill sergeant" at New York Military Academy. Dobias had treated him roughly when he was a boy but also instilled in him a fighting spirit. Trump has often spoken of himself as a military-school product, a fighter, and an athlete, and as he asserts these elements of his identity in our first interview, he lays claim to the highest testosterone level in the room. He is, undoubtedly, hormonally blessed, which would account for his competitive nature. It is also probably true that being bundled off to a military academy where he had to "learn to survive" affected his ability to empathize with others. This may explain his statement that "the most part, you can't respect people because most people aren't worthy of respect."

In the exchange that follows this flash of candor, I tell Trump that many people offer respect to others as a matter of course and withdraw it if offended. He thinks this is "nice" but inconsistent with what life has taught him. "I think I probably expect the worst of people because I've seen too much. But I think it's a very nice trait to have." Remarkably, for a person sitting on a pile of cash, in a concrete tower with a commanding view of Manhattan, Trump describes his life as a struggle. "Life is about survival," adds Trump. "It's always about survival."

In our roughly ten hours of conversation, Trump reveals the most about himself when he touches on the subjects of competition and human nature. He approaches all of life as an unending contest, which explains why he often uses the word *winner* when describing himself and calls people he dislikes *losers*.

"I believe in hard work. I believe in being prepared and all that stuff. But in many respects, the most important thing is an innate ability."

"And you knew this as a kid?"

"No, I never thought of it as a kid."

"Do you think you had it even then?"

"Always."

"When you look back at yourself then?"

"I had it. I always had it."

At various moments Trump returns to the idea that he is better at many things, from golf to business, because of his genetic gifts. "I'm a big believer in natural ability." He would even say, "I have a natural ability *for land* [emphasis added]." This belief in the Trump bloodline would be explained more bluntly by Donald Jr., who says, "I'm a big believer in racehorse theory." Gesturing upward, to the heavens and his father's office on the floor above, he adds, "He's an incredibly accomplished guy, my mother's incredibly accomplished, she's an Olympian, so I'd like to believe genetically I'm predisposed to better than average."

In an era when economic inequality is a growing public concern, genetic superiority is a handy justification for stupendous wealth, whether it is inherited or earned. (In the case of Donald Trump, both apply.) Not surprisingly, social scientists have found that the rich and powerful are more likely than others to credit "innate ability" for their status. But while nature can favor some people, so many forces shape us that settling on one as determinative is a kind of magical thinking. Magical too is the power of positive thinking, the Norman Vincent Peale philosophy that encouraged optimism as a solution to virtually all of life's problems. Trump imbibed the reverend's message as a boy at Marble Collegiate Church and has subscribed to his views all of his life. "I am a believer in positive thinking. A big believer," he says. "But I'm also a big believer in guarding against a downside, because the upside will take care of itself. I've always said that." This is the essential paradox of Trump's personality. He is the fellow who declares himself "a winner" but also expects conflict and criticism. He said he expects more if he decides to run for president in 2016.

Trump repeatedly hinted that he had already decided to run in 2016, when he would turn seventy, and even mused about the possibility that Mark and I, who are New Hampshire natives, might help him in that politically vital state. It was difficult for us to imagine Trump as a serious candidate and we thought it more likely that his interest was a matter of marketing himself and not true political ambition. In a potential GOP field of roughly twenty, others also seemed to be publicity-seekers. Among them, Trump led the pack when it came to daring. After Hillary Clinton declared her candidacy he sent out a social media message that asked, "If Hillary Clinton can't satisfy her husband what makes her think she can satisfy America?" When an uproar ensued, the post disappeared from Trump's account and his aides explained that he did not write it himself. However the words did garner attention for Trump and likely thrilled the political Right's most partisan troops.

The power of controversy was never lost on Trump, who considered almost every kind of attention beneficial to his public image. "I think my honesty gets me in trouble," he explained. "I think I'm so honest that it gets me in trouble. I'm a very smart person, I could give an answer that's perfect and everything's fine and nobody would care about it, nobody would write about it, or I could give an honest answer, which becomes a big story."

"Will that hurt you or help you politically, being that honest and forthright?" asked Mark.

"I think it will help me. I think people are tired of politically correct people, where everything comes out 'The sun will rise and be beautiful.' I think people are really tired of politically correct. I just attacked the Central Park Five settlement. Who's going to do that? . . . You know what you have to do? You have to fight them then, tooth and nail. Like when I get sued by a lightweight like Schneiderman, a total dope, not respected, driving business out of New York."

The Central Park Five were the teenagers who had been arrested and charged with the notorious assault and rape of a young woman in Central Park in 1989. Trump had made a singular contribution to the public furor around the case with his full-page newspaper advertisements imploring the state to "BRING BACK THE DEATH PENALTY." Freed when DNA evidence proved someone else committed the crime, the men sued, and in 2014 the City of New York paid them a total of $40 million, or $1 million each per year of imprisonment, as a settlement. This event prompted much public soul-searching about the rush to judgment in the case, but Trump called the settlement "a disgrace" and complained, "These young men do not exactly have the pasts of angels." When we spoke, at the time of the settlement, Trump said, "I spoke to a detective who is sure that they attacked her."[6]

Confident as he was in that New York City detective, Trump was equally dismissive of the state's top law enforcement officer, Attorney General Eric Schneiderman. The detective was reliable because he backed Trump. Schneiderman was a bad guy because he had filed suit over Trump University, which was not a university but rather an expensive (some paid in excess of $30,000) how-to-get-rich training program. The statute of limitations barred most of the attorney general's case, but he had been able to proceed on his complaint that Trump operated an unlicensed educational institution.

In our conversations Trump talked of Schneiderman as someone who is "very terrible" and "a stupid guy." It seemed likely that the attorney general would gain little with his suit. In late 2014 a judge found Trump U. had failed to meet state licensing requirements, but other actions Schneiderman cited in his complaint fell outside various statutes of limitations and would not be considered by the court. The judge delayed assessing a fine against Trump.

More serious for Trump were federal court rulings in the Southern District of California, which allowed two suits brought against Trump and Trump University to proceed. In *Cohen v. Trump*, a judge permitted anyone in the nation who bought Trump University courses after 2007—thousands of people—to join a class action suit alleging that Trump had violated a civil anti-racketeering statute. In the other, *Makaeff v. Trump University,* a judge permitted only residents of three states to be involved in a suit initiated by a woman who said she had spent about $60,000 on Trump University offerings. In a countersuit alleging defamation, Trump's attorneys noted that Makaeff had previously endorsed

Trump University. When a judge dismissed the countersuit, he noted in his opinion that "victims of con artists often sing the praises of their victimizers until the moment they realize they have been fleeced." Trump's attorney Jill A. Martin told the press that "there are no facts to support any claim against Mr. Trump. Regardless, and despite having nearly five years to do so, the plaintiffs have been unable to quantify any measure of damages. As a result, we believe that the classes should be decertified and the cases dismissed." Toward this end, Trump's team sought to have the cases thrown out of court. They failed, and the parties proceeded toward trial. Although no one could predict the outcome at the courthouse, Trump faced the unpleasant prospect of hardworking people testifying that their experience with Trump University left them feeling like suckers.

Donald Trump may have understood how the plaintiffs felt. In one of his earliest press interviews he had recalled how he had watched various dignitaries, including Robert Moses, overlook the great engineer Othmar Ammann at the ceremony that marked the opening of the Verrazano-Narrows Bridge in 1964. What young Trump noted was not that Moses and the others had been unfair, but that Ammann was a "sucker," and Trump vowed to himself that he would never let such a thing happen to him. In the decades that followed, he would make suckers out of lots of people, including New Yorkers who loved the Bonwit Teller friezes, depositors of the banks that enabled his excessive borrowing in the 1980s, and investors who bought stock in his casinos. Depending on your standard, the suckers might also include:

- Voters who considered Trump a serious presidential candidate.
- Birthers who thought he was right about President Obama.

• Buyers who lost money on a busted development in Mexico bearing his name.
• Scottish officials who saw only a tiny fraction of the $1.5 billion development Trump promised if they let him build a golf course on an environmentally vulnerable site.[7]

Some of the people who bet on Trump and lost are less than sympathetic figures. It's hard to work up concern for a politician who uses his power to push a project through and then feels let down. In many cases, however, it is not the targets of Trump's manipulation who matter but the bystanders. With the birther claims, Trump hurt the American people as a whole as he spread a conspiracy theory that was rooted in the irrational fears of those Americans who could not accept the president's skin color and name. Trump wasn't solely to blame for this state of affairs. Many program hosts on Fox News encouraged him even as the network's biggest star, Bill O'Reilly, knocked down the birther arguments.

Trump saw no downside in his birtherism. In our conversations he repeats that he is interested in running for president again in 2016 because his business experience shows he can deal with "people that are tougher and smarter than the people Obama has to deal with. Believe me." He considers deal-making to be the measure of a man and adds, "Obama never made a deal except for his house, and if some Republican did that deal, they'd be in the hoosegow—you know what I'm talking about with the house, right?" I tell him, "I have no idea," but later learn of a fizzled effort to get the press to treat Obama's purchase of a home in Chicago in 2005 as the product of some shady dealings. Shadiness is in the eyes of the beholder, and in the case of Obama's home there was little to see.

Looking forward to his own possible campaign in 2016, Trump says he is ready for reporters who would be unstinting in their investigations of his past, from his Vietnam-era draft deferments due to bone spurs to the birther crusade.

"I'll expose them as being very dishonest, and it may work and it may not. Ultimately it's hard to beat the press. The press is so dishonest. But I will go after them. It's hard to beat the press, but the good news is there's some very honest media. I have Twitter, I have Facebook—between Twitter and Facebook I'll be at five million people by the time your book comes out. That's more than the biggest media company."

In fact, at 2.5 million Trump had a little more than 10 percent of CNN's following on Twitter. Among other media outfits *The New York Times* and the BBC both claimed more than double Trump's total, while *Time* and the satirical news site *The Onion* bested him by more than 1.5 million followers. But though he was wrong on the numbers, Trump was right about his main point, which was that he could bypass the gatekeepers in the press to reach people directly with his messages. Trump said he did his own writing online, and given the wide range of tones in his comments, this seemed true. A devoted tweeter, his online statements address everything from a doctor in New York with the Ebola virus— "Obama's fault"—to the notion that the Big Apple could actually benefit from global warming, if the phenomenon is real, because it suffers from uncomfortable cold snaps in the winter.

Unlike many other prominent businessmen approaching age seventy, Donald Trump is so well versed in pop culture that he is willing and able to comment on the romantic lives of young stars. When actress Kristen Stewart had an affair, he wrote that she had "cheated on" her boyfriend Robert Pattinson "like a dog." He said that singer Katy Perry should be wary of John Mayer because "he dates and tells." As a TV star, he understands the importance of keeping up with trends and fashion to remain relevant. He also stays true to his hit-back-harder philosophy.

"Cher said some nasty shit," says Trump, referring to the singer/actress. "So I took on Cher. I knocked the shit out of her and she never said a thing about me after that. Bette Midler said something. I said, 'Bette Midler is unattractive both inside and out.' Okay. That was the last time. That was it. She was done."

Midler had joined the backlash against Trump's offer to pay $5 million to charity if President Obama made public his Harvard transcript. Obama's supporters considered this demand, which had never been made of any previous president, part and parcel of an insulting effort to delegitimize him. Midler, recalling the fight over Trump's real estate developments tweeted, "The man who ruined New York seeks to ruin the nation. Show some respect, if not for the man." She also poked fun at "the terrible dye job" Trump had done on his hair. Cher, in her tweets, complained about Macy's department store offering Trump-branded wares and called Trump a "LOUDMOUTH RACIST CRETIN, WHO'D LIE LIKE 'HIS RUG' TO GET SOME CHEAP PRESS." She also called him a "flaming asshole." "Cher should spend more time focusing on her family and dying career!" Trump replied, later adding, "I don't wear a 'rug'—it's mine. And I promise not to talk about your massive plastic surgeries that didn't work."

These "Twitter wars" demonstrated the perils of an age that finds celebrities expressing themselves in bursts of unmediated opinion. It's hard to imagine the female stars of a bygone era—Ella Fitzgerald? Patsy Cline?—

typing out the words *flaming asshole* and making the document available to everyone in the world. But it is a fact of the media age that public conversation is being continually degraded. The process, which recalls Daniel Patrick Moynihan's concept of "defining deviancy down," has made for more frank, and plainspoken debates but it has also brought everyone closer to the gutter. In this rhetorical environment, victory often goes to the loud and the profane rather than the reasoned and considered. And while Trump may contribute to the decline of civil discourse, he is hardly alone.

Indeed, in their battles with Trump, neither Cher nor Midler comported themselves in a ladylike fashion. In light of this record, Trump would say, "There's a very unfair double standard" applied to verbal brawls when men and women are at odds. Men hold no obvious advantage in an online dispute, and Twitter wars—has anyone ever won one?—and the Internet abound with examples of both men and women expressing themselves in the least dignified ways. Addressing his critics, Trump adds, "They'll say, 'How can you talk about a woman like that?' Or, 'How can you talk about somebody like that?' So she'll knock my hair, which is fine. It's fucking my hair. But she'll say, 'Oh, he wears the worst wig I've ever seen.' Right? So then I'll hit her and they'll say, 'How can you say something bad about her?' I say, 'Well, what did she say about me?'"

In Trump vs. Midler, and Trump vs. Cher, the sides were evenly matched, and Donald did have a point when it came to who struck first. Coming from a man who readily explains that his temperament hasn't changed much from his days in first grade, his complaint is to be expected. When my colleague Mark broached the subject of Trump's tweet about Kim Novak at the 2014 Academy Awards ceremony—Kim should "sue her plastic surgeon"—Trump also expressed himself in first-grader mode:

Michael: Did you feel bad after that?

Donald: A little bit. But, you know . . .

Michael: Why did you do it?

Donald: Because if she's putting herself out there like that . . . By the way I wasn't the only one. There was . . .

Michael: I'm sure everybody noticed it.

Donald: Kim Novak.

Michael: Yeah, but you said it.

Donald: No, I said that she should "sue her plastic surgeon." Well, in one way . . .

Michael: Aw, this is . . . poor old lady.

Donald: No, I don't know. She's not old. I mean, she's . . .

Michael: She's like eighty years old.

Donald: I know. I didn't think I got in trouble. No, I thought some people thought it was great and other people thought . . . that's why I have five million people, I guess, you know.

Michael: It was provocative.

Donald: It was provocative, yes.

Michael: So was that an impulse?

Donald: I used to think she was beautiful, by the way.

Michael: She was.

Mark: Oh, she was.

Donald: But she got on the stage and . . . don't forget she's been away. She got on the stage and I said, "Holy shit."

Mark: It was shocking.

Michael: Did you write that in the moment?

Donald: It was so shocking that you . . . I did. I wrote it at the moment.

Mark: Okay. That's what I was wondering. I mean, you're thinking about the consequences of that when you're putting yourself out there with that kind of a statement?

Donald: With Twitter you'll say things that you can regret because you're doing them instantaneously, okay? But you're being very honest. That's nothing compared to me. They're always knocking the shit out of my hair.

A phone call interrupted us and we never returned to the topic of Novak. Trump did draw criticism for his very public dig, and Novak had felt so bullied and humiliated by his comment and others that she retreated to her home and didn't go out in public for weeks. The controversy did have a positive side, as it inspired a great deal of public comment about cosmetic procedures, body image, and the modern obsession with youth and appearance. As a man who seems most comfortable when in combat—financial, sporting, verbal—Trump seemed perplexed by the idea that Kim Novak had suffered as a result of his casual remark. But to his credit, he wasn't put off by the questions about his behavior. Trump hates to talk about the past, but comes alive when challenged in the present, as demonstrated when he once noted, "Interesting session we're having today."

◆

By repeated measures, the majority of Americans don't like Donald Trump. In 2011, experts at the firm that issues the celebrity Q Score ratings said that for every one person who liked Trump, more than four did not. More recently, in 2014, 61 percent of New Yorkers responding to a *Wall Street Journal*/Marist College poll said they had an unfavorable view of him. In liberal corners of the Internet Trump's image is used to illustrate the biggest problem in the economy, which is the steadily widening gap between the super-rich and everyone else. Yet, people continue to watch his TV show and purchase branded products from him in numbers sufficient to make his fortune grow.[8]

What Trump understands is that anyone he might offend by, say, calling Obama "Psycho!" rejected him long ago, and those who like him draw nearer when he does this sort of thing. In a nation of 300 million people, a following as small as 20 percent is such an enormous market that he doesn't need anyone else. This is the same calculus that the Fox cable news network uses as it designs its programming. For many businesses it is better, in a world of almost infinite options, to cultivate a proportionally small but intensely loyal following of repeat customers (or viewers) than to win the mild approval of everyone else.

Trump also understands that even while Americans may suspect the economic game is rigged to favor the rich, they still want to be rich themselves. His rise to prominence in 1978 coincided, almost exactly, with the moment when median wages stopped growing and the earnings of those in the highest ranks took off. At that same time the mass media became swollen with lifestyle and celebrity "news," a kind of pornography of wealth and fame. As the public feasted on images of excess, Trump's face was associated with all the tantalizing pleasures that money could buy. Obscured by hype, the facts of his life didn't matter as much as the idea of him. Anyone who tried to grasp the "real" Trump was likely to fail. As the ninety-two-year-old doyenne of gossip Liz Smith tells me, "I've known him forever, and I can't figure him out."

◆

During lunch at the restaurant that occupies the ground floor of her apartment building, Smith recalls the time she suggested that Trump be honored as a "living landmark" by the New York Landmarks Conservancy. Many of Trump's friends and enemies have received this award, including Graydon Carter, and Trump had surely contributed as much to the life of the city as such landmarks as Brooke Shields and Tommy Tune. But the conservancy is a stuffy group, said Smith, and they rejected Trump. With the kind of compassion one might show for a poorly behaved boy who received a spanking, Smith says she knows the conservancy hurt Trump's feelings, and she feels bad about it.[9]

Boyish, even at his advanced age, Donald Trump can charm in a way that invites kind concern. He once said to me, as he spoke of a good deed, "See, I have a heart." We were standing at his office door at the time, and I reflexively touched his shoulder and said, "I know." In that moment I wanted to believe that the bombast is all a joke. Then I remembered the language he uses to attack people who disagree with him. They are, in his words, "ugly" (many, including Arianna Huffington). They are "stupid" (many, including Obama). They are "scumbags" (the above-mentioned Carter and others). They live like "pigs" (Scottish farmer Michael Forbes).

And they are "losers" (George Will, Rosie O'Donnell, Cher, Mark Cuban, Rihanna, Karl Rove, etc., etc.) The name-calling is more style than substance. Sticks and stones. More significant are all those who have lost money, or peace of mind, in their dealings with Trump. They may not think he has a heart.

◆

Donald Trump's cardiac status is an element of an overarching question that writers and filmmakers and even psychologists have long tried to answer. In 2011, William Cohan of *The Atlantic* magazine explored the puzzle in a piece titled "What Exactly Is Donald Trump's Deal?" Cohan properly credited Trump as "a skillful developer, a highly creative thinker, and an extraordinary deal maker," motivated by money as a method of scorekeeping. A year later, writing in the *Chicago Tribune,* columnist Clarence Page said Trump shows how to turn "audacious and even obnoxious narcissism into pure gold."[10]

Trump was offered as a journalist's paragon of narcissism at least as far back as 1988. The academics and psychologists got involved a few years later and would go on to make the diagnosis of Trump into a kind of professional sport. Trump makes an appearance in texts for the profession, including *Abnormal Behavior in the 21st Century* and *Personality Disorders and Older Adults: Diagnosis, Assessment, and Treatment.* He also appears in books for laypeople such as *The Narcissism Epidemic: Living in the Age of Entitlement; Help! I'm in Love with a Narcissist;* and *When You Love a Man Who Loves Himself.*[11]

Many recent books about narcissism echo Christopher Lasch's landmark *Culture of Narcissism* (1979), a lament that would have us place Trump in "an age of diminishing expectations." Lasch saw an epidemic of self-involvement emerging as young adults with a weak sense of identity sought continual affirmation in attention, material comforts, and exciting experiences. What Lasch feared, Donald Trump lived with more verve than anyone else on the planet. Others may have matched him in one category, such as fame. But no one equaled him on all three levels of narcissistic achievement.

Although his detractors are repulsed, Trump would say that in his aggressive pursuits he is a true expression of the American ideal. He *does* represent aspects of well-established cultural norms. Repeated studies have determined that Americans *do* value individualism more than other peoples and are more willing to call attention to themselves. We revere those who take risks in pursuit of the big score, even when they fail, and we tolerate wide gaps in wealth, health, and even life expectancy to preserve our chance to become winners, no matter the odds. We are also inclined to brag and promote ourselves at a level that would be unseemly anywhere else. Donald Trump may blow his horn a little louder than other Americans, but he is playing the right tune.[12]

Present at the beginning of his run, when he was defining himself as an emblem of his age, Donald Trump's first wife, Ivana, recalls herself as a naïve, young woman who wasn't especially interested in wealth or fame when she left Czechoslovakia for Montreal in the 1970s. She lived with a boyfriend and worked as a model and ski instructor. She says that indeed she was a competitor in the 1972 Sapporo Olympics and "finished seventh in the downhill," but no record of this seems to exist. According to Sports-Reference.com, Bernadette Zurbriggen of Switzerland placed seventh in the downhill, and no one named Ivana competed at all. No Czech skiers, male or female, even traveled to the games.

Ivana makes her Olympic claim and describes her

early life during an interview at her town house on the East Side of Manhattan, half a block from Central Park. Once as famous as her husband, she has retreated from public life. In our time together she speaks in a soft, halting voice. She moves slowly, and her face seems almost frozen by cosmetic intervention. About her years immediately before Donald, she says:

"I was instructing the top guys or girls in ski school. And then I would go back home to Montreal and modeling."

"Did you like your life then?"

"Yes."

"Were you happy?"

"Yes."

"You didn't have a strong ambition to be very wealthy or very famous?"

"Not at all."

Ivana readily recalls happier episodes from the early years of her marriage to Donald, and the details of her successes as his business partner. She's direct about the woman Donald left her for, saying, "She's a stupid girl. She doesn't have a brain." But when I ask what she thinks motivates her former husband, she struggles to answer and says, "I think he wants to be noticed." A moment later, when I ask if she feels she has "figured out" Donald, she first says, "Yeah, I figured it out," then adds, "Well, I really don't know."

Ivana survived a hurricane named Donald but is, twenty years after her divorce from him, still a little off-balance. The Trump children are more forthright in their evaluations of their father. Eric, the youngest son of Donald and Ivana, says, "There's no more all-American guy than him." He says that his father is "a supergenius in a very, very practical way" who could be compared with Winston Churchill, Andrew Carnegie, and John D. Rockefeller. More careful in her replies to my questions, Ivanka interprets her father's id-driven behavior as, not meanness, but candor. "He is going to say exactly what he is thinking. He doesn't need to hear what the question is or the story is in advance so he can craft an answer." Donald Jr. is more expansive:

"Listen, he's a polarizing guy. Okay? There is no question. There are not guys out there that probably say, 'Yeah, Trump's okay.' There are guys that say, 'I love Trump! He's the greatest guy in the world!' Or he's their least favorite human being in the whole world. That said, that person who hates Trump the most still wants to get their picture with him when he walks by. That person still wants to shake his hand. That person is still sort of mesmerized by him in his presence."

More than his siblings, Donald Jr. is willing to offer a more rounded assessment of the whole matter of growing up Trump. He recalls that when he was young he asked to be sent to boarding school to escape the glare of publicity during his parents' divorce. He recognizes that his father contributed substantially to the modern media frenzy over celebrities, which encourages outlandish statements and has normalized events that would have once been shocking:

"He himself was one of the figures that changed the way the media looks at celebrity, the way that media treats the sort of brashness of what's reported today. The boundary line has grown—there really is nothing off-limits anymore. It doesn't matter who you are or what it is, there is no boundary. Some of the covers of the *New York Post* at the time [of the Donald/Ivana divorce] were probably what made a big part of that switch—but now it's commonplace. But when you think of this stuff in 1989, 1990, that's a long time ago. And before that it was a very different world. He's definitely someone that's formed what media is today because of it."

Seen in the light of a mediated age, which requires

extreme efforts to gain attention, Donald Trump Sr.'s self-promotion, displays of wealth, and even his hair make sense for someone who is intent on being noticed. Poke fun if you will, but the painstakingly constructed swoosh and artificial glow of Trump's coiffure make him instantly recognizable. Without it, he might stand in front of Trump Tower and escape notice. With it, he is mobbed. His hair has drawing power, even if he didn't set out, in the beginning, to cultivate a billboard atop his head. In the beginning he sought to escape looking bald. But he was, as usual, ahead of the culture. In the years after Trump adopted his style, cosmetic surgery, hair replacement, skin-smoothing injections, and unnatural hair color were adopted by women and men in all social classes. Instead of something shameful, these vanities became enviable signs of wealth and status that people discussed quite openly. Ask Donald Trump about his hair and he's likely to invite you to pull on it. (I declined.)

In all of his posturing and style, Trump is perfectly in sync with his generation, whom Tom Wolfe skewered in his 1976 essay "The 'Me' Decade." As the country, and Trump's cohort, passed through various stages—Studio 54 glitz, Reagan-era glamour, late-eighties retrenchment, postnineties inequality—Trump was in step. This uncanny consistency leads Donald Jr. to argue that his father is not more persona than person, insisting, "It's not an act. It's not 'How can I wake up and be more like Donald Trump today?' You can't do that for thirty-five years. You can do that for a few weeks, but not for thirty-five years."

◆

In the winter of his life, Donald Trump remains fully committed to his pursuits, which include fighting, consuming, and marking the planet with his name. He finds nothing shameful in this but, when prodded, will admit to just a bit of self-doubt. In one of our talks he asks, "Have you ever heard of Peggy Lee? 'Is That All There Is?' It's a great song because I've had these tremendous successes and then I'm off to the next one because it's, like, 'Huh, is that all there is?' That's a great song actually, a very interesting song, especially sung by her, because she had such a troubled life."

Trump has offered his observations about the Peggy Lee line to other interviewers, which makes me think that he keeps it in reserve for a moment when he's supposed to demonstrate self-awareness. Later when I read over a transcript of the interview, it becomes obvious that what he says next is more telling. Referring to Lee's lyric I say, "Do you ask yourself that sometimes too?" He replies:

"No, I don't want to think about it! I don't like to analyze myself because I might not like what I see. I don't like to analyze myself. I don't like to think too much about the past—other than to learn. The only thing I like about the past is to learn from it, because if you make a mistake, you want to learn from it. Now, I'd much rather learn from other people making mistakes. I read a lot. I read a lot of stories about success and failure, because it's much cheaper to learn from other people's mistakes than your own. I can tell you of many, many mistakes that people made, and that's much better than if I make those mistakes. So the thing I like about the past is you can learn from people's mistakes and also learn from people's triumphs."

"You said you read a lot. Is there something that has influenced you a lot?"

"Well, when I say I read a lot, I'm talking about current reading of the press and the media. I would love to read. I've had many bestsellers as you know, and *The Art of the Deal* was one of the biggest-selling books of all time—that's really what started this whole thing, I think, *Trump: The Art of the Deal*. Now in all fairness, it became a number-one bestseller for many, many months, and the reason is because of what I had done before. So I was well-known before I did the *Art of the Deal,* but that was a big breakthrough. I think the tremendous success of *The Apprentice* becoming the number-one show on television, that was a big break for me."

A linguist or psychologist could write at length on Trump's conversational style. After the briefest reflection, he slams the door on introspection and turns immediately to consider other people and their failures. A mention of books leads him to discuss his own book and its sales and then the corresponding success of his TV show. Invariably he looks for ways to turn the conversation to the theme of his triumphs. In fairness, our conversation is about *him,* but it's hard to escape noticing that even as he notes a genuine success, he can't resist exagerrating. *Trump: The Art of the Deal* sold well, but an "all-time" bestseller it is not.

Untangling any single Trump claim, like his reference to his book, requires great effort and generally yields little of value, though it can be amusing to challenge him on certain claims. When he told me the western coast of Ireland is like "Florida" and a certain Scottish farm is called "a killing field," I got him to admit that both statements were products of his own mind, and nothing more. However, while the specifics of his assertions do not matter, his compulsive effort to present—and have others accept—his view of himself and the world he inhabits does. If Trump is, as his son says, authentically Trump, then all of this effort is sincere and necessary to his self-concept. I would have liked to ask Trump about this, but after I interviewed his son, and his second wife, Marla Maples, who spoke of him in glowing terms, Rhona Graff called a halt to our sessions. The reason? I had spoken to someone on the Trump list of enemies, the writer Harry Hurt, who had offended Trump way back in 1993. I had mentioned to Marla Maples that I had spoken to him. It seemed she had then shared this fact with her ex.

Left to conclude my study without Trump, I could reflect on the challenges of his childhood. His mother had been sickly; his father was demanding and often absent. Both abandoned him to a military school that was, by modern definitions, brutal. Yet his parents also provided him with ample support, and he would be the first to insist they were loving and generous. Other factors must be weighed. Foremost seems to be the extraordinary time Trump occupied. In 1946, the year he was born, America was on the cusp of a prosperity the world had never before seen. An explosion of mass media was making image-making and celebrity elements of daily life. A fiercely intelligent child, growing up rich and privileged at this time, would think that anything was possible. Add enormous ambition, and he would try to achieve it.

The factors that influenced Trump's development were present in the lives of many of his peers, whom Christopher Lasch found to represent the culture of narcissism. But Lasch doesn't suggest that these souls are worthy of contempt, even though they often injure others. They are, themselves, harmed by a spiritually hollow society that exalts and rewards the self-promoter and the supersalesman while relegating everyone else to isolated anonymity. In the time since Lasch made his argument, the forces he observed have grown more powerful, and the financial rewards to those who can harness them have increased. The result has been an epidemic of narcissism and its component parts, which include grandiosity and self-loathing. Taken together, these feelings produce both the insatiable desire to be seen as a winner and dread of being regarded as a loser.

For Lasch's literary descendants, the Trump represented in so many accounts is the prime example of the pathology of our age. But none of these works consider him fully. Yes, he can be boorish and obnoxious and is unnecessarily cruel. But considering the world as he found it, Trump should also be regarded as a genuinely successful man who triumphed in the winner-take-all game. He is a living expression of the values of his time. Wealthy and universally recognized, he established himself in the public mind first as a developer, but went on to occupy two more prominent (some would say similar) positions—game-show host and politician. In these roles the self that he constructed came to fit him perfectly. With cameras forever fixing him in technology's version of the pool where Narcissus saw his reflection, he should be excused for thinking he has some sort of magic inside him.

Certain that he was special and superior, Trump finally decided to offer his leadership skills to the United States of America and the wider world. On June 16, 2015, hundreds gathered in the atrium of Trump Tower and waited for him to ride down the escalator to the strains of the Neil Young anthem—"Rockin' in the Free World." Filled with painful allusions to social dislocation, the dystopian lyrics of the song contrasted with the stirring beat and powerful chords sounded by the guitars in the recording. However they matched the view of the nation's condition that Trump would paint in his speech.

Waving and signaling thumbs up, Trump was preceded on the stairs by his wife, Melania, who stood as motionless as a mannequin as the escalator carried her to the ground floor. In the cheering crowd, Marla Maples' former publicist Chuck Jones watched with a sense of wonder and appreciation. He felt that Trump had a real shot at the nomination and would vote for him if he got the chance. (He was also relieved that security guards had permitted him to enter the lobby.)

Trump offered roughly forty minutes of stream-of-consciousness commentary beginning with complaints about how Japan, China, and Mexico take advantage of the United States. "When do we beat Mexico at the border?" asked Trump, blending immigration with trade. "They're laughing at us, at our stupidity. And now they are beating us economically. They are not our friend, believe me. But they're killing us economically.

"The U.S. has become a dumping ground for everybody else's problems," added Trump, who then paused for a smattering of applause. "Thank you. It's true, and these are the best and the finest. When Mexico sends its people, these aren't the best and the finest. They're not sending you. They're not sending you. They're sending people that have lots of problems, and they're bringing those problems with us. They're bringing drugs. They're bringing crime. They're rapists. And some, I assume, are good people.

"But I speak to border guards and they tell us what we're getting. And it only makes common sense. It only makes common sense. They're sending us not the right people. It's coming from more than Mexico. It's coming from all over South and Latin America, and it's coming probably—probably—from the Middle East. But we don't know. Because we have no protection and we have no competence, we don't know what's happening. And it's got to stop and it's got to stop fast." Trump's solution? He would "build a great, great wall on our southern border. And I will have Mexico pay for that wall."

In the course of his remarks, Trump often sounded sour notes—"the American dream is dead"—and he lurched from economic issues to terrorism to nuclear-treaty negotiations to health care. In each case, he argued that President Obama and others were not capable leaders, but that he would be up to any presidential task. The difference came down to his skills as a negotiator, he noted, as well as raw talent and God's favor. "I will be the greatest jobs president God ever created," said Trump. "Our country needs a truly great leader, and we need a truly great leader now. We need a leader that wrote *The Art of the Deal*."

When Trump concluded his remarks he glanced skyward, raised his hand, and Neil Young's song began to play again. He then looked to his right to see members of his family glide onto the stage. The women each appeared with finely colored hair ranging from brassy to subtle blond. The men wore fine dark suits. He embraced each, rather stiffly, and altogether, they could have been mistaken for models gathered to be photographed for a clothing catalog. After a few minutes of posing for the cameras, the group departed and the crowd dispersed.

On the morning after Trump's announcement, editors of the New York *Daily News* added a red nose and lips to his picture and plastered it on the front page of the paper under the headline, "Clown Runs for Prez." Other subheads read, "Trump Throws Rubber Nose in GOP Ring" and "Ad Libs Circus Speech to Formally Announce." Comedians had a field day with many of Trump's statements. David Letterman, the former talk-show host, emerged from retirement to present his "Top Ten" list of "Interesting Facts About Donald Trump." Among them was the "fact" was that "during sex he calls out his own name." Jon Stewart, who was about to leave his long-running gig as host of *The Daily Show* crowed, "Thank you, Donald Trump, for making my last six weeks the best six weeks. He is putting me in some kind of comedy hospice where I'm getting straight morphine."

But while Trump's announcement was fodder for

comics, his comments on Mexico and immigration disturbed those who understood the facts surrounding the issue. In actuality, illegal immigrants were less likely to commit crimes than others, and Mexican Americans had long experience with violence and disruption at the hands of those who deemed them to be lawbreakers. In the early part of the twentieth century, dozens of Mexican Americans were lynched. In 1943, American military men conducted organized attacks on Mexican American youths in the so-called Zoot Suit Riots. In the 1950s and 1960s, government agents periodically swept through Mexican American neighborhoods to make mass arrests. This history informed reactions among Latino leaders who consider Trump's comments to be dangerously inflammatory.

Among Trump's business partners, the concern about his comments was more practical than political. With Latinos making up the single largest ethnic group in the country, his harsh words would alienate millions of consumers. With this in mind, executives at NBC announced that the network would no longer feature Trump on *The Apprentice*, and the Univision Spanish-language TV network canceled its deal to air his Miss Universe pageant. Other Trump partners including Serta, Macy's, and the Perfumania fragrance company severed ties with him. The Professional Golf Association of America pulled a tournament from one of his courses. The sports TV network ESPN also withdrew a tournament from a Trump course and NASCAR, the stock-car racing outfit, canceled plans for an event at a Trump property in Florida.

As partners left him, the Trump brand was dented and his company's revenues were affected. However, as a multibillionaire, he could afford the losses. When Republican rivals including Jeb Bush, Marco Rubio, and Lindsay Graham criticized his statements, Trump dismissed them as weak on the immigration issue. Many mainstream Republican leaders were concerned about Latino voters, few of whom supported the GOP in 2008 and 2012. Trump blithely predicted he would eventually win over these voters. In the meantime, he was happy to enjoy the rabid support of Republicans who approved of what he was saying.

More ordinary politicians, pundits, and journalists struggled to explain Trump's early success and parse his statements. Few understood the psychological background to his pursuit. For Trump, who by his own estimate was the same person he was as a needy child, there would never be enough power, attention, or wealth. Then there was the style of his rhetoric and reasoning. Trump spoke in such a disjointed and ungrammatical way that fact-checking his statement was an exercise in futility. Consider just the opening lines from a transcript of his address:

> So nice, thank you very much. That's really nice. Thank you. It's great to be at Trump Tower. It's great to be in a wonderful city, New York. And it's an honor to have everybody here.
>
> This is beyond anybody's expectations. There's been no crowd like this. And, I can tell, some of the candidates, they went in. They didn't know the air-conditioner didn't work. They sweated like dogs.
>
> They didn't know the room was too big, because they didn't have anybody there. How are they going to beat ISIS? I don't think it's going to happen.

Aside from his "thank you's," it is impossible to determine just what Trump was trying to say, although he clearly wanted to mention his opponents in the primary race and compare them to sweating dogs who couldn't deal with the threat of the Islamic terrorist group ISIS.

Accented in Trump's tough-guy tone, these statements communicated the feeling of plain-spoken English but were more like the deliberate doublespeak of carnival barkers. In fact, his message was so convoluted that listeners would have to fill in much of the meaning themselves. How, for example, would he bill Mexico for a border fence? This didn't seem to matter to him. Also, it didn't matter to Trump that he has changed his mind on abortion rights, moving from being "very pro-choice" to "very pro-life." Nor did it matter to him that he had shifted from favoring universal health care to opposing health-care reform under President Obama. What did matter was his own belief in the natural abilities handed down to him by his German and Scottish forebears.

Approaching age seventy, Trump also possessed a fortune great enough to fund a presidential run without any help from donors. However, he was running out of time. If he was ever going to be president, the time was 2016. If he spent $50 or $100 million on the effort to win the nomination it would actually be a less-than-extravagant indulgence for a man of his means. If he lost, the experience of participating in debates and barnstorming around the country would be invigorating and ego affirming. If he won, he could extend the experience through the general election and, perhaps, move into the one residence in the nation that he might imagine is more prestigious than Trump Tower.

◆

A few years ago, some in the psychiatric profession proposed that narcissism, which had long been regarded as malignant, be reconsidered. "Narcissism is not a disease," suggested psychiatrist Peter Freed of Columbia University. "It's an evolutionary strategy that can be incredibly successful—when it works."[13] Who would better represent this successful strategy than

Trump? Consider the flourishing of all-about-me technologies that have been adopted by so many hundreds of millions of people. Facebook, Twitter, Instagram, and even the selfie photographs that bloom by the millions online are all expressions of the kind of self-promotion that Trump has practiced for profit throughout his life. The only difference is that he did it first, and on a much grander scale.

In a world where many habitually broadcast photographs of their sandwiches just before they are eaten, we no longer agree that intense self-regard is a sign that something is wrong. It may, instead, be a reasonable reaction to life in a society where extension of the self, through media, is an accepted way to escape feeling insignificant. Donald Trump is not a man apart. He is, instead, merely one of us writ large. Given his intense desire to distinguish himself as special, if not sui generis, he is likely to find this conclusion disturbing. It is, for the rest of us too.

ACKNOWLEDGMENTS

Thomas Dunne, perhaps the ablest publisher in New York, deserves all the credit for the conception of this work. He and editor Peter Joseph made it much better with their excisions, queries, and suggestions.

My research began with a shelf-ful of preceding works, including books by Wayne Barrett, Harry Hurt, and Gwenda Blair, who established the Trump record of the 1900s. Wayne and Harry were both generous with their time and shared supporting documents that they had preserved. (Wayne even turned me loose in his voluminous and valuable archive.) I received additional kind assistance from fellow writers Neil Barsky, Tom Fitzsimmons, and Liz Smith, who is also an officially recognized living landmark of New York City. Timothy L. O'Brien's provocative *TrumpNation* proved informative when it comes to the Trump style, as did Donald's own books, most especially his first, *Trump: The Art of the Deal*.

In addition to an armful of books, articles, and brochures, Donald Trump gave me and my colleague, Mark D'Agostino, about ten hours of his time. Our interview sessions, which took place in his Trump Tower home, were not governed by any explicit ground rules, but at times Donald did insist some comments were "off the record." Fortunately these numbered less than a handful, and the restriction did not affect either the tone or quality of the account I was able to make of his life. He was the first person I ever interviewed, in more than thirty years of this work, whoever demanded secrecy after he said something good about himself.

Besides Donald, I received the help of various Trumps, including his children Donald Jr., Ivanka, and Eric. Their mother, Ivana, was also generous with her time, and so too was the second Mrs. Trump, Marla Maples. In the Trump Organization offices I found all of the executives, especially Rhona Graff, George Sorial, and Meredith McIver, generous and accommodating. They were most helpful in providing me with background materials and connecting me to Theodore Dobias and Robert Utsey, who discussed Donald Trump's early years.

Many people agreed to be interviewed for this book, and most spoke without reservation. They are quoted in these pages and I am grateful for their help. I owe special thanks to a handful of Scots, including researcher/writer Andy Wightman, Martin and Gina Ford, David and Moira Milne, and Michael and Sheila Forbes. Bill Lawson, genealogist on the Isle of Lewis, provided detailed information on the MacLeod clan of Tong, and I was informed about Aberdeen, city and shire, by Councilor John Cox and Robert Collier of the Chamber of Commerce.

I also received reliable, timely, and thorough assistance from Dunstan Prial, Jonathan Anzalone, Amy Choi, Jeff Katz, and Laura Tillman. Amy D'Antonio offered both her editorial services and her perspective on key concepts. Copy editor Steve Boldt taught me tricks that, as an old dog, I should already know.

Most of all this work has been informed by a decades-long conversation about ideas, psychological concepts, and the human heart with my most important ally and collaborator, Toni Raiten-D'Antonio.

NOTES

PREFACE TO THE 2016 EDITION

1. Ben Schreckinger, "Trump on Protester: 'I'd Like to Punch Him in the Face,'" *Politico,* February 23, 2016.

2. Transcript of Donald Trump's December 30 speech in Hilton Head, S.C., *Kansas City Star,* January 20, 2016.

3. Eric Bradner, "Donald Trump Stumbles on David Duke, KKK," *CNN.com,* February 29, 2016; and Jane C. Timm, "Donald Trump's History of Talking About David Duke and White Supremacists," *MSNBC.com,* February 29, 2016.

4. Paul Kane, "Paul Ryan Rejects Trump's KKK Comments, But Not His Candidacy If He Wins GOP Nomination," *Washington Post,* March 1, 2016.

5. Ashley Parker and Maggie Haberman, "Donald Trump's Backers Express Deep and Diverse Support," *New York Times,* March 1, 2016.

6. Amanda Hess, "Welcome to Donald Trump's Internet Bunker, Where Reality is Negotiable," *Slate,* March 3, 2016.

7. Robert Schlesinger, "This Too Shall Pass," *U.S. News & World Report,* November 24, 2015.

8. Nate Silver, "Dear Media, Stop Freaking Out About Donald Trump's Polls," *FiveThirtyEight.com,* November 23, 2015.

9. Alexander Burns, Maggie Haberman, and Jonathan Martin, "Inside the Republican Party's Desperate Mission to Stop Donald Trump," *New York Times,* February 27, 2016.

10. Philip Rucker and Robert Costa, "The Republican Party's Implosion over Donald Trump's Candidacy Has Arrived," *Washington Post,* February 28, 2016.

11. Alexander Burns, "Anti-Trump Republicans Call for a Third-Party Option," *New York Times,* March 2, 2016.

12. Sandy McIntosh, "Culture of Hazing: Donald Trump, Me & the End of New York Military Academy," *Long Island Press,* October 5, 2015.

INTRODUCTION

1. Chris Grygiel, "Obama Slams Trump: 'Did We Fake the Moon Landing?,'" *Seattle Post-Intelligencer,* April 30, 2011, http://blog. seattlepi.com/seattlepolitics/2011/04/30/obama-slams-trump-did-we -fake-the-moon-landing/; for video see https://www.youtube.com /watch?v=UIkxoq0agNo; and Dean Schabner and Ryan Creed, "Donald Trump 'Honored' to Be Butt of Obama, Seth Meyers Jokes at Correspondents' Dinner," ABC News, May 1, 2011, http:// abcnews.go.com/Politics/donald-trump-honored-butt-obama-seth -meyers-jokes/story?id=13503379.

2. "Romney Leads GOP Field as Trump Pops Up," *Wall Street Journal,* April 6, 2011; "Donald Trump: Political Apprentice," *Variety,* February 19, 2011; and Hunter Walker, "Poll: New Yorkers Do Not Like Donald Trump," *Business Insider,* March 6, 2014.

3. Erik Hayden, "Jon Stewart vs. Donald Trump: Throwaway Joke Devolves into Name-Calling," *Hollywood Reporter,* May 3, 2013, http:// www.hollywoodreporter.com/live-feed/jon-stewart-donald-trump -throwaway-451612; and "Donald Trump Drops Bill Maher Lawsuit," *Huffington Post,* April 2, 2013, http://www.huffingtonpost.com/2013/04 /02/donald-trump-drops-bill-maher-lawsuit_n_2999605.html.

4. "Donald Trump: Political Apprentice," *Variety,* February 19, 2011; and "Trump: Sam, Tebow Reactions Show US in Politically Correct 'Hell,'" *Newsmax,* http://www.newsmax.com/US/Donald-Trump -Michael-Sam-Tebow/2014/05/12/id/570817/.

5. For an example of the Gilded Age anti-education argument see Andrew Carnegie, *The Empire of Business* (New York: Cosimo Classics, 2007), 80.

6. Wayne Barrett, *Trump: The Deals and the Downfall* (New York: HarperCollins, 1992), 79.

7. George Gilder, *Wealth and Poverty* (New York: Basic Books, 1981), 304–15, and *Wealth and Poverty: A New Edition for the Twenty-First Century* (Washington, D.C.: Regnery, 2012), 102.

8. "How Young People View Their Lives, Futures and Politics: A Portrait of 'Generation Next,'" Pew Research Center, Washington, D.C., 2007.

9. Deposition taken for *Donald Trump v. Timothy O'Brien,* Superior Court of New Jersey, Camden County.

10. P. T. Barnum's fame is noted in Leo Braudy, *The Frenzy of Renown* (New York: Vintage, 1997), 498. For "Face of a Dog!" and other examples of egregious behavior, see Ann Holmes, "On Donald Trump's Sexism," *Washington Post,* April 30, 2011, http://www .washingtonpost.com/lifestyle/style/column-anna-holmes-on-donald -trumps-sexism/2011/04/21/AFmSfEHF_story.html

I. THE TRUMPS OF BROOKLYN, QUEENS,

AND THE KLONDIKE

The most substantial source for this chapter is Gwenda Blair,
The Trumps: Three Generations That Built an Empire (New
York: Touchstone, 2000). Others include:

1. William R. Conklin, "F.H.A. Official Got $48,500 Law Fees from
Family Firm: Agency Head for This State from '35 to '52 Tells
Senate Inquiry He Did No Wrong," *New York Times,* August 25,
1954; "Projects in This Area, Connecticut, and New Jersey, Named
by the Housing and Home Finance," *New York Times,* June 12, 1954,
13; Charles S. Egan, "Housing Inquiry Lists 'Windfalls,'" *New York
Times,* June 12, 1954, 1; Associated Press, "F.H.A. Corruption, Graft
Laid to Powell," *New York Times,* September 13, 1954, 1; testimony
from official transcript *FHA Investigation: Hearings Before the
Committee on Banking and Currency, Subcommittee on Housing
and Urban Affairs,* US Senate, 83rd Cong. (Washington, D.C.: US
Government Printing Office, 1954). For Eisenhower see Blair,
Trumps, 182–83. For Eisenhower and Zeckendorf: "Zeckendorf Tells
President About Big SW Development," *Washington Post,* July 9,
1954. For Teapot Dome quote: "Contempt Action Threatened in FHA
Probe," *Washington Post,* July 13, 1954, 4.

2. The story of Friedrich Trump's adventures in the West, return to
Germany, and life in New York is well told in Blair, *Trumps,* 41–102;
Trump's citizenship declaration on file US District Court Seattle.

3. http://www.flu.gov/pandemic/history/1918/the_pandemic/index
.html.

4. The tale of New York's rise is told in Donald L. Miller, *Supreme
City* (Simon & Schuster, 2014). For housing prices and the economic
cycles of the first half of the twentieth century, see Price V. Fishback
and Trevor Kollmann, *New Multi-City Estimates of the Changes in
Home Values, 1920–1940,* National Bureau of Economic Research
Working Paper No. 18272 (August 2012).

5. James Truslow Adams, *The Epic of America* (Boston: Little,
Brown, 1931).

6. Foreclosures from *Statistical Abstract of the United States 1970*
(US Department of Commerce), 690. For real estate crisis in New
York see "Fifteen Parcels Go Under Hammer," *New York Times,*
January 11, 1934, 38; and "Home Owners Ask More Protection,"
New York Times, March 28, 1934, 3.

7. Gwenda Blair reveals Trump's role in the Lehrenkrauss affair
thoroughly in *Trumps.* See also "Notes of Social Activities in New
York and Elsewhere," *New York Times,* August 16, 1930, 12;
"Mrs. Lehrenkrauss Gets Decree," *New York Times,* October 7, 1932,

2; "Lehrenkrauss Corp. in Receivership Suit," *New York Times,* December 7, 1933, 24; "Mortgage House Faces New Inquiry," *New York Times,* December 10, 1933, n3; "Receivers to Keep 4 Concerns Active," *New York Times,* December 12, 1933, 42; "Lehrenkrauss Home Bought by His Firm," *New York Times,* December 15, 1933, 5; "Plea to RFC Bared by Lehrenkrauss: Mortgage Operator at Inquiry into Bankruptcy Admits He Sought $1,000,000 Loan," *New York Times,* December 21, 1933, 6; "3 Named Trustees for Lehrenkrauss: Close to 3,000 Persons Try to Get into Meeting of the Bankrupt Firm's Creditors," *New York Times,* January 16, 1934, 33; "Brooklyn Banker Indicted in Theft," *New York Times,* January 24, 1934, 11; "Brooklyn Banker Submits to Arrest," *New York Times,* January 25, 1934, 2; "3 in Lehrenkrauss Failure Are Re-Indicted for Theft," *New York Times,* February 27, 1934, 13; "5 Years in Prison for Lehren-krauss," *New York Times,* March 8, 1934, 42; and "Two Mining Stocks Under State Inquiry," *New York Times,* March 11, 1934, 20.

8. "Builders Get Plaque: FHA Officials Attend Opening of Brooklyn Model Home," *New York Times,* August 12, 1936, 36.

9. For Bernays see Larry Tye, *The Father of Spin: Edward Bernays and the Birth of Public Relations* (New York: Picador, 2002).

10. For mobsters in the building trades see Alan Block, *East Side–West Side: Organizing Crime in New York, 1930–1950* (New Brunswick, N.J.: Transaction Publishers, 1983), especially 225–26.

11. For Capehart greeting see Blair, *Trumps,* 193.

2. THE BOY KING

1. For Leverhulme and Lewis see Roger Hutchinson, *The Soap Man: Lewis, Harris and Lord Leverhulme* (Edinburgh: Berlinn, 2005).

2. *Iolaire* disaster, Stornoway Historical Society, http://www.stornowayhistoricalsociety.org.uk/iolaire-disaster.html.

3. Life in the Trump household from various sources including Jerome Tuccille, *Trump* (New York: Donald J. Fine, 1985): Blair, *Trumps*; and Harry Hurt, *The Lost Tycoon: The Many Lives of Donald. J. Trump* (New York: W. W. Norton, 1993).

4. For "king' and "killer" see Hurt, 13.

5. Blair, *Trumps,* 231–33; and John Brodie, "Where Playing to Win Was Born," *Spy,* March 1990, 36.

6. Steven B. Levine, "The Rise of American Boarding Schools and the Development of a National Upper Class," *Social Problems* 28, no. 1 (October 1980): 63, http://www.jstor.org/stable/800381; Charles Frederick Hoffman, "The Growing Importance of Military Schools," *School Review* 56, no. 10 (December 1948): 597; Fred Kniss, review of *Practicing Virtues: Moral Traditions at Quaker and Military*

Boarding Schools, by Kim Hays, *American Journal of Sociology* 100, no. 4 (January 1995): 1067; and James Q. Wilson, "In Loco Parentis: Helping Children When Families Fail Them," *Brookings Review* 11, no. 4 (Fall 1993): 14.

7. Kenny Gallo, *Breakshot: A Life in the 21st Century American Mafia* (New York: Pocket Books, 2010), 27.

8. Richard Hofstadter, *Anti-Intellectualism in American Life* (New York: Random House, 1963), 356–58.

9. Michael J. Haupert, "The Economic History of Major League Baseball," https://eh.net/encyclopedia/the-economic-history-of-major-league-baseball/.

10. Richard Weiss, *The American Myth of Success: From Horatio Alger to Norman Vincent Peale* (Champaign: University of Illinois Press, 1988), chap. 7, "The Amerrican Mystique of the Mind."

3. APPRENTICE

1. "Lefkowitz Calls Wagner Fete the 'Ultimate' in 'Immorality': Terms $25,000 in Pledges 'Shakedown Reminiscent of Boss Tweed'—Gerosa Asks Charter Inquiry on Mayor," *New York Times,* October 1, 1961, 66.

2. Barrett, 65–72; and Edith Evans Asbury, "Housing Windfall Yielded 1.8-Million," *New York Times,* January 27, 1966, 1.

3. Edith Evans Asbury, "Mitchell Defends Huge Housing Fee: Ex-Senator Tells Inquiry His Firm Received $427,633; Aide Got $575,000," *New York Times,* January 28, 1966, 1.

4. "Profiteers in Housing," *New York Times,* January 29, 1966, 26.

5. "Steeplechase Park Planned as the Site of Housing Project," *New York Times,* July 1, 1965, 33; Martin Tolchin, "Coney Landmark Is Sold to Trump: Apartments May Rise in Steeplechase Park," *New York Times,* July 2, 1965, 60; Mccandlish Phillips, "Return of Coney Island: Amusement Area, Badly Hurt Last Year, Is Attempting to Win Back Customers," *New York Times,* April 13, 1966, 31; Steven V. Roberts, "A Park Is Backed for Coney Island: Developer Who Bought Site Calls Plan Wasteful," *New York Times,* October 20, 1966, 59; Charles G. Bennett, "Park Usage Voted for Steeplechase: City to Seek $2-Million Aid to Buy Coney Island Tract," *New York Times,* May 23, 1968, 47.

6. Marie Brenner, "After the Gold Rush," *Vanity Fair,* September 1990.

7. Edward C. Burkes, "Growth of Poverty in City Creating New Poor Zones: Rapid Spread of Poverty in City Creates Entire New Zones of Poor Residents Here," *New York Times,* April 10, 1972, 1; and

William J. Collins and Robert A. Margo, "The Economic Aftermath of the 1960s Riots in American Cities: Evidence from Property Values," NBER Working Paper No. 10493, May 2004, doi:10.3386/w10493.

8. David K. Shipler, "The Changing City: Housing Paralyzed by a Conflict of Powerful Forces; Apartments Are Scarce and Construction Lags," *New York Times,* June 5, 1969, 1.

9. *Daily Pennsylvanian* editorial of January 14, 1955, quoted in William Whyte, *The Organization Man* (Simon & Schuster, 1956), 93.

10. David Card and Thomas Lemieux, "Going to College to Avoid the Draft: The Unintended Legacy of the Vietnam War," *American Economic Review* 91, no. 2 (May 2001): 97–102.

4. FEAR CITY

1. For rent control in New York see W. Dennis Keating, "Landlord Self-Regulation: New York City's Rent Stabilization System, 1969–1985," *Urban Law Annual; Journal of Urban and Contemporary Law* 31 (January 1987).

2. Judith DeSena and Timothy Shortell, eds., *The World in Brooklyn: Gentrification, Immigration, and Ethnic Politics in a Global City* (Lanham, Md.: Lexington Books, 2012); and Larry Littlefield, "Has New York City Recovered From the 1970s?: Public Policy in New York City and State," https://larrylittlefield.wordpress.com/.

3. Martin Tolchin, "South Bronx: A Jungle Stalked by Fear, Seized by Rage," *New York Times,* January 15, 1973, 63.

4. Walter Kerr, " 'Paris Is Out' Can Leave Kerr Out," *New York Times,* February 22, 1970, D5.

5. For "Some were vain . . . " see *Trump: The Art of the Deal* (New York: Random House, 1987), 97. For Steinbrenner, Le Club, etc., see Michael Thomas, "Want a Hot Treatise on the Insanity of Riches?," *New York Observer,* June 28, 1999, http://observer.com/1999/06/want-a-hot-treatise-on-the-insanity-of-riches/.

6. Richard Severo, "Igor Cassini, Hearst Columnist, Dies at 86," *New York Times,* January 9, 2002, B8; and "Le Club, Restaurant of Jet Set, Cited for Health Code Violations," *New York Times,* September 7, 1974, 43.

7. Tom Wolfe, "Dangerous Obsessions," *New York Times,* April 3, 1988, Books, 1. Details of Cohn's life from Sidney Zion, *The Autobiography of Roy Cohn* (Secaucus, N.J.: Lyle Stuart, 1988); and Nicholas von Hoffman, *Citizen Cohn* (New York: Doubleday, 1988).

8. Von Hoffman, 414, 415; and Barrett, 133.

9. Joseph P. Fried, "Trump Promises to End Race Bias," *New York Times,* June 11, 1975, 47.

10. Martin Gilens, *Why Americans Hate Welfare: Race, Media, and the Politics of Antipoverty Policy* (Chicago: University of Chicago Press, 2000), 103–20.

11. For a complete explication of coded race speech see Ian Haney Lopez, *Dog Whistle Politics: How Coded Racial Appeals Have Reinvented Racism and Wrecked the Middle Class* (New York: Oxford University Press, 2014).

12. Jack Newfield and Wayne Barrett, *City for Sale: Ed Koch and the Betrayal of New York* (New York: HarperCollins, 1988), 149.

13. Maurice Carroll, "A Major but Unobtrusive Factor in Carey Victory," *New York Times,* September 15, 1974, 37.

14. Fred Ferretti, *The Year the Big Apple Went Bust* (New York: Putnam, 1976).

15. T. J. Englis, *The Westies: Inside the Hell's Kitchen Irish Mob* (New York: G. P. Putnam's Sons, 1990).

16. For Palmieri see Robert A. Wright, "Is $25,000 a Month Enough?," *New York Times,* August 20, 1972, F5.

17. For Eichler homes and X-100, see www.eichlernetwork.com.

18. The story of Trump and the Penn Central properties is told in thorough detail in Barrett, 91–150. Robert D. McFadden, "Penn Central Yards' Sale Is Approved by U.S. Court," *New York Times,* March 11, 1975, 38.

19. "Bank Aide Admits Taking $392,000: Issued False Loans to Get Money for Gaming Debts," *New York Times,* March 11, 1975, 39.

20. "John N. Mitchell Dies at 75; Major Figure in Watergate," *New York Times,* November 10, 1988, 1.

5. DONALD SAVES MIDTOWN

The tale of Trump and the Penn Central is well told in Hurt, 83–94.

1. Michael Stern, "Italian Developer Proposes Huge South Bronx Project," *New York Times,* February 6, 1975, 1.

2. For value of Commodore see William G. Connolly, "In Hotels, the Key Is Occupancy, and It Is Up a Little," *New York Times,* December 17, 1972, R1.

3. James Fearon, "Texaco Is Moving to Westchester: Half of Work Force Here to Be Transferred; Management to Stay; 40 in Area Those Who Will Move," *New York Times,* July 19, 1973, 28; and "Schrafft's Restaurant Closing After 44 Years," *New York Times,* March 28, 1974, 35.

4. Edward Ranzal, "Talks Slated on Commodore Hotel Deal," *New York Times,* April 23, 1976, 39.

5. Glenn Fowler, "Commodore Plan Is Called Unfair: Some Competitors Deplore Tax Abatement for Hotel," *New York Times,* April 9, 1976, 20.

6. Carter B. Horsley, "New Offer Is Made for the Commodore," *New York Times,* April 10, 1976, 16.

7. Charles Kaiser, "Last Guest Checks out of the Commodore Hotel," *New York Times,* May 19, 1976, 37.

8. For evil of the *Post* see *Columbia Journalism Review* 18, no. 5 (January/February 1980): 22–23.

9. Marie Brenner, "After the Gold Rush," *Vanity Fair,* September 1990.

10. Carter B. Horsley, "In Environs of Grand Central, New Strength," *New York Times,* April 30, 1978, R1.

11. Paul Goldberger, "The Commodore Being Born Again," *New York Times,* January 11, 1978, 20.

12. Judy Klemesrud, "Leona Helmsley: Power Becomes Her," *New York Times,* July 22, 1980, B15.

13. Barbara Goldsmith, "The Meaning of Celebrity," *New York Times Magazine,* December 4, 1983, 75.

14. Tom Wolfe, "The 'Me' Decade and the Third Great Awakening," *New York,* August 23, 1976.

15. Timothy O'Brien, *TrumpNation: The Art of Being The Donald* (New York: Warner, 2005), 53.

16. Judy Klemesrud, "Donald Trump, Real Estate Promoter, Builds Image as He Buys Buildings," *New York Times,* December 1, 1976, 82.

17. James B. Jacobs and Ellen Peters, "Labor Racketeering: The Mafia and the Unions," *Crime and Justice* 30 (2003): 229–82; and Alan Block, *East Side–West Side: Organizing Crime in New York, 1930–1950* (New Brunswick, N.J.: Transaction Publishers, 1983).

18. Interview.

6. TOWERING TRUMP

1. Bryan Miller, "Maxwell's Plum, a 60's Symbol, Closes," *New York Times,* July 11, 1988, B1.

2. Interview.

3. Patricia Lynden, "Where the Donald Trumps Rent," *New York Times,* August 30, 1979, C1.

4. For the plan for a second apartment see Barrett, 5.

5. Robert D. McFadden, "Developer Scraps Bonwit Sculptures," *New York Times,* June 6, 1980, B5; and James B. Jacobs, *Gotham Unbound: How New York City Was Liberated from the Grip of Organized Crime* (New York: New York University Press, 1999), 108–9. See also Ronald Goldstock, *Corruption and Racketeering in the New York City Construction Industry: Final Report of the New York State Organized Crime Taskforce* (New York: New York University Press, 1991; Selwyn Raab, "Irregularities in Concrete Industry Inflate Building Costs, Experts Say," *New York Times,* April 26, 1982, A1; and "Links Among 3 Companies," *New York Times,* April 26, 1982, B6.

6. Barrett, 194; and O'Brien, 70.

7. Barrett, 196; Selwyn Raab, "Key Teamster Leader Is Convicted of Labor Racketeering by L.I. Jury," *New York Times,* October 9, 1982, 1.

8. Erika L. Paulson and Thomas C. O'Guinn, "Working-Class Cast: Images of the Working Class in Advertising, 1950–2010," *Annals of the American Academy of Political and Social Science* 644 (2012): 50–69. For a comprehensive analysis see also Karen Sternheimer, *Celebrity Culture and the American Dream* (New York: Routledge, 2011), especially 186–213.

9. For a deep analysis of Reagan's rhetoric see Michael Weiler and W. Barnett Pearce, *Reagan and Public Discourse in America* (Tuscaloosa: University of Alabama Press, 1992), especially 106–8; and Katy Waldman, "The Science of Truthiness," http://www.slate.com/articles/health_and_science/science/2014/09/truthiness_research_cognitive_biases_for_simple_clear_conservative_messages.html.

10. For lower-wage jobs replacing high-wage ones see Katherine S. Newman, *Falling from Grace* (New York: Vintage Books, 1989), 25–27.

11. Marlene Lee and Mark Mather, "U.S. Labor Force Trends," *Population Bulletin* 63, no. 2 (June 2008); Juliet B. Schor, *The Overworked American* (New York: Basic Books, 1991), 355; Sheldon Cohen and Denise Janicki-Deverts, "Who's Stressed?: Distributions of Psychological Stress in the United States in Probability Samples from 1983, 2006, and 2009," *Journal of Applied Psychology* 42, no. 6 (2012): 1320–34; Thomas A. Durkin, "Credit Cards: Use and Consumer Attitudes, 1970–2000," *Federal Reserve Bulletin,* September 2000; and Chris Kraul, " 'Nothing Down' Investment Writer Charged Back Taxes, Penalties," *Washington Post,* September 25, 1987, F3.

12. Garry Wills, *Reagan's America: Innocents at Home* (New York: Penguin, 2000), xiii–xv.

13. Kevin Phillips, *The Politics of Rich and Poor* (New York: Random House, 1990), 17, 157; and Herbert Mitgang, "Recounting the Lowlights of the Reagan Years," *New York Times,* March 20, 1991, C15.

14. O'Brien, 66.

15. Blair, *Trumps,* 325; and William E. Geist, "The Expanding Empire of Donald Trump," *New York Times Magazine,* April 8, 1984, 31.

7. CELEBRITY DONALD

1. Interview with Barrett.

2. Patricia Lynden, "Where the Donald Trumps Rent," *New York Times,* August 30, 1979, C1.

3. Wayne Barrett, "Like Father, Like Son: Anatomy of a Young Power Broker," *Village Voice,* January 15, 1979, 1; and Wayne Barrett, "Donald Trump Cuts the Cards," *Village Voice,* January 22, 1979, 1.

4. Robert D. McFadden, "Builder Says Costs Forced Scrapping of Bonwit Art," *New York Times,* June 9, 1980, B3; Marilyn Bender, "The Empire and Ego of Donald Trump," *New York Times,* August 7, 1983; and William E. Geist, "The Expanding Empire of Donald Trump," *New York Times Magazine,* April 8, 1984, 28.

5. Ada Louise Huxtable, "The Tall Building Artistically Reconsidered," *New Criterion,* November 1982.

6. Jack Newfield and Wayne Barrett, *City for Sale: Ed Koch and the Betrayal of New York* (New York: HarperCollins, 1988), 3.

7. Josh Barnabel, "The Mayor Expresses His Concern with Trump Plan for a Stadium," *New York Times,* December 13, 1984, B2; and Frank Lynn, "The Koch Re-Election Campaign Has Taken In $2.8 Million So Far," *New York Times,* January 16, 1985, B5.

8. Gloria Steinem, "Shaw Did Write 'Tootsie-Wootsie,'" *New York Times,* December 12, 1967, 155.

9. William E. Geist, "The Expanding Empire of Donald Trump," *New York Times Magazine,* April 8, 1984, 28.

10. Graydon Carter, "Donald Trump Gets What He Wants," *GQ,* May 1984, 170.

11. Patricia Leigh Brown, "Gatekeepers to the Famous and the Powerful," *New York Times,* November 19, 1991.

12. Gregory S. Kavka, "Hobbes's War of All Against All," *Ethics* 93, no. 2 (January 1983): 291–310.

13. Gwenda Blair, *Donald Trump: Master Apprentice* (New York: Simon & Schuster, 2005), 84.

8. DONALD IN SUCKERLAND

1. Phillip H. Wiggins, "Casino Operator's Profit Soars in Third Quarter: $6.7 Million for State Casino Net," *New York Times,* November 10, 1978; and Kathleen Hughes, "Clinic Aids Compulsive Bettors," *New York Times,* November 25, 1984, NJ14.

2. Donald Janson, "2 More Casinos Due for Atlantic City; but Casino Panel Forces Harrah's and Golden Nugget to Part with Officers Under Cloud; Trial Runs Have Begun; 6 Issued Permits So Far; Tough Stance on Executives," *New York Times,* December 23, 1980, 43; Donald Janson, "Behind the Split Casino-License Decisions," *New York Times,* March 10, 1985, NJ1; and "Wrong Bets in Atlantic City," *New York Times,* March 11, 1985, A18.

3. Paul Schwartzman, "She Kicks Sand in Trump's Face, Sneers at The Donald's Bucks," *New York Daily News,* July 26, 1998, 7.

4. George Anastasia, "Land Rush Has Impeded Renewal," *Philadelphia Inquirer,* June 1985, 1.

5. Hurt, 134.

6. Ibid., 148.

7. Ibid., 140–41.

8. Ibid., 149; also Bill Johnson, "Gambling-Firm Stocks Could Put Investors in the Chips This Year, Some Analysts Say," *Wall Street Journal,* January 17, 1985, 1; and Steve Swartz, "Holiday, Trump Drafting Terms to End Rocky Alliance over Atlantic City Casino," *Wall Street Journal,* November 11, 1985, 1.

9. Trump's fortune estimated at $100 million, *Fortune,* November 21, 1988. America had 153 centimillionaires in 1965 according to Leslie A. White, *Modern Capitalist Culture* (Walnut Creek, Calif.: Left Coast Press, 2008), 491.

10. Bill Johnson, "Golden Nugget Chairman Wynn Takes His Biggest Dice Roll in Bid for Hilton," *Wall Street Journal,* April 11, 1985, 1.

11. For Williams and further details on this kind of scheme see Haynes Johnson, *Sleepwalking Through History* (New York: W. W. Norton, 2003), 227–37.

12. Robert Kuttner, "Why Work Is More and More Debased," *New York Review of Books,* October 23, 2014, 52.

13. Laurie P. Cohen, "Holiday Corp.'s Stock Trades Actively on Possible Bid from Donald Trump," *Wall Street Journal,* September 29, 1986, 1.

14. Julie Amparano, "Trump Matches Pratt Proposal to Control Resorts, and His Prospects Seem Stronger," *Wall Street Journal,* March 9, 1987, 1.

15. Julie Amparano, "Trump, Griffin Reach Truce over Resorts—Entertainer to Buy Firm; Trump to Keep Casino and Some Other Assets," *Wall Street Journal*, April 15, 1988, 1.

16. O'Brien, 100–102.

17. *New York*, September 12, 1988, 27.

18. "Judge Says Trump 'Harassed' Tenant," *New York Times*, November 10, 1983, B7; and Sydney H. Schanberg, "Donald Humbug," *New York Times*, February 7, 1984, A25.

19. "Trump and Residents Settle a 5-Year Dispute," *New York Times*, December 21, 1986, 44.

20. Hurt, 171.

21. O'Brien, 68.

22. Von Hoffman, 3–40, 464; Barrett, 292–93; and Marilyn Chase, "Cohn Is Said to Get White House Assist on AIDS Drug Test—Ailing Attorney Is Receiving New Medication AZT at Government Hospital," *Wall Street Journal*, August 1, 1986, 1; Albin Krebs, "Roy Cohn, Aide to McCarthy and Fiery Lawyer, Dies at 59," *New York Times*, August 3, 1986, 1; Bill McAuliffe, "*Playgirl* Readers Say Keillor Has Sex Appeal," *Minneapolis Star and Tribune*, August 5, 1986, B1; and Anthony Rotundo, *American Manhood* (New York: Basic Books, 1993), 284–93.

9. LUCK RUNS OUT

1. http://www.abcmedianet.com/web/showpage/showpage.aspx?program_id=002279&type=maples.

2. Barrett, 184, 389.

3. Harry Berkowitz, "The Manager Behind the Mogul," *Washington Post*, September 23, 1989, E39.

4. "Lightweight" and "piece of garbage" from "There They Go Again," *Philadelphia Inquirer*, December 2, 1987, C2.

5. Margot Hornblower, "Private Prosperity, Public Corruption; Politicians Take a Cut of the Profits," *Washington Post*, August 21, 1987.

6. For the complete story of corruption in the Koch administration see Jack Newfield and Wayne Barrett, *City for Sale: Ed Koch and the Betrayal of New York* (New York: Harper & Row, 1988). See also Alan Feuer, "Up from Politics, Almost," *New York Times*, October 1, 2004; and *Trump: Art of the Deal*, 243–45.

7. Hurt, 190.

8. Adell Crowe, "Trump Ad Only Advice," *USA Today*, September 3, 1987, 4A.

9. Interview with Dunbar.

10. Fox Butterfield, "New Hampshire Speech Earns Praise for Trump," *New York Times,* October 23, 1987, 3.

11. Laura Keirnan, "No Respect," *Boston Globe,* November 1, 1987, 10; and Larry Eichel, " 'Draft Trump' Committee in N.H. Gets Visit from the Non-Candidate," *Philadelphia Inquirer,* October 23, 1987, A3.

12. Kevin Phillips, *The Politics of Rich and Poor* (New York: HarperCollins, 1990), chap. 6, "The New Plutography of 1980s America"; http://hypertextbook.com/facts/2005/MichelleLee.shtm; "Income and Inequality: Millions Left Behind: A Report Based on the Work of Woodrow Ginsburg, Former Chair, Economic Policy Committee," 2012 update by William Rice, Director of Policy and Programs, ADA Education Fund, with help from Mary von Euler, 8th ed. (Washington, D.C.: Americans for Democratic Action Education Fund, 2012); Thomas Piketty, *Capital in the Twenty-First Century* (Cambridge, Mass.: Belknap Press, 2014), 24; and Russell S. Whelton, "Effects of Excessive CEO Pay on U.S. Society," Saginaw Valley State University, https://support.google.com/mail/bin/answer.py?hl=en&answer=21289.

13. Nixon letter courtesy of Donald Trump.

14. Susan C. Faludi, "Behind the Scenes Ghostwriting Booms," *Wall Street Journal,* September 5, 1990, A1; Christopher Lehmann-Haupt, "Books of the Times," *New York Times,* December 7, 1987, C29; Jeannie Williams, *USA Today,* December 15, 1987, 2D; and Elizabeth Mehren, "Donald Trump: The Art of the Party," *Los Angeles Times,* December 20, 1987, 10.

15. From interviews with Jones and Fitzsimmons.

16. Ron Alexander, "From Astor to Minnelli, Greetings to the Rainbow Room," *New York Times,* December 10, 1987, B1.

17. Neil Barsky, "Trump Again Seeks to Delay Loan Payment—Payout for Airline Shuttle Is Due in Three Weeks; Bailout Pact Seems Safe," *Wall Street Journal,* September 20, 1990, A4; Doug Carroll, "Who's Looking at Eastern; Deals Would Benefit All Parties," *USA Today,* October 7, 1988, 1B; and Paula Span, "The Selling of the Shuttle; How Donald Trump Forged Another Deal," *Washington Post,* October 23, 1988, H1.

18. For Carson's losing investment see Henry Buskin, *Carson* (Boston: Houghton Mifflin Harcourt, 2013): 272–74.

19. Glenn Plaskin, "Trump: 'The People's Billionaire,' " *New York News,* March 12, 1989.

20. Joe Feagin and Melvin Sike, *Living with Racism: The Black Middle Class Experience* (Boston: Beacon Press, 1995), 187; and

Walter Goodman, "A Poll of Viewers' Feelings About Racial Issues," *New York Times*, September 8, 1989, C24.

21. Jonathan Van Meter, "That's Why the Lady Is a Trump," *Spy*, May 1989, 86–88; and "Dear Donald," *Spy*, May 1989, 98–100.

22. Blair, *Trumps*, 293–94; and Hurt, 243–44.

23. David Johnston, "For A.C. Casinos, Cash Has Slowed at Critical Time; Some Worry That for the First Time, the City's Gambling Capacity May Exceed Its Gamblers," *Philadelphia Inquirer*, November 20, 1988, F5; Bob Drogin, "For Atlantic City, Casino Jackpot's Still a Long Shot," *Los Angeles Times*, August 1, 1989, 1; David Johnston, "A Human Toll Adds to A.C.'s Troubles," *Philadelphia Inquirer*, October 15, 1989, C1; and Neil Barsky and Pauline Yoshihashi, "Three Executives of Trump Casinos Die in Air Crash," *Wall Street Journal*, October 11, 1989, 1.

24. Adam Smith, *The Roaring '80s* (Summit Books, 1988), 204–5.

25. Blair, *Trumps*, 404; and Hurt, 247.

26. Michele Digiralomo, "Analyst Angers Trump, Is Fired; Report Questioned Taj Mahal's Prospects," *Philadelphia Inquirer*, March 24, 1990, A1; "Analyst Who Was Fired Sues Trump," *Boston Globe*, July 11, 1990, 40; Ann Hagedorn, "Philadelphia Analyst Fired After Trump Threatened to Sue—Real Estate Tycoon Angered by Comments on Market for His Taj Mahal Casino," *Wall Street Journal*, March 26, 1990, C5; Randall Smith, "Wall Street Takes Tough Line on Leveraged Companies," *Wall Street Journal*, February 7, 1990, C1; Bryan Burrough, "RJR Nabisco: An Epilogue," *New York Times*, March 12, 1999, 23; and Neil Barsky and Pauline Yoshihashi, "Trump Is Betting That Taj Mahal Casino Will Hit Golden Jackpot in Atlantic City," *Wall Street Journal*, March 20, 1990, B1.

27. Neil Barsky, "Shaky Empire: Trump's Bankers Join to Seek Restructuring of Developer's Assets—Wary About His Cash Flow, They Might Force the Sale of Certain Properties—Loans Seem to Be Up to Date," *Wall Street Journal*, June 4, 1990, 1; David Johnston, "Bankers Say Trump May Be Worth Less Than Zero," *Philadelphia Inquirer*, August 16, 1990, 1; and Diana B. Henriques with M. A. Farber, "An Empire at Risk—Trump's Atlantic City; Debt Forcing Trump to Play for Higher Stakes," *New York Times*, June 7, 1990, 1.

28. John R. O'Donnell with James Rutherford, *Trumped!: The Inside Story of the Real Donald Trump—His Cunning Rise and Spectacular Fall* (New York: Simon & Schuster, 1991), 138–43; Barrett, 16; and James Barron, "Almost Everybody's Playing Stomp-the-Trump," *New York Times*, June 30, 1990, 1, 27.

29. Susan Lee, "The Down Side of the Donald," *The New York Times*, July 14, 199, BR24; Lee Siegal, *Not Remotely Controlled: Notes on*

Television. (New York, Basic Books, 2007) 269; Pat Widder, "The Trump Slump," Fort Lauderdale *Sun Sentinel*, June 30, 1991, 10f; David S. Hilzenrath, "Tape Portrays Trump Creditors' Fear, Anger; Bankruptcy Worries Led to Casino Deal," *Washington Post*, November 29, 1992, 24.

30. Hurt, 245–46.

31. David Hilzenrath and Michelle Singletary, "Trump Went Broke, but Stayed on Top; Fearing a Bankruptcy Quagmire, Lenders Made Deals with Developer," *Washington Post*, November 29, 1992, 1; David Johnston, "Taj Mahal to File for Bankruptcy," *Philadelphia Inquirer*, January 30, 1991, B1; Alison Cowan, "Taj Mahal Casino Contractors Say Trump Is Slow to Pay Cash," *Austin American-Statesman*, May 4, 1990, 3; and Neil Barsky, "Donald Trump Gets $3 Million in Chips off the Old Block—Father Helps His Son Make Casino Bond Payment, but Will Deal Crap Out?," *Wall Street Journal*, January 21, 1991, C13.

32. David Johnston and Barbara Demick, "Uncertain Days for Executives in Trump's Empire," *Philadelphia Inquirer*, June 17, 1990, E1.

33. "Raucous Support for Ivana Trump," *New York Daily News*, February 15, 1990.

34. Charlotte Hays, *The Fortune Hunters: Dazzling Women and the Men They Married* (New York: Macmillan, 2007), 158–62; and Hurt, 272–77.

35. John Taylor, "Trump the Soap," *New York*, March 5, 1990, 30–37.

36. James Barron, "Herald of Trump Trouble Is Sorry for 'Media Circus,'" *New York Times*, February 17, 1990, 30.

37. Hurt, 333.

38. Ibid., 385.

39. Ibid., 354; and Barrett, 9.

10. TRUMP THE SPECTACLE

1. Blair, *Trumps*, 443.

2. Duncan Norton-Taylor, "How Top Executives Live," *Fortune*, July 1955.

3. Richard Cohen, "Wretched Excess, 1989; How the Steinbergs Put the Nouveau Back in Riche," *Washington Post*, August 20, 1989, 1; and Margot Dougherty, David Hutchings, and Fred Hauptfuhrer, "Ali-Dada's Arabian Night," *People*, September 4, 1989.

4. "Study: High Suicide Rate for Farmers," *Philadelphia Inquirer*, October 14, 1991, C12; Jay Romano, "Thousands Lose Homes in Mortgage Foreclosures: Mortgages from an Era of 'Boom

Psychology' Can Be Difficult to Pay Off," *New York Times,* April 26, 1992, NJ1; and Kevin Phillips, *The Politics of Rich and Poor* (New York: HarperCollins, 1990), 206–7.

5. Bob Greene, "Million Idea: Use Greed for Good," *Chicago Tribune,* December 15, 1986; and John F. Dickerson, "Battling Boesky's Penniless (He Says) and Barred from Wall Street, Ivan Boesky Pulls a Raid on His Ex-Wife's Fortune," *Time,* May 3, 1993.

6. For "image means" see *Trump: Surviving at the Top* (New York: Random House, 1990), 11; David Johnston, "Banks Sell Trump on Art of Allowance," *Chicago Tribune,* June 25, 1990, 1; Joseph P. Kahn, "Imitation Maples Was Forbes' Joke on Trump," *Boston Globe,* April 6, 1990, 69; Jim Hankins, "Soviet Comic Getting Serious: View Profile," *Austin American-Statesman,* December 15, 1990, A22; "Vanishing Villains; Hollywood Casts About for Replacement Rogues," *Washington Post,* April 15, 1990, 1; Kim Foltz, "Trump, the Brand Name, Faces a Tarnished Image," *New York Times,* February 22, 1990, D22; Valerie Helmbreck and Peter Johnson, "Sawyer's 'Primetime' Scoop: Marla Maples," *USA Today,* April 18, 1990, 1D; and Mike Meyer, "The Whirlwind Tour," *Minneapolis Star Tribune,* June 2, 1991, 1G.

7. Howard Kurtz, "Marla: 'I Love Him'; Trumps' Problems Weren't Her Fault, She Tells Sawyer," *Washington Post,* April 20, 1990, C1.

8. Marie Brenner, "After the Gold Rush," *Vanity Fair,* September 1990; Liz Smith, "Trump Fuming over Article, Vows to See Editor in Court," *Orange County Register,* August 21, 1990, F4; and Liz Smith, "Donald Faces Up to Barbara on Friday's '20/20' Interview," *Orange County Register,* August 16, 1990, K4.

9. Mark Feeney, "Donald Trump as Chump," *Boston Globe,* August 16, 1990, 77.

10. Michael Lewis, "Trump Fights Back," *New York Times,* September 2, 1990, A3.

11. Kevin Phillips, "A Capital Offense; Reagan's America," *New York Times,* June 17, 1990, A26.

12. James Warren, "Stay Tuned for 'Masterpiece Network,' " *Chicago Tribune,* August 1991.

13. Susan Heller, "Chronicle," *New York Times,* June 27, 1991, B6; and Jeannie Williams, "Notorious and Uproarious in N.Y.," *USA Today,* January 9, 1991, D2.

14. "Trump Says He Asks Dates to Take AIDS Test," *Saratoga (N.Y.) Daily Gazette,* June 29, 1991, B11; and Lori Brown, "Trump Plans for Safe Dating," *Austin American-Statesman,* June 29, 1991, A24.

15. "Return Engagement: Was She Trumped, Er, Dumped? No Way! Marla Maples Has Donald—and a $250,000 Ring—Wrapped Around Her Finger," *People,* July 22, 1991.

16. Hurt, 385–87; Sue Carswell, "Trump Says Goodbye Marla, Hello Carla," *People,* July 8, 1991; Susan Heller Anderson, "Chronicle," *New York Times,* June 27, 1991, B6; "Personalities," *Washington Post,* June 29, 1991, C3; Benjamin Weiser, "Fugazy Admits Perjury," *New York Times,* June 6, 1997, 9; and "Return Engagement: Was She Trumped, Er, Dumped? No Way! Marla Maples Has Donald—and a $250,000 Ring—Wrapped Around Her Finger," *People,* July 22, 1991.

17. Sierra Helen, "2 More Presidential Candidates Squaring Off in Court; Seattle Suburb Goes with the Floe; Scarlett, Rhett Get Top Lip Service; Making a Point on Fragrances; The Donald, Again," *Chicago Tribune,* February 6, 1992, 24.

18. Susan Bickelhaupt and Ellen O'Brien, "Not Singing Marla's Praises," *Boston Globe,* May 30, 1995, 58.

19. Hurt, 417–19.

20. Julie Baumgold, "Fighting Back," *New York,* November 9, 1992, 36.

21. O'Brien, 204; and Richard T. Pienciak, "Marla Against the Ropes," *New York Daily News,* October 20, 1997, 5.

22. O'Brien, 2, 204–5.

23. Roxanne Roberts, "They Do, They Do, Already! Six Years, One Baby and a Zillion Bucks or So Later, the Trump-Maples Merger," *Washington Post,* December 21, 1993, B1; "Trump-Maples Wedding Will Be Lavish," *Chicago Tribune,* December 19, 1993, 4; and Howard Kurtz, "The Emperor's Old Clothes," *Washington Post,* September 2, 1990, X5.

11. NEW TRUMP

1. Interview.

2. Hubert Herring, "Business Diary," *New York Times,* May 9, 1992, A2.

3. Tracey A. Reeves, "Trump Decries Indian Gaming," *Seattle Times,* October 6, 1993.

4. Timothy O'Brien, "What's He Really Worth?," *New York Times,* October 23, 2005.

5. O'Donnell, 252–53, 269–73.

6. Peter Truell, "A Saudi Prince Fond of High-Profile Investing," *New York Times,* April 12, 1995, D6; Calvin Sims, "Rich Saudi Bails Out Disney Unit," *New York Times,* June 2, 1994, D1; and David Stout and Kenneth Gilpin, "Trump Is Selling Plaza Hotel to Saudi and Asian Investors," *New York Times,* April 12, 1995, A1.

7. Kurt Eichenwald, "Art of the Public Offering: Trump Plans to Sell Stock," *New York Times,* March 31, 1995, D2; and "Trump Gets $295 million in Sale of Stock, Debt," *St. Louis Post-Dispatch,* June 8, 1995, 7C.

8. Linda Sandler, "Heard on the Street: Trump Castle Junk Bonds Attract Gamblers Itching to Bet on the Empire's 'Iffiest' Casino," *Wall Street Journal,* January 2, 1996, 18.

9. Blair, *Trumps,* 438–41.

10. Elizabeth Kolbert, "Trump's Loss Is a Victory for Taste," *New York Times,* August 3, 1998, 1.

11. Charles Bagli, "Partnership in Deal for Empire State Building," *New York Times,* March 19, 2002, B3.

12. Christine Smith, "Selina Scott: Why Did I Say No to Warren Beatty?," *Mail Online,* June 5, 2009.

13. Interviews with Scott and Brocklebank. Also Severin Carrell, "Great Scott, It's Trump v. Selina, Round Two," *Guardian,* August 6, 2009.

14. Associated Press, "Donald Trump Regretting Not Asking Out Princess Diana," *Bowling Green (Ky.) Daily News,* December 2, 1997, 16C.

15. Richard T. Pienciak, "All-Biz Donald Repelled Marla: 'I Wanted a Man Who Would Read Stories with Me to My Baby . . . That's Important,'" *New York Daily News,* October 19, 1997, 3; and "Marla Against the Ropes," *New York Daily News,* October 20, 1997, 5.

16. "Other Shoe Drops For Publicist Maples' Aide Guilty In Foot Fetish Case," *St. Louis Post-Dispatch* Feb. 17, 1994, 2; Barbara; Ross, Larry McShane, "Heel Hound! Maples' Shoe-Fetish Stalker At It Again, Pleads Not Guilty to Nutty Email Rants," *New York Daily News,* June 28, 2012, 9; Rebecca Rosenberg, "Marla Maples' Stalker Sentenced to 60 Days in Jail," *New York Post,* March 21, 2014.

12. CANDIDATE TRUMP

1. Sam Roberts, "In New York, Black and Hispanic Strongholds Become More White," *New York Times,* December 15, 2010, A17; Katrina vanden Heuvel, "A Populist Insurgency in New York City: Mayor Candidate Bill De Blasio Would Bring Needed Change to N.Y.C.'s 'Two Cities,'" *Washington Post,* August 14, 2013.

2. "Trump's Castle Is Shifting to Publicly Held Company," *New York Times,* June 26, 1996, 2; James Sterngold, "Long Odds for the Shares of Trump's Casino Company," *New York Times,* March 9, 1997, 4; and Floyd Norris, "Worse Odds Than Roulette: Buying Trump Casino Stock," *New York Times,* September 24, 1999, C1.

3. Jeffrey Toobin, "The Dirty Trickster: Campaign Tips from the Man Who Has Done It All," *New Yorker,* June 2, 2008.

4. "Naked City," *Spy,* December 1989, 32.

5. Frank Rich, "Who Doesn't Want to Be a Millionaire," *New York Times,* November 20, 1999, A13.

6. O'Donnell, 62; and Hurt, 53–55.

7. "Giuliani Gets 46 to Clinton's 43 in New York Senate Race, Quinnipiac College Poll Finds; Voters Say No Thanks to Trump, Beatty, Buchanan," October 5, 1999, https://archive.is/AnZ3T.

8. Corky Siemaszko, "Trump Mulling White House?," *New York Daily News,* July 12, 1999, 4; Tracie Rozhon, "Fred C. Trump, Postwar Master Builder of Housing for the Middle Class, Dies at 93," *New York Times,* June 26, 1999, B7; Joel Siegel, "Trump 'Stump' Fee—100 G," *New York Daily News,* December 2, 1999, 4; Jo Mannies, "Trump Is Still Uncertain About His Candidacy Here," *St. Louis Post-Dispatch,* February 9, 2000, B9; Chrisopher Carey, "Success Guru Anthony Robbins Brings National Motivational Tour Here," *St. Louis Post-Dispatch,* February 9, 2000, C1; and Adam Nagourney, "Reform Bid Said to Be a No-Go for Trump," *New York Times,* February 14, 2000, 18.

9. Donald Trump, "What I Saw at the Revolution," *New York Times,* February 19, 2000, A15.

10. Corky Siemaszko, "Trump Slams Bush on Iraq," *New York Daily News,* July 9, 2004, 7.

11. Peter Sanders, "Trump to Return over $17.5 Million to Shareholders," *Wall Street Journal,* March 29, 2005, A2.

12. Henry S. Farber, "Overworked America: 12 Charts That Will Make Your Blood Boil," Princeton University CEPS Working Paper No. 171, June 2008; Dave Gilson, "Why 'Efficiency' and 'Productivity' Really Mean More Profits for Corporations and Less Sanity for You," *Mother Jones,* July/August 2011; Rick Ungar, "The Retirement Crisis Is Here for Millions—Income Inequality Now Set to Wreak Its Ugly Revenge," *Forbes,* March 19, 2013; John Cassidy, "American Inequality in Six Charts," *New Yorker,* December 18, 2013; and Jon Greenberg, "MSNBC's Melber: Congressional Wealth Climbed While Median American Saw No Change," *Tampa Bay Times,* February 11, 2014.

13. Deborah Schooler, L. Monique Ward, Ann Merriwether, and Allison Caruthers, "Who's That Girl: Television's Role in the Body Image Development of Young White and Black Women," *Psychology of Women Quarterly* 28, no. 1 (March 2004): 38–47; Mike Featherstone, "Body, Image and Affect in Consumer Culture," *Body & Society* 16, no. 1 (March 2010): 1193–221; Michael Wolf, *The*

Entertainment Economy (New York: Three Rivers Press, 1999), 79; and Ed Shane, *Disconnected America: The Consequences of Mass Media in a Narcissistic World* (Armonk, N.Y.: M. E. Sharpe, 2001).

13. TRUMP THE TV SHOW

1. January Golab, "The Loneliness of the Long Distance Runner," *Los Angeles Magazine,* January 1996.

2. Brian Lowry, "Reality and Voyeurism Heading to Summer TV," *Los Angeles Times,* February 4, 2000, F1.

3. Donna Petrozzello, " 'Survivor' & the City: South Pacific Contest Ends in Central Park," *New York Daily News,* May 19, 2002, 3.

4. Bernadette Wegenstein and Nora Ruck, "Physiognomy, Reality Television and the Cosmetic Gaze," *Body & Society* 17, no. 4 (December 2011): 27–54.

5. "Economic Trends, 2000–2010," http://www.decisionanalyst.com. Also, David Weil, *The Fissured Workplace: Why Work Became So Bad for So Many and What Can Be Done to Improve It* (Cambridge, Mass.: Harvard University Press, 2014).

6. Annaliese Griffin, "A Profile of Matias Reyes," *New York Daily News,* April 5, 2013; and Sarah Burns, *The Central Park Five* (New York: Random House, 2011).

7. Bill Carter, *Desperate Networks* (New York: Random House, 2007), 277–82.

8. From interviews with Rancic, Burnett, Trump.

9. James Traub, "The Anti-Trump," *New York Times Magazine,* December 20, 1998, 62.

10. Matthew Gilbert, " 'Apprentice' Isn't Business as Usual," *Boston Globe,* January 8, 2004, 1; Suzanne Ryan, "When Race Enters Boardroom, 'Apprentice' Really Heats Up," *Boston Globe,* January 29, 2004, C1; and Jennifer Pozner, *Reality Bites Back* (Berkeley, Calif.: Seal Press, 2010), 165–68.

11. Gal Pennington, "Viewers Speak: Enough Already with Reality," *St. Louis Post-Dispatch,* December 16, 2004, F1; Brooks Barnes, "Martha Stewart Gets Low Ratings in Show's Debut," *Wall Street Journal,* September 23, 2005, B2; " 'Idol' Ads Fetch Record Prices," *St. Louis Post-Dispatch,* September 25, 2005, 20; "Donald Ducks," *Chicago Tribune,* October 21, 2005, 72; "Stewart Hoped to Let Trump Go," *Chicago Tribune,* November 1, 2005, 16; Bill Hutchinson, "Donald to Martha, She Signs Off with a Veritably Homeric Paean to Humankind's Most Trusted Friend, Hubris," *New York Daily News,* February 20, 2006; "And Finally," *Chicago Tribune,* February 22, 2006, 56; "Stewart's Show a Mistake for All, The Donald Says,"

Deseret News, February 22, 2006, A2; Bill Hutchinson, "Trump 'Fired' Up. Rips Martha for Blaming Him for the Failure of Her Show," *New York Daily News,* February 22, 2006, 4; Bill Hutchinson, "You Moron, Says Trump," *New York Daily News,* February 23, 2006, 10; Don Kaplan, "Poison Penn Calls Trump a Horror Show," *New York Daily News,* November 25, 2012, 12; and Patrick Day, "Penn Jillette Speaks His Mind, as Is His Wont," *Los Angeles Times,* February 3, 2013, D16.

12. David Pauly, "He's Fired! Image Can't Pay the Bills as Real World Gives Reality TV Star Trump the Boot," *Pittsburgh Post-Gazette,* August 15, 2004, D2.

13. Christina Bikley, "Moving the Market: Trump Hotels Files Chapter 11; Donald Trump's Stake Will Drop," *Wall Street Journal,* November 23, 2004, C3; and David Segal, "He's the Top; His Casino Business May Be Down, but Donald Trump Is on a Roll," *Washington Post,* September 9, 2004, C1.

14. Timothy L. O'Brien and Eric Dash, "Now, Reality for Trump Looks More Like 'Survivor,'" *New York Times,* September 24, 2004, C1.

15. "'Lost' Cause," *Pittsburgh Post-Gazette,* November 11, 2005, D2.

16. From Trump's deposition in *Donald J. Trump v. Timothy L. O'Brien.* See also Alex Frangos, "Trump on Trump: Testimony Offers Glimpse of How He Values His Empire—Worth Rises, Falls 'with Markets and Attitudes and with Feelings, Even My Own Feeling,'" *Wall Street Journal,* May 18, 2009, 1.

17. Troy Graham, "Dismissal of Trump Lawsuit Is Asked: A 2005 Book Cites Sources Alleging 'The Donald' Was Not a Billionaire. He Says His Public Image Suffered," *Philadelphia Inquirer,* May 19, 2009, B1; and Peter S. Goodman, "Trump Suit Claiming Defamation Is Dismissed," *New York Times,* July 16, 2009, B5.

18. "Ivana Weighs In on Donald-Rosie Rhubarb," *St. Petersburg Times,* January 25, 2007, 2B; Tom Jicha, "The View's Ratings Are Coming Up Rosie," *South Florida Sun-Sentinel,* January 15, 2007, D1; John Maynard, "Trump Fumbles, but NBC Still Wins," *Washington Post,* January 10, 2007, C7; "Trump, O'Donnell Take Off the Gloves," *Chicago Tribune,* December 21, 2006, 27; Adam Lisberg, "Donald Rips 'My Nice Fat Little Rosie.' Mogul Threatens to Sue 'View' Star in Miss USA Storm," *New York Daily News,* December 21, 2006, 3; "Adding a Few New Barbs to the Crown; It's Getting Ugly Fast as Donald Trump and Rosie O'Donnell Spar over the Miss USA Flap," *Los Angeles Times,* December 22, 2006, E36; "Quick Takes: Ratings, Conflict Up with O'Donnell," *Los Angeles Times,* December 23, 2006, E2; "People," *St. Louis Post-Dispatch,* December 29, 2006, A2; and Karen Thomas,

"O'Donnell Leads Trump in Unpopularity Contest," *USA Today,* January 9, 2007, D2.

14. "THE BEAUTY OF ME"

1. Tina Brown, "Donald Trump, Settling Down," *Washington Post,* January 27, 2005, C1.

2. Tom McNichol, "The Art of the Upsell: How Donald Trump Profits from 'Free' Seminars," *Atlantic,* March 17, 2014.

3. Ben Montgomery, "Trump U in Tampa: inside one-day real estate seminar," *The Tampa Bay Times,* June 14, 2008.

4. Ben Montgomery, "Trump U in Tampa: inside a one-day real estate seminar," *Tampa Bay Times,* June 4, 2008; Douglas Feiden, "Trump U Hit by Complaints From Those Who Paid Up to 30 G and Say They Got Very Little In Return," *Daily News,* New York, May 30, 2010; Tom McNichol, "The Art of the Upsell: How Donald Trump Profits from 'Free' Seminars," *Atlantic,* March 17, 2014.

5. John Chase and Rick Pears, "The Self-Styled Consumer Advocate Has Run Unsuccessfully for Office for More Than 3 Decades," *Chicago Tribune,* February 10, 2006; and Matthew Mosk, "An Attack That Came out of the Ether," *Washington Post,* June 28, 2008.

6. For a complete history see Matthew W. Hughey and Gregory S. Parks, *The Wrongs of the Right: Language, Race, and the Republican Party in the Age of Obama* (New York: New York University Press, 2014), especially 45–48. See also Ben Smith and Byron Tau, "Birtherism: Where It All Began," *Politico,* April 22, 2011.

7. Jonathan Zimmerman, "Donald Trump, the 'Birthers,' and the GOP's Moment of Truth," *Christian Science Monitor,* April 26, 2011, 23.

8. Jeff Zeleny, "The Caucus: Trump Will Speak at CPAC," *New York Times,* February 10, 2011. Quotes from Trump speech via YouTube.

9. Maggie Haberman, "Bill O'Reilly Pounds Birther Donald Trump," *Politico,* March 30, 2011.

10. For "Part of the beauty of me" see http://abcnews.go.com/Politics /donald-trump-president-trump-weighs-sheen-palin-obama/story ?id=13154163.

11. Tim Jones, "Family Portraits: Strong Personalities Shaped a Future Senator, Barack Obama," *Chicago Tribune,* March 27, 2007; and Robert Farley, "Donald Trump Says President Obama's Grandmother Caught on Tape Saying She Witnessed His Birth in Kenya," *PolitiFact,* April 7, 2011.

12. Andrew Peyser, "Reality Intrudes on the Donald Show," *New York Post,* April 28, 2011; and Josh Benson and Maggie Heberman, "FAQ: How Did New Hampshire Like Donald Trump," *Politico,* April 28, 2011.

13. "Donald Trump to Release Financial, Tax Information at the 'Appropriate Time,'" ABC News, April 27, 2011.

14. www.motherjones.com/mojo/2011/donald-trump-poll-gop-plummet.

15. Ashley Parker, "Road to G.O.P. Nomination Has a Trump Tower Exit," *New York Times,* September 27, 2011, 13; Sara Forden, Bloomberg News, "Trump Says He's Decided 'in My Mind' to Pursue the Presidency," *Honolulu Star-Advertiser,* May 2, 2011; "Romney Leads GOP Field as Trump Pops Up," *Wall Street Journal,* April 6, 2011; Carson Griffin, Brian Niemeitz, and Lisa Lang, "Kids Ask Don: Chill on Bam," *New York Daily News,* November 24, 2012, 19; and Tony Hicks, "Donald Trump Drops Suit Against Bill Maher," *Oakland Tribune,* April 1, 2013.

15. A NOT-SO-INNOCENT ABROAD

1. Interviews with Balmedie residents.

2. "It is crucial we embrace": *Evening Express,* April 15, 2006, 6; and Trump flies in to see golf venue: BBC News, April 28, 2006.

3. Gerard DeGroot, "With Extinction on Its Mind, Scotland Wants Population Growth," *Christian Science Monitor,* February 19, 2004, 9; and North Sea oil: facts and figures, February 24, 2014, http://www.bbc.com/news/uk-scotland-scotland-politics-26326117.

4. "How Jack of Clubs Came Up Trumps for Donald," *Edinburgh Scotsman,* May 14, 2006; "Trump Tells McConnell of Scots Business Venture," *Edinburgh Scotsman,* October 25, 2005; and http://www.scotland.gov.uk/Resource/Doc/216107/0057771.pdf.

5. Martin Ford, "Deciding the Fate of a Magical Wild Place," *Journal of Irish and Scottish Studies* 4, no. 2 (Spring 2011).

6. "Trump Threat to Ditch 300 Million Scottish Golfing Resort," *Edinburgh Scotsman,* April 1, 2006.

7. Interviews with Forbes, Munro, Milne.

8. Interviews with Griffin and Forbes.

9. Interviews of the Fords.

10. Graeme Baxter, "Open for Business?: An Historical, Comparative Study of Public Access to Information About Two Controversial Coastal Developments in North-East Scotland," *Information Research* 19, no. 1 (March 2014).

11. http://www.aberdeenshire.gov.uk/committees/files_meta/802572870061668E802573C50042E4EF/291107isc.pdf.

12. Interview with Ford. See also Martin Ford, "Deciding the Fate of a Magical Wild Place," *Journal of Irish and Scottish Studies* 4, no. 2 (Spring 2011).

13. Severin Carrell, "Heir of Stornoway: Trump's Flying Visit to the Family Home," *Guardian*, June 9, 2008. For Leverhulme's adventures in Lewis see Roger Hutchinson, *The Soapman* (Edinburgh: Berlinn, 2003).

14. Fred A. Bernstein, "Trump's Adventures in the Land of Golf," *New York Times*, July 6, 2008, BU20. See also David Ewen, *Chasing Paradise* (Edinburgh: Black and White, 2011), 90–93, 106, 110–12.

15. Sarah Lyall, "Debate on Trump Project Takes the Low Road," *New York Times*, May 4, 2009, A12.

16. Carolyn Churchill, "Trump Accuses Menie Estate Landowner of Living in Pigsty," *Edinburgh Herald*, May 27, 2010; "Donald Trump Criticises Actions of Councillors Who Opposed Golf Resort Plans," BBC, April 2009; Severin Carrell, "Donald Trump Issues Abusive Statement Against Golf Course Opponent," *Guardian*, November 24, 2009; Severin Carrell, "Film-Makers Arrested on Site of Donald Trump's Scottish Golf Resort," *Guardian*, September 12, 2010; letters from attorney Ann Foulds to Christine Gore, Aberdeenshire Council, dated February 2 and March 9, 2009, http://www.andywightman.com/docs/faulds_gore4March2009.pdf and http://www.andywightman.com/docs/draftCPOorder.pdf; "Trump Accused of Buying Government Expertise," *Edinburgh Herald*, September 27, 2009; and "Sarah's a Trump Card in Donald's Controversial Golf Development," *Edinburgh Herald*, May 29, 2009.

17. Ewen, 193.

18. Andrew Bolger, "Trump Vows to Press On with Scottish Resort," *Financial Times*, May 26, 2010; Trump letter dated April 17, 2012; and "Money Talks as Europe's First £100M Course Hits Its Schedule for Opening," *Edinburgh Scotsman*, November 16, 2011.

19. Alastair Robertson, "The Role of Police and Council in Trump Golf Course," *Glasgow Daily Record*, May 16, 2016; Peter Woodifield, "Trump's Spat with Salmond over Scots Wind Turbines Escalates," *Bloomberg*, April 24, 2012; Rod Mills, "Donald Trump Pulls Plug on Second Scottish Golf Course in Wind Farm Row," *Glasgow Scottish Daily Express*, February 13, 2014; and "Has Trump International Golf Links Failed Scotland?," http://www.globalgolfermag.com/matthewmooreblogspot/has-trump-international-golf-links-failed-scotland/.

POSTSCRIPT: UNDERSTANDING DONALD

1. Mark Singer, "Trump Solo," *New Yorker*, May 19, 1997.

2. "Donald Trump Talks 2012, Calls Obama the 'Worst President Ever,'" Fox News, April 14, 2011; and Trump on *The Situation Room*, CNN, December 11, 2007.

3. http://www.ontheissues.org/celeb/Donald_Trump_Abortion.htm.

4. Chris Mooney, "Donald Trump's Climate Conspiracy Theory," *Mother Jones,* January 27, 2014; Torie Bosch, "Donald Trump Enters Anti-Vaccine Quack Territory," *Slate,* April 3, 2012; and Yamiche Alcindor, "Anti-Vaccine Movement Is Giving Diseases a 2nd Life," *USA Today,* April 8, 2014.

5. All quotes from Trump, his children, and his ex-wives are from interviews.

6. "Donald Trump: Central Park Five Settlement Is a 'Disgrace,'" *New York Daily News,* June 21, 2014.

7. Gonzalo Curiel, Order in *Makaeff v Trump University LLC*— United States District Court for the Southern District of California, June 17, 2014. For the class action ruling, see Order Granting Class certicication, *Cohen v. Trump,* 3:13-cv-02519-GPC-WVG (S.D. Cal. Oct. 27, 2014), available at http://zhlaw.com/wp-content/uploads/2014 /10/Order-Granting-Class-Trump-RICO.pdf. For the baja condo resort that went bust, Los Angeles Times, Nov. 27, 2014, http://www .latimes.com/business/la-fi-mo-donald-trump-settles-baja-mexico -condo-resort-lawsuit-20131127-story.html.

8. Robert Klara, "Brand Trump: How the Developer-cum-TV-Star-cum-Presidential-Candidate Became a Living Product," *Adweek,* May 2, 2011.

9. Interview with Smith.

10. Clarence Page, "Our Mirror-Kissing Culture," *Chicago Tribune,* June 6, 2012.

11. Robert Lenzer, "He's His Own Trump Card: New York's Biggest Wheeler-Dealer Looking for Bigger, Better Deals," *Boston Globe,* October 23, 1988, A1; Ken Khoury and Dick Raspa, "The Business of Media: Organizing Carnival by the New Entrepreneurs," in *Modern Organizations and Emerging Conundrums: Exploring the Postindustrial Subculture of the Third Millennium,* ed. Richard Goodman (Lanham, Md.: Lexington Books, 1999); Michael Oriard, "Muhammad Ali: The Hero in the Age of Mass Media," in *Muhammad Ali: The People's Champ,* ed. Elliott Gorn (Urbana: University of Illinois Press, 1995); and David Elkind, "Miseducation: Young Children at Risk," *Pediatrics* 83, no. 1 (January 1, 1989): 119–21.

12. Michael Lewis, *The Culture of Inequality* (Amherst: University of Massachusetts Press, 1993, vi–xvi; Andy Molinsky, "Common Language Doesn't Equal Common Culture," *Harvard Business Review Online,* April 3, 2013; and Andy Molinsky and Dorie Clark, "How to Adapt to American-Style Self-Promotion," *Harvard Business Review Online,* April 7, 2014.

13. Casey Schwartz, "Is It Time to Redefine Narcissism?," *Daily Beast,* December 2, 2010.

BIBLIOGRAPHY

Ariely, Dan. *The (Honest) Truth About Dishonesty.* New York: HarperCollins, 2013.

Axelrod, David. *Believer: My Forty Years in Politics.* New York: Penguin Press, 2015.

Baida, Peter. *Poor Richard's Legacy.* New York: William Morrow, 1990.

Barrett, Wayne. *Trump: The Deals and the Downfall.* New York: HarperCollins, 1992.

Bellah, Robert N., et al. *Habits of the Heart.* Berkeley: University of California Press, 1985.

Blair, Gwenda. *The Trumps: Three Generations That Built an Empire.* New York: Touchstone, 2000.

———. *Donald Trump: Master Apprentice.* New York: Simon & Schuster, 2005.

Boorstin, Daniel J. *The Image.* New York: Vintage Books: 1992.

Braudy, Leo. *The Frenzy of Renown, Fame and Its History.* New York: Vintage Books, 1986.

Burnett, Alistair. *Aberdeen.* Gloucestershire, UK: NPI Media Group, 1999.

Burns, Sarah. *The Central Park Five.* New York: Vintage Books, 2011.

Bushkin, Henry. *Johnny Carson.* New York: Houghton Mifflin Harcourt, 2013.

Cashman, Sean Dennis. *America in the Gilded Age.* New York: New York University Press, 1984.

Ehrenreich, Barbara. *Fear of Falling.* New York: HarperCollins, 1989.

———. *Nickel and Dimed.* New York: Henry Holt, 2001.

———. *This Land Is Their Land.* New York: Metropolitan Books, 2008.

Ewen, David. *Chasing Paradise.* Edinburgh: Black and White, 2011.

Feagin, Joe R. *The New Urban Paradigm.* Lanham, Md.: Rowman & Littlefield, 1998.

Ferretti, Fred. *The Year the Big Apple Went Bust.* New York: G. P. Putnam's Sons, 1976.

Frank, Thomas. *One Market Under God: Extreme Capitalism, Market Populism, and the End of Economic Democracy.* New York: Anchor Books, 2000.

————. *What's the Matter with Kansas?* New York: Metropolitan Books, 2004.

————. *Pity the Billionaire: The Hard-Times Swindle and the Unlikely Comeback of the Right*. New York: Henry Holt, 2012.

Frank, Robert H. *The Darwin Economy: Liberty, Competition, and the Common Good*. Princeton, N.J.: Princeton University Press, 2011.

Freeland, Chrystia. *Plutocrats: The Rise of the New Global Super-Rich and the Fall of Everyone Else*. New York: Penguin Books, 2012.

Gabler, Neal. *Life: The Movie*. New York: Vintage Books, 1998.

Goldstock, Ronald. *Corruption and Racketeering in the New York City Construction Industry*. New York: New York University Press, 1990.

Hofstadter, Richard. *The Paranoid Style in American Politics*. New York: Vintage Books, 2008.

Hollinger, David A., and Charles Capper. *The American Intellectual Tradition*. New York: Oxford University Press, 2011.

Hunter, James. *The Making of the Crofting Community*. Edinburgh: John Donald, 2000.

Hurt, Harry. *Lost Tycoon: The Many Lives of Donald J. Trump*. New York: W. W. Norton, 1993.

Hutchinson, Roger. *The Soap Man*. Edinburgh: Birlinn, 2003.

Jacobs, James B. *Gotham Unbound*. New York: New York University Press, 1999.

————. *Mobsters, Unions, and Feds*. New York: New York University Press, 2006.

Johnson, Haynes. *Sleepwalking Through History*. New York: W. W. Norton, 2003.

Katz, Michael B. *The Undeserving Poor: From the War on Poverty to the War on Welfare*. New York: Pantheon Books, 1989.

Kluger, Jeffrey. *The Narcissist Next Door*. New York: Riverhead Books, 2014.

Koch, Edward I. *Citizen Koch*. New York: St. Martin's Press, 1992.

Lachman, Seymour P., and Robert Polner. *The Man Who Saved New York: Hugh Carey and the Great Fiscal Crisis of 1975*. Albany, N.Y.: Excelsior Editions, 2010.

Lapham, Lewis H. *Money and Class in America*. New York: Weidenfeld & Nicolson, 1988.

Lasch, Christopher. *The Culture of Narcissism: American Life in an Age of Diminishing Expectations*. New York: W. W. Norton, 1979.

Lawrence, Ken. *The World According to Trump*. Kansas City, Mo.: Andrews McMeel, 2005.

Lopez, Ian Haney. *Dog Whistle Politics: How Coded Racial Appeals Have Reinvented Racism and Wrecked the Middle Class*. New York: Oxford University Press, 2014.

Marshall, P. David. *Celebrity and Power: Fame in Contemporary Culture*. Minneapolis: University of Minnesota Press, 1997.

Milne, David. *It's Only Sand*. Balmedie, UK: MilHouse Publishing, 2009.

Nackbar, Jack, and Kevin Lause. *Popular Culture: An Introductory Text*. Bowling Green, Ohio: Bowling Green State University Popular Press, 1992.

O'Brien, Timothy L. *TrumpNation: The Art of Being The Donald*. New York: Warner Business Books, 2005.

O'Donnell, John R., with James Rutherford. *Trumped!: The Inside Story of the Real Donald Trump—His Cunning Rise and Spectacular Fall*. New York: Simon & Schuster, 1991.

Perlstein, Rick. *The Invisible Bridge: The Fall of Nixon and the Rise of Reagan*. New York: Simon & Schuster, 2014.

Pierce, Charles P. *Idiot America: How Stupidity Became a Virtue in the Land of the Free*. New York: Anchor Books, 2009.

Pozner, Jennifer L. *Reality Bites Back: The Troubling Truth About Guilty Pleasure TV*. Berkeley, Calif.: Seal Press, 2010.

Rush, George, with Joanna Molloy. *Scandal: A Manual*. New York: Skyhorse Publishing, 2013.

Sexton, Don. *Trump University Marketing 101*. Hoboken, N.J.: John Wiley and Sons, 2006.

Shorris, Earl. *A Nation of Salesmen: The Tyranny of the Market and the Subversion of Culture*. New York: W. W Norton, 1994.

Sinclair, Upton. *The Brass Check: A Study of American Journalism*. Urbana: University of Illinois Press, 2003.

Smith, Adam. *The Roaring '80s*. New York: Summit Books, 1988.

Smith, Liz. *Natural Blonde*. New York: Hyperion Books, 2000.

Sternheimer, Karen. *Celebrity Culture and the American Dream: Stardom and Social Mobility*. New York: Routledge, 2011.

Trump, Donald J. *Trump: The Art of the Deal*. New York: Random House, 1987.

———. *Trump: The Art of the Comeback*. New York: Times Books, 1997.

———. *Trump: Think Like a Billionaire*. New York: Ballantine Books, 2005.

———. *Think Big: Make It Happen in Business and Life*. New York: Collins Business, 2007.

———. *Trump: Never Give Up*. Hoboken. N.J.: John Wiley and Sons, 2008.

Tuccille, Jerome. *Trump: The Saga of America's Most Powerful Real Estate Baron*. New York: Donald I. Fine, 1985.

Twenge, Jean M., and W. Keith Campbell. *The Narcissism Epidemic: Living in the Age of Entitlement*. New York: Atria, 2009.

Veblen, Thorstein. *The Theory of the Leisure Class*. Oxford, UK: Oxford University Press, 2007.

Weiss, Richard. *The American Myth of Success*. Urbana: University of Illinois Press, 1969.

Whyte, William H., Jr. *The Organization Man*. New York: Simon & Schuster, 1956.

Wolf, Michael J. *The Entertainment Economy*. New York: Three Rivers Press, 1999.

INDEX

ABC, 239, 286, 374

Aberdeen Evening Express, 390, 395, 404, 405

abortion rights, 423, 451

Adams, Cindy, 162, 264–65, 267–68, 269–70, 287

Adams, James Truslow, 31–32

Adams, Joey, 162, 287

Adler, Alfred, 197

advertising, 83–84, 198, 236–37, 276–77

affirmative action, 252, 378

air rights, 164–65, 169

alcohol, 29, 78, 92, 202–3

Aguilar, Patricia, xvi

Alibi (race horse), 260

Allen, Robert G., 182

Alzheimer's disease, of Trump, Fred, 322

The America We Deserve (Trump, D.), 323

American Dream, 31–32, 278, 447

American Express, 328

American Institute of Architects, 184

American royalty, 240

Americana Hotel, 81, 82, 135

Ammann, Othmar, 66, 429

Amtrak, 119

Amusing Ourselves to Death (Postman), 330

Anderson, Kurt, 248

Antichrist, Obama, B., as, 373

Anti-Intellectualism in American Life (Hofstadter), 60

antiwar activities, 90–92

Apple, 12

The Apprentice, 4, 16–17, 340–52, 383–84, 423, 444
    "the cobra" on, 346
    falling viewership for, 361
    Mexico and, 449
    publicity from, 346–47
    Scotland and, 406
    Stewart, M., on, 348–50

Archie Bunker (fictional character), 252

Argovitz, Jerry, 230, 264

aristocracy, 6–8

arson, at Trump Tower, 177–78

asbestos, 295

Aspen, Colorado, 265–66

The Atlantic, 438

Atlantic City
    gambling in, 12, 204–27, 255–60, 299–300
    Las Vegas and, 205
    organized crime in, 207

Atlantic City Convention Hall, 206

Atlantic Monthly, 368

autobiographies, 243–44

Avant Garde, 197

Axelrod, David, 420

baby boom, 8

The Bachelor, 335

The Bachelorette, 335

baldness, 317, 347

Bally's, 205, 215–16

Bancroft, Anne, 230

bankruptcy, 213, 261–64
    in Great Depression, 31–42
    of middle class, 279
    of Penn Central, 114–15, 123
    of Resorts International, 254

bankruptcy (*continued*)
  of Taj Mahal, 261, 276
  of Trump Castle, 280
  of Trump Hotels and Casino
    Resorts, 327, 351
  of Trump Plaza, 280
  of Zeckendorf, 117
Barbarians at the Gate (Burrough
  and Helyar), 285
Barbizon Hotel, 225
Barclay Hotel, 127
bargain prices, 208
Barnum, P. T., 13
Baron, John (false identity),
  173–75, 191, 256, 265, 422
Barrett, Wayne, 120, 122, 169,
  187–90
  on Cohn, 224
  criticism of, 284, 421
  on 100 Central Park South, 222
Barrows, Sydney Biddle, 287
Barry, Maryanne Trump. *See*
  Trump, Maryanne
Barsky, Neil, 256, 259, 264
baseball, 61
Basinger, Kim, 289, 290
Bass, Robert M., 219
Baumgold, Julie, 294
Baxter, Anthony, 412
Bay Ridge, 38
BBC, 306, 412, 414, 431
Beach Haven, 21–24
Beame, Abe, 81, 111–15, 118, 162,
  189
  Barrett and, 189
  Carter, J., and, 141
  reelection attempt of, 138
Bear Stearns, 214
Beatty, Warren, 158, 321
beauty pageants, 206, 228–29, 327,
  359, 361, 449
Belmont, August, 37
Benanav, Jonathan, 255
Berger, David, 119, 121–22
Berkowitz, Harry, 233
Bernays, Edward, 39–40
Best & Co., 164
Biaggi, Mario, 110–11
Big Brother, 333, 334

Biltmore Hotel, 127
bin Laden, Osama, 327, 383
Birmingham, Alabama, xi
birth, 3, 50
birthers
  Corsi and, 378–79
  CPAC and, 372–74
  Obama, B., and, 2, 369–86, 423,
    430
  O'Reilly and, 430
Black and White Ball, 219
blackout, 139, 140
blacks, 87–88, 89
  education of, 252, 316, 380
  lawsuits and, 104–10
  welfare and, 108–9
Blair, Gwenda, 117
Blanton, Smiley, 69, 71
Blavatnik, Leonard, 11
Bloom County, 280
Blue Gemini (film), 230–31
Board of Estimate, 42, 76, 136,
  137
Board of Water Supply, 141
bodyguard/chauffeur, 153, 154–55,
  277
Boeing 727, 259, 390, 405
Boeing 747, of Talal, 300
Boeing 757, 11
Boesky, Ivan, 279–80
Bonfire of the Vanities (Wolfe),
  248
Bonwit Teller, 163–64, 168,
  429
  demolition of, 171–75
books, 15–16, 328–29. *See also
    specific titles*
  on money, 7–8
  by Stewart, M., 348
Boorstin, Daniel J., 83
Booz Allen Hamilton, 330
The Boston Globe, 236, 284
Boston Properties, 168
Bowden, Mark, 261
Bowery Savings Bank, 138, 143
Bradley, Bill, 322
brand name, 12–13, 357
Breakfast at Tiffany's (Capote),
  163

Breakshot (Gallo), 55
Breathed, Berkelcy, 280
Bren, Donald, 11
Brenner, Marie, 142, 283
Brooklebank, Ted, 306, 307
Brooklyn, 95–126
    Democratic Party in, 111, 189
    poverty zones in, 88, 95
    Trump, Fred, and, 36–37
Brooklyn Rapid Transit Company, 37
Brown, Tina, 283, 364
Bruni, Carla, 288–89, 290
Buchanan, Patrick, 319–20, 378
Buffett, Warren, 129
bullying at military school, xxi, 17, 59, 222
Bulmer, Jeff , 280
Bulworth (film), 321–22
Bunshaft, Gordon, 95
Burnett, Mark, 333, 334–48
Burns, Sarah, 339
Burrough, Bryan, 285
Busey, Gary, 383
Bush, Barbara, 282
Bush, George H. W., 271–72
Bush, George W., 321, 323, 326, 377, 423
Bush, Jeb, xii, 449
Business Investment Incentive Program, 135
Business Week, 200

Caesar's, 205, 212
Caine, Michael, 418
Caliandro, Arthur, 297
campaign contributions, 167–68
    to Carey, 120
    by Helmsley, H., 145–46
    to Koch, 195
    to Nixon, R., 287
    to Torricelli, 299
Capehart, Homer, 21–23, 37, 44–45
Capone, Al, 299
Capone, Louis, 41
Capote, Truman, 163, 219
Capshaw, Kate, 296

Carey, Hugh, xxi, 120–23, 135, 139, 145
Carlin, George, 217, 331
Carnegie, Andrew, 7, 25
Carnegie, Dale, 50–51
Carnegies, 6
Caro, Robert, 302
Carpenter, Kelli, 360
Carson, Johnny, 92, 184–85, 249–50
Carter, Graydon, 199–200, 248, 383, 421, 437
Carter, Jimmy, 141, 180
Carter hotel chain, 136
Cartier jewelers, 164
Cartland, Barbara, 198
Cash, Dave, 62
Cashmore, John ("Cashbox"), 82
Cassini, Igor, 101
Cassini, Oleg, 101
Castro, Fidel, 320
CBS, 323
CBS News, 379
celebrities
    advertising and, 83–84
    from beauty pageants, 228–29
    Bernays and, 39
    Le Club and, 100–101, 103
    Helmsleys as, 146–47
    Maples as, 287–88
    Maxwell's Plum and, 157–58
    publicity and, 146–47, 153, 187–203
    Q score for, 3, 436
    from reality television, 335–36
    sex tape scandals of, 361–62
    shamelessness of, 287
    television about, 197–98
Celebrity Apprentice, 351, 383
Central Park
    jogger's rape in, 251, 294, 339, 380, 427–28
    Wollman Rink in, 232–33, 336
Ceresney, Andrew J., 356, 358
Chalk's International Airlines, 221
Charles, Prince of Wales, 183, 201
Chase Manhattan Bank, 232
Cheney, Dick, 92
Cher, 198, 385, 432–33

Chicago, McCormick Place in, 114
Chicago Tribune, 250–51, 371, 376, 438
childhood, 46–72
China, xv, 373, 382
Choate, Patrick, 326
Chrysler Building, 130, 143
Cimco, 233
Citibank, 247, 261
Citizen Cohn (von Hoffman), 226
Citizen Koch (Koch), 233
Civil Rights Division, of Department of Justice, 104–10
climate change, xv, 5, 423
Clinton, Bill, 15, 92, 318, 326
Clinton, Hillary, xvii, 269, 364, 370, 373, 426
Le Club, 100–101, 103, 195
CNN, xi, xiii, 323, 431
"the cobra," 346
Cody, John, 178–79
Cohan, William, 438
Cohen, Michael, ix–x, 372
Cohen v. Trump, 428
Cohn, Roy, xxii, 19, 101–10, 419
    Barrett and, 189
    Cody and, 178–79
    death of, 226
    disbarment of, 223–24, 225
    Eichler and, 120
    Friedman and, 141–42
    HIV/AIDS and, 224–26
    politics and, 167–68
    prenuptial agreement by, 159–61
    Stone, R., and, 236
    at Studio 54, 149
Coking, Vera, 206
Colbert, Stephen, 181
Collins, Gail, 13–14
Collins, Nancy, 297
Collyer, David Sorin, 292
Columbus Circle, 303
comedians, 1–2, 4, 14, 448–49
Commodore Hotel, 127, 128–31
    Barrett and, 189
    Carter hotel chain and, 136
    demolition of, 143, 144

Friedman and, 141–43
    Hyatt Corporation and, 132, 133–34, 143, 145
    tax breaks for, 135–37
concrete, 177–78
Coney Island, 80–82, 86, 88, 135
Conger, Darva, 335
Congressional Campaign to Exterminate Jew Power in America, 369
Conner, Tara, 359
Conrail, 119
Conroy, Pat, 55
Conservative Political Action Conference (CPAC), 372–74
conspiracy theories, 377–78
convention center, 114–15, 124, 125–26
Cooper, Pat, 287
corporate takeovers, 215–16
Corsi, Jerome, 376–77
Cosell, Howard, 141
Cothrans, Shirley, 228, 229
Coué, Émile, 70
coverture, 159
CPAC. *See* Conservative Political Action Conference
Crafts, Wilbur Fisk, 7
Crippled America (Trump, D.), xv
crofts, 403
Crowley, Terry, 62
C-SPAN, 382–83
Cuba, 320
The Culture of Narcissism (Lasch), 149, 438–39
Cuomo, Mario, 139, 236

D'Agostino, Mark, 419, 433–35
Daily News, 111, 249, 324, 367, 385, 448
    on Knauss, 363
    on O'Donnell, R., 360
    Trump, Ivana, and, 267
    on wedding to Maples, 297
The Daily Show, 4
Dallas, 180
Dalton (Ga.) *Daily Citizen,* 268

Dare to Succeed: How to Survive and Thrive in the Game of Life (Burnett), 336
Darth Vader (fictional character), 304
Death of a Salesman (Miller), 51
death penalty, xv, 139, 251–52, 427
deferment, for draft, 92–93
Demm, William, 36
Democratic Party, 138
  Barrett and, 189
  in Brooklyn, 111, 189
  FHA and, 37–43
  National Convention of, 92
  Trump, Fred, and, 37–43, 74, 77
De Niro, Robert, 230
Department of Justice, 104–10
deregulation, 9
Designing Women, 291
Dewey, John, 52
Diana, Princess, 198, 201, 308
DiBono, Louis, 42
Dic-Underhill Concrete, 177
Diener, Lawrence, 255
Dimon, Jamie, 420
Dinkins, David, 196
discipline, 54, 55–60
disease of extravagant expectations, 83
Disney, Walt, 81
divorce
  from Maples, 308–9
  from Trump, Ivana, 273–75
DJT stock offering, 301–2, 314
Dobias, Theodore ("Maje"), xxi, 55–60, 93, 424
Doctorow, E. L., 302
dog-whistle language, 109
Dole, Robert, 239
Donahue, Phil, 242
Donald J. Trump Special Dunes, 415
"Donald's Rules of Success," 325
dot-com bust, 338
Douglas, Buster, 267
Dowd, James, 342, 350
draft, 92–93
drugs, at Studio 54, 149

Drumpf, Friedrich. *See* Trump, Friedrich
Duke, David, xiii–xiv
Dunbar, Michael, 237–38
Duncan, Dan, 11
Dynasty, 180

E. Trump and Son, 30, 31
The Early Show, 323
East Flatbush, 36–37
Eastern Airlines, 246–48, 249, 254
Easton, Nina, 220–21
Ebola, 431
Eco-Challenge, 333
Economic Forum, 390
education, 7, 11
  of blacks, 252, 316, 380
  disinterest in, 90
  at Fordham University, 63–68
  at Kew-Forest School, xx, 52–53
  at NYMA, xx–xxi, 54–63
  Trump, Fred, and, 10
  Trump University, 365–68, 428–29
  at University of Pennsylvania, 68, 84, 89–90, 91–92
  at Wharton School of Finance and Commerce, 89–90, 93
"Effective Speaking and Human Relations" (Dale Carnegie course), 50–51
Ehrlichman, John, 107
Eichler, Edward ("Ned"), 116–21, 125, 127, 132
Eisenhower, Dwight D., 20, 43
Eldridge, Russell, 224–25
electricity blackout, 139, 140
Elizabeth II (Queen), 47, 249
Elliott, Osborn, 140
Ellison, Larry, 10
Empire State Building, 98, 119, 304–6
Entertaining (Stewart, M.), 348
Entertainment Tonight, 197, 292
The Epic of America (Adams), 31–32
Equitable Life Insurance Company, 137–38, 143, 168

Ernst & Young, 351
ESPN, 194, 449
Esquire, 327
Estess, Mark, 255, 317
Expedition Robinson, 333–34

Face the Nation, 319
Facebook, 431
Falber, Harry, 59
Falcon Crest, 180
fame, 12–13, 227, 288. *See also*
     celebrities
   of Cohn, 109
   of Griffin, M., 221
   of Manigault-Stallworth,
     346–47
   of Maples, 271
   at NYMA, 61
   of Steinbrenner, 101
Fannie Mae. *See* Federal National
     Mortgage Association
Fazio, Tom, 397
FBI. *See* Federal Bureau of
     Investigation
Federal Bureau of Investigation
     (FBI), xi, 104, 299
Federal Housing Administration
     (FHA), 19–24, 37–38, 41, 43
Federal National Mortgage
     Association (Fannie Mae), 38
Feeney, Mark, 284
Felder, Raoul L., 160
Felix Happer (fictional character),
     391
Femina, Jerry Della, 277
FHA. *See* Federal Housing
     Administration
Fichtners, Christiane, 228, 229
FilmTV Daily, 231
Finch, Jennie, 350–51
fiscal crisis, 111–14
Fitzgerald, F. Scott, 30
Fitzsimmons, Thomas, 230–31,
     244, 268
Flatbush, 36–37, 40, 88
Foerderer, Norma, 200, 237, 282
For Love Alone (Trump, Ivana),
     291–92
"For the Love of Money," 372

Forbes, Malcolm, 278, 280, 284
Forbes, Michael, 396–97, 402–3,
     408–10, 411, 412, 414
Forbes, Sheila, 402
Forbes (magazine), list of richest
     people in, 12, 284, 312–13,
     321, 327, 354
Ford, Gerald, 111, 112–13
Ford, Martin, 400–401, 404–5,
     410
Fordham University, 63–68
foreclosures, 31–42, 130
Fortune, 200, 278
Four Seasons, 100
Fox News, 315, 368, 374, 430
Fox News Sunday, 319
Frankel, Bethenny, 349
Fred C. Trump Convention Center,
     166
Freed, Peter, 451
Frengut, Renee, 277
Freud, Sigmund, 39
Friedman, Stanley, 141–43, 235
Friedrich, Otto, 249–50
Fugazy, William, 290–91
Fullam, John P., 119, 121, 122

Gabler, Neal, 39
Galbreath and Company, 304
Gallo, Kenny, 55
Gallup Poll, 12, 360–61
gambling
   in Atlantic City, 12, 204–27,
     255–60, 299–300
   Hilton and, 365
   Indian tribes and, 299
   organized crime and, 209
Gap, 12
garbage strike, 112
Gates, Bill, 11, 129
gay marriage, 423
Geffen, David, 10
General Electric Pension Trust, 303
"General Order No. 6," 59
Genesco, 163–64
Genova, Mario di, 135
Gentlemen Prefer Blondes, 163
gentrification, 313
germophobia, 285

Gifford, Frank, 289, 290, 292
Gifford, Kathie Lee, 289–90, 292
Gigante, Vincent ("Chin"), 172
Gilded Age, 6–8
Gilder, George, 9
Giuliani, Rudolph, 196, 235, 364, 381, 419
Glenfiddich whisky, 414
Gliedman, Tony, 233, 261
Global Scot, 393, 415, 417
global warming, 423
Gold Elite program, 365
gold rush, 21–23
Goldberg, Jay, 274
Goldberger, Paul, 144, 145
Golden Nugget, 209, 215
Goldsmith, Barbara, 147
Goldstein, Donna, 107, 109
golf resort, in Scotland, 387–417
Goodman, Randolph, 262
Gorbachev, Mikhail, 238–39
Gordon Gekko (fictional character), 15, 279
Gore, Al, 323, 326, 332
gossip columns, 287
GoTrump .com, 365
Gotti, John, 356
Goulds, 6
GQ, 199
Grace, George, 43–44
Grace, Thomas G. ("Tommy"), 37–38, 43–44
Graff , Rhona, 422, 445
Graham, John, 8
Graham, Lindsey, 383, 449
Grand Central, 130 –31
grandiosity, 150, 446
Great Depression, 8, 31–42
Great Dunes of Scotland, 414–15
Great Gatsby (Fitzgerald), 30
greed, 15, 77, 279, 391
Greedlock, 234
greenmailing, 212, 213, 215
Greenpoint, 88
Gregory, Dick, 217
Griffin, Merv, 216–17, 220, 254, 258
Griffin, Tom, 387, 394–99, 416
Guccione, Bob, 206

Guideposts, 71
Gulf of Mexico oil spill, 420
Gulf+Western Building, 303–4
Gumbel, Bryant, 252
Guterman, Gerald, 278

Haberman, Maggie, 377–78
hair, 317–18
Hall, G. Stanley, 52
Hampton, Lionel, 231
Handley, Kaye, 257
hard work, 51, 54
Harding, Warren G., 21
Harrah's, 209–10, 211–14
Harris, James, 366
Hart, Gary, 270, 272
Hatch, Richard, 335, 384
Hawkins, Ashton, 174
Hawtree, Martin, 397, 416
health care reform, 451
hedonism, 16
Hell's Kitchen, 115, 124, 125–26
Helms, Jesse, 224
Helmsley, Harry, 135, 145–47, 148, 305
Helmsley, Leona, 145–48, 269, 305, 419
Helmsley Palace, 145
Helmsley Park Lane, 146
Helyar, John, 285
Herrera, Carolina, 296
high-achievers, 6
highways, in Manhattan, 97–98
Hill, Napoleon, 69–70, 329
Hilton, William Barron, 205, 212–14, 364–65
Hispanics, 88, 89
HIV/AIDS, 224–26, 288
Hixon, Verina, 176, 178, 179
Hobbes, Thomas, 202
Hobday, Neil Peter Whyte, 387–89, 396, 404, 409, 410
Hoffman, Abbie, 217
Hofstadter, Richard, 60
Holiday Inn, 210, 214–15, 218
Holocaust, 319
Home Title Guarantee, 35
homosexuality
    of Cohn, 101, 224

homosexuality (*continued*)
  of Forbes, Malcolm, 284
  of Koch, 139
  in military service, 320, 423
  of O'Donnell, R., 360
Hoover, J. Edgar, 107
Hotel Astor, 134
House Wreckers Union Local 95, 173, 174
Hoving, Walter, 168–69
"How to Be Successful in America" (Lowry), 96
HRH Construction, 67–68, 98, 121, 123, 232–33
Hubbard, Elbert, 7
Hudson Waterfront Associates, 302
Hughes, Howard, 250, 285
Hulcy, D. A., 278
Humphrey, Hubert, 326
Hurt, Harry, III, 160–61, 208, 263, 289, 317
Hussein, Saddam, 370
Huxtable, Ada Louise, 97, 191–92
Hyatt Corporation, 132, 133, 143, 145
Hyde, Stephen F., 255

Iacocca (Iacocca), 243
Iacocca, Lee, 243
Icahn, Carl, 213
The Image: A Guide to Pseudo-Events in America (Boorstin), 83
immunizations, 5
Imus, Don, 291
income inequality, 10
Indian tribes, 299
Indiana Jones (fictional character), 336
inflation, 10
innate ability, 425
insider trading, 213
Interborough Rapid Transit Company, 37
Invesco Trust, 301
Iraq War, 326–27
Is That All There Is? (Lee, P.), 443

Isle of Lewis, 47–50, 400, 403, 405–7, 417
"It Ain't Necessarily So," 307

Jackson, Michael, 184
Jamaica Estates, 44–45, 46–47
Japan, 373
Javits, Jacob, 126
Jay Bulworth (fictional character), 321–22
Jeopardy, 217
Jewish Anti-Defamation League, 319
Jillette, Penn, 351
Jobs, Clara, 116
Jobs, Paul, 116
Jobs, Steve, 116, 330
Johnson, Lyndon B., 108, 161
Johnson, Philip, 134
Jones, Chuck, 231–32, 244, 270, 310–11
Jones, David, 324
junk bonds, 209, 254, 256, 301

The Kansas City Star, xii
Kashiwagi, Akio, 300
Kaszycki, William, 172, 173
Kaszycki & Sons, 171
Kazan, Abraham, 76
Kefauver, Estes, 42–43
Kemp, Jack, 239
Kennedy, Caroline, 296
Kennedy, Jacqueline Bouvier, 159, 165
Kennedy, John F., xx, 71
Kennedy, Michael, 274
Kennedy, Robert F., 188
Kent, Robert, 255
Kent State, 91
Kerner Commission, 116
Kerr, Walter, 100
Kew-Forest School, xx, 52–53
Keynes, John Maynard, 37
Khomeini, Ayatollah Ruhollah, 238–39
King, Don, 243
King, Larry, 281
King, Martin Luther, Jr., 88
Kitt, Eartha, 219

Kiyosaki, Robert, 353–54
KKR. *See* Kohlberg Kravis
    Roberts
Klemesrud, Judy, 148, 151–52, 239
Knauss, Melania, 360, 363–64,
    375
Koch, Edward I., 139–41, 193–96,
    419
    Commodore Hotel and, 143
    Myerson and, 139, 196, 229, 234
    Olympic Tower and, 166
    100 Central Park South and, 223
    Wollman Rink and, 232–33
Kohlberg Kravis Roberts (KKR),
    256
Kolbert, Elizabeth, 303
Korean Broadcasting System, xviii
Koskinen, John, 132,
    136–37
Kravis, Henry, 256
Kristol, William, xviii
Ku Klux Klan, xiii
Kushner, Harold, 248

La Guardia, Fiorello, 126
"the Ladies Mile," 163
Lambert, Benjamin, 132
Lambert, Lawrence, 263
Lancaster, Burt, 391
Lapidus, Morris, 68, 81, 85–86,
    135
Larry King Live, 323
Las Vegas, 205
Lasch, Christopher, 149–50,
    438–39, 445–46
Late Show, 260
lawsuits, 13, 14, 355–61
    for alleged housing
        discrimination, 104–10, 189
    Cohn and, 104–10
    by Department of Justice,
        104–10
    by Griffin, M., 217
    by Holiday Inn, 214–15
    on Indian tribe gambling
        business, 299
    against Maher, 386
    NFL and, 223
    against O'Brien, T., 421

100 Central Park South and,
    221–23
by Roffman, 257–58
against Trump University,
    367–68, 428–29
Leach, Robin, 197–98, 277, 286
Lee, Peggy, 219, 443
Lee, Spike, 252
Leerhsen, Charles, 283–84
LeFrak, Samuel J., 104–5
Lehmann-Haupt, Christopher,
    242–43
Lehrenkrauss, Beatrice, 34
Lehrenkrauss, Charles, 34
Lehrenkrauss, J. Lester, 34
Lehrenkrauss, Julius, 34–35
Lehrenkrauss, Lester, 34
Lehrenkrauss & Co., 34–36
leisure class, 25–26
Lemmon, Jack, 231
LeRoy, Mervyn, 157
Lescaze, William, 65
Letterman, David, 260, 379–80,
    408, 448
*Letters from a Self-Made
    Merchant to His Son*
    (Graham), 8
Lever, William (Lord
    Leverhulme), 48, 406–7, 417
Levner, Lawrence, 160
Lewis, Michael, 285
Lews Castle, 406–7, 417
Liasson, Mara, xvii
libel, 189–90, 283, 359
Liddy, G. Gordon, 147
lifestyle, 197–98, 240
Lifestyles of the Rich and Famous,
    197–98, 227, 277, 286
Lilliputian Bazaar, 164
Limited-Profit Housing Companies
    act of 1955, 67
Lindenbaum, Abraham, 74–75, 77
Lindsay, John V., 77, 87, 97, 113,
    164, 302
Little Nell, 265
Live with Regis and Kathie Lee,
    290
living landmark, by New York
    Landmarks Conservancy, 437

Local Hero (film), 390–91
Lokey, Michelle, 356
Lombardi, Vince, 56
Lone Star Gas, 278
Lorenzo, Frank, 247
Los Angeles Convention Center, 353
Los Angeles Times, 220–21
Lost Tycoon (Hurt), 161, 317
lottery, for draft, 92–93
"Love on the Rocks" (Smith, L.), 267
Lowry, Albert J., 96–97, 182
Lucky Sperm Club, 3, 212, 364
luxury, 12, 95–96, 145, 277

Macari, Thomas, 171–72
Machrihanish Dunes, 416
Mackinnon, James, 404
Macy's, 449
Madden, Kevin, xvii
Madonna, 289, 290
Mafia. *See* organized crime
Maher, Bill, 4, 385–86
Mailer, Michael, 309
Makaeff v. Trump University, 428–29
Make-A-Wish Foundation, 342–43
Malkin, Peter, 305
Malone, Sarah, 412, 417
"The Man Who Has Everything" (Walters), 239–40
Manhattan, 74, 95–126
    Americana Hotel in, 81, 82
    gentrification of, 313
    luxury apartments in, 95–96
    politics in, xxii, 118
Manhattan House, 95
Manhattan Inc., 200
Manigault-Stallworth, Omarosa, 346–47, 350–51
Manufacturers Hanover, 143
Maples, Marla, 228–32, 244–46, 248, 253–59, 264–75, 280–83
    Baron and, 256, 265
    Bruni and, 288–89
    celebrity of, 287–88
    on *Designing Women,* 291

divorce from, 308–9
engagement to Trump, 291
Forbes, Malcolm, and, 280
No Excuses and, 270–71
Playboy and, 270
pregnancy of, 295
prenuptial agreement with, 295–96, 309–10
on *PrimeTime Live,* 281–82
recollections of, 444–45
reconciliation with, 289–90
reported breakup with, 291, 292
Trump, Ivana, and, 254, 255–56, 266
in *Vanity Fair,* 274
wedding to, 296–97
in *The Will Rogers Follies,* 292, 298
Mar-a-Lago, 225, 263, 277, 300, 364
Marcos, Imelda, 287
Marder, Murrey, 110
Market Insights, 277
marriage, 152–53. *See also* Maples, Marla; Trump, Ivana
    gay, 423
    to Krauss, 364
    Trump, Fred, and, 244
Martin, Andrew, 369–70
Martin, Jill A., 429
masculinity, 87
Massachusetts Mutual Life Insurance Company, 143
Maxwell's Plum, 157–58
Mayer, John, 432
mayor, consideration as, 196
McCain, John, xv, 371, 373, 376, 383
McCarthy, Joseph, 19–20, 103, 110, 371
McCloskey, Pete, 236
McConnell, Jack, 391–96, 417
McCormick Place, 114
McCrary, John ("Tex"), 64
McDonald's, 328
McGraw, Phil ("Dr. Phil"), 379
McKenna, William, 20
McRae, Ron, 375–76
Me Decade, 15, 148, 149, 442

Meet the Press, 319
Menie Estate, 387–90, 397, 398,
    402, 407, 415
Menie Sand Sheet, 394–95
Meriwether, Lee, 229
Merrill Lynch, 254
Merv Griffin Resorts, 261
MetLife Building, 127
Metropolitan Museum of Art, 171,
    174
Mexico, xv, 5, 373, 447, 449
Meyers, Seth, 1–2, 382–83
middle class, 8, 124, 183, 279
    Republican Party and, 315
    in suburbs, 96
    white flight of, 87, 88
Midler, Bette, 292, 432–33
Midtown, 127–55
military school, xx–xxi, 54–63
military service, 92–93
    homosexuality in, 320, 423
    NYMA as, 93–94
Milken, Michael, 15, 209, 279–80
Miller, Arthur, 51
Miller, Dennis, 282
Miller, George, 299
Miller, Jeffrey, 124–25
Miller, John, 289, 290
Milne, David, 388, 402, 409–10,
    412–13
Minnelli, Liza, 219, 297
Miss America, 206, 228–29
Miss Universe, 327, 449
Miss USA, 359, 361
Mitchell, Don, 278
Mitchell, John N., 123, 125
Mitchell, MacNeil, 76
Mitchell-Lama program, 67–77
Modern Screen, 269
Monroe, Marilyn, 163, 229
Monte Cristo, 26–27
Moon, Sun Myung, 128
moral obligation bonds, 123, 125
Morgan, J. P., 6, 25
Morris, Dick, 323
mortgages, 31–42, 67, 130
Mosbacher, Georgette, 268
Moses, Robert, 65–66, 429
Moynihan, Daniel Patrick, 433

Mr. Green, 175
Munro, Susan, 387–89, 402, 412,
    413–14
Murdoch, Rupert, 140
Muslims, xi, xv
Mussolini, Benito, 55
Myerson, Bess, 139, 196, 229, 234

Nappear, Matthew, 32
narcissism, 149–50, 438–39, 445,
    451
NASCAR, 449
The Nation, 39
A Nation of Salesmen (Shorris),
    286
National Convention, of
    Democratic Party, 92
National Enquirer, 321
National Public Radio, xvii
NBC, 195. *See also The
    Apprentice*
    Miss Universe and, 327
    Survivor on, 335–36
Neaher, Edward, 106
New Age movement, 290
New Arctic Restaurant and Hotel,
    28
New Deal, 37
The New Explorers, 286
New Jersey Casino Control
    Commission, 214
New Jersey Generals, 194
New York (magazine), 196, 200,
    222, 271–72, 294–95
New York Bank for Savings, 128
New York Central Railroad, 129
New York Committee for a
    Balanced Building Bloom,
    170
New York Foundling Hospital,
    208
New York Landmarks
    Conservancy, 437
New York Military Academy
    (NYMA), xx–xxi, 54–63,
    423–24
    bullying at, xxi, 59
    fame at, 61
    masculinity and, 87

New York Military Academy
      (*continued*)
   as military service, 93–94
   sports at, 61–62, 424–25
   superiority of, 60
New York Post, 267–68, 441
   on divorce, 273
   Koch and, 139–40, 196
   on Maples, 269–70
   Murdoch and, 140
New York State Commission of
      Investigation, 75–77
The New York Times, xvi, xxii, 13,
      38, 66, 76–77, 222
   advertising in, 236
   on *The Apprentice,* 341
   Beame and, 111
   on campaign contributions, 167
   on divorce, 273
   father's obituary in, 322
   gossip column in, 287
   Helmsleys and, 148
   New York Post and, 140
   on Olympic Tower, 277
   publicity in, 151–53, 198–99
   on renting to blacks, 108–9
   Steeplechase Park and, 81
   Trump, Fred, and, 191
   Trump, Ivana, and, 191
   on *Trump: Surviving at the Top,*
      285
   on Twitter, 431
The New Yorker, xvi, 315, 379, 422
New Yorker Hotel, 128
Newsday, 289
newspapers, 6. *See also specific*
      newspapers
   advertising in, 236–37
   for sports, 61
Newsweek, 200, 270
NFL, 223
Nichols, Mike, 282
Nicholson, Jack, 265
Niebuhr, Reinhold, 70–71
9/11. *See* September 11, 2001
98percentapproval .com, 368
Nixon, Pat, 180
Nixon, Richard, xv, 106, 107, 180,
      242

The Boston Globe and, 284
   Buchanan and, 319
   Sawyer and, 281
   Steinbrenner and, 287
   Stone, R., and, 236
   Watergate scandal and, 125, 147
No Excuses (jeans), 270–71
Nothing Down: How to Buy Real
      Estate with Little or No
      Money Down (Allen), 182
nouveau riches, 3
Novak, Kim, 418, 433–35
Now Get Out of That, 333
nuclear-arms-treaty negotiator, 13
NYMA. *See* New York Military
      Academy

Obama, Barack
   as Antichrist, 373
   birthers and, 2, 369–86, 423, 429
   criticism of, 420, 423
   Ebola and, 431
Obama, Sarah, 375–76
O'Brien, Conan, 317
O'Brien, Timothy L., 14, 149, 296,
      355–59
   criticism of, 421
   lawsuits against, 421
O'Connor, Paul, 413
O'Donnell, John, 255–56, 260–61
O'Donnell, Rosie
   on *Survivor,* 336
   on *The View,* 359–61
   at wedding, 297
Olnick, Robert, 120
Olympic Tower, 164–70
   air rights for, 164–65
   campaign contributions and,
      168
   home in, 277
   multiuse plan for, 165
   Onassis and, 164–65
Olympics, Trump, Ivana, in, 156,
      439–40
On Photography (Sontag), 83
Onassis, Aristotle, 159, 164–65
One Astor Plaza, 134–35
100 Central Park South, 221–23
O'Neal, Shaquille, 364

The Union, 431
OPEC. *See* Organization of
    Petroleum Exporting
    Countries
Open Housing Center, 104–10
O'Reilly, Bill, 374, 430
Organization of Petroleum
    Exporting Countries (OPEC),
    372–73
organized crime
  in Atlantic City, 207
  Cody and, 178–79
  Cohn and, 103
  in concrete business, 177
  gambling and, 209
  in Indian tribe gambling
    business, 299
  protection money for, 213
  Tammany Hall and, 42
  Trump, Fred, and, 41–44
The Other Woman (lingerie), 270

Paar, Jack, 216
Pacino, Al, 101, 230
Paerdegat Woods, 40
Pagnozzi, Amy, 297
Palmieri, Victor, 115–21, 125, 127,
    128, 132, 136–37, 166
Pan Am, 143
Pan Am Building, 127
Paramount, 303
Paris Is Out! (play), 100
partnerships, 208–9
Pattinson, Robert, 432
Paul, Jerry, 301
Paulsen, Pat, 322
Pauly, David, 352
Peale, Norman Vincent, xx, 69–72,
    156, 297, 325, 357, 426
Pearce, Henry, 138
Pei, I. M., 65
Penn Central, 99–100, 127–28,
    132–33, 166, 189
  bankruptcy of, 114–15, 123
  convention center and, 114–15,
    124, 125–26
  Midtown and, 127–55
  Westpride and, 302
Penthouse, 228

People, 201–2, 208, 227, 266, 289,
    360
Perfumania, 449
Perot, Ross, 318–19
Perry, Jack, 392
Perry, Katy, 432
Persian Room, at Plaza Hotel, 219
Peter Cooper Village, 119
Phillips, Kevin, 10, 180, 285–86
Phillips, Stone, 308
Phillips, Thomas, 248
Phinney, Richard, 412
Photoplay, 180
Pickens, T. Boone, 213
Pickford, Mary, 65
Pittsburgh Post-Gazette,
    375
Planning Commission, 84–85, 118
Plaskin, Glenn, 266
Playboy, 261, 266, 270, 335, 384
Playgirl, 226–27
Plaza Hotel, 218–20, 300
Plunkitt, George Washington, 25,
    43, 142
poison pill strategy, 215
political correctness, 427
Politico, 377
politics. *See also* campaign
    contributions; Democratic
    Party; presidential candidacy;
    Republican Party
  The Apprentice and, 16
  Cohn and, 167–68
  Commodore Hotel and, 142–43
  Dunbar and, 237–38
  Helmsley, H., and, 145–46
  in Manhattan, 118
  Trump, Fred, and, 36, 85
The Politics of Rich and Poor
    (Phillips), 10, 285
Polshek, James, 304
Ponzi scheme, 35
pop culture, 431–33
popularity, 6, 12
Porgy and Bess, 307
Port Authority of New York and
    New Jersey, 98
Port Sunlight, 48
Post, Marjorie Merriweather, 225

Postman, Neil, 330
Pottinger, J. Stanley, 106–7
poverty zones, 88–89, 95
Powell, Clyde L., 20, 22, 43–44
power, 6, 325
The Power of Positive Thinking
(Peale), xx, 69
PR. *See* public relations
Prejean, Carrie, 361–62
prenuptial agreement
with Maples, 295–96, 309–10
with Trump, Ivana, 159–61, 274
presidential candidacy, x–xviii,
238–39, 430–31, 446–49
of Clinton, H., 426
of Reform Party of the United
States of America, 318–32
President's Advisory Commission
on Intergovernmental
Relations, 141
Press and Journal, 395, 401, 402,
405, 417
Pressman, Gabe, 225
PrimeTime Live, 281–82
Prince (singer), 265
Pritzker, Jay, 134
Pritzker family, 132
private jets, 10–11, 259, 277, 300,
324, 390, 405
Professional Golf Association of
America, 449
Prohibition, 41
Project X, 392
prostitution, 26, 28
pseudo-events, 83–87
Public Broadcasting Service, 286
public relations (PR), 39–40,
82–84
publicity, 13, 146–47, 153,
187–203
from *The Apprentice,* 346–47
for Helmsleys, 148
in *The New York Times,* xvi,
151–53
by Trump, Fred, Jr., 82–83
for Trump, Fred, 74
for *Trump: The Art of the Deal,*
236
for Zeckendorf, 64

Putin, Vladimir, 420
Putnam Securities, 301

Q Score, 3, 436
al-Qaeda, 327, 383
Queenan, Joe, 248

race riots, 87–88
racehorse, 260
theory, 425
Rancic, Bill, 342, 347
Ravitch, Richard, 98, 121, 122–23,
135, 136
Reagan, Nancy, 180, 226
Reagan, Ronald, 9, 180–81, 213,
237, 238, 326
Cohn and, 226
Steinbrenner and, 287
tax cuts of, 180, 291
*Real Housewives of New York
City,* 349
reality television, 330–31, 333–61.
See also The Apprentice
Reddit, xvi
Redford, Robert, 151
Reems, Harry, 151
Reform Party of the United States
of America, xiii, 318–32
Regan, Donald, 181
Relaxation Plus, 130
Remnick, David, 379
Republican Party, xiv, xvii–xviii, 69,
237, 315, 318
birthers and, 371
Cohn and, 107
Mexico and, 450
Stone, R., and, 315–16
Res, Barbara, 144–45, 167,
175–76, 184, 261, 294
Resorts Casino Hotel, 205, 261
Resorts International, 216, 217–18,
221, 254
respect, 1, 53, 79
RestNet Tea Party, 371
Reston, James, 181
Results 2000, 324–25
Reyes, Matias, 339
Rice, Donna, 270, 272
Rich, John, 384

Rich Dad Poor Dad (Kiyosaki), 353–54

Richardson, Elliot, 107

Rickey, Branch, 69

Rigell, Scott, xviii

Riverside South, 302–4

Rizzo, Frank, 113

RJR Nabisco, 256, 285

Robards, Jason, 230

robber barons, 25

Robbins, Tony, 324–25, 331

Robinson, Anne, 346

Rockefeller, John D., 7, 25, 27

Rockefeller Center, 195

Rockefellers, 6

"Rockin' in The Free World" (Young), 446

Rockwell, Rick, 335

Roffman, Marvin, 254–55, 257–58

Rogaine, 347

Romney, George, 106

Romney, Mitt, xvii, xviii, 92, 374, 384–85

Roosevelt, Franklin Delano, 37

Roosevelt Hotel, 127

Rosenbaum, William, 43

Rosenthal, A. M., 140

Ross, Diana, 101

Royal Society for the Protection of Birds, 401

Rubenstone, Edward, 122

Rubio, Marco, xiii, xvii, 449

Ruggiero, Steve, 314

Russell, Bertrand, 217

Ryan, Paul, xiv

Saarinen, Eero, 81

Salmond, Alex, 403, 415, 417

Sarkozy, Nicolas, 288

Saturday Night Live, 347

Sawyer, Diane, 281, 282

"Scale of Punishment," 59

Scalia, Antonin, 282

Schafer, Henry, 3

Schanburg, Sidney H., 222

Schieffer, Bob, 379

Schneider, Karen, 290

Schneiderman, Eric, 367–69, 427, 428

school of hard knocks, 7

Schrafft's restaurant, 130

Schwartz, Tony, 235, 243

Schwartzkopf, Norman, 325

Schwarzman, Stephen, 10

Scotland
  golf resort in, 387–417
  greed in, 391
  housing in, 415
  Isle of Lewis in, 47–50, 400, 403, 405–6, 417
  Menie Estate in, 387–89, 390, 397, 398, 402, 407, 415
  Menie Sand Sheet in, 394–95
  Trump, Donald, Jr., in, 399, 411, 412
  windmills in, 387, 394–95, 415, 416
  zoning in, 391

Scott, Janney Montgomery, 257–58

Scott, Selina, 306–8

Scottish Wildlife Trust, 401

Scutt, Der, 134–35, 145, 152, 250
  Bonwit Teller and, 168
  Trump Tower and, 171, 192

Sea Shell Guest House, 206, 208

Second Gilded Age, 9–14

"The Secret to Donald Trump's Hair," in *Time*, 317

Secrets of the Millionaire Mind, 328

Securities and Exchange Commission, 300

Segal, David, 352

Self-Mastery Through Conscious Autosuggestion (Coué), 70

self-promotion, 15, 17, 21, 442, 452

self-surveillance, 84

September 11, 2001, xv, 327, 370

Serta, 449

sex tape scandals, of celebrities, 361–62

sexist comments, 294

sexual harassment, 175, 356

sexuality, 100, 149. *See also* homosexuality

Shields, Brooke, 437

Shorris, Earl, 286

Siegel, Stanley, 153
Silent Majority, xv
Silver, Nate, xvii
Simmons, Russell, 353
Simon, Paul, 292
Simpson, O. J., 297
Sinatra, Frank, 284–85
Singer, Mark, 422
Site of Special Scientific Interest (SSSI), 389, 394
60 Minutes, 225
Smith, Adam, 256
Smith, Liz, 5, 249, 267–69, 273, 284, 437
    Helmsleys and, 147
    on wedding to Maples, 297
"social X-Rays," 271
Solomon, Peter J., 166
Son of Sam, 139, 140
Sontag, Susan, 83–84
Soprano, Tony (fictional character), x
Sorial, George, 399–400, 404, 409, 411
Spanish flu, 29
Spears, Britney, 365
Special Committee to Investigate Crime in Interstate Commerce, 42–43
speculation, 10
Spellman, Joseph, 57, 66
Speyer, Jerry, 344
Spielberg, Steven, 184, 249
sports, 61–62, 194–95, 424–25
Sports -Reference.com, 439
Spy, 248–49, 253, 269
SSSI. *See* Site of Special Scientific Interest
St. Louis Post-Dispatch, 324
St. Moritz Hotel, 208
Star Wars, 304
Stark, Abe, 81–82
Starrett City, 119–20
Starrett Corporation, 119
Status, 101
Steeplechase Park, 79–81, 84–86
Steinberg, Gayfryd, 278
Steinbrenner, George, 101, 195, 287, 419

Steinem, Gloria, 197–98
Steingut, Stanley, 135
Stern, Henry J., 167
Stevens, Stuart, xvii
Stewart, Andrew, 348
Stewart, Jon, 4, 448
Stewart, Kristen, 431–32
Stewart, Martha, 348–50
Stockman, David, 9
Stone, Oliver, 279
Stone, Roger, 236, 315–18
Storr, Debra, 404, 410
Streisand, Barbra, 158, 230
student deferment, 92
Studio 54, xxi, 149, 442
Stuyvesant Town, 119
suburbs, 87, 96
Sunshine, Louise, 166, 233
superiority, 5, 13, 52, 60, 168
Super Tuesday, xiv
survival, 424
Survivor, 334–37
Sutton, Percy, 138
Sylvania Electric, 278
Syrovatka, George, 156, 157, 158

Taitz, Orly, 371
Taj Mahal, 216, 246, 254, 256, 258, 259, 261, 276
Talal, Al-Waleed bin, 300
Talese, Gay, 66
Tammany Hall, 42, 77, 81
Tampa Bay Times, 366
Tapper, Jake, xiii
tax breaks, 77, 85, 135–37, 193
tax cuts, 9, 180, 241, 291
Taylor, John, 271–72
Tea Party Express, 371
Teapot Dome, 21
television. *See also specific programs and networks*
    about celebrity, 197–98
    Griffin, M., and, 216–17
    reality, 330–31, 333–61
    sports on, 194–95
    Trump: The Art of the Deal and, 236
    wealth and, 180
Television City, 196

Tepedino, Frank, 62
Texaco, 130
That Something (Woodbridge), 7
theater career, 63
The Theory of the Leisure Class (Veblen), 25
Think and Grow Rich (Hill), 69–70
Thompson, Kay, 219
"Tiffany location," 163
Tiffany's, 168–69
Tilyou, George, 79
Time, 200, 250, 282, 317, 431
The Times, of London, 402
Times Square, 130
Tocqueville, Alexis de, 6
Today, 335–36, 340–41
Tolchin, Susan, 322
Tomasello, William ("Willie"), 41–42, 43
Tonight, 216, 323
Toobin, Jeffrey, 315
Top Scot, 414
Torricelli, Robert, 299
Tosti, Matthew, 74–76
tourism, 114
Towery, Vecepia, 336
Tripping Up Trump, 410
Trudeau, Garry, 284
Trump, Barron William (son), 364
Trump, Donald. *See specific topics*
Trump, Donald, Jr. (son), 162, 211, 273, 425, 441
  in Scotland, 399, 411, 412
Trump, Elizabeth (sister), 50
Trump, Elizabeth Christ (grandmother), 28
Trump, Eric (son), 211, 273, 440
Trump, Fred (father), xix–xx, 9, 13–14, 19–45, 51–54, 154, 322–23
  Commodore Hotel and, 144
  Democratic Party and, 37–43, 74, 77
  "Effective Speaking and Human Relations" (Dale Carnegie course) and, 50–51
  Eichler and, 118–19

FHA and, 19–24, 37–38
  graft and profiteering by, 19–24
  marriage and, 244
  Midtown and, 131
  Mitchell-Lama program and, 67–77
  Mr. Green and, 175
  New York State Commission of Investigation and, 75–77
  The New York Times and, 191
  organized crime and, 41–44
  Peale and, 69–72
  at Planning Commission, 84–85
  politics and, 36, 85
  PR and, 39–40
  publicity for, 74
  Res and, 176
  Steeplechase Park and, 84–86
  Tammany Hall and, 77, 81
  Trump Castle and, 264
  Trump Tower and, 176
Trump, Fred, Jr. (brother), 50, 51–52, 78–82, 86–87, 202–3
Trump, Friedrich (grandfather), 26–29
  alcohol and, 29, 78
Trump, Ivana (wife), 156–62, 250–51, 271–72
  for advertising, 276–77
  Daily News, Post and, 267–68
  divorce from, 273–75
  Eastern Airlines and, 246–47
  Helmsley, L., and, 269
  on her children, 273
  For Love Alone by, 291–92
  Maples and, 255–56, 266
  The New York Times and, 191
  in Olympics, 156, 439–50
  Plaza Hotel and, 246
  prenuptial agreement with, 159–61, 274
  recollections of, 439–40
  Res and, 176
  Spy and, 248–49, 253, 269
  Taj Mahal and, 246
  Trump Plaza and, 211
  Walters and, 268
  wedding to, 161–62
Trump, Ivanka (daughter), 211, 273

Trump, Mary Anne MacLeod (mother), xix, 47–50, 307, 309, 405–6

Trump, Maryanne (sister), 50, 53, 323, 406

Trump, Robert (brother), 50, 51–52, 257

Trump, Tiffany (daughter), 295, 298

Trump: The Art of the Comeback (Trump, D.), 296, 309

Trump: The Art of the Deal (Trump, D.), 15, 235–36, 242–44, 443–44

Trump Castle, 214, 264, 280

"Trump effect," 185–86

Trump Entrepreneur Initiative, 367

Trump Hotels and Casino Resorts, 314, 315, 323, 327, 351

Trump: How to Get Rich (Trump, D.), 328, 406

Trump International Hotel and Tower, 304

Trump Management Corporation, 104

Trump: Never Give Up (Trump, D.), 406

Trump Plaza, 206, 280, 301
    Harrah's at, 211–14
    O'Donnell, J., and, 260–61

Trump Princess (yacht), 10, 259, 280

Trump Shuttle, 246–47, 259, 261–62

Trump: Surviving at the Top (Trump, D. and Leerhsen), 283–84

Trump: Think Like a Billionaire (Trump, D.), 328

Trump Tower, ix, x, 169–70, 175–79, 277
    apartment sales at, 183–86, 193
    The Apprentice at, 340, 341
    arson at, 177–78
    concrete for, 177–78
    Huxtable and, 191–92
    Koch and, 193–94
    Res and, 175–78, 184
    Trump, Fred, and, 176

Trump University, 365–68, 428–29

Trump Village, 67–68, 74–76

Trumped! (O'Donnell, J.), 255, 260

Trumpf, Friedrich. *See* Trump, Friedrich

TrumpNation (O'Brien, T.), 355–59

Tune, Tommy, 437

Turner, Jim, 107

Twain, Mark, 4, 6

20/20, 239, 241, 242

21 Club, 100, 158

Twin Towers, 98

Twitter, 4, 385, 431, 432, 435

two-dimensional society, 39

Tyson, Mike, 267, 419

UDC. *See* Urban Development Corporation

United States Football League (USFL), 194–95, 223

University of Pennsylvania, 68, 84, 89–90, 91–92

Univision, 449

Unleash the Power Within (Robbins), 325

Unlimited Power (Robbins), 325

Urban Development Corporation (UDC), 123, 135, 136, 142

Urban League, 104, 106, 108

USAir, 261–62

USFL. *See* United States Football League

U.S. News & World Report, xvii

Utsey, Robert, 154–55, 162, 380

Van Meter, Jonathan, 253

Vanderbilt, Cornelius, 25, 128–29

Vanderbilts, 6

Vanity Fair, 274, 283, 421

Veblen, Thorstein, 25

Ventura, Jesse ("the Body"), 319

Vermeil, Dick, 325

Verrazano-Narrows Bridge, 65–66, 429

Viacom, 303

Vietnam War, xxi, 90–92, 125, 217

The View, 359–61

The Village Voice, 187–88, 189
von Hoffman, Nicholas, 224, 226
vulgarity, 16

Wagner, Robert F., 74, 77, 87
Waldorf-Astoria, 365
Walesa, Lech, 12
Walker, Jimmy, 30
The Wall Street Journal, xvi, 194,
    211, 259, 358, 382, 436
  on DJT, 301
  on greenmailing, 215
  on Sorial, 399
  on Taj Mahal, 256
  on Trump Castle, 264
  on Trump Hotels and Casino
    Resorts, 327
Wallace, Mike, 225
Walters, Barbara, 224, 239–40,
    241, 265, 281, 283
  as disloyal, 295
  Scott, S., and, 306
  Trump, Ivana, and, 268
  on *The View,* 359–60
Warner, Harry, 157
Warner, Peter, 173
Washington Correspondents
    Dinner, 282
The Washington Post, 110, 233,
    236, 273, 287, 352
Watergate scandal, 125, 147
Waterside Plaza, 98
Watson, Thomas, 69
*We Got Fired! . . . And It's the
    Best Thing That Ever
    Happened to Us,* 329
wealth
  birth to, 3
  from fame, 12–13
  hedonism and, 16
  Helmsley, H., and, 145
  housing and, 6
  power and, 6
  Reagan, R., and, 180–81
  television and, 180
  vulgarity and, 16
Wealth and Poverty (Gilder), 9
weddings
  to Krauss, 364

  to Maples, 296–97
  to Trump, Ivana, 161–62
Weekly Standard, xviii
Weinman, Rosalyn, 316–17
"Welcome to Fear City," 112
welfare, 88, 99, 105, 108–9, 380
West Side Story, 54
Westbrook, Pegler, 110
Westin Hotels, 131–32, 219
Westpride, 302
whales, in gambling, 300
Wharton School of Finance and
    Commerce, 89–90, 93, 152,
    279
Wheel of Fortune, 217
*When Bad Things Happen to
    Good People* (Kushner), 248
Where's the Birth Certificate?
    (Corsi), 377
White, Mary Jo, 356
white flight, 87, 88
White House Correspondents'
    Dinner, 1–2
white supremacy, xiii–xiv
Whitman, Meg, xviii
Who Moved My Cheese?, 328
Who Wants to Be a Millionaire,
    334
*Who Wants to Marry a Multi-
    Millionaire?,* 335
Why We Want You to Be Rich
    (Trump, D. and Kiyosaki), 354
Whyte, Peter. *See* Hobday, Neil
    Peter Whyte
Wightman, Andrew, 416
Wilde, Oscar, 347
wilding, 251, 294
The Will Rogers Follies, 292, 298
Williams, Edward Bennett, 213
Williams, Mark, 371
Williams, Vanessa, 228, 229
Willy Loman (fictional character),
    51
Winchell, Walter, 110
windmills, in Scotland, 387,
    394–95, 415, 416
Winfrey, Oprah, 292, 320, 364
Winklmayr, Alfred, 272
Wiseman, Carter, 304

The Wizard of Oz, 157
WNBC, 195
Wohlfert-Wihlborg, Lee, 201–2
Wolf, Michael J., 330
Wolfe, Tom, 15, 148, 149, 248,
    271, 442
Wollman Rink, 232–33, 336
Wood, Harmon and Company, 37
Woodbridge, William, 7
World Trade Center, xv, 98
Wright, Frank Lloyd, 116
Wynn, Steve, 209, 212–14

yachts, 10, 259, 277, 280
Yale Club, 127

Yokoi, Hideki, 304–6
Yorty, Sam, 113
Young, Neil, 446, 448
You've Been Trumped
    (documentary), 412, 414

Zeckendorf, William, 20, 63–65,
    117
Zingone, Renzo, 127–28
zoning, 82, 86, 170
    air rights and, 164–65
    in Scotland, 391
Zuccotti, John, 118
Zucker, Jeffrey, 340–41
Zurbriggen, Bernadette, 439